No More Worlds to Conquer

No More Worlds to Conquer

The Black Poet in Washington, DC

Brian Gilmore

Georgetown University Press / Washington, DC

Library of Congress Cataloging-in-Publication Data

Names: Gilmore, Brian author
Title: "No more worlds to conquer" : the Black poet in Washington, D.C. / Brian Gilmore.
Description: Washington, DC : Georgetown University Press, 2025. |
Includes bibliographical references and index.
Identifiers: LCCN 2025014592 (print) | LCCN 2025014593 (ebook) | ISBN 9781647126544 hardcover | ISBN 9781647126551 paperback | ISBN 9781647126568 ebook
Subjects: LCSH: American poetry—African American authors—History and criticism | American poetry—Washington (D.C.)—History and criticism | African American poets—Washington (D.C.) | Poets, Black—Washington (D.C.) | LCGFT: Literary criticism
Classification: LCC PS153.B53 G55 2025 (print) | LCC PS153.B53 (ebook) | DDC 810.9/896073—dc23/eng/20250709
LC record available at https://lccn.loc.gov/2025014592
LC ebook record available at https://lccn.loc.gov/2025014593

∞ This paper meets the requirements of ANSI/NISO Z39.48-1992 (Permanence of Paper).

EU GPSR Authorised Representative
LOGOS EUROPE, 9 rue Nicolas Poussin,
17000, LA ROCHELLE, France
E-mail: Contact@logoseurope.eu

26 25 9 8 7 6 5 4 3 2 First printing
Printed in the United States of America

Cover design by James Keller
Interior design by Paul Hotvedt

As always, for my parents, Dorothy Pearl and Wilmer Isome Gilmore

&

For my bestie from elementary school, Ronnie Beavers,

&

for Reuben Jackson and Peter J. Harris

All writers need communities . . .

—Meta DuEwa Jones, “Understanding the New New Black Poetry,” *Souls*

Contents

Preface: "We Wear the Mask"

Between 1898 and 1901, Paul Laurence Dunbar lived here in Washington, DC, in the city's LeDroit Park section of the city. It was only for a short time, but he was already well known and famous in the nation's poetry circles. He wasn't the first Black person to write poetry or want to be a professional poet, but he was the most well-known Black poet in the late nineteenth century.

He came to the city initially and was connected to all the key communities: the academic world, the local Black poetry world, the larger poetry world of Washington, DC, and its segregated realities.

Dunbar did readings in DC, and other areas around the area through churches and social clubs, connected with the Black professionals, and collaborated with other artists. He is not the beginning of Black poetry in the city, but he is a symbolic crossroad. His famous wife, the writer and then suffragist Alice Dunbar Nelson, was also in Washington much of this time until the couple split permanently before Paul's death.

On some level, Dunbar's success as a poet mirrored the path Black America was on at the time. The city didn't even have a high school for Black students until 1870, and that was just after the Civil War. Dunbar was born in 1872 in Dayton, Ohio. It would make sense that some of his generations would begin to take a different path from most of their forebears. Dunbar's life would not be in the fields; it would be the life of an artist and creative intellectual, and he would not be alone. He would be without question the most important Black poet of his generation.

Dunbar was literary energy at the time, and at a desperate political time for Black people in America as they became aware of the suffocating racist backlash that occurred once Reconstruction ended and the door on freedom was slammed shut yet again. But Dunbar navigated this murky arrangement. Other Black poets in the city saw his example, and read his work. From that, they could define themselves, speak to their times, and move forward.

No More Worlds to Conquer: The Black Poet in Washington, DC is history, reflection, literary life, and politics in the Black poetry community of DC, since Dunbar came to live and work in the city. It considers what began when he came here and what did develop here and continues to develop even as I try to document and make creative sense of 100 years of Black poetry in the city. Much came after Dunbar departed the city. Kelly Miller's daughter, May Miller, emerged as a writer and student at Howard University. May Miller would be a major figure in the city for the next seventy years. And there were also other visitors who made a difference and made small lasting contributions to the city.

Between 1924 and 1926, Langston Hughes lived and wrote in Washington. Hughes's time here has, like Dunbar, taken on even more importance over the decades. Other local Black poets began to emerge both in the city and outside of it. William Waring Cuney. Georgia Douglas Johnson. And, of course, though also a short-lived star of the word, Jean Toomer.

By the late 1930s and 1940s before the war, poetry among Black poets was vibrant and beginning to establish its historical circles. Sterling A. Brown is editor of the Federal Writers' Project. Black poets live and work in the city, and they make significant cultural contributions to the national literary scene. The postwar period for Black poets in Washington, DC, is less certain and lacks the identity and certainty of the prewar period. Yet, the Black poet pushes on. Black poets' desire to create differently is their strength.

By the 1950s the push to desegregate the city took shape. This is very important as well to understanding Black poetry in the city. It developed mostly in its own space, in its own communities. There were few serious opportunities outside of Black America for Black poets, though occasionally, as is shown in the book, some poets were able to enter less-traditional spaces. And then there were spaces that were more than welcoming and wanted African American poets in their space.

All through this time, the established circles did remain: The Black poets have their own scene, they push into the city's existing institutions slowly, and the academic communities continue to thrive and push literature as well. People might not become Washingtonians per se, but they do become part of the Black poetry scene. The late Gaston Neal, a poet from Pittsburgh who lived and worked in the city for about forty years, defined it best when he once called himself a "Washingtonian" even though he was born and raised in Pittsburgh.

The institutions would also begin to accept Black poets and Black poetry as part of the real world. Robert Hayden and Gwendolyn Brooks would serve as poetry consultants to the Library of Congress in the '70s and '80s respectively. E. Ethelbert Miller, one of the leading contemporary American poets, came to DC in 1968 to attend Howard University. He became a poet and never left.

Kenneth Carroll became a poetry institution in the city in his own right. A spoken word movement that emerged in the 1990s joined ranks with hip-hop culture and created a completely new range of expression in the city.

No More Worlds to Conquer is a way of putting the Black poet of Washington, DC, in the proper context over the long haul, through a series of literary movements, and developments. It answers the questions as to why the black poetry scene in Washington remains strong and visible and continues to produce outstanding writers of note. It is also hoped that the reader will understand why black poets come here to live and work, as well as perhaps why they don't feel a need to remain much of the time. Why despite preconceived notions about the city of government Black poetry and literature has thrived here and continues to thrive and is an essential part of American Literature in the United States. This story is not all the story, but it is one story, from the vantage point of just one poet, who inherited the great legacy nurtured and advanced in the city. A story that continues to grow in statute and importance. Of course, it is impossible to mention every poem, every significant event in the city and in its surrounding suburbs. But that is not intentional. That is the nature of this kind of adventure. This is hopefully a beginning, a charge to others to use the mediums artists and writers have at their disposal and tell our stories.

Acknowledgments

THANKS MOST OF ALL TO MY PARENTS, DOROTHY PEARL GILMORE AND WILMER ISOME GILMORE.

To all of the writing teachers and great elders who exposed me to writing and literature as a boy, teen, and college student. Ms. Lewis, my third grade teacher at LaSalle Elementary; David Chrisman, of Archbishop Carroll High School; Father Carney, of Archbishop Carroll; Keith Schlegel (Frostburg State), and Richard Trask (Frostburg State).

Thanks for my family—Elanna, Adanya, Lirit, Pannonica, my sibs: Keith, Allison, Mike, and my extended families all over the United States, especially the offspring of Hazel and Aquila Gilmore and the Santuc family of South Carolina.

Thanks for Andy Fogle, the poet, and Hope LeGro, of Georgetown University Press, who together made this happen. Andy passed me the ball, Hope called the play; hopefully, I made the basket.

Marcia Davis, the writer-editor who gave me my first writing gig that resulted in my obsession with the local history of Black poets.

Also thanks to the following individuals and institutions who helped this happen in some way, some much bigger than others: *Emerge Magazine, The Washington Post, Beltway Poetry Quarterly*, and Kim Roberts, *Alehouse Press Magazine*, for publishing the first essay on Paul Laurence Dunbar.

To the true heavy lifters in the world of research and archival materials who helped this come together:

Sylvia Brown, Special Collections—Williams College,
Williamston, Massachusetts

Kathy Shoemaker, Rose Library—Emory University

Howard University—Moorland-Spingarn Library

Tulane University

Charles Sumner Library and Archives

Jen & Dalton, Gelman Library—Special Collections, GWU

Yale University—Library

NYC Public Library and Arthur Schomburg Research Center

Syracuse University—Library

Paul Breman

Ohio Historical Society

Tamar Meekins, William Bland and everyone at Robert Ades and Associates, Paul Breman, Hope LeGro, E. Ethelbert Miller, Haki Madhubuti, Gaston Neal, Howard Shorter, Linette Marie Allen, Jennifer King, Dalton Alves, all the staff at Special Collections—Gelman Library—George Washington University, Emory University Rose Library, Kathleen Shoemaker, Kimberly Springle, Sumner School Archives, Charice M. Thompson, Moorland-Spingarn Library—Howard University, Aldon Nielsen, Schomburg Center and NYC Public Library, Amber Zu-Bolton, Kenneth Carroll, Joel Dias-Porter (Renegade), Terrance Hayes, D. Stover from Landover, Jewel Neal, Michael Wallace, Jabari Asim and family, *The Progressive Magazine*, Matt, Bill, Norman, and all the other editors of that great publishing institution, Marcia Davis, *Alehouse Press Magazine*, *Beltway Poetry Quarterly*, Madeira School, Cynthia Davis, Verner Mitchell, University of Maryland, College Park, Robert Koulish, Brandee Pettus, Harpreet Kaur, Christine, Justine, Evan, Diego, "Dean" Russell, etc., Michigan State University, Joan Howarth, David and Veronica, Jesse, and all of my MSU Clinical Law family, Catherine and Stephen, Matt Fletcher, American Poetry Museum, Sankofa Books (Haile and Family), Kurt Schmoke, Howard University, David Chrisman, Robert Hoderny, Keith Schlegel, LaSalle Elementary School, Katie Davis, Silvana Straw. I know I left many people out but not by design. One Love to All.

1

Love Song

In the third grade, at Jessie LaSalle Elementary, just around the corner from my house in Washington, DC, I first embraced the poetry of Paul Laurence Dunbar, the Black poet. Mrs. Lewis was my teacher. The entire class was assigned homework. Select any poem, commit it to memory, and then recite it in front of the class. Thinking back, I didn't think much of it. I was shy and didn't like speaking in front of people, but I didn't fret for some reason. After a search through literary paperbacks, my father kept in the house, I selected Dunbar's "We Wear the Mask."[1] My very best friend in the world then, Ronnie Beavers, a schoolmate, picked a Dunbar poem too: "Negro Love Song." We went through all the books together.

To this day, I can still remember reading the poem. It took me hours to memorize it to the point where I was fearless.

We Wear the Mask
We wear the mask that grins and lies,
It hides our cheeks and shades our eyes,—
This debt we pay to human guile;
With torn and bleeding hearts we smile,
And mouth with myriad subtleties.

Why should the world be over-wise,
In counting all our tears and sighs?
Nay, let them only see us, while
   We wear the mask.

We smile, but, O great Christ, our cries
To thee from tortured souls arise.

We sing, but oh the clay is vile
Beneath our feet, and long the mile;
But let the world dream otherwise,
We wear the mask!
—*Paul Lawrence Dunbar*

My first poetry reading. My first real encounter with the majesty of verse. At the time I read the poem, I did not know what it meant. I also did not know that Paul Laurence Dunbar had once lived and wrote in my city between 1898 and 1901. Once I found out, the poetry reading meant even more to me.

Whenever I read poetry, I again imagine that I am standing in front of Mrs. Lewis's class, nervous and excited. Poetry is in my hands, head, and heart. People sit attentively and are listening. I think about it even more after I learned of Dunbar's time here and the subsequent connections made.

Emancipation

In October 1896 the Black American poet Paul Laurence Dunbar, the poet whom I first discovered in third grade at LaSalle Elementary School, came to the city of Washington, DC. Dunbar had come to give his first official poetry reading in the city before the public at large. Dunbar was a rising star in the poetry world and the Black poetry world at the time. His first collection, *Oak and Ivy*, had been published in 1893, and his rise as a serious professional poet continued every year. It is hard to imagine such a time when there was just one African American poet whom the entire country took seriously. Yes, there were many other African American writers and poets, but Paul Laurence Dunbar in 1896 was Black poetry in America.

In 1893 Dunbar had consciously embraced poetry as his profession. Offered a chance to apprentice as a lawyer in his hometown of Dayton, Ohio, Dunbar spurned the opportunity. Instead, he traveled to Chicago and the World's Fair, where the great orator Frederick Douglass hired him as a clerk. Douglass, in charge of the "Hayti" exhibition at the fair, gave Dunbar a chance to read his works and present Black poetry as serious art. Dunbar also met and began corresponding with Rebekkah Baldwin, a schoolteacher from DC. Baldwin would still be writing to Dunbar a year later. She would find an unsure poet on her hands in need of some encouragement:

> Paul, if you could only throw off the cloak of skepticism that envelopes you so completely and let the radiance of faith and trust enter your soul, how much happier you would be! . . . Why should you, my dear Paul, with all the music of the muses murmuring in your soul, why, I say, should you constitute yourself into a morbid social chemist weighing and analyzing the smiles, tears, tones, emotions and expressions of your friends.[2]

Dunbar listened to Baldwin. Baldwin was not just a friend whose counsel Dunbar trusted; he likely loved her deeply as something more than a friend. Thereafter, Dunbar did not let any inner doubt deter him from his path toward a life of letters, and in 1896 that ascent was in full bloom.

Dunbar's reading in Washington was held on October 19, 1896, at the Church of Our Father.[3] Before the reading, an announcement appeared in local newspapers and was penned by Robert H. Terrell. Terrell, a distinguished member of Washington's African American community, had been appointed justice of the peace in 1901 by President Theodore Roosevelt. Terrell graduated from the prestigious M Street High School, attended Harvard, and obtained a law degree from the Howard University School of Law in 1890. He practiced law in the city and in 1925 would be the first African American appointed as judge in the city's Municipal Court. In 1891 he married the future Mary Church Terrell, who as a civil rights pioneer and activist would make the Terrell name even more famous than her husband did.[4]

In 1896 as the reading approached, the lawyer Terrell gave Dunbar a hero's welcome to his city: "Mr. Dunbar's distinction is a unique one. He is a literary character in its best sense and is the first negro-American who has ever given marked evidence of that order or ability, rich imagination and great originality, such as command the attention of critics."[5]

On October 19, 1896, Dunbar appeared at the Church of Our Father. The Reverend Dr. Jeremiah Rankin, president of Howard University at the time and well-known local member of the clergy, introduced him to the people of the city. Rankin described Dunbar as a Black poet on a "great mission."[6] Dunbar appropriately began the program with "Ode to Ethiopia," his famous poem of race pride. The poem was part of his 1895 published volume *Majors and Minors* and has been described over the years as a poem of "racial and national patriotism."[7] The middle stanza, an aside to Blacks for race pride, is the most well-known portion of the poem:

> Be proud, my race, in mind and soul
> Thy name is writ on Glory's scroll
> In characters of fire
> High 'mid the clouds of Fame's bright sky
> Thy banner's blazoned folds now fly
> And truth shall lift them higher.[8]

Dunbar's performance included appearances by local musicians from the city. His voice was described as "deep, musical," with "a natural style of elocution."[9] "Ode to Ethiopia" was followed with more of the same, as Dunbar dazzled the local crowd with his softer poems such as "The Poet and His Song" and the very well-known "When Malindy Sings."[10] "When Malindy Sings" is the kind of poem that haunts Dunbar's literary career to this day. It is a poem full of the fake dialect that many Blacks and literary critics have found troubling and stereotypical but poems, nonetheless, whites and white audiences wanted Dunbar to recite. According to literary critic Eleanor Alexander, these dialect poems that Dunbar became famous for among whites are part of the "Plantation School" of writing created by "European-Americans" that evoke a "nostalgic image of the South." The genre perpetuates "racial inferiority," because Blacks present themselves in a jovial mood, satisfied with their position in society at the bottom rung of the country's civic structure.[11]

Dunbar's choice to write and recite such poems was a paradox for him for his entire literary life. Literary critic Ralph Story, in a September 1983 article on Dunbar, wrote that "the reading public" viewed this style "as a novelty" and that it placed "restraining parameters on the substance and style of his work and on whatever popularity he accrued.[12] According to Story, a black man as an artist, in society was "constrained by tons of propaganda" and "institutionalized injustice." Poems of this type are the kind of poems that led *The Washington Post*, in the review of the program, to declare that Dunbar is a "master of darkie dialect."[13]

A review of Dunbar's reading in *The Washington Post* reported that serious poems such as "Ode to Ethiopia" and others from his book *Majors and Minors* were equally appreciated by the audience. The Washington, DC, literary audience was seeing the poet for the first time in all his glory.

Not long after his Church of the Father reading, Dunbar continued to gain in stature nationally and internationally. He gave another reading in the DC area to benefit the Manassas Industrial School in Virginia.[14] The reading, held at the historic Fifteenth Street Presbyterian Church, located right downtown just blocks from the White House, was another celebrated local literary event. The Manassas Industrial School was an educational remnant of postslavery America. It was a school founded in 1894 for "colored" children. It was located across the river in Virginia in the heart of the country where the great war to end slavery had been waged so furiously.

"Mr. Dunbar's character poems are so favorably known," *The Washington Post* wrote on December 11, 1896, before the reading, "that a pleasant evening is assured."[15] Dunbar shared the bill with the Selika Quartet, a group that provided music for the evening.

The Fifteenth Street Presbyterian Church was a good place for such a performance because the church was a huge institution in the local Black community. The church had been founded in 1841 in the city with the specific purpose of organizing a church for "people of color" and "consideration of the propriety of forming a colored Presbyterian Church and Congregation in this city."[16]

Dunbar did not disappoint. On an evening of bad weather in the city, there were, according to *The Washington Post*, "as many white people as those of his own race" in attendance in the "crowded" auditorium of the church. After the music performance and introductions, Dunbar took over and showed himself well: "Mr. Dunbar's appearance was greeted with loud and continued applause. He spoke in the deep, strong voice, rich in feeling and pathos. His gestures and manner were those of an accomplished elocutionist, and his magnetism appealed strongly to the audience."[17]

This warm reception in the city for Paul Laurence Dunbar, Black poet, in his first big literary sojourn in Washington, DC, was a precursor to bigger things, and for the city as a town of Black poetry.

Reconstruction

Paul Laurence Dunbar, the first star African American poet in America, was a child of Reconstruction. He was born June 27, 1872, at 313 Howard Street, in Dayton, Ohio. The writer and historian Henry Louis Gates refers to the period as "chaotic" and "exhilarating" but "ultimately devastating."[18] Reconstruction is also described as a period of "extraordinary excitement," a "time in America could finally become that land of freedom that it had promised to be since the very beginning."[19] It was time when Black people sat in the House of Representatives and the Senate in the US Congress and when poor whites and poor Blacks found "common cause with one another."[20]

But as Black people began to achieve some sense of normalcy and gains in society in many essential aspects of a normal upward life, a fierce backlash and wave of terror erupted in the United States from whites and white hate groups. The pushback would last for decades and was rooted in racial violence. Reconstruction would eventually be stopped in its tracks, and white supremacy would rule the nation. Black boys like Paul Laurence Dunbar born in the middle of a period of so much hope would have to figure out a way forward despite the obstacles in their way.

Dunbar's parents reflect an intimate part of this sordid history. His mother, Matilda, and his father, Joshua, were former slaves. Dunbar's father's story as it relates to the war and slavery is particularly noteworthy.

According to Benjamin Brawley, in his study of Dunbar's life, *Paul Laurence Dunbar*, Joshua Dunbar was "among the slaves who escaped from Kentucky to Canada by 'underground railroad' in the years before the Civil War."[21] Joshua Dunbar, though safely in Canada, did not lose touch with or ignore the struggle for freedom he had left behind in America. When war broke out, he returned to the states and joined the Fifty-Fifth Regiment of Massachusetts, the "second regiment of Negroes recruited in the North."[22]

Paul's mother, Matilda Murphy, already a widow with two sons, and Paul's father, Joshua, met after the war and settled in Dayton, Ohio. The marriage bore Paul before Joshua Dunbar eventually deserted the family. Matilda Dunbar was left to raise them all and to work as a domestic washerwoman to do so. Yet Paul still had developed love and respect for his father in the short time they were together as a family.

It was no accident that the boy Paul became a great man of letters; his mother made sure that would happen. Matilda Dunbar introduced him to poetry as a child and worked tirelessly to see that he would embrace the word and always seek success in learning. Her work as a washerwoman helped her son Paul to obtain entry into Central High School in Dayton, where he, the only Black in the class, soared academically despite racism in Dayton as well. Dunbar participated in the debating society, served as editor of the school's paper, and was president of the school's literary society.[23]

After excelling in high school and finding the path to college tricky and expensive, he took a job working as an elevator boy in Dayton.[24] He began selling his poetry at his job and eventually took a loan from a friend in 1893, publishing his first collection of poetry, *Oak and Ivy.*

Not long after, he received an offer from a judge for an apprenticeship to learn to be an attorney (to read the law), but he passed on it. He decided to travel to the World's Fair in Chicago and seek work. It was there that he met the great orator Frederick Douglass and became his clerk at the Haitian exhibit for $5 per week.

The City

By the end of the nineteenth century in the city of Washington, life for Black people, like most Black people in the United States in the post-Reconstruction period, changed dramatically. In her seminal study of race relations in the city before 1965, *The Secret City: The History of Race Relations in the Nation's Capital,* Constance McLaughlin Green describes life in the city as "a drastic shift in attitude."[25] According to Green, the city became more focused on "material progress" and discarded any "concern for racial justice."[26]

Washington was where Black people "had made greater strides than anywhere else in the United States." Black people gained the right to vote there before the passage of the Fifteenth Amendment and were participants in local government and lawmaking during the early part of Reconstruction. While Washington was a city full of African slaves in the early nineteenth century by 1840, "free Blacks" outnumbered Black slaves by nearly 3 to 1.[27] By 1850 there were 8,158 free Blacks, 2,113 Black slaves, and 29,730 whites.[28] Following the end of the war, over 8,000 Blacks registered to vote in the city, and despite racial hostility there, they continued to make incremental gains. But once the nation overall descended into its white supremacist underpinnings, the whites of DC accepted this push toward a segregated, racial-caste-oriented country. They "concluded that most" Black people would "never make good citizens."[29] In addition, the Blacks, as well, ceased to fight vigilantly for one another against this racial pushback.[30] Jim Crow laws emerged after the end of Reconstruction and with the case of *Plessy v. Ferguson* in 1896, the coming century would prove to be a challenge racially. Paul Laurence Dunbar's life as poet began at this time.

Black Poet Laureate

In 1896 *The Washington Post* declared Dunbar "the poet laureate" of the "colored race." It was well deserved. Sterling A. Brown, the city's most important poet, mused many years later that Dunbar "gave readings" of his poetry "reciting it with the gusto of a Negro peasant."[31] Brown's words on Dunbar confirm that Dunbar was accepted by many establishment whites as the "poet laureate" of the "colored race" but also that his connections to ordinary Black people was even more authentic. Dunbar was from among the ordinary Black people of America with a pedigree that could not be dismissed easily. He was a high school graduate but poor. He worked as an elevator boy in Dayton, Ohio, and it was only the goodwill of white benefactors that enabled him to publish and sell his poetry. J. Saunders Redding in his seminal work of literary criticism, *To Make a Poet Black*, wrote of Dunbar that "no Negro of finer artistic spirit has been born in America."[32]

Dunbar's great days in Washington were followed by more of the same: requests for readings. His home in Dayton became bombarded with such requests and by 1897, right before he settled in Washington, DC, and before his eventual marriage to the writer Alice Moore, Dunbar took his very-well-known trip to England to work the literary circuit of America's father nation.

Dunbar, the poet, was the toast of England for months. The blatant indignities of Jim Crow America were vanquished temporarily. Dunbar's writings (his art) were taken seriously; Britain "welcomed him with the same generosity it had offered his black fellow countrymen." London, where Dunbar stayed, "turned out her most learned and distinguished men to meet and hear him" at the event.[33]

After his triumphant but introspective tour of England that lasted until summer 1897, Dunbar began his official longer sojourn in the city of Washington that would build upon his earlier performances and connections there. He would leave his mark in the city not just by who he was as a poet but as a notable resident. Dunbar was a professional writer.

He held himself out as a professional scribe in every manner of his being despite any other work he had to do to support himself and his mother. He took on the pursuit of writing and human interaction around his writings as not just a financial living but also his identity. It was why he came to the East Coast of the United States in the first place. He would reside and write in Washington, DC, but there was also New York City not far away.

His life would also include Alice Moore, a captivating woman of Creole stock from New Orleans he had taken notice of as far back as 1895. Moore was an exceptional literary artist as well who had achieved her own notoriety as a writer before she even met Dunbar. The two would marry, even though Moore's family was against the union.[34]

Dunbar also received some very good news at this time as well. Librarian of Congress John Russell Young[35] in October 1897 offered Dunbar an appointment to work at the Library of Congress in DC. At last, the poet laureate could relax about money for the moment and be a poet. His home base would be Washington, even though he would travel widely reading his work. He was described upon the appointment as the "colored poet" in the announcement that he would be working at the Library of Congress, again another clear recognition of his status as the Black poet of his generation and of that time.[36] Dunbar had obtained the job not only because he was the "colored poet" of the day but also because of connections. Daniel Murray, assistant librarian at the Library of Congress and the second Black person ever employed there, was instrumental in Dunbar's hire. Dunbar worked for Murray during his appointment. Murray is a literary figure of note in his own right.

Col. Robert G. Ingersoll, a prominent veteran of the Union Army during the Civil War, also had worked behind the scenes to find employment for Dunbar with Murray at the library. It was thus all set now—Dunbar could marry Alice Moore, and the couple could take their place in Washington among the many other Blacks of the day who found the city to be tolerable for a variety of reasons.

They were married on March 6, 1898, in New York City, and the lovers, with the intense relationship that seemed to always be headed toward its well-known sad ending, settled in LeDroit Park. This made sense for a professional African American couple thinking outside the norm, dreaming of a better life.

Located just blocks from the campus of Howard University, the neighborhood became one of the many neighborhoods that formed the core of Black life in the city during Dunbar's brief sojourn there. Dunbar and his wife, Alice, lived next door to Robert and Mary Church Terrell, and other notable African Americans were also jammed into the neighborhood. Their address was 321 U Street NW. For the city of Washington, it was an artistic coup that Dunbar had come to live and work there. The former elevator operator was, indeed, the first important Black poet to live and work in America. And he was right there in Washington, DC, with his partner, Alice Dunbar.

The Literary Life

It is often said that Paul and Alice Dunbar became part of the "colored elite" of the city of Washington. This seems to be undisputed. It was a unique city for African Americans anyway, even though all the evils that had occurred to most African Americans such as chattel slavery, segregation, and discrimination occurred there as well. But the city had its own racial history and customs that allowed many African Americans to carve out a better life. Dunbar, well read and sharp with words, made his singular contribution to the nurturing of an African American poetry tradition in the city because of this unique paradox.

Dunbar's essay from *Harper's Weekly*, "The Negro in Washington" (1901) is one of the best sources over the years for providing an honest depiction of Black life in the city at the turn of the century.[37] Dunbar had no reason to exaggerate or lie; he was not from Washington, DC, and it wasn't likely he would remain there indefinitely. As a famous poet, a famous Black poet, his presence and readings were in demand. Washington was a city of singular importance when Dunbar was there, and it was particularly important to African Americans.

"It is the delicately blended or boldly differentiated light and shade effects of Washington negro life that are the despair of him who tries truthfully to picture it,"[38] Dunbar writes of the city. His use of "light" and "shade effects" seem almost deliberate, contrived, as if Dunbar is telling the reader that there are color and class issues within the race among Blacks.

"It is the middle-class negro who has imbibed enough of white civilization to make him work to be prosperous."[39] The passage is optimistic, though Dunbar is not so foolish as to forget where he is living. "But he has not partaken of civilization so deeply that he has become drunk and has forgotten his own identity." In these passages Dunbar is not only musing about African Americans in general, but he is talking about life for Black people in Washington, DC.

Dunbar also uses the piece to specifically identify aspects of life in Washington for Blacks that are, in fact, well known through the African American world at the time. Dunbar clearly observes the daily work of Black women working as servants for privileged whites when he refers to the presence of black "mammies" in the Nation's Capital, something he calls "a real bit of the old South." He sees these Black women with "laundry work" and with a "little baby carriage" and notes that they came to the city when it was "indeed the Mecca for colored people."

There are Black women serving as waitresses as well, according to Dunbar, as he notes observing "the old lady who leans over the counter of a tiny and dingy restaurant on Capitol Hill and dispenses coffee and rolls and fried pork to her colored customers." These women are often made fun of, according to Dunbar, as they too are a remnant of the old South, that mythical place that the Blacks of Washington, DC, seemingly forget still exists and that will always be a part of them. In the Fourteenth Street Corridor, the streets where Black people were forced to create their own world, Dunbar observes something remarkably different from "mammies" with laundry and babies or "mammies" serving as waitresses.

"Colored men have made money here," Dunbar also writes, "and some of them have known how to keep it."[40] Dunbar also notes their power locally, challenging long-held stereotypes of black failure when he points out that several black men are on the local board of trade and that a Black man "drafted" the city's assessment law. Dunbar also is quick to note that the Black community where he lives is a neighborhood of professionals—"so many" that Dunbar would be too busy counting the Black lawyers and doctors working and living in the city.

Dunbar wrote a second essay about his time in Washington, DC, which also provides a portrait of the city. It appeared in *The Saturday Evening Post*. By this point, he was essentially gone from the city. Dunbar's official stay was cut due to illness. His work, at the Library of Congress working in the dusty shelves of the country's premier repository of written works, brought on a bout of tuberculosis. Dunbar had spent fifteen months working at the library.

Dunbar's health problems forced the Dunbars to sell their home in the city's LeDroit Park district. Alice and Paul, always so focused on his work and his stature as a writer, moved to Colorado, where the air was fresh and where Paul could continue to pursue these literary dreams and hopes in a better state of health. This did not end his attachment to the city, but it did cut short his stay.

But the marriage soon fell apart. It was Paul's fault. His self-medicating drinking habits and brutish treatment of his wife led to destruction of the union. Paul would return to Dayton eventually, where he would die in 1906. Alice Dunbar-Nelson, his widow, an important literary and public figure in her own right, worked hard after his death to keep his memory and work alive despite their split at the end. Her literary career, on hold during her marriage to Dunbar, resumed.

Ms. Dunbar married again and continued to write and publish. She also aggressively involved herself in the movement for women's suffrage. One wonders what might have been had she not married Paul Laurence Dunbar. Alice Dunbar-Nelson was a very capable writer of high talents. Her marriage to Dunbar did not change that, but it did change her career trajectory. His death at such a young age also shifted the narrative where the initial focus of his life and hers would always be him.

But the city of Washington would never forget the elevator boy poet from Dayton, Ohio and his wife, Alice Dunbar-Nelson, no matter how brief their time in the city. Paul became an infinite gift to the city. To this day, a city high school bears his name. Many of the Black poets who would follow his example as professional poets would graduate from that high school and lead the life Dunbar sought to live in just thirty-four productive but very short years.

2

The Washingtonians

The Washingtonian
Possessed of this city, we are born
Into kinship with its people.
Eyes that looked upon
Cool magnificence of space,
The calm of marble,
And green converging on green
In long distances,
Bear their wonder to refute
Meaningless dimensions,
The Old-World facades.

The city is ours irrevocably
As pain sprouts at the edge of joy,
As grief grows large with our years.
New seeds push hard to topsoil;
Logic is a grafted flower
From roots in a changeless bed.
Skeleton steel may shadow the path,
Broken stone snag the foot,
But we shall walk again
Side by side with others on the street,
Each certain of his way home.[1]
—*May Miller*

Black Women and Art

When Henry Lincoln Johnson, an African American lawyer living in Atlanta, Georgia, was appointed recorder of deeds in the District of Columbia in 1910, the history of Black poetry in Washington, DC, was set on a historically special and specific course. Johnson was the husband of the poet Georgia Douglas Johnson, a seminal figure in Black poetry in the city for most of the twentieth century.

On September 28, 1903, the couple was married in Atlanta. Henry Lincoln Johnson was a "nationally known public figure" in Atlanta,[2] and he and his bride, Georgia, were graduates of Atlanta University. Mr. Johnson would also graduate from the University of Michigan Law. Mrs. Johnson would study music at Oberlin in Ohio.[3] On October 15, 1903, the couple received guests at their home at 428 Houston Street in Atlanta.[4]

This combination of political aspirations and creative drive would coalesce in the future, when the couple moved to Washington, DC, in 1910. Johnson would become engaged in politics and support Woodrow Wilson, the staunch segregationist president who was elected in 1912. Yet, while Johnson would spend his time in the city in politics, it would be his wife, Georgia, who would leave the larger literary legacy. The decision of the power couple to move to the District of Columbia altered literary history in Washington, DC.

By the early 1920s, the Johnson home at 1461 Street NW in Washington, DC, would become a centerpiece of early African American twentieth-century literary activity. Johnson's role in creating a literary space for Black writers and poets in her home would draw Langston Hughes, W. E. B. Du Bois, James Weldon Johnson, May Miller, and Zora Neale Hurston, writers who are household names today in academic as well as literary circles.[5] The forging of this space was more than just happenstance.

The city remained fertile ground for Black poetry and poets after Paul Laurence Dunbar departed. It was attractive to Black professionals, and that included African American writers and artists. In December 1902 James E. McGirt, a poet from Greensboro, North Carolina, visited the city, and it was mentioned in local media. McGirt, a college graduate and laborer, a contemporary of Dunbar, would go on to have quite a notable, though short, literary career.

The Washington Post referred to McGirt as "this new aspirant for poetry laurels"[6] during his visit, a reference to the declaration of Paul Laurence Dunbar as the "Poet Laureate of the Negro Race." It was predicted by the *Post* that it wouldn't be long before McGirt would "take his place by the side of Paul Laurence Dunbar." McGirt, however, would eventually settle in Philadelphia and enjoy a fruitful writing career.

In addition to McGirt, James Corrothers, another well-known Black poet, would also visit the city and be noted in the local media. Corrothers was a good friend of Paul Laurence Dunbar and was quite prolific in his own right. Yet, he would not become synonymous with the building Black literary scene in the city and would not leave the impact that Dunbar did in the city. He would publish widely, including in James Weldon Johnson's (no relation to Georgia Douglas Johnson or her husband, Henry Johnson) *The Book of American Negro Poetry*, a leading anthology of verse published in 1922.[7]

Georgia Douglas Johnson was also included in that celebrated anthology along with many other writers from Washington, DC, or writers who had ties to the city. By 1922 Johnson would be fully established as a poet in the city and connected to the Black literary life there.

In 1916–17, she published her first collection, *The Heart of a Woman, and Other Women,* but she had been actively pursuing the arts before that time. In November 1913 her musical production *Your Eyes Are Like Violets* was published. It was published by the P.J. Music Company of New York City, which specialized in publishing "credible music productions by colored music writers."[8] Two years later, in April 1915, Johnson published two additional songs—"Regal Rose" and "Within My Inmost Heart."[9] In addition to having her skills as a song composer recognized, Johnson was also cited for her talents in writing "prose" and "short stories" and "poetical effusions."[10]

Johnson finished and wrote two "movie picture scenarios," both of which were picked up by a leading New York City film firm.[11] At the time, Johnson was furiously writing poems, songs, short fiction, and a photoplay entitled *Blood Yoke,* which appeared in Pittsburgh and dealt with the issue of color.[12] In 1917 her poem "Exodus" stirred the public locally. Johnson was studying "library management" at the time at Howard University when the poem appeared.[13] The poem, unlike much of her other early work, was directly related to the struggle of Black people. It dealt with why African Americans were leaving the South for a different life in the North.[14]

Johnson, who migrated from Atlanta to Washington, DC, herself, could certainly comment on such an experience:

Hegira (The Exodus)
Oh, black man, why do you northward roam, and leave all the farm lands bare?
Is your house not warm, tightly thatched from storm, and a larder replete your share?
And have you not schools, fit with books and tools the steps of your young to guide?
Then what do you seek, in the north cold and bleak, 'mid the whirl of its teeming tide?

I have toiled in your cornfields, and parched in the sun,
I have bowed 'neath your load of care,
I have patiently garnered your bright golden grain, in season of storm and fair,
With a smile I have answered your glowering gloom, while my wounded heart quivering bled,
Trailing mute in your wake, as your rosy dawn breaks, while I curtain the mound of my dead.

Though my children are taught in the schools you have wrought, they are blind to the sheen of the sky,
For the brand of your hand, casts a pall o'er the land, that enshadows the gleam of the eye,

My sons, deftly sapped of the brawn-hood of man, self-rejected and impotent stand,
My daughters, unhaloed, unhonored, undone, feed the lust of a dominant land.

I would not remember, yet could not forget, how the hearts beating true to your own,
You've tortured, and wounded, and filtered their blood 'till a budding Hegira has
blown.

Unstrange is the pathway to Calvary's hill, which I wend in my dumb agony,
Up its perilous height, in the pale morning light, to dissever my own from the tree.

And so I'm away, where the skyline of day sets the arch of its rainbow afar,
To the land of the north, where the symbol of worth sets the broad gates of
combat ajar![15]
—*Georgia Douglas Johnson*

"Hegira" was not included in her singular collection, *The Heart of a Woman*, but that is mostly because the poem didn't fit thematically. Johnson was not a confrontational poet. Jessie Faucet, who would become a celebrated fiction writer during the Harlem Renaissance, reviewed *The Heart of a Woman* for the *Journal of Negro History*: "In this work, Mrs. Johnson, although a woman of color, is dealing with life as it is regardless of the part that she may play in the great drama. Here she is a woman of that imagination that characterizes any literary person choosing this field as a means of directing the thought of the world."[16] William Stanley Braithwaite, the poet who had encouraged Mrs. Johnson to write a full volume of poetry, wrote the introduction to *The Heart of a Woman*.[17] His introduction is also mentioned in a review in *The Crisis* magazine. Braithwaite, an African American who traced his family background to British Guiana, describes Johnson's collection as "intensely feminine" and "deeply human." His mother was an "American black who could pass for white," and Braithwaite's professional career as a writer, critic, and teacher played out in a similar manner.[18] Braithwaite describes the book as poetry about "the emancipation of women" that is "yet to be fully accomplished," a book about the "reality of a woman's heart and experience with astonishing raptures."[19]

The collection itself is dedicated to her husband, Henry, and is a fine collection of rhyming verses that rarely stray from the mood of emotional love. Johnson seeks to take the reader deep into the soul of a woman. *The Heart of a Woman* set the stage for Johnson's emergence in the next decade as a key local and national figure in Black poetry. She would firmly establish her place in what would come to be known as the "genteel" poetry school along with Anne Spencer.

By 1921 she would begin to convene literary salons in her home at 1461 S Street NW in Washington, DC, on Saturday nights. Among the writers who would eventually appear at Johnson's salons would be May Miller, the daughter of Kelly Miller and a graduate of Howard University.

If you read the early personal writings of poet and playwright May Miller when she was just a teenager, you soon understand how it is that she became a prolific writer and so well respected. Her command of the English language on the page is self-evident in these early days. The first time I lost myself in the musings of Miller was as she was writing as a young student at Howard University. In one of her many letters to her older brother, Kelly Jr., May Miller writes on January 18, 1918, the following: "Examination is all that one can hear on campus. Every other student seems to be writing a fifty-page theme."[20]

Later in the same letter, a passage concerns the now-legendary Howard University–based theater organization Stylus: "The Stylus held its initiation last Saturday night. The way in which its new members acted was interesting. They learned passages from the Bible with more earnestness than in a Sunday school class. One member suggested we initiate the whole student body so that all the students may know one biblical passage."[21]

Miller was only eighteen years old at the time she wrote the letter and was involved in the founding of a Stylus literary society at Howard University in 1917. She is a child of the city's Black striver class, those African Americans who were able to navigate the difficulties of America's racial caste system through determination, family, community ties, and education. She is one of the bridge-building poets in the city, an African American poet able to find acceptance in many literary circles there.

Miller's success as a writer and as a public figure in Washington for much of the twentieth century is hardly surprising also because of her father, Kelly Miller. Kelly Miller attended Howard University on scholarship and would eventually create the school's sociology department.[22] He was dean of the school of arts and sciences at Howard from 1907 to 1919, and he was a prolific writer of essays and commentary in many of the nation's leading newspapers and magazines.[23] It is Miller's home where Paul Laurence Dunbar lodged when he first came to DC in the 1890s.

It is often suggested that May Miller's presence and role in the history of Black poetry in the city is understated. This is not true. Miller is a major literary figure locally and nationally. Michael Harper—late, great poet, and author of the legendary volume of poems *Dear John, Dear Coltrane*—described May Miller as "a teacher and culture bearer with a great heart and soul; she has never withdrawn from the complexities and contractions of the world."[24]

Local writer Myra Sklarew, herself a significant literary presence in the city of Washington, DC, once wrote that "to read across May Miller's life is to read across the history of 20th century America."[25]

Robert Hayden, the Detroit poet and once the poetry consultant to the Library of Congress, wrote that May Miller "writes with quiet strength, lyric intensity" and that she "is perceptive and compassionate."[26]

And the poet O. B. Hardison describes May Miller as a poet who writes with "an authentic note of love and warmth."[27] It isn't just the kind words and tributes May Miller receives here. It is the fact that the words are coming from a cross section of some of America's great literary figures and minds. Local DC writers and writers with national prestige such as Robert Hayden all name May Miller as a major writer.

May Miller was born in Washington, DC, on January 26, 1899, one of the five children of Kelly Miller and Anna May Miller. The family lived at 430 Bryant Street NW on the campus of Howard University. African American intellectuals of the day such as the poet Paul Laurence Dunbar entered the Miller home because of May Miller's father. And on some level, this is how and where the Dunbar literary legacy was passed to May Miller. This is so even though May Miller never actually met the elevator boy turned Black poetic superstar.

Dunbar first came to see Miller's father well before May was even born. Dunbar was likely gone from the city by the time young May Miller was aware of her world on that day. But Dunbar still made a connection with the little girl, who would go on to become one of the city's most important writers. According to May Miller, in an interview with Grace Cavalieri, Dunbar, on one of his early visits to the Miller home before May was born, inscribed a book for their newborn son, Kelly. Though Dunbar's gesture was for her older brother, and she was not even yet born, she still savored the moment.

"I was born a little bit late for this," she said to Cavalieri. "But my oldest brother was a baby when Paul Laurence Dunbar visited the house. And when he asked my mother, what shall I give the baby . . . my mother said, your first book, Mr. Dunbar. And he wrote on the flyleaf of that book, a poem to my brother."[28]

Miller said that her brother never cared much for poetry despite Dunbar's gift to him. Miller embraced Dunbar's literary gift of poetry for herself. "I should have been born then, and that book should have been dedicated to me," she told Cavalieri during that interview. "That book is in a bookcase in my home," she added.[29]

It is probable that Miller was going to pursue the arts and, most likely, a literary life anyway. Yet, Dunbar's presence in her family space made it more likely, not to mention her father's promotion of literature in the home to his children.

In 1913 Miller was only fourteen years old but began to get published. She received a check for .25 cents from the School for Progress in Philadelphia for a story she had written. The check was accompanied by a letter from the School Progress League, where she was informed that the "story" she had "submitted" would be published by the league in August 1913.

"We are very well pleased with your efforts and hope that you will try again very soon." Miller was also invited to "write and tell us what you think of School Progress at the same time you acknowledge the receipt of your check."[30]

The poem accepted for publication was about Venus, the goddess of love. Miller has said more than once that she never cashed that check. Many years later she said that the poem was "god-awful." Yet, she also admits that she was "scratching" words from her very early years. She was basically a writer from birth, almost.

One year later after that early success, Miller published again. This time her writings appeared locally in *The Washington Post*. It was another contest, and fifteen-year-old

Miller earned $3 for a story called "Wireless in Squirreldom." The story was printed in full in the newspaper on October 4, 1914.[31]

Once again, Miller's command of the English language is self-evident from beginning to end: "Kind Aunt Anna: I guess you will be very much surprised on receiving this 'wireless' and much more so on finding it from squirreldom. Yes, I am Shadetail, the squirrel, and the proud proprietor and inventor of the wireless system in squirreldom. But to my surprise, Aunt Anna, you know that even in squirreldom each word costs a nut when sending a wireless."[32]

Today, Miller's short work of fiction would likely be called flash fiction due to the brevity of the story. The story is the musings of Shadetail the squirrel, who becomes the pet of a family for two years. It does show off Miller's early love of nature, which would appear again and again in her poetry as she rose in the local literary scene. It is a theme she would make part of her personal aesthetic.

"Fettered Genius"

Before their later connections in the 1920s at Georgia Douglas Johnson's literary salons, it is hard to say whether Miller and Johnson met. Miller is just a teenager developing a writing voice. Johnson, on the other hand, is publishing volumes of poetry and getting noticed in other parts of the country. But they are continuing to build upon the individuals and institutions that came before them. Miller would attend Dunbar High School (M Street High School would be named for Paul Laurence Dunbar after his death). Miller would attend Howard University and become involved in Stylus, the drama club at the college. Both Black women writers didn't know it, but they were also part of a long tradition of African American poetry in America.

By embracing life as poets as Dunbar did prior to them, they were also forging what Keith D. Leonard calls the "Black bardic" tradition.[33] Leonard refers to this tradition in his book *Fettered Genius*. It is a tradition that dates back from Dunbar to George Moses Horton, Francis Harper, and then, of course, Phillis Wheatley.[34] It is poetry where the poets demonstrate their own excellence as poets and, in turn, fight the struggle for racial upliftment.

By maintaining the struggle against racial oppression and seeking true self-consciousness in America, Black poets have asserted their right to full humanity and equality in society. Dunbar, according to Leonard, "initiated self-conscious ethnic self-definition in African American poetry."[35] Leonard adds that he doesn't do this through his "dialect" poetry, which was the poetry that the masses preferred. Dunbar does it by committing in his poetry to "racial uplift ideology" according to Leonard, "the dominant black principles of the time."[36] Dunbar is at his best, Leonard admits, when he uses Standard English in his poetry but also the cultural folklore of Black people that is also part of his dialect poetry.

While Leonard does not mention May Miller as part of this tradition, this does not mean she doesn't fit the model. She does. Her instinctive command of the English language in all her writings makes that self-evident. This is part of Leonard's assertion in elevating these Black poets to a level of excellence and racial uplift without having to necessarily speak directly on the racial oppression issue.

Leonard does devote considerable time to Georgia Douglas Johnson in *Fettered Genius*. On some level, she fits Leonard's ideal even more than Dunbar does. Johnson navigates the world as a Black poet who does not necessarily see writing about race to be the escape. Many years later, according to Leonard, Johnson will write to the poet Arna Bontemps and tell him that "it seems to me an art to forget those things that make the heart heavy."[37] By succeeding as a poet, this is when one leaves the "chains behind."[38]

Johnson, according to Leonard, was a poet who emphasized "the ultimately liberating relationship between this imagination and its claim to dignity on one hand and its circumscribing, oppressive world on the other."[39] Johnson, though she would become an important player during the Harlem Renaissance as it came together forcefully in the city of Washington, DC, was not the kind of poet that the period is most famous for historically. Johnson was, in fact, quite the opposite, but according to Leonard her overall place in African American letters is secure.

Miller and Johnson, and more than likely many others, became writers in a city that was being constructed and deconstructed politically, socially, and culturally. In other words, Washington, like most of the rest of the country, was in a state of transformation. It was decades after the Civil War and the sabotage of Reconstruction by the country's white supremacists' elements, but the effects were self-evident. The old history of the city is a Jim Crow history, but the post–Civil War history is as troubling as the city's most recent history as a progressive place, where liberal and racial politics still finds itself imprisoned behind constitutional controls that defy America's founding ideals.

Well before Miller and Johnson began writing poetry about love and the human experience and all but avoided racial ideals, the nation's capital emerged after the war as one of the country's early experiments with Black equality. Black men gained the right to vote after the war and were instrumental in voting into office a biracial ruling body. According to historians George Derek Musgrove and Chris Myers Asch, the right to vote for Black men in the Reconstruction period "desegregated the municipal bureaucracy, provided jobs to a burgeoning Black middle class, implemented massive public works projects, and supported the expansion of what became the nation's best Black public school system."[40]

In addition, "city leaders also passed anti-discrimination legislation that remained on the books well into the next century and provided the legal foundation for the city's post–World War II civil rights movement. DC developed a reputation as a haven for Black advancement, attracting some of the nation's top Black intellectuals and political figures, including famed orator Frederick Douglass."[41]

It was great initial progress, but it all crashed and burned in 1874, when the city's chief executive, Alexander Shepherd, his administration, and the Board of Public

Works were all accused of reckless spending, and the city lost most of its power and independence. The power Black people had gained in 1867 during Reconstruction led to a white conservative backlash against a biracial government in the nation's capital.[42] While the attack upon Shepherd and the rights of the locals was the final act, the move to shutter the rights and gains of Black people in the city was the motive for the racist actions of Congress.

This is the city Johnson and Miller were a part of the early years of the twentieth century. Woodrow Wilson, elected president in 1912, also provided more satisfaction to white Americans uninterested in serious racial change in the city and nation. Wilson, a staunch segregationist, decided to segregate much of the federal workforce when he arrived in office in 1913.[43]

Members of the Wilson administration and an organization known as the National Democratic Fair Play Association pressed hard to separate Black workers from white workers in the federal government workplace.[44] Considering many local African Americans worked in the federal government, these actions sent a clear message that Jim Crow America was going nowhere and was going to continue to try to maintain its presence.

W. E. B. Du Bois, the great intellectual and editor of *The Crisis* magazine, published a letter in the magazine directly to President Wilson taking him to task for his actions: "Sir, you have now been President of the United States for six months and what is the result? It is no exaggeration to say that every enemy of the Negro race is greatly encouraged; that every man who dreams of making the Negro race a group of menials and pariahs is alert and hopeful," Du Bois's letter reads.[45]

Du Bois also points out that many African American clerks found themselves working in separate rooms at various agencies. Only after intense agitation from African Americans did the policy change some, though it wasn't repealed totally.[46] Under the conditions of racial segregation already imposed in the city, it is no wonder that the African American population socially and culturally began to build and settle into their own institutions and put their cultural stamp on these associations.

The creation and establishment of the Black male-run social organization known as the MuSoLit are evidence of Black Americans in the city building their own. The organization, which focused on music, social life, and literature, to bring about "improvement in the race," got off to a triumphant beginning in 1905 with several events. While MuSoLit was founded in 1905 in the city, records for the organization only exist as of 1915 onward, mostly through news clippings, to document the group's role in helping shape Black cultural society in Washington, DC.[47]

May Miller's father, Kelly Miller, was intimately involved in the organization from the beginning. It was invitation only and specialized in music, literary, and social studies.[48] In February 1910 MuSoLit devoted its program to paying tribute to Abraham Lincoln and Frederick Douglass, two individuals instrumental in changing the country and ending slavery. This was a very characteristic event for the organization. The members used music, poetry, and oratory to pay tribute to important individuals in African American history and culture. On May 9, 1911, the organization held one of its biggest early gatherings, when it met to celebrate Paul Laurence Dunbar, the poet, who had lived in the city from 1898 to 1901.[49]

While it is a good thing that the African American community in the city had a very prominent literary and cultural club, its impact was limited. For one, women could not join the organization, and second, the organization was focused upon recruiting certain types of Black people, mainly those lucky enough to have obtained professional status or certain educational credentials. This would only have a limited effect on literature's development in the city.

Washington, DC, itself made it clear in December 1915 how it felt about Dunbar and his time there. The city was considering renaming the M Street High School, and Dunbar's name was one of two at the top of the list in late 1915.[50] On January 8, 1916, Mrs. Helen Davis, president-general of the "Dunbar Literaries," of 516 Tenn. Avenue, wrote a letter to the city's commissioners endorsing naming the high school after Dunbar.[51] With great passion, Mrs. Davis wrote, in part, the following:

> His books can be found in nearly every other home in Washington; our society has been largely instrumental in making it possible. He is recited or quoted in nearly every public and private entertainment of note. His life and work have evoked the highest encomium, not only from eminent authors but from eminent people in both public and private life, national and international.
>
> Gentlemen, we kindly request you to hold out the lantern of hope, by naming the school after our own taciturn, energetic, and frugal Paul Lawrence Dunbar, to the great number of children, whose parents, like those of Dunbar are honest toilers in the humbler walks of life; that they may be encouraged to toil on to the goal, knowing that at last just recognition will be their reward from those higher up.[52]

The school was named for Dunbar not long afterward, in 1920.[53] It is one of the single-most important symbolic moves in the history of the city toward establishing a legacy of excellence in education and literature. At the time, Mrs. Davis likely was unaware, but she had set in motion the true spirit of Dunbar's literary life in the city and, in effect, had also spoken for and to a long list of great and important Black poets. Many would walk the halls and learn at the school named for Mr. Dunbar and carry that spirit of life as a poet out into the world.

3
We Swear by *Cane*

I co-facilitated a poetry workshop between 1995 and 1997 at Lamond Riggs Library in Washington, DC, on Saturday mornings. The library is located right down the street from my home on Kennedy Street NE. My co-facilitators are legends of the world of letters now. Yona Harvey, a Kate Tufts Discovery Award recipient, author of several books of poems, and one of the first Black women in America to write for Marvel Comics. Ta-Nehisi Coates, National Book Award winner, MacArthur fellow, and author of *Between the World and Me*—a book for the ages. I was older than them and sort of the unofficial leader of the workshop, but looking back it was just a group of young, hungry poets who loved words. I was older, so in the African tradition they were nice enough to let me take the lead.

Other poets came by to help run the workshop regularly. A. Van Jordan, author of many volumes of poetry now and a professor of creative writing at Stanford. Ernesto Mercer, one of my writer friends and colleagues in the city of Washington and, like me, a DC local. Our workshops were the quietest moments of my early poetry life. Most of the time one of us would begin by sharing a poem from an established poet. One of my favorite poets to share was Jean Toomer.

Toomer's 1923 book *Cane* was where I found the deep well of beautiful verse to use in the workshop. His poetry was about the city where we were working and writing. His poetry was also different, it had its own voice, and it also took us places we could only imagine before but now we could see in our minds. Toomer also received even more respect because he was from Washington, DC, born there in 1894.[1] *Cane* is a unique work of literature that arguably changed American literature. *Cane* is, by best descriptions, a culmination of a lot of experiences for the writer, Jean Toomer. He had lived in white and Black communities in Washington. He had lived in New York and lost both of his parents (one by desertion, the other due to death).[2]

He had also attended several colleges but writing eventually steals his heart. And then he also by chance meets the writer Waldo Frank and the public intellectual Alain Locke. Without Frank and Locke, Toomer still becomes a writer more than likely, but perhaps his path is different.

The Poet

On Christmas 1919 the poet Jean Toomer wrote a letter to Georgia Douglas Johnson in Washington, DC. It was one of several letters he would write to Douglas. Toomer, a DC native, was in New York City at the time, and Douglas was in Washington. Toomer had taken a job working in shipyards in New York City for ten days but made it clear in the brief note that he was done with it and would be a writer.

A full Xmas to you and those you love.
Most of my energies have gone in work, work at the shipyards.
Now, I know of their life, so I've quit.
I'll have more time to write.[3]

It seems no accident that Toomer, the developing writer, and Georgia Douglas Johnson, the very first of the significant Black poets living in Washington, DC, in the post-Dunbar period, would find one another. In a city like Washington, with a confident but insular Black writing community, Black writers and especially the Black poets eventually found each other. You get the impression as well that Toomer, at the time, was eager to find his way in the literary world and Douglas, who had found her footing to a degree, would be a rich resource for the young poet and someone he could relate to easily.

Toomer and Johnson also have similar but different backgrounds. Johnson, born in Atlanta, well educated, is married to a politician at the time. Her marriage is why she is living in Washington, DC. Toomer also has strong political connections. His grandfather is P. B. S. Pinchback, a famous Louisiana politician and one of many Black politicians elected to office during Reconstruction. Jean Toomer bounces around some as a young child, but he is mostly with his grandfather.

After Toomer's father, Nathan Toomer, deserted Jean's mother, Nina Pinchback, and the family, Toomer and his mother moved in with her parents, the Pinchbacks. They lived on Bacon Street, Washington, DC, a predominantly white neighborhood of working-class and middle-class families. Toomer and his family, the Pinchbacks, were African American under America's very auspicious "one drop rule" even though they could pass for white. However, Toomer's grandfather, P.B.S. Pinchback, sent Jean to Black schools in the city, and that included the all-Black M Street High School (renamed for Paul Laurence Dunbar in 1916).

Toomer experienced a transient, unstable life. His mother remarried, and she moved to New York. But she died in 1910, and Jean then settled permanently with his grandparents. P.B.S. Pinchback was Jean's biggest, early influence anyway. Historically he is a giant of an American. According to W. E. B. Du Bois, in his seminal social and political history, *Black Reconstruction*, Pinchback was born in Georgia, and "was the son of a white man."[4] He was also "white in appearance" (with a few drops of Negro blood, according to Du Bois) and was educated up North in Cincinnati, just across the slavery line in Ohio.[5] He was highly intelligent and made captain in the Union Army.[6]

Pinchback eventually settled in Louisiana, and during Reconstruction, when African Americans gained the right to vote, he became lieutenant of the state of Louisiana from 1871 to 1872.[7] He also served briefly as governor for forty-three days, the first Black governor of a state in US history.[8]

Eventually, after Reconstruction collapsed, he settled North, in Washington, DC, and even took a job in New York for a while to support his family. By the time Jean came back to live with him, Pinchback had moved to the U Street Corridor in the heart of Black America's culturally thriving city.[9] It was a change for the young Toomer. He had once fit comfortably into the city's white community in their neighborhoods, even though he attended Black schools. Now, young Jean resided in the heart and soul of Black America. And not only that, but the literary gumbo that would soon become the Renaissance was quietly taking shape right in the community where he now found himself. But before any of that would occur, Jean Toomer would produce a work of art that predates the magical surge of art and identity that is the Harlem Renaissance. That work is *Cane*.[10]

Meeting the Maestro

In America, the most important intellectual to many is named John Locke. John Locke is quite responsible for America's doctrine of private property and the advancement of slavery. Yet in Black America, one of the most important intellectuals is Alain Locke. Alain Locke is like many African Americans in Washington, DC, early in the twentieth century. A giant of a man, though he wasn't giant in size. A Rhodes scholar, and longtime Howard University professor of philosophy, Locke is a key framer and player in the Renaissance. He is also central to the power and influence of the Black literary tradition in Washington, DC, even today as his legacy resonates more and more each year.

He was born in Philadelphia, but by 1912 he was an associate professor at Howard University. He would leave Howard University to obtain his PhD from Harvard University, and by the early 1920s he would return to Howard, where he would teach and create for decades. It is not certain when Toomer met Locke or judging by his letters to Locke when he felt comfortable reaching out to Locke. But it is likely sometimes in the early 1920s, when Toomer was beginning to pursue the writing trade in a very serious manner, just like Paul Laurence Dunbar had done at the turn of the century. Toomer had yet to return to his home city of Washington, DC, from New York, but he did contact Locke in April 1920, when he was living in New York, precisely to try to meet Locke.

By the summer 1920, Locke and Toomer had met: Toomer wrote Locke and referenced the fact that they had a "talk last evening." It was an important connection to consider how Locke would influence Black writing in the nation and in Washington over the next decade.

They met after many years of wandering by Toomer. He aspired to be a writer, but one also must live and mature. Toomer spent time in Wisconsin, Chicago, and New York. He attended college in all three of these places. He took jobs trying to sell cars door-to-door in Chicago. He worked at a shipyard in Newark, New Jersey. It gave Toomer an appreciation for the working class, but it didn't knock him off his path to be a writer and work in the arts.

In 1920, living in New York, Jean Toomer was furiously writing to many people, contemplating his writing life. In January 1920 he wrote to Georgia Douglas Johnson in DC again and told her of trying to connect with W. E. B. Du Bois at *The Crisis* so he would read some of his writings.[11] Though Du Bois didn't remember Toomer when Toomer got in touch with "the Doctor," Toomer was encouraged enough by Du Bois's response to declare that he would send Du Bois "some of my writings." "I've got a bunch of sentences and phrases stacked away for use," Toomer also wrote. "And many, many new experiences and thoughts. They're all collecting in my mind."[12]

A month later, February 1920, Toomer again wrote to Johnson, and it is obvious he is devoted to writing, describing his time as "the biggest of my life." He does promise Johnson that he will be in Washington, DC, soon to describe to her "the evolutions of his life."[13] He is also writing to Lola Ridge, Lewis Mumford, and Alain Locke. He is trying to figure things out.

It can probably be said that between 1920 and 1922 is Jean Toomer's birth as a writer. All his communications by letter talk about writing and wanting to be a writer. In 1920 he wrote to Lola Ridge, Georgia Douglas Johnson, and Alain Locke from New York, and writing is an obsession for him at this point. He has made his decision.

His correspondence at the time indicates he is in contact more regularly with Georgia Douglas Johnson and Alain Locke. He is also visiting some of the early gatherings at Georgia Douglas Johnson's home in the U Street area. He is comfortable enough with Locke by this point that he tells him, "I certainly would like to have you join us."[14] It is also important because he is surely comfortable with the scene at Johnson's home and the writers who attend the meetings.

But, in the summer of 1922, Toomer also connected with the writer Waldo Frank.[15] They met at a party in New York City but didn't talk. Later, their paths crossed in Central Park, New York, and their friendship was born. This friendship laid the foundation for Toomer to embrace the experiences and reflections that would produce *Cane*. Frank also became Toomer's frequent recipient of letters once Toomer moved back to Washington.

The return to DC and the South had to happen as well. The return to the city would bring his intellectual growth as a writer full circle. Washington in 1920–22 was the heart of Black America. The Black people in the city had built a cultural and intellectual homeland. They were segregated in their neighborhoods, but they shaped life there down to all the most important details. The schools, churches, businesses, and civic and community associations worked to support the lives of Black people in the city.

Toomer now lived in the African American community and likely witnessed the strivers' culture among Black people that Washington, DC, became famous for over the years. There were specific reasons that the city began to develop in such a manner. During Toomer's childhood and teen years, "the number of blacks pursuing an education after high school grew dramatically."[16]

In addition, by 1900 "the number of black Washingtonians in school after the age of twenty was only 157; two decades later, the figure had climbed to 541."[17] Black Washington also had "a well-financed segregated school system with a wide array of other, large public institutions that employed educated blacks."[18] Black Washington outnumbered other major cities with significant Black populations in the number of clergies, teachers, and physicians in significant numbers. Several hundred African Americans also worked in the government.[19]

Historian Steven Mintz partially explains the vibrant Black cultural community that Toomer was part of when he lived with his grandparents on U Street. Mintz describes Black Washington at the turn of the century as possessing "a self-conscious leadership class" that was "committed to racial equality and to the moral and intellectual uplift of the black population." Many of them, according to Mintz, traced "their ancestry back to prominent black abolitionist leaders, professionals, and political figures of the mid-nineteenth century."[20] This did create a class divide in the city among African Americans. Toomer was a witness to these divisions in the Black communities in DC. But Toomer was uniquely situated to witness it all because of his appearance.[21]

Cane also is the product of Toomer spending time in the South, in Georgia specifically as a schoolteacher in Sparta, Georgia.[22] It was a job he obtained by chance, and one that came with considerable logistical challenges, as his grandparents depended upon him greatly. His letter in November 2021 to Alain Locke sums up the impact the experience in Georgia had on the writer Jean Toomer. "There is poetry here," Toomer writes, "and drama, but the atmosphere for one in my position is almost prohibitory."[23]

Toomer also tells Locke that he is "a natural born teacher . . . I'm clearing hurdles altogether too high here, but I can't help it. I leap, and then look back to see the bewildered expression on my pupil's faces."[24] Toomer also tells Locke of what he has observed in Sparta: "99 percent of the people who write and talk about the Negro hardly know his name. Artistically, the field is virgin."[25]

Toomer's biographer, John Chandler Griffin, is certain that if Toomer had not spent those few months in Georgia, *Cane* would never have been written.[26] The book is Toomer's manifesto. It is the culmination of his experiences in Black Washington and in the Black Belt of Georgia. It is probably more accurate than most sociological studies of Black people during that period.

In summer 1922 one of Toomer's most famous pieces of writing, "Seventh Street," was first published by *Broom Magazine*. "Seventh Street" will go on to be a fixture in the DC section of the *Cane*, and it screams with the vibrant and raw life of post-war Washington. In addition, in November 1922, Toomer appeared at the downtown YMCA in Washington discussing his writings.[27] Toomer was furiously writing and editing the book at the time.

Toomer's writings in *Cane* became a search of self, and a search for his Black self as well. Toomer could pass just like his grandfather, but he chose not to do so. He decided to write honestly and to live honestly, something his newly found friend Waldo Frank never did during his writing life. Frank, like Toomer, was Black under America's one drop rule, but he chose to remain behind the veil of America's caste system. Toomer elected to come from behind the wall and speak to the Black experience and to America from the vantage point of a human being. The writings inspired by his visits to the South were critical, as was his multifaceted life in Black Washington, DC.

The book appeared in the summer of 1923, and Toomer's world would change dramatically. The goal he had been chasing, that many writers chase, simply to be accepted as a writer, was obtained. His entry had been properly announced as well in the newspaper of record, *The New York Times*, in August 1923.[28] The book received immediate attention from critics and reviewers, but African American newspapers found the book of most interest. The *New York Age* described Toomer, in an article announcing the book's entry into the world, as a "Negro from Washington DC."[29]

The book is described as a book "of Negro life in Georgia, that has aroused considerable interest."[30] The *Pittsburgh Courier* devotes full attention to the book in its pages on December 22, 1923.[31] Floyd Calvin, while impressed with the unique nature of the book, still declares that "Negroes generally will not understand *Cane*. They will hate it and its author except for the parts which are against white people." Calvin adds that "a number of white people will feel the other way." The book is also, according to Calvin, "not for or against us, racially," but "it is a great book." He recommends for more writers to follow its broad outline.[32] Toomer's publisher, Liverlight, surely wants the book to succeed. It takes out an ad in *The New York Times* announcing the book's arrival.[33]

"To such recent literature of the negro as Stribling's *Birthright*, Du Bois's *Darklight*, and O'Neill's *Emperor Jones*," the ad reads, "has been added a new interpretation of negro life, *Cane* by Jean Toomer."[34] Yet the ad, while a great score for Toomer, conforms to the racist madness of the times in America in publicizing the books. This is not more stereotypically racist than other such moments, but it would be wrong not to call it out.

This racist description read as follows: "*Cane* by Jean Toomer presents emotions, dramatic, genre pictures (in Washington and Georgia) of negro life whose rhythmic beat, like the primitive tom-toms of the African jungle, you can feel because it is written by a man who has felt it historically, poetically, and with deepest understanding."[35] The book's arrival was also effectively launched by Waldo Frank's famous introduction, which helped place the book in and out of context. Frank's high praise for his friend and colleague is somewhat famous now even a century later:

> A poet has arisen in that land who writes, not as a Southerner, not as a rebel against Southerners, not as a Negro, not as apologist or priest or critic: who writes as a poet. The fashioning of beauty is ever foremost in his inspiration: not forcedly but simply, and because these ultimate aspects of his world are to him more real than all its specific problems. He has made songs and lovely stories of his land . . . not of its yesterday, but of its immediate life. And that has been enough.[36]

Frank calls the book in "more ways than one," "a harbinger of the South's literary maturity: of its emergence from the obsession put upon its minds by the unending racial crisis—an obsession from which writers have made their indirect escape through sentimentalism, exoticism, polemic, 'problem' fiction, and moral melodrama."[37]

Is Frank injecting his own vision onto Toomer's work? It is doubtful. *Cane*'s beauty is in its distance from race but also its closeness. Toomer's time in many worlds and many places gives him that distance, but also once he links up the DC Black literary community, an understanding and closeness. *Cane*, for Toomer, according to Frank, is an "unafraid creation," the "work of a man of twenty-seven" who is perhaps "a literary force of whose incalculable future I believe no reader of this book will be in doubt."[38]

But now Jean Toomer, the ambiguous racial writer of Washington, DC, is launched, and many assert him to be something new and bold in the city and in America. Though *Cane* is often called a novel and is compared to Sherwood Anderson's *Winesburg, Ohio*, *Cane* is more a series of interrelated sketches of Black life in America. The book has fifteen poems, six vignettes, seven stories, and a play.[39] While many have situated the book within the Harlem Renaissance period, others have resisted that easy categorization.

The book has also received titles such as "avant-garde" and "experimental" and many other outlier descriptions, but it isn't, if one understands Toomer's influences.[40] Sherwood Anderson and James Joyce (*Dubliners*) were Toomer's models, and they both wrote books that were very similar. In the modern era, Jabari Asim's *A Taste of Honey* has some of *Cane*'s organizational patterns. If there is one part of the book that probably speaks to the uniqueness and power of the book, it is the vignette narrative called "Seventh Street."

For Black poets in DC, it is a favored work. Toomer is writing about the city and captures it like he is a painter in this excerpt:

> Seventh Street is a bastard of Prohibition and the War. A crude-boned, soft-skinned wedge of nigger life breathing its loafer air, jazz songs and love,

> thrusting unconscious rhythms, black reddish blood into the white and whitewashed wood of Washington. Stale soggy wood of Washington. Wedges rust in soggy wood . . . Split it! In two! Again! Shred it! . . . the sun.[41]

Few poets and writers at the time are writing as Toomer writes here. The writing has a certain freedom and audacity to it, a certain humanity free of fear. It is again likely because Toomer is part of the city of Washington as neither white nor Black. He exists in a space he can determine and where he can write honestly about what he observes. *Cane's* reception in the world of literature is unquestionably a big moment. It is also quite a moment in Black DC. It is notable that the book doesn't sell a huge number of copies but does reach a second printing. It is a book that takes a snapshot of a point in time in Black Washington, DC, and in Black America. It reaches a second printing but does not endure for years and years. It soon drops off the radar and became a relic of time. Yet, by the 1960s *Cane* has reemerged and is embraced by a new legion of Black poets.

The legendary anthology *Black Voices,* edited by Abraham Chapman and published in 1968 describes Toomer as "the most promising of the talents and original voices of the Negro Renaissance."[42] Chapman, who selects multiple pieces from Toomer, writes that "Toomer raised the innovation of literary experimentation of the 20s and the modernist mode to new levels of artistic achievement in racial expression by an American Negro."[43] *Cane* is especially a book embraced by Black DC writers who have been drawn to the history of Black life in the city. Local poet Kenneth Carroll remembers discovering Toomer as a student at the University of the District of Columbia (UDC): "I first heard about Toomer oddly enough on Gil Scott-Heron's song, 'Cane.' Then my freshman year at UDC, I read Toomer and was blown away with the beauty and pain of the stories in *Cane.*"[44]

Gil Scott-Heron, on his 1978 recording "Cane," proudly announces at the beginning of the song that Jean Toomer's *Cane* inspired it. Scott-Heron lives in DC in the 1970s, and teaches at the University of the District of Columbia. Two characters in *Cane*—Karintha and Becky, the subject of deep narratives by Toomer in the book—are the crux of the song Scott-Heron composes and records.

Poet Yona Harvey has a similar story of encountering *Cane* and Toomer. Harvey, originally from Ohio, was attending Howard University and came across the new printing of the book, which was enjoying a long-lasting renaissance by that point. The book also had an impact on her. That is the book's true and lasting importance. Once it comes back into print in the late 1960s, it becomes a permanent fixture in the lives of DC Black poets. Toomer, however, is living in obscurity outside Philadelphia. He dies there in 1967.

Yet, his gift to all the young Black poets of the city was solidified. Toomer had done what every poet who followed would aim to do: to be an honest poet dedicated to his art. And this is what all the Black poets I met in the city desired to do—to be true to our own voice and to be honest. While it will be endlessly debated whether *Cane* was part of the Harlem Renaissance, as Chapman suggested in his description of Toomer, there were other signs of increased literary activity among Black poets in the city, supporting the view that something was already in motion before the official Renaissance was declared in 1925 by Alain Locke. James Weldon Johnson, a Renaissance figure, then, a writer, songwriter, and lawyer, edited a collection of poetry in 1922 that backs this view.

Johnson's *The Book of American Negro Poetry* was published in 1922, and it created quite a stir on its own. It also featured more than several writers with ties to Washington, DC. Included were Georgia Douglas Johnson, Jessie Faucet, and Gwendolyn Bennett.[45] Even more important, Weldon Johnson is considered a disciple of Paul Laurence Dunbar.[46]

Along with *Cane*, the publication of this anthology is essential to understanding the development of Black poetry in the early twentieth century before the Renaissance. And its strong connections to the Black poets of the city of Washington, DC, cannot be denied. Johnson's anthology has been described as "a milestone in the progress of the Negro author."[47] The book establishes "a theory of 'Negro literature' which, given the outburst of expression immediately following, is fructified and extended."[48] The *Journal of Negro History* writes that Johnson is attempting to show the "greatness of the Negro as measured by literature and art."[49] This philosophical approach resembles what Alain Locke is beginning to put together at Howard and what other African Americans writers and artists are embracing.

The Shadow

In addition to *Cane* and Johnson's seminal anthology, something as remarkable occurred at this time in Black poetry, though far less known. Lewis Grandison Alexander, a poet and theater artist born and raised in Washington, DC, began to experiment with the Japanese poetry form known as the "haiku" or as it's also known—"hokku." Considering the form had barely made inroads into the creative space of any American writers at the time, Alexander's exploration of the form demonstrates how free and fertile the early 1920s period was in DC for African American poets and artists.

The hokku form is centuries old, but the first very well-known haiku written by an American poet is Ezra Pound's "In a Station of the Metro," in 1913 in *Poetry Magazine*.[50] For Alexander to be credibly working with the form not long after Pound is ambitious. It is possible Alexander is the first African American professional poet to work in the form. In his hokku offerings, he also breaks many of the accepted rules of convention in several of the poems, including the following:

My soul like a tree
Sways above dry leaf autumn
Be kind, oh wind god.[51]

Before his hokku explorations, Alexander participates in the Howard Players at Howard University.[52] The Howard Players, over the years, will become a favored destination for many Black poets who study on campus.

Alexander writes deeply about his hokku in *The Crisis* magazine in December 1923. His essay "Japanese Hokkus"[53] can serve as an essay today on the topic, as Alexander is careful to not just explain the form but to also write about Bashō, a poet Alexander calls the "greatest epigrammatist" of all time. Even though many concede that Alexander goes his own way with the form, this is not because Alexander does not fully grasp the form. According to Alexander, it is "not enough" to say that a "hokku is a seventeen syllable poem." Alexander writes that the "real value" of the form is not the "physical directness" but the "psychological indirectness." What is "suggested" is what really matters and not "what is said."

Recent attention to Alexander is likely to increase, and that is a good thing. Alexander is the uncle of the legendary John Thompson Jr., who was also born and raised in Washington, DC. Thompson, and who died in 2020, is an institution in the city. He was coach of the men's NCAA basketball team at Georgetown University from 1972 to 1999. He is the first African American coach to win a Division I Men's NCAA Basketball Championship. Most just say, he coached "The Hoyas."

Thompson had a stellar career himself in the city, but his contribution is to DC's sports folklore. He was a star on the Archbishop Carroll High School boys' team that won fifty-five straight games between 1959 and 1960.[54] He played at Providence College, was All-American there, and then played two years in the NBA with the Boston Celtics, where he became friends for life with the great Bill Russell, as Russell's backup.[55]

But Thompson quit the NBA, returned to Washington, and eventually became an educator/coach of some legend. He stressed excellence on and off the court for his players and immersed himself in the struggle for equal justice for African American student-athletes throughout his coaching career. He took the Georgetown Hoyas to three NCAA Championship appearances and won the title in 1984 with Patrick Ewing, his most famous player, as his anchor. He was inducted into the Basketball Hall of Fame in 1999.

Following Thompson's death in 2020, his autobiography, *I Came as A Shadow* (written by Jesse Washington), was published.[56] It is in this book that Thompson celebrates Lewis Grandison Alexander, his uncle and his mother's brother. For those who have not heard of Alexander, it is an introduction. The title of his autobiography is from Alexander's poem "Nocturne Varial." The first lines read: "I came as a shadow / I stand now a light."[57]

Lewis Grandison Alexander came to live with his sister (Thompson's mother) when Thompson lived on Benning Road in Southeast, Washington, DC. Alexander attended public schools and was visited by Langston Hughes and Countee Cullen while living at the Benning Road location. He was also involved in several DC theatrical companies.

"Lewis made an extremely positive impression on me, and I loved him dearly," Thompson wrote in his autobiography. "He was the first person I knew in the world who made a mark with his intellectual abilities."[58] Alexander made such an impact on Thompson that Thompson named his second-born son Lewis Grandison Alexander Thompson, in tribute to his late uncle. Unfortunately, Thompson's second son died just ten days after birth.

Alexander's triumph in literature, along with Toomer's *Cane*, said loudly that African American poets in Washington, DC, would endure. Many years later, Alexander's great-niece Tiffany Thompson (daughter of John Thompson) would become a key player on the Washington Black poetry scene in various poetry collectives and at several poetry venues. It is this kind of lineage that demonstrates the strong bonds that had already developed in the city during the early part of the twentieth century among African American poets.

4
Renaissance

Sterling Brown and I agreed that Washington DC has always had a group of Black literary figures who were big. . . . There is no getting away from it, by the time the renaissance came in New York, many were prepared for it because they had been writing.
—*May Miller (commenting on Washington, DC, and the Harlem Renaissance)*

I taught at Michigan State University for eleven years, between 2010 and 2021. One of my most engaging experiences there was when I was asked to moderate a film called *The Art of the Steal.* It is a film about the theft of the art collection of Dr. Albert C. Barnes by the city of Philadelphia and other forces. The film explains how the city of Philadelphia, along with its corporate art establishment, was able to take control of one of the greatest art collections in the world and commodify it against the desires of its creator and owner during his life, Dr. Barnes.

Dr. Barnes was a world-famous art collector, educator, philanthropist, and physician who was a bit of a rival to many thinkers and art world players at the time. Barnes also respected African American art and the humanity of African people. In a 1925 essay, "Negro Art and America," Dr. Barnes wrote that the "New Negro Renaissance" began as early as 1895.[1] Dr. Barnes traced the movement back to two African Americans: Booker T. Washington, the educator, and Paul Laurence Dunbar, the poet.

"Their combined influences brought a new epoch for the American Negro," Barnes wrote. While Washington pushed self-sufficiency through "business life," Dunbar opened "new fields of beauty" for African Americans. Black people in America cast aside "unjust persecution" for "race pride," according to Barnes, and a poet, who came to live in Washington, DC, at around this time, was a major player.[2] Barnes wrote that it was because of Dunbar that many poets came to be at that time as well. They followed the "path"; they yielded to the call of "art," which was but a "new genius" of Black expression, according to Barnes. Dr. Barnes, in writing specifically about

Dunbar, made the case of Dunbar's importance to the launch of the Black Renaissance in America and Black poetry.

Some people don't accept Barnes's view because he based it on his personal observations. But his take is consistent with the belief of other scholars of the Renaissance, such as historian David Levering Lewis, author of *When Harlem Was in Vogue.*[3] Even before Barnes's essay, in January 1921, things were happening in DC.

The poet Jean Toomer writes to Howard University philosophy professor Alain Locke and is thinking hard. Toomer has written to Locke previously and has sought out meetings with Locke, the intellectual who is most responsible for helping launch the Renaissance. Toomer's January 1921 letter to Locke expresses a certain mission. Toomer tells Locke of meetings he has with Georgia Douglas Johnson, Mary Burrill, and other DC writers for the purpose of "historical study of slavery and the Negro."[4] He also told Locke that "we need something to cement us."

At the time of Toomer's communications to Locke, African Americans had been living second-class lives in America. The *Plessy v. Ferguson* "separate but equal" case had declared Black people the hated race of the nation. In 1919 there were race riots in Washington. The historian Carter G. Woodson was almost murdered. In 1922 the Lincoln Memorial was dedicated. Some African Americans were invited to the event but had to sit in a segregated section. The response to white supremacy from African Americans was culture and art. Their culture and their art.

In Washington, DC, a city of vibrant Black life in America, where African Americans had pushed at society's oppressive norms for generations, Toomer was certain that this developing cultural energy was strong and obvious. Years later, in the March 1925 of *Survey Graphic* magazine, Professor Alain Locke was able to describe what Toomer felt was happening in America and in DC among writers much more specifically.

The Movement

Professor Alain Locke was born September 13, 1885, in Philadelphia, Pennsylvania.[5] He attended public schools in that city and eventually graduated from Harvard in 1907 with Phi Beta Kappa honors.[6] Locke was the first African American Rhodes scholar and came to work at Howard in 1912, though he continued his studies in Berlin and again at Harvard. In 1916, while at Howard University, Locke and Dr. Thomas Montgomery Gregory founded the Stylus literary society.[7] Many of the early Washington, DC–based poets would contribute in some way to the organization. May Miller, the DC poet inspired by Dunbar, was there when Stylus was founded. Locke also had his own connections to Dunbar.

On February 9, 1907, on the first anniversary of Dunbar's death, Locke delivered a speech-essay about Dunbar at an African American A.M.E. Zion Church (Rush Memorial A.M.E. Zion) in Cambridgeport, Massachusetts. Locke was studying at

Harvard at the time. According to his biographer, Jeffrey C. Stewart, Locke tried to get the essay on Dunbar published, but it was rejected.[8] So he delivered his essay on Dunbar celebrating the poet's legacy and aesthetics in much the same manner that Anglo-Saxon intellectuals sought to uplift their writers.

Locke did not represent all African American literature then; he was just a student. But by the time he made it to Howard University and connected with the Black middle-class literati in Washington, DC, he would have a role to play in the city. Middle-class African Americans were more likely to be able to afford books to read anyway, and this was Locke's audience and circle. Locke would teach for over forty years at Howard, but he also sought to make sense of African American literature and culture in the early twentieth century. Locke called the period "The New Negro," which became the thematic organizing principle in the March 1925 issue of *Survey Graphic.*

African Americans, as oppressed and exploited Americans, understood individually and collectively what they were experiencing. Communities like those in Harlem and Washington and others could articulate that growing dissent and isolation. The poets and artists had been creating long before the famous *Survey Graphic* issue of March 1925 and Locke's essay "Enter the New Negro." Locke just was uniquely able to articulate these feelings into a movement statement, a manifesto on a certain level. "In the last decade something beyond the watch and guard of statistics has happened in the life of the American Negro,"[9] Locke wrote in *Survey Graphic.* It reads much like Toomer's 1921 letter to Locke, where he says, as mentioned earlier, "we need something to cement us."[10] Locke's lecture on Dunbar back in 1907, delivered initially to barely an audience, embodied the same concept.

In addition to Toomer reaching out to Locke by letter, Locke connected with the poet Langston Hughes in Paris. Hughes's reputation as a serious writer and poet led Locke to pursue him in Paris and tell Hughes about his upcoming *Survey Graphic* special issue. Locke wanted poets and poems, and Hughes was on his list. Hughes's poetry would be prominently featured. Angelina W. Grimké, Georgia Douglas Johnson, and Jean Toomer, poets based in Washington, DC, at this time, also had poetry included.

But, for the most part, in the *Survey Graphic* Harlem issue and the subsequent book, *The New Negro,* poetry is not given much space. Locke's shepherding of the movement into cohesion is very clear, though. Locke calls the period and the surge of creative activity a "Negro Renaissance" and articulates the connections between the art being created in the present with the past.[11] His anthology *The New Negro* is a complete statement politically and culturally.[12]

Shortly after Langston Hughes and Locke connected in Paris as Locke put together his *Survey Graphic* issue, Hughes arrived in Washington, DC. He would spend sixteen months writing and working in the city. Hughes had his designs on perhaps attending Howard University with Locke's help and rooming with his middle-class relatives in the city. But none of it was to be. Hughes fell into life as a working-class Black person in a city with clear African American class issues. It would be an issue many Black people discovered in DC over the years. Washington was a city for African Americans and a city with a significant Black presence and culture. But economics and culture impacted the ability of African Americans to become cohesive.

During his time writing and working in the city, Hughes would find himself mostly working but also trying to write. Hughes wrote to a friend, the arts patron Carl Van Vechten, and told him about his disjointed travels in the capital. As Hughes noted to Van Vechten so long ago, he was pleased to have found a job that left his afternoons free, the time he hoped to spend writing.

Washington, despite Hughes's general complaints about his life there, was important in his life. His residency there became a mixture of memories, a place of personal sadness and public success, of political trepidation, and a final moment of quiet triumph. Hughes lived in Washington between 1924 and 1926, and it was, as his biographer Arnold Rampersad says, an important time in his development as a writer and a person: "By the time he left the city in 1926 . . . he had a far more concrete sense of who he was and who he wanted to be than he ever had."[13]

That is no small point. When Hughes arrived in the city at age twenty-two, he'd already lived a year in Mexico with his estranged father, penned and published the famous poem "The Negro Speaks of Rivers," and seen much of the world through his travels as a young seaman. "I arrived in Washington with only a sailor's pea jacket protecting me from the winter's winds. All my shirts were ragged, and my trousers frayed. I am sure I did not look like a distinguished poet when I walked up to my cousin's porch in Washington Negro society section, LeDroit Park," Hughes later wrote in his biography, *The Big Sea*.[14]

Hughes was not a man of means, though he had well-off relatives in Washington. He had, as Rampersad noted, an "odd class location—upper-class by virtue of his family connections, lower-class by virtue of his poverty."[15] There would be no funds to attend Howard. Hughes grew disenchanted with Washington thereafter and its sharp class lines among African Americans, including in his own family.

Much to his relatives' consternation, Hughes took a job in a laundry, earning $12 a week. As he would write in *The Big Sea*, "Cultured colored Washington did not find it fitting and proper that a poet should work in a wet wash laundry."[16] He and his mother and brother (who had come to Washington before Hughes) had been living with some of those wealthier relatives but eventually moved to an apartment not far from the laundry at 1749 S Street NW. He would also rent a room at the YMCA on 12th Street NW, just below U Street.

Living with his mother in Washington was an important experience, Rampersad said. It deepened Hughes's resolve. "She wanted him to . . . support her rather than live the bohemian life of the struggling artist; he knew he wanted to be a writer."[17] Hughes poured his unhappiness and frustrations into his work. "I felt very bad in Washington, so I wrote a great many poems," Hughes wrote in *The Big Sea*.

In Washington, DC, a city where African American poets had the best chance at opportunities, Hughes saw life there in stark terms. Washington was a Jim Crow city like all the other American cities. It was segregated, and many of the more educated and well-to-do African Americans wanted no part of the working-class African Americans. Hughes found solace on Seventh Street, the area just below Howard University. "From all this pretentiousness Seventh Street was a sweet relief," Hughes would write. "Seventh Street is the long, old, dirty street, where the ordinary Negroes hang out, folks with practically no family tree at all, folks who draw no color line between mulattoes and deep dark browns, folks who work hard for a living with their hands."[18]

It was the same Seventh Street Jean Toomer wrote about in his book *Cane*. It was here, Rampersad said, that Hughes "probably learned more about African American music as a reflection of the culture as a whole than he had ever known."[19] Seventh Street helped to further shape Hughes's aesthetic and deepen his commitment to art that celebrated the life of the common man and woman. After the laundry job, Hughes worked briefly for Carter G. Woodson, the legendary historian and author of *The Miseducation of the Negro*. It was a job that would seem perfect for the aspiring intellectual. But that didn't last either.

Hughes then began working at the Wardman Park Hotel. Known today as the Marriott Wardman Park Hotel, it is filled with elegant rooms named for US presidents and figures from the American Revolution—Thomas Paine, Ethan Allen, and Nathan Hale among them. But there was nothing for the great American poet and writer until decades later, when the story got larger and larger. An exception was one evening in 1925, when Hughes spotted the well-known poet Vachel Lindsay dining at the hotel. He hastily wrote out samples of his verse and dropped them beside Lindsay's plate. Impressed, Lindsay later read the busboy poet's work to his audience. It changed Hughes's life—for a moment. Reporters mobbed Hughes the next day, and he soon found his face plastered in newspapers: He was wearing his busboy uniform. That incident and the famous photograph would leave a lasting impression in the city and on Hughes's life and work.

Though stories remain that Lindsay "discovered" Hughes at the Wardman, the truth is that Hughes had already been published in national journals, and Alfred Knopf had already agreed to publish Hughes's first collection of poetry, *The Weary Blues*. Alain Locke had tracked Hughes down all the way in Paris to have him agree to let him publish his work in the *Survey Graphic* Harlem issue. The encounter with Lindsay was a flash in the media spotlight, but Hughes had been well on his way before that meeting.

"I want to go to college, probably Lincoln College, Pennsylvania, a college for Negroes," Hughes told Josephine Tighe Williams of *The Washington Star* when she picked up the busboy story.[20] This was one of Hughes's reasons for working—to earn money for his education.

Hughes was unable to afford Howard University back then, as even with the job he was barely making ends meet. He was spending time with Washington's better-known Black writers. Alain Locke (whom he already knew) was one, as was May Miller, Angelina Grimké, and many others gathered at writer Georgia Douglas Johnson's house at 1461 S Street NW on Saturday nights for her celebrated salons. Johnson served food and drink to her guests, who would talk into the evening. Hughes participated in these literary salons, though, as he would note, he still worried about his uncertain future: "I didn't know what was going to happen to me," he wrote in *The Big Sea*. Zora Neale Hurston, the writer and folklorist of African American culture, attended the salons. She had come to DC in 1920 to attend Howard University, which she did.

Finally, in early 1926, luck came Hughes's way. He met the local DC poet and singer Waring Cuney by chance. Cuney grew up a stone's throw from Hughes's comfort zone of Seventh Street, the strip Hughes fell in love with during his time in the city. Cuney was born and raised at 503 Florida Avenue NW, in the heart of Black Washington at the time. Cuney urged Hughes to apply to Lincoln University in Pennsylvania, where Cuney was already a student. Though not as well known as Hughes, Cuney would forge his own legacy during the years before World War II. Cuney and Hughes stayed in touch all their lives, and Hughes would return again and again to the city for various reasons, including poetry readings.

The key person to all these connections and lifelong friendships is still Georgia Douglas Johnson and her Saturday night literary gatherings. Hughes fondly describes Johnson as a "charming woman poet" who serves the poets and guests "cake" and "wine."[21] The regular group of literary lovers and figures talk "poetry," "books," and "plays," according to Hughes.[22]

The attendees at the salons were a mixture of well-known literary players and less-known artists and professionals: Marita Bonner, Dutton Ferguson, May Miller, Lewis Alexander, Esther Popel, Zora Neale Hurston, Richard Bruce Nugent, John P. Davis, Willis Richardson, Hallie Elvara Queen, and Clarissa Scott Delaney. Hughes also mentions Alain Locke being present and Angelina Grimké, longtime teacher at Dunbar High School, as a regular "Saturday nighter" as well.

Zora Neale Hurston, who attended Howard University, thought a great deal of what Georgia Douglas Johnson was doing in her home with the local Black poetry community. Her July 18, 1925, letter to Johnson from Roselle, New Jersey, said as much: "I was mighty pleased to get a letter from you. This is my chance to say what a wonderful poet you are. No, what a soulful poet I know you are," Hurston wrote. Her time in the city was over by then. She wrote in the same letter: "Please let me be a friend of yours. I need you."[23] The sisterhood the two had developed, and respect is self-evident.

No surprise that the DC poet May Miller would find her spot at the Johnson salons where Hughes and Hurston also found a safe space. Miller was an established writer with strong connections to Howard University and the upper-middle-class segments of Black Washington. She had even met Hurston and talked her into attending Howard University rather than Baltimore's Morgan State University, another storied historically Black college in America.[24]

There were notable poets but also fiction writers and dramatists at the salon and many of them were not born in Washington, DC, but as was the tradition, they had landed in the nation's capital. The city was a cultural and literary magnet for African Americans interested in culture, politics, law, medicine, and literary pursuits. Dunbar High School, the school named for Paul Laurence Dunbar, was "the" high school for African Americans nationwide. Howard University was "the" university for them. Among the lesser-known attendees mentioned here who were poets is Esther Popel. Popel was a poet, was a longtime middle school teacher, and was born in Harrisburg, Pennsylvania. She taught at Shaw Junior High and Francis Junior High, schools still operating in Washington, DC, today.

While Popel did not publish many poems, her 1934 poem, "Flag Salute," remains much anthologized today and a work of art much recognized.[25] When it was published by The NAACP's *The Crisis* magazine in 1933, it was highly controversial. It is a poem in response to the lynching of George Armwood in Princess Anne County, Maryland.[26] According to various sources, Armwood was used by his white employer to rob a white woman named Mary Denston. The robbery likely went wrong. Initially, Armwood was provided with safe passage out of the Eastern Shore likely because he didn't rape anyone. Denston was seventy years old; Armwood was twenty-eight.

Armwood was brought back to the location of the crime, and jailed. Soon a mob of 2,000 people broke into the jail and slaughtered Armwood. Popel's poem mocks "The Pledge of Allegiance" using Armwood's murder as a backdrop.

Clarissa Scott Delany, another of the poets who attended the salons, is probably the most tragic poet of the Renaissance period. Delany, aunt of the now legendary writer Samuel Delany, who had not even been born when she died in 1927, only published four poems in her life. Delany was a regular attendee at Johnson's salons on Saturday nights, and she was dedicated to the craft. Born in Tuskegee, Alabama, she was the daughter of Emmett Jay Scott, who was an assistant to Booker T. Washington.[27] She graduated from Wellesley College and made Phi Beta Kappa. She taught at Dunbar High School for a few years and established a Poetry Club at the school while she taught there. When she died, the school paid tribute to her in its 1928 yearbook: "Written indelibly on our own minds and hearts is the record of our teacher, who achieved what few other women achieved, that is 'complete success.' "[28]

Delany's death in 1927 released an ocean of grief in the Washington, DC, literary community and in many other circles. *Opportunity* magazine, along with the *Pittsburgh Courier*, took the time to pay her a special tribute following her death by publishing her poem "Solace," which seemed to speak to the moment:

Solace
My window opens out into the trees
And in that small space
Of branches and of sky
I see the seasons pass
Behold the tender green
Give way to darker heavier leaves.

The glory of the autumn comes
When steeped in mellow sunlight
The fragile, golden leaves
Against a clear blue sky
Linger in the magic of the afternoon
And then reluctantly break off
And filter down to pave
A street with gold.
Then Bare, gray branches
Lift themselves against the
Cold December sky
Sometimes weaving a web
Across the rose and dusk of late sunset
Sometimes against a frail new moon
And one bright star riding
A sky of that dark, living blue
Which comes before the heaviness
Of night descends, or the stars
Have powdered the heavens.
Winds beat against these trees;
The cold, her gentle rain of spring
Touches them lightly
The summer torrents arrive
To lash them into a fury
And seek to break them—
But they stand.
My life is fevered
And a restlessness at times
An agony—again a vague
And baffling discontent
Possesses me.
I am thankful for my bit of sky
And trees, and for the shifting
Pageant of the seasons.
Such beauty lays upon the heart
A quiet.
Such eternal change and permanence
Take meaning from all turmoil
And leave serenity
Which knows no pain.[29]
—*Clarissa Scott Delany*

The publication by the *Pittsburgh Courier* via *Opportunity* contained the following tribute entitled "Superbly Poised for Life; And Quietly She Left It"[30]—"In the death of Clarissa Scott Delany, the buoyant, newly hopeful ranks of the younger Negro group were touched. With a well-trained and restlessly searching mind, a magnificent and sturdy idealism and all the impetuous zeal of youth, she was superbly poised for life, and quietly she left it."[31]

Black and White

In 1928 Lewis Grandison Alexander is one of a few African American poets from Washington who are included in a poetry anthology, *Black and White*.[32] The anthology is the work of J. C. Byars Jr., who selected all the work for Crane Press. The anthology includes sixty-three poems, mostly from white writers, but four African American poets are included. Considering the time, in a mostly segregated America, de jure, and de facto, this is quite remarkable. Also included are Angelina Grimké, the Dunbar High School teacher; Walter Everette Hawkins, a postal worker with strident and quite direct politics; and Georgia Douglas Johnson, the quiet keeper of the city's Black poetry scene at the time. Alexander has haiku (*The Washington Post* calls the form "hokku") published in *Black and White*, something very novel for the times. His haiku gets Alexander a solid mention in *The Washington Post* review of the book.[33]

Black and White is full of poets from "all walks of life," *The Post* reports in its review in January 1928.[34] Considering that the city has government workers, this should not be a surprise. In addition, and consistent with that ideal, Washington, DC, is also described as a city that has always been "very kind to creators of verse."[35] It is surely kind in this instance to allow four Black poets to step out of their segregated space and briefly become part of the larger literary community of the city. The attention does not launch careers, but it does demonstrate that the city has remained one all its own.

Donald Jeffrey Hayes's review of the anthology in *The Chicago Defender* is entitled "Interracial Poetry."[36] The book, according to Hayes, is "more than deserving of a space on your bookshelf." He describes it as a "brooch of many-colored stones" that is as "remarkable for its social attitudes as it is for its wealth of poetic gems." Mary White Ovington's review in *The Philadelphia Tribune* takes the same tact but even more forcefully when she writes about the importance of the anthology: "This book is of interest to me largely because this young compiler, born in Virginia, has drawn no color line but has included in his volume colored as well as white."[37] Ovington also writes that the anthology would be "cold without" these Black poets and reprints one of Alexander's hokku in full. Ovington's review and the other attention the anthology receives at the time demonstrated again the uniqueness of the overall poetry scene in the nation's capital. These Black poets can find an audience for their work outside their immediate neighborhoods and their literary circles. Alexander, Johnson, and Grimké also have poetry published the previous year in Countee Cullen's well-known poetry anthology, *Caroling Dusk*. That anthology is very well known among African

American poets and critics and includes work by several other DC writers and writers with strong connections to the city.

Jessie Faucet—the writer, novelist, and Dunbar High School teacher—has poetry in *Caroling Dusk*, as do Sterling A. Brown, Waring Cuney, and Alice Dunbar-Nelson. Cullen also includes all four of the poems that the rising poetic star Clarissa Scott Delany completes before her tragic death ("Joy," "Solace," "Interim," and "The Mask"). The strength of those poems demonstrates such possibilities for Delany and the loss her death was to the American poetry world.

Safe Space

The following year, 1928, the momentum of the movement and the Black poets of Washington, DC, continued. Lewis Grandison Alexander completed editing an issue of *The Carolina Magazine*, a student-run magazine at the University of North Carolina.[38] Alexander assembled the issue by contacting many poets he knew and had worked with in those years. The issue was dedicated to showcasing the "various transitions in Negro verse" at the time. The university was inspired to produce the issue because of George Moses Horton, an African American poet born in slavery in North Carolina who is closely associated with the university.

The poets included in the issue of *The Carolina* in May 1928 include Langston Hughes, William Waring Cuney, Georgia Douglas Johnson, Jessie Faucet, Mae V. Cowdery, Carrie W. Clifford, James H. Young, Alice Dunbar-Nelson, Donald Jeffrey Hayes, Angelina W. Grimké, Sterling A. Brown, Edward Silvera, John F. Matheus, and Arna Bontemps.

Alexander's poetry was also included along with two important essays. Charles S. Johnson, of Howard University, offered a piece, "Jazz, Poetry, and the Blues"; and Alain Locke was the second essayist, with "The Message of the Negro Poets." The publication was a singular triumph for Alexander, among his other literary works, but also for the Black poets in Washington, DC, all of whom can be traced to Georgia Douglas Johnson's Saturday night salons, which had been going strong for years.

It is apparent that during the 1920s, Johnson's salons were convened very consistently. While the meetings were mostly the bourgeois crowd of Howard University and Dunbar High School and the occasional transient artist or government worker, Johnson's maintenance of the gatherings is what counted most. She had invited Alain Locke to such a gathering as far back as August 1920. This is consistent with Jean Toomer's insistence on organizing a collective in the city.

It is also notable that Johnson's space was socially flexible and safe. Many attendees who came to Johnson's home on Saturday nights would identify as LGBTQ today. Locke was gay, though closeted, and so was Lewis Alexander, though it is unclear if Alexander was openly gay back then. Richard Bruce Nugent was also gay, and Mary Burrill, according to Jeffrey Stewart, in his monumental Alain Locke biography, *The New Negro*, was "the lesbian lover of Lucy Slove," a dean at Howard University at the time.[39] Countee Cullen, who was gay, appeared at the salons, and of course it has been at least strongly suggested and/or confirmed from at least one source that Langston Hughes was gay.[40]

Regardless, the overall sentiment back then was Johnson's salons were a safe space for African American artists navigating the world at a time of great change in the country. The camaraderie of the Black DC poets is impressive for that reason alone, for these writers to consistently gather and build and advance a tradition. Her salons were somewhat of a training ground for writers, a test zone for literary talents and free creativity. Many of the poets who came to live and write in the city found exactly what they were looking for before they sought out bigger audiences in New York City.

And again, like the poets and artists that Alexander featured and presented in *The Carolina Magazine* issue in 1928, Johnson's roster of talent and guests at her home (affectionately called "Halfway House") contained those writers and many others. While those writers were drawing attention in the literary world, Johnson's home was "where that work found its first audience."[41] This is where the "writers struggled" in Johnson's "safe and supportive" environment. The Black poets "shared their work and critiqued the writing of their peers; the review they received from one another was constructive; it helped shape the work they later published."[42]

Johnson's contribution surely cannot be taken lightly either. There was no indication that anything of this nature existed during the years when Dunbar lived and wrote in the city. There is also no indication that May Miller had been exposed to such a widespread welcoming group until she began to attend the salons in the 1920s. Miller and Johnson, the two Black women poets who got the energy started a decade or so before the salons reached their apex, were also working and writing plays. Many of DC's Black poets and those Black poets passing through for a taste of the community cast off into the world of letters elsewhere. But many stayed and kept building the legacy that we know today.

5
Images

At Nina Simone's last Washington, DC, live performance—in May 2000, three years before her death—she performed a song based on William Waring Cuney's poem "No Images." Simone delivered a raspy but captivating a cappella performance of the song that is a poem. Simone prefaced the performance of the song by stating that the song was for the West Indian servant women who had come to toil in America but who would never know their true beauty in such an oppressive society.

I was at the concert. "No Images" is a poem set to music, written in 1926 by Cuney (or as he has been known over the years, Waring Cuney). It was written and made immortal during the Renaissance cultural period of African Americans in the 1920s and is one of the most anthologized poems in the history of African American literature. Cuney, if the history of the African American poet in DC is to be discussed accurately, might be the most important poet born and raised in the city next to Sterling Brown. His work is the feeling of the city. He is the voice of African Americans who came to build the town, the essence of a race seeking freedom and citizenship on its terms. Paul Laurence Dunbar came to the city and laid pieces of literary foundation for the poetry scene, and Cuney did his part as well.

William Waring Cuney, the poet and songwriter, came into the world on May 6, 1906, in Washington, DC. This is the same year Dunbar died in Dayton, Ohio. Cuney was born to a middle-class African American family. His father, Norris Wright Cuney, was a career government worker at the US Government Printing Office. His mother, Madge Louise Cuney, a woman well connected in the established African American Republican circles of the day, was a public school teacher. He was a twin at birth; his brother, Norris Wright, by all indications, was like Waring, raised to respect and love one another and to look out for each other in the world.

Cuney was reared in the neighborhood known today as "Shaw" (it was not called "Shaw" when Cuney lived there) at 503 Florida Avenue NW. His father's brother Lloyd Cuney, an employee of the Government Printing Office, lived just down the street at 328 U Street NW. John Cuney, a painter, and another of his father's brothers, lived for a time at 503 Florida Avenue NW as well.[1]

The African American Cuneys of Washington, DC, are part of the recent noble past of Black America; they were descendants of a Black politician from Texas named Norris Wright Cuney.[2] The African American Cuney family of Texas can be traced back to Phillip Minor Cuney, a planter and slaveholder from Texas.[3] Like many wealthy white landowners in the nation's antebellum period, Phillip Cuney, while married, maintained a relationship with one of his female African American slaves.[4] In this case, Adeline Stuart, born in 1818, with roots in faraway Alexandria, Virginia, was the subject of Cuney's sexual escapades.[5]

The sixteen-year relationship between Stuart and Cuney resulted in eight children and, eventually, her freedom in 1859.[6] Cuney not only openly acknowledged his Black (mulatto) children, but he took the time, effort, and financial resources to ensure that they would have a better chance in the world by educating them. Three of his sons born because of his relationship with Stuart—Nelson, Norris, and Joseph—were eventually sent to George B. Vashon's very well-known and prestigious Wylie Street School for Colored Youth (later Wylie Street School for Blacks) in Pittsburgh, Pennsylvania, for education. Cuney paid for all of it.[7]

Cuney's father and brother's namesake are both named Norris Wright Cuney, the same name as that of the well-known Republican politician from Texas, Norris Wright Cuney. But Norris Wright Cuney, the Black man who carved out a life and a legacy in Texas when Black people were being driven out of the American world and into the oppressive world of Jim Crow, was not Waring's father, though his father had the very same name and was Norris Wright Cuney's nephew. Cuney's grandfather was named John Nelson Cuney.

Cuney's days in Washington included education at Armstrong High School, where he and his twin, Norris, excelled as students. Waring was president of the senior class at Armstrong in 1923.[8] Meanwhile, Norris was the arts editor for the school yearbook, *The Reflector*.[9] Waring was in the school's Cadet Corps for 1922 and in the school orchestra. He read the final address of the senior class of 1923 to the faculty, and he also prepared a paper for education week at the legendary Metropolitan Baptist Church.[10]

Cuney's paper is notable because he is a student of Armstrong High School, the school most focused on vocational training.[11] Cuney's paper breaks free from those confines, suggesting he was already thinking back when he was just seventeen of a more expansive education, and a freer life. Apprenticeships in vocational training, Cuney wrote, forced the young student to abandon "intellectual training." The student "did not receive any training in such studies as mathematics, the sciences, or the foreign languages." Cuney asserts that "intellectual training is essential in the pursuit of a trade." Cuney calls for trade training but also instruction in the sciences, foreign languages, in English, and in English literature.

Waring's participation in music in high school does suggest the path his creative life would take. According to Rosey E. Pool, in her 1962 anthology, *Beyond The Blues*,

Cuney always aspired to be a singer and his brother, Norris, wanted to be a pianist. Cuney kept chasing his poetry and song dreams back in the 1920s. But first came poetry and that chance meeting with Langston Hughes in 1925 during Hughes's time living in the city. Cuney would develop a close friendship with Hughes, and they would remain in touch off and on until the 1960s.

Yet Cuney also, like most African American poets in the city at the time and nationally, was influenced by the example of the poet Paul Laurence Dunbar. His presence in the city was there every day for Cuney, as his high school, Armstrong, and Dunbar High School were on the same block, and the schools partnered as one ROTC program.[12]

Also, his second cousin Maud E. Cuney (Hare), a musician, knew Dunbar personally and collaborated with him musically in Chicago in 1902 before Waring was born.[13] Maud Cuney was a big influence on Waring's decision to pursue music as a vocation, and according to Cuney biographers Cynthia Davis and Verner D. Mitchell, she "would have shared stories of her association with the famous poet."[14] In addition, Davis and Mitchell note that Cuney was "most explicit" about Dunbar's influence on his poetry.

In 1926 Cuney's poem "No Images" was published in *Opportunity* magazine and shared the first and second prizes for poetry that year. Cuney wrote the poem when he was eighteen and originally submitted the poem under a pseudonym. No explanation has ever been given for this decision, but according to the June 1926 issue of *Opportunity*, the prize for "No Images" was awarded to Cuney, but he submitted the poem as "Ford Kramer." At the time, Cuney was a student at Lincoln University in Pennsylvania. The *Pittsburgh Courier* reported on the award in its May 8, 1926, issue: "Mr. Kramer's poem, 'No Images' . . . was especially praised by the judges." The judges who praised Cuney's now-famous poem are notable as well. William Stanley Braithwaite, James Weldon Johnson, Alain Locke, Robert Frost, Clement Wood, William Rose Benét, and Vachel Lindsay, all men, judged the contest. The poem is in the naturalist tradition of literature:

No Images
She does not know
Her beauty,
She thinks her brown body
Has no glory.
If she could dance
Naked
Under palm trees
And see her image in the river,
She would know.
But there are no palm trees

On the street,
And dishwater gives back no images.[15]
—*Waring Cuney*

Paul Breman, one of the few publishers who kept tabs on Cuney for years, hails the poem as an "indomitable presence."[16] The writer, poet, and critic Lorenzo Thomas describes it as "an immortal poem," and the "very model of a New Negro Movement Renaissance poem."[17] Thomas contends that "No Images" is a "model of accessibility and clarity" and "a perfect Imagist poem."

In the famous 1929 German anthology of African American poetry *Afrika Singt*, "No Images" was included, along with writings from Jean Toomer and Jessie Fau-cet.[18] In 1927 "No Images" was published by a publication called *FORUM: A Magazine of Controversy*, founded by Isaac L. Rice. Rice was, among other things, a social reformer.[19] At the time, to get published in *FORUM* was the equivalent of *Harper's Magazine* or *The Atlantic* monthly.

Cuney's work was not missed by many editors at this time either, as he personally evolved as a writer. Countee Cullen included seven of his poems, including "No Images," in his anthology *Caroling Dusk*, for example. Lewis Grandison Alexander published him in that famous issue of *The Carolina Magazine*. Cuney, on some level, is the quintessential Black poet from Washington. The city is where he was educated and raised and where he became a poet. It is also where he connected with the larger national Black community of poets. Yet, like many Black poets born in the city, or who came to the city for education and opportunity, Cuney departed and was back and forth to the city over the years, even though DC was officially his home base.

By 1927 Cuney was blending poetry and songwriting into one, as his aspirations to sing had taken a larger part of his time. He had continued to attend Lincoln University, but by 1927 he was attending the New England Conservatory of Music in Boston. He had sung in the glee club at Lincoln University, so his love of music thrived over time. He departed the university in 1927 before graduation to devote himself completely to music. He took two voice classes at the conservatory in 1927, and he still used his Washington, DC, address at 503 Florida Avenue NW.

This is also likely the time that Cuney connected with African American writers and artists in the Boston area. They were also part of the same African American Renaissance going on in America. According to members of a group of African American writers in the Boston area known as the Saturday Evening Quill Club, Cuney began attending their gatherings in 1927, though it is not known how regularly.[20]

The writers in the Quill, as it has been referred to over the years, included many notable Black writers of the period in addition to Cuney. Dorothy West was a regular attendee to meetings, as was Helene Johnson and visual artist Lois Mailou Jones, who would go on to teach at Howard University for forty-six years. Eugene Gordon, a journalist and 1917 graduate of Howard University, was the engine for the Quill and for its publication—*The Saturday Evening Quill.*

Cuney's poems appeared in the June 1928 issue of the magazine, which only lasted three issues. Gordon, a very politicized writer, left the country to write in Russia.[21] Cuney, on the other hand, connected with the Boston writers. One of the writers he became friends with within the Boston area was Roscoe Conklin Wright, a multigenre writer connected to the Black Boston writing scene.[22] Wright's daughter Mary Meekins confirmed her father spoke of being friends with Cuney when he was hanging out in the Boston area with the Black writers on that scene back at that time.[23] Boston also was a chosen destination for Waring Cuney because of family.

Maud E. Cuney (Hare), from Washington, DC, is Cuney's second cousin.[24] Maud Cuney Hare is fully dedicated to a life in music eventually in Boston, and she is well connected with the New England Conservatory. Waring does attend the school and at some point even stays with his cousin Maud.[25] Gossip pages mention in August 1927 that he is in Washington visiting his mother and brother.[26]

In 1930 Cuney was part of a classic anthology of just four poets—*Four Lincoln University Poets*—William Allyn Hill, Edward Silvera, Langston Hughes, and Cuney.[27] But for Cuney and Hughes's chance meeting in the city during Hughes's residency in DC, the book would never have been published. Yet, all four of the poets spent some time in Washington at some point. It is again a testament to the city's well-developed and cohesive African American community because of segregation. While Cuney was gone from the city by the time the anthology was published, Edward Silvera was living there in 1931. Silvera would die in 1937.

In 1931, as a sign of Cuney's slow ascent into the pantheon of significant African American poets, his poetry was included in an updated version of James Weldon Johnson's anthology *The Book of American Negro Poetry*. The book was originally published in 1922, and it was a precursor of things to come among African American poets in general and in the city. The publication now had forty authors instead of thirty-one and 184 poems instead of 116. Also published in Johnson's anthology in the updated version is Sterling A. Brown, another poet born in Washington, DC. Cuney and Brown are hardly rivals, but of the writers who came up in the city in the first half of the century, they are exploring many of the same cultural and aesthetic traditions: the blues, folk music, and gospel, the daily struggle of men.

Strong Man, Race Man

The poet Sterling A. Brown, a fixture at Howard University for over forty years, was a "race man," that familiar ideal in African American history and folklore. So many over the years have attempted to define the concept, even my own father, who often called certain Black men (Brown certainly) race men. The best definition of the term "race man" comes from the book *Black Metropolis*, the famous sociological study by St. Clair Drake and Horace R. Cayton, two African American sociologists.[28]

Cayton and Drake's *Black Metropolis*, subtitled "A Study of Negro Life in a Northern City," is about Chicago in the 1940s. When it was originally published in 1945 Richard

Wright, the famous writer with ties to the city, wrote the introduction and called the book a "landmark of research and scientific achievement."[29]

Cayton and Drake define "race man" as having what they describe as a "dual sense." On the one hand, "it refers to any person who has a reputation as an uncompromising fighter against attempts to subordinate Negroes" (African Americans). The other meaning of the term, according to Cayton and Drake, is derogatory, referring to people who "pay loud lip-service to 'race pride.' "[30]

When African Americans use the term referring to one of their own, it is the former and not the latter. Brown, in the eyes of the many who knew him, were taught by him, or befriended by him, was a race man, the uncompromising fighter. When he died in 1989, he had lived the life of a race man. His life spanned nearly the entire twentieth century, making him an ideal historical actor in American history.

Sterling A. Brown's father, Sterling N. Brown, had been born into slavery in Tennessee. Sterling N. Brown, like the son, was an intellectual. Sterling Brown, the son, would have a chance to rise from the challenges faced by his father and by his mother, Adelaide, who also had been born into slavery in east Tennessee (Roane County). The elder Sterling Brown described the area as noteworthy "for its healthfulness, general thrift and fair-minded people."[31] Brown's father was "at least seven-eighths Caucasian and possibly one-eighth Negro," and like many who had been enslaved he did not know his "family record," nor was it recorded in public records.

And like Frederick Douglass, it bothered him for all his life.[32] The Reverend Sterling N. Brown was born into a large, impoverished family, and so he worked for years to support the family and professional life that would take shape at Fisk University and Oberlin College.[33] He worked in Cleveland as a minister and then finally made his way to DC in 1889, where he became a pillar of Black Washington. Somehow, slavery and poverty had not broken him and didn't lay a glove on him.

Sterling A. Brown, his son, would be born in Washington, DC, on May 1, 1901, and would grow up on the campus of Howard University. He had five older sisters. The Brown family was a "struggling middle class" family, as Rev. Brown presided over Lincoln Congregational Church, a church that still stands today. Brown's mother, Adelaide Allen, was also a Fisk University graduate and valedictorian of her class. W. E. B. Du Bois was at Fisk when the father, Sterling, and Adelaide attended.

Brown's father passed the concept of "esprit de corps,"[34] to his son. Rev. Brown sank his heart, soul, and effort into the betterment of African Americans in the United States. His son, Sterling, would do the same. Adelaide Allen Brown gave young Sterling the love of literature.[35]

Brown's mother would read the poetry of Paul Laurence Dunbar to him. While Brown would eventually embrace the imagist poetry of Carl Sandburg and others, Dunbar was a part of him deeply as well. Brown praised Dunbar for standing tall in life as a professional Black poet and his writing excellence but also criticized his art for its shortcomings, mainly the dialect poems, which did not quite accept fully the full essence of the African American experience and of the ordinary Black folk.

In a certain way, Sterling Brown, though it was not necessarily intentional, was groomed for this role. He was born in Washington during a time of great change and a reckoning for the city's African American population. He attended public schools, which also included matriculation at Paul Laurence Dunbar High, the best high school for African American students in the country at the time. Not only was Dunbar a magnet for local African American populations, but African Americans around the country sought to get their students to attend.

The faculty at Dunbar was world class and included many writers of the day who would distinguish themselves in the world of letters. This was segregation at work. The Black talent could not work outside of the African American spaces in the city, so the talent of Black educators was concentrated. It is a reality that the Black population accepted but with a level of quiet determination. Brown, in his famous 1944 essay "Count Us In," stressed that African Americans took a realistic approach to life in America.

"Advances have been made, but the Negro was so far behind in opportunity that he does not let his glance linger on the gains; he looks ahead along the road to full participation,"[36] Brown wrote. It was no different in Washington, even among the African Americans with the best opportunities in a city where things were the same racially for Black people.

Those opportunities for Brown for education and a richly diverse city full of African American professionals, working-class people, and those living in abject poverty, gave Brown the educational vitae that would lead him to Williams College in Massachusetts, and then Harvard College, for a master's degree. But Brown would never forget the more ordinary people he met along the way—all of them.

His writing was simply a profound change and represented the kind of art and scholarship most Black writers either could not make so deeply or simply did not want to create by probing deep into their own experiences and opinions. Brown was that crossroads of class, race, and color in the African American community. Brown himself represented that paradox. He was light in skin color and his beloved wife, Daisy, was even lighter.

But Brown would have none of it. He was African American, in spirit, culture, and in heart. As Brown would say in a speech at Williams College in 1973:

> I am an old Negro, and I am proud of it. My students get angry because I do not use the word "black." I do use the word "black." If a person wants to call themselves black. Fine . . . I have had a love of Africa since I was a child. But I do know a lot of people who are talking about going to Africa are going to stop by Paris on the way over.[37]

Such are the complexity and strength of Sterling A. Brown.

In March 1925, in the official newsletter for Omega Psi Phi Fraternity, Inc., Sterling A. Brown would publish his first poem. It was the start of a long life as a bard.

The newsletter is called *Oracle*, and Brown's poem, a sonnet, is titled "For a Certain Youngster."[38] While Brown would spend most of the next sixty years challenging Western thought and formal concepts in literature, Brown's mastery of the sonnet in the poem is self-evident. He presents a reflective work of verse that demonstrates the skills he would apply for the rest of his life but also his willingness to speak of a universal humanity.

Southern Roads

In 1922, while finishing his studies at Williams College, Sterling Brown came to be who he would be for the rest of his life. Just as I was pretty sure in 1985 that I was going to be a poet and work in public service in some capacity, Brown had done the same by 1922. One of his professors, George Dutton, was giving a lecture on Joseph Conrad, the Polish writer and author of, among other works, *Heart of Darkness*. It was suggested by Professor Dutton that Conrad wanted to help his people in Poland in some manner and that Conrad likely brooded over the challenge presented to him.

Brown said that Dutton looked at him when he related the challenge set before Conrad. Brown took the moment as a challenge to himself and the plight of the African Americans in the United States. Brown said he knew what Professor Dutton "meant." To Brown, he was saying, "Don't get fooled by any lionizing," and surely "don't get fooled" by being allowed to exist and sit among "selective clientele." Brown knew there was "business out there" that he had to "take care of," and that business was his people, African Americans. Brown said he never forgot that moment when his eyes locked in with Dutton's either.[39]

Brown described the Dutton lecture as a turning point in his professional life. And after bouncing around the South for several years and teaching there, Brown's true turning point arrived when he came to teach at Howard University in 1929. Brown would remain there for over four decades, teaching, publishing, advocating, and creating a body of work unparalleled in American literature. He also mentored many of the poets who would shape American literature and African American literature, and who would build an important Black literary scene in Washington, DC.

What Brown lacked in quantity, he exceeded most in quality and importance of work. And where most feared to tread, Brown did over and over. His people, as he noted, became his work and his mission, and he honored the opportunity at Howard and in the academic world with aesthetic choices that continue to luminate and teach today. The Washington, DC, Black poets are nothing without Sterling Brown. Gaston Neal, E. Ethelbert Miller, Kenneth Carroll, Jennifer Smith, Darrell Stover, and Laini Mataka are the poets they are at least, in part, because of Sterling Brown's work and example.

Brown was outspoken but also humble, unique, and singularly an individual. He was also respectful of those who came before him. It is no accident that he could and did demonstrate a mastery of old poetic traditions, though it is most important that Brown embraced Black culture and Black life. In 1932, with the publication of *Southern Road*, his first full collection of poetry, he changed African American poetry forever. It is a book that continues to grow in stature and influence today.

It is no surprise that Brown struck out on his own as a poet. Brown, though he was born in Washington, DC, where the Harlem Renaissance was embraced, never bought into the notion of the "Harlem Renaissance." He never accepted the minimization that such a label affixed on African Americans, despite his respect for those who created during the period. Many years later, Brown put the period in proper context. "The New Negro is not for me a group of writers centered in Harlem during the second half of the twenties," Brown wrote in 1955.[40] He also stressed that most of the writers of the period were not from Harlem. Harlem was used as a "show window" or a "cashier's till." It was surely not Black America at the time, necessarily.

Also, the short period of the so-called movement to Brown rendered it slightly false in description. Black poets and writers in his hometown of Washington were major players in the surge of Black art and poetry in the 1920s and before the 1920s. Brown also mentioned several DC writers when he noted the poets who played a big part in the period. Waring Cuney, Georgia Douglas Johnson, Angelina Grimké, and Jean Toomer are affectionately mentioned by Brown as "the more important poets" of the New Negro period.[41] Brown also called the period a time when white-controlled publishing houses finally reached out and published some Black writers. According to Brown, before the period if you saw a Black person in the office of a publishing house in New York, they were probably a messenger.[42]

Sterling Brown's arrival at Howard and onto the national poetry scene occurred at a time of great distress. The country was on the cusp of the Great Depression. While Washington, DC, was somewhat sheltered from the effects, white supremacy and its entrenched policies caused African Americans to feel the effects of the economic downturn disproportionately. Jobs traditionally held by African Americans in the city, such as "janitors, bellhops, waiters, elevator operators, and barbers," were taken over by whites as whites "asserted superior claims" to the work.[43] Washington was still a Jim Crow city when Brown returned home. It was segregated in every aspect for the most part, though the city itself, because it is the seat of the national government, offered opportunities.

"Long Gone"

James Weldon Johnson wrote the original introduction to Sterling Brown's *Southern Road*. Johnson had included Brown in the revised edition of his poetry anthology, *The Book of American Negro Poetry*, published in 1931. He spoke highly of Brown in the preface and in his autobiographical introduction. Johnson called Brown one of "the outstanding poets of the younger group."[44] Brown was not included in the original 1922 version of the anthology, as he was still just a college student at the time.

Johnson wrote that Brown, "more than any other American poet . . . has made thematic use of Negro folk epics and ballads." Johnson added that "a false note is rarely heard" of Brown's work and that he "really absorbed the spirit of" folk poetry, "made it his own, and, without diluting its primitive frankness and raciness, truly re-expressed it with artistry and magnified power."[45]

Johnson has similar praise in his introduction to *Southern Road*. He groups Brown in with many of the emerging Harlem Renaissance poets deemed the "Younger Group." Claude McKay, Jean Toomer, Langston Hughes, Countee Cullen, and finally Brown, who was the last to emerge. Brown's timing is also important because though he is associated with the Harlem Renaissance period by critics, he is not truly a part of it in timing. Johnson describes all these poets, including Brown, as less direct on race issues, "less didactic and imploratory" as well. They are not "regardful," according to Johnson, of the "white environment."[46]

Johnson specifically described Brown's poetry as "fine" and "unique" and as having discarded the minstrel dialect that was typical of the Dunbar period and after. Brown, according to Johnson, "adopted the common, racy living speech of the Negro in certain aspects of real life."[47] Brown found his niche and voice in American literature in the folk poetry of African Americans, the traditions and cultural epics and ballads, like "Stagolee" and "John Henry."

Brown's decision was a bold artistic choice. Considering the shadow of class within the African American community, and especially Howard University, Brown had stepped outside of his class with his poetry. He was drawn to the lives of ordinary people and not just their lives but their humanity.

In 1932 he was published in the anthology series *Folks Say*.[48] Brown appeared in vol. 4, edited by B. A. Botkin. The volume was called *The Land Is Ours*. Botkin was a folklorist and scholar who taught at various universities and spent much of his career in this field, including time in the Federal Writers' Project, where Brown would likewise work. Botkin published an impressive array of Brown's works in an unlikely publication. Not only is part of Brown's "Slim Greer" series here but also "Long Track Blues," "Call Boy," "Putting on Dog," "A Bad, Bad Man," and "Rent Day Blues." The publication of this work was a prelude to what Brown had in store with the publication of *Southern Road* the same year. Brown was again focusing on the ordinary people of Black life in America, and he wrote how they talked and created the spaces where they lived and struggled.

Most of these poems are in *Southern Road*.

Sterling A. Brown dedicated the book of poems *Southern Road* "To My Mother." It was his mother whom he would acknowledge many years later, who read poetry to him as a boy, including the poetry of Paul Laurence Dunbar; thus, it was the obvious choice. His father, the distinguished minister and Howard University professor at the School of Divinity, had died in 1929.

Brown acknowledged the publications where his poetry began to find an audience: *The Carolina Magazine, Contempo, The New York Herald Tribune, The Crisis, Palms, Theatre Arts Monthly, Color, Folks Say,* and *Ebony and Topaz*. It is true that Brown's decision to shift the focus of his literary offerings from nonfiction to poetry had been important for African American Literature overall.

His poetry was also accepted at this time in *The Anthology of American Negro Poetry* edited by V. F. Calverton. V. F. Calverton is a pseudonym for the writer George Goetz. Goetz, a radical reformer and author, was founder and editor of *Modern Quarterly*, an independent Marxist journal. *Modern Quarterly* was especially created to provide a forum for Black intellectuals.[49] This poem resulted in a letter to Brown praising the power of his art and seeking more.

Edward Buckman writes to Brown from New York City on January 15, 1930, and asks Brown if he could recite "Long Gone" on the radio.[50] "The purpose of this letter is to discover whether you would be willing to allow me to read your poem, 'Long Gone,' in programs of radio readings." Mr. Buckman writes that he always chooses poems in the "first person" and that he aims for "naturalness" in reading the readings, to "steer the reader as far away as possible from the usual elocutionary technique."

It is unclear whether Brown allowed his work to be read on the radio by Buckman, and it is unclear whether Buckman is the Edward Buckman who did work on Broadway in New York City in the 1920s. But one thing for certain was the power of the book *Southern Road*. Most of Brown's great poems are in this collection, except for "Old Lem."

The most notable and well-known poems are "Strong Men," a poem Brown wrote in 1929; "Southern Road"; "Odyssey of Big Boy"; and his all-time classic, "Ma Rainey." *Southern Road* also includes the "Slim" poems and the very personal "After Winter," a poem that made Brown cry when he would read it aloud.

"After Winter" is about his family and their life on a farm his father purchased in Laurel, Maryland. Brown mentions two of his sisters in the poem—Clara and Grace—and he mentions himself—"the little feller." Life there had an impact on Brown, considering he grew up on the Howard University campus and its intellectual environment. It allowed Brown to stay in touch with the ordinary things in life.

Originally, *Southern Road* is published by Harcourt, Brace, and Company in 1932. It immediately garners attention in the literary world. While many critics, such as Henry Louis Gates, try to write Brown out of the Black Renaissance period that began in the 1920s, Brown rejects such an idea.[51] Brown believes that the Renaissance that began many years ago lasted much longer than a few years, as is suggested. Brown contends that the period stretched well into the 1930s. This means that Brown considers *Southern Road* part of everything that had been going on before and after his entry into the scene.

Most of the responses to the book were very good and reflect the fact that Brown had broken through artistically. He did not sound like anyone, and he didn't even sound like any African American writer. One of the first reviews was from Louis Untermeyer in *Opportunity* magazine:

> This review must begin with a confession. I had seen separate poems under the name Sterling Brown. I had heard his praises here and there, but, with

> the skepticism of one who reads too much, I imagined Brown was merely another Negro poet—gifted as so many of the younger writers are—another of James Weldon Johnson's interesting but not important enthusiasms. I was wrong. "Southern Road" is sufficient to correct and rebuke me, even without Johnson's discriminating foreword.[52]

Untermeyer, a well-respected self-taught poet, writer, and editor, was prolific throughout his life.[53] He not only wrote many books of his own, but he produced many anthologies of note. Untermeyer mentioned that Brown, in his poetry, does not adopt the attitude of the "Negro as entertainer" in his work, though "Brown's humor is significant." Brown "does not paint himself blacker than he is, nor does he slouch in grotesque or falsely sentimental verse to win the applause of a white audience," wrote Untermeyer. According to Untermeyer, Brown "laughs at the whites as lightly as he ridicules the follies (and occasional pretentiousness) of the black and tans."[54]

Southern Road is also reviewed by the writer Wallace Thurman, the author of the timeless classic work of fiction *The Blacker the Berry: A Novel of Negro Life*. Thurman, like Untermeyer, admits that he was skeptical of Brown when he came to *Southern Road*. And like Untermeyer, Thurman changes his mind. Thurman's exposure to Brown was his early work, in the 1920s. Brown, at that time, was a new college graduate and had not pivoted to writing poetry in the manner that would define his life. Thurman is so impressed with Brown's verse in *Southern Road* he writes that Brown must have been "holding out," or it is he (Thurman) who has "overlooked" Brown and his poetry. Thurman describes the poems as "excellent."[55]

Thurman describes Brown's poetry as not "conventional or stereotyped," and poetry that is intelligent and sensitive with a "sense of adventure." Brown is unafraid of poetry that is "essentially negroid," according to Thurman, and he notes Brown's use of the hymn "When the Saints Go Marching In" as proof of Brown's ferocious independence and Blackness on the page.

Poetry Magazine's review of Brown's *Southern Road* is racist and dismissive. The review does not identify the author, and it is very short:

> A negro student who has progressed in his poetical technique to the point indicated by the youthful stanzas in Part Four of this volume, can no longer consider himself a primitive, and must achieve, in attempting to go back to his racial beginnings, more than a mongrel effect. He has followed Housman, Shakespeare, and other masters of English lyricism too far. His salvation lies in following them farther.[56]

The journal makes no effort to analyze Brown's art honestly. Brown's book rejects most of what western literature is, and so Brown is likewise rejected by an establishment journal.

The New York Times describes *Southern Road* as a "notable new book of negro poetry," a book where "race" is on every page, but it is "race that is neither arrogant nor servile."[57] The poetry contains "bitterness," but it is not the bitterness of Black people in America but the "bitterness of all men." The *Times* singles out "Maumee Ruth" and "Sam Smiley" as two examples of poems by Brown that fit this mode. Brown proves in *Southern Road* that African American writers can make a "genuine and original contribution to American literature."[58]

While some of the review is overtly condescending, it still is a very good review for Brown's first book. The review was so good that the *Pittsburgh Courier* made note of the review in the *Times*. *Southern Road* also was reviewed by *The American Mercury*, a popular and respected publication at the time.[59]

With such high acclaim for a first book, Brown had ascended to the top of the African American poetry world. He also was Washington's most important Black poet by far now, as he was homegrown and educated. His life and literary aesthetics were rooted in the land in and around the city and African American life.

The high opinion of *Southern Road* would not diminish either. Writers and other literary figures wrote Brown directly, asking to obtain copies. Nancy Cunard and Elmer Carter, editor of *Opportunity* magazine, each praised the book highly and sought copies directly from Brown.[60] Alain Locke declared that the book launched a new era in poetry. In addition, years later Henry Louis Gates described it as "artistic achievement" that "ended the Harlem Renaissance."[61] *Southern Road* "undermined all of the New Negro's assumptions about the nature of the black tradition and its relation to the individual talent." The poetry, "composed in dialect . . . also had as their subjects distinctively black archetypal mythic characters, as well as the black common man whose roots were rural and Southern."[62]

As a result of *Southern Road*, Brown's literary life would be quite different. He would never become a commercial literary force in America like his colleague Langston Hughes or Paul Laurence Dunbar before that. However, his reputation would be forever that of a giant of authentic American poetry, Black culture, and the intellectual successor to W. E. B. Du Bois. Brown would maintain a teaching post at Howard University for over forty years, becoming an iconic figure in the city of Washington, DC, on the campus of Howard University, and throughout Black America.

6

A Photograph

In 2009 I wrote a short essay for the National Museum of African American History and Culture about a photograph taken by a photographer from the Scurlock Photography Studio. The museum, in its development stages at the time, was curating an exhibition on the Scurlocks, a family of Black photographers who documented the history of Black Washington, DC.[1] The legendary family business began with Addison Scurlock, who started the company and then continued for decades with his two sons, Robert and George.[2] Paul Gardullo, the curator of the exhibit, asked me to write the essay.

The single photograph was taken in 1947 of an African American middle school girl at Bruce-Monroe Middle School. She is standing in front of a school classroom reading poetry before a small marquee announcing, "Poetry Week." There are other poets on the marquee—Paul Laurence Dunbar, Walt Whitman, and Langston Hughes. The young girl is a student in Ms. Duckett's class.[3] Bruce-Monroe Middle School had once been a school for white children in the city. White parents in 1913 had advocated for the school to be so.[4] However, by 1931 the school became a "colored" school. Washington, DC, and its social and legal Jim Crow arrangements remained racially segregated in the 1930s.[5] Poetry Week was a big deal in not only the 1920s and 1930s but many decades later in the United States in many public schools. The celebration was founded by Anita Browne of the General Federation of Women's Clubs in New York.[6] In Washington, as Poetry Week had its birthing moments in 1936, the heyday of the Black cultural Renaissance receded.

The African American poets who had emerged during the period of the Renaissance remained at work. Georgia Douglas Johnson, Jean Toomer, Alain Locke, Sterling Brown, May Miller, and many others had matured and settled into their artistic and professional lives. Georgia Douglas Johnson continued to write and organize salons. May Miller taught in the nearby Baltimore public schools, where she would remain for twenty years. Jean Toomer continued to write, but his literary moment had passed. Importantly, Sterling Brown, at Howard, and William Waring Cuney, in various spots, continued to create art rooted in the city's politics and African American aesthetics.

Cuney is writing poetry as well and is also songwriting. He maintains contact with Brown and in 1935 sends him several poems, which have not been published anywhere.[7] The poems include "Judgment Morning," "After Prayer Meeting," "Walking Papers," "No Lie," "Weary Traveler," and "Flight." The poems are all dated December 16, 1935, and are all written in Cuney's singular blues and gospel style that had come to define his work. "After Prayer Meeting" is one such example of Cuney's mastery of simple phrasings:

After Prayer Meeting
The Elder
sure preached
down this evening
I know he gave
The Sinnahs a fright.
Good-night, Sister Lee
Good-night

Good-night, honey
I'm so sleepy
I'm yawning
But if I'm living
and nothing happens
I'll see you
Sunday morning[8]
—*Waring Cuney*

With these poems, Cuney challenges the notion that he is a poet with just one notable poem, "No Images."

Brown, at this time, had just purchased a house uptown at 1222 Kearney Street, NE, in a neighborhood that is called Brookland today. Brown wrote about the experience of settling into the community in *The Washington Star*, responding to the newspaper's State Department correspondent, Jeremiah O'Leary, who blamed "white flight" in the neighborhood on Pearl Harbor. Brown, with wit and style, begged to differ:

> The exodus of the Irish and WASPs cannot be blamed on Pearl Harbor. I am afraid that my family was one of the dire causes of white flight. Moving from our previous home when it was purchased by Howard University, my mother bought two lots in Brookland and built one home for herself and two daughters, and one for my wife, myself and our adopted son. When the

homes were completed, "For Sale" signs in the neighborhood seemed to sprout overnight.[9]

Brown also pointed out to readers the distinguished individuals and neighbors who visited him at his home. Ralph Bunche, E. Franklin Frazier, Mike Daugherty, Ben Botkin, Angus McDonald, Gunnar Myrdal, Jerre Mangione, John Hammond, Charles E. Smith, Fred Ramsey, Gordon Gullickson, and Alan Lomax all visited Brown regularly.[10]

The Brookland neighborhood was tailor-made for African American professionals during DC's Jim Crow years. It was "economically stable" according to Sandra Fitzpatrick and Maria R. Goodwin in their book *The Guide to Black Washington.*[11] Two Black architects in the development of the community, Hilyard Robinson and Howard Mackey, built many homes in the neighborhood, including homes for Ralph Bunche and historian Rayford Logan, two distinguished intellectuals.[12] Robinson and Mackey would eventually direct Howard University's school of architecture.

Just as Brown did not bite his tongue regarding the discrimination in his new neighborhood, he also did not bite it when talking about African American literature up until that time. In his seminal work of literary criticism *The Indignant Generation: A Narrative History of African American Writers and Critics, 1934–1960*, Lawrence P. Jackson describes Brown, at this time, as rejecting "an entire stratum of American literature" in how it described and treated Black life. It was "false," Jackson writes of Brown's position.[13]

Most important, according to Jackson, Brown was "unafraid to offend whites or burn bridges."[14] The stereotypes imposed upon African Americans, Brown noted, were driven by a quest for profit during the slave trade, and these stereotypes carried over into Brown's time. When the intense Renaissance period faded, Brown looked back upon it as a missed opportunity. The liberal ideas led by Carl Van Vechten had diminished the impact of Black art that was free and honest in its representations. Brown said that Van Vechten had corrupted the Harlem Renaissance, and he referred to the latter as a "voyeur" and "terrible influence."[15]

Considering Brown was at the Capstone of "Negro education," Howard University teaching, he was marking his territory and assuming the role he would play for the next fifty years in Washington, DC, and in Black America. Brown was not just a poet and teacher; he was the official critic of Black American cultural life.

Work for Writers

Jerre Mangione's name as a visitor to Sterling Brown's home connects the next and other part of Brown's life as a poet and public scholar currently. It explains Brown's influence, stature, and singular voice in the African American struggle in America. Mangione was national coordinating editor of the Federal Writers' Project during the Great Depression and FDR's New Deal. Brown would play a big part in that work even while still maintaining his teaching duties. Brown was brought onto the Federal

Writers' Project (FWP) by Mangione during the Great Depression and worked on the project from 1936 to 1940.[16]

Brown, riding the wave of *Southern Road* and teaching at Howard University, was in high demand for all sorts of cultural activities. The FWP was just one such project. Brown's major accomplishment at FWP was the completion of the Washington, DC, guidebook. FWP's goal was to publish a guidebook for each US state and the District of Columbia (Washington, DC).

FWP began on July 27, 1935.[17] Its creation fell under the Works Progress Administration, a federal agency created to confront the calamities and poverty of the Great Depression.[18] FWP was where writers could find their way to a certain degree during very lean times in America and the world. The federal government established the agency to provide writers with a means of subsistence. Sterling Brown was the project's national editor of Negro affairs.[19] Brown received high praise for his work on the guidebook and for his honesty.[20] Many years later, Mangione noted how society ignored the problems African Americans faced in America and how the guidebook sought to ignore these issues as well. Brown's writings, according to Mangione, were the exception.

Mangione wrote that Brown's "chapter on the subject constituted the most forthright analysis of the plight of blacks in Washington ever to be published under government auspices."[21] Mangione wrote that Brown presented "well-tempered" prose that "enunciated a forceful indictment of the forces in White America that kept Negroes subjugated in the ghettos of the nation's capital, some in the very backyard of the Capitol itself." Brown declared in the guidebook that in Washington, DC, there is a "denial of democracy" to African Americans, "at times hypocritical and at times flagrant."[22] The key to Brown's success at FWP is the fact he had a plan. He wanted the guidebooks, especially the book from Washington, to reflect the reality of life for African Americans in segregated America, de facto and de jure.

Southern Road, his celebrated book of poems from 1932, was cited as one reason why he was chosen as the national editor of Negro affairs. Considering the kind of poetry Brown wrote and the kinds of people Brown found most important, it was obvious his work at FWP would speak to the ordinary Black citizen. Brown, in his work at FWP, was apt to describe the hard work and struggle of African Americans to establish churches, community organizations, public schools, educational boards, and other civic institutions.

Brown criticizes the lack of literature in Washington, DC. Considering literature is Brown's life's work, the DC guidebook's statement that there is "little literature even attempting to do justice to the facets of Negro life in Washington D.C." is truth telling.[23] Brown's assessment of the time cannot be discounted. There is poetry being written by African Americans in the city, and some of it is connected to Howard University. In addition, poets such as Georgia Douglas Johnson remain actively involved in writing circles but none of serious note as during the 1920s. The energy created by the poets in the city from back in the 1920s is being replicated in other cities and countries. In particular, the African writers associated with France have been inspired by the "Renaissance" writers of the United States to start the "Negritude" movement. But, as for DC itself, the poets who were the important figures have matured as professional writers.

Waring Cuney, Brown's lifelong friend, though he had been away from the city mostly over the years, would make the locals proud from a distance in a sort of swan song of creativity in 1941. Cuney, who had spent time in Boston, and even in Rome several times to study music (in 1934 he told Langston Hughes by letter this was his fourth time studying in that city),[24] would eventually settle in the Bronx, in New York City. He would list his address as an apartment at 1122 Tinton Avenue, in the Bronx, for much of his later life.

There is a strong suggestion that Cuney is also in DC a lot at the time as well as off and on. Arna Bontemps writes to Cuney several times seeking permission to use his poems for a youth anthology called *Golden Slippers*.[25] And this could be true, though it is quite unclear. Bontemps does ask Cuney via letter if Washington is more exciting than New York, though it is unclear what is meant by the question. He also mentions Cuney's "blues" as well but sadly informs Cuney he can't use the poems because they don't allow "cussing in school rooms."[26] Cuney is likely spending time in both cities. In 1938 he is an assistant to Langston Hughes for a play Hughes is producing at the time.[27]

In 1941 Cuney's constantly evolving blues/folk/gospel style came to great use when he collaborated with the folk singer Josh White on White's album *Southern Exposure*.[28] White had become well known as a folk singer when progressive politics and folk music became a cultural and political force in the States. In 1941 White recorded the album *Southern Exposure* through Eric Bernay's Keynote Records. The recording has taken on a kind of cult status today.

Cuney, like White, was on a similar but quieter path. He was a poet, singer, and songwriter. He was doing cultural work loosely connected to progressive causes. It worked well for the album: White's singing and Cuney's songwriting. Richard Wright wrote the foreword liner notes. Wright described the songs and poems White performed and Cuney had written as "images we all know and see each day . . . images . . . that run through these blues"; and a "surer guide than facts and figures" of the "state and quality of feeling existing among Negro folk."[29]

White performed the song/poems from the album live in August 1941 at Ralph's Bar and Grill in the Sugar Hill neighborhood in New York City.[30] The great blues composer W. C. Handy was in attendance and paid high tribute to the work on the album by White and Cuney. From Howard University, Arthur Davis, the distinguished professor, and Sterling Brown, the poet, were in attendance. Aaron Douglas, the great artist from Fisk University, also attended the performance. The album itself is described as a collection of "familiar stories telling of want and privation and discrimination" and "stories we read day after day in newspapers—songs of discrimination in national defense and in the Army and Navy—songs about poor wages and housing, the poll tax, voting, and unions."[31]

Cuney was involved later in 1941 in Washington organizing the W. C. Handy Music Festival, of which he was director. Josh White and Cuney were both slated to perform, and Paul Robeson was chosen as special guest at the festival. The festival and Cuney's involvement in the planning of it again proved his affinity for progressive ideals.[32]

The festival was part of a gathering of Black students in the city—the National Negro Youth Conference. It was a highly anticipated event and nationally organized. Cuney was specifically responsible for organizing a birthday tribute to the great W. C. Handy, who was turning sixty-eight at the time of the conference. On October 18, 1941, just before the conference, Cuney was in Washington as a member of the organizing committee.[33] The conference was held over three days, and Handy did appear. The writer Richard Wright also appeared and presented a paper at Dunbar High School in opposition to Adolph Hitler.[34]

The success with Josh White and Cuney's collaboration in prewar politics was sort of the "last hurrah" for Waring Cuney before the war. In December 1941, with the attack on Pearl Harbor by Japan, America entered World War II. Cuney officially entered military service on July 29, 1942.[35] He would be away for more than three years and would return as a decorated war hero.

Negro Caravan

Sterling Brown's statement regarding African American poetry continues into the 1940s. First, Brown; Arthur Davis, a Howard University professor; and Ulysses Lee, a Howard graduate and Lincoln University professor, publish the African American literary anthology *The Negro Caravan*.[36] The book is still talked about today as a big deal, even though it was originally published in 1941. Many of DC's significant Black poets of the first half of the twentieth century are published in the book. But the poetry section itself is small considering the length of the anthology. This is consistent with Brown's statement in the FWP guidebook regarding African American literature. Notably, Angelina Grimké, the longtime English teacher at Dunbar High School, is included, as are Cuney, Georgia Douglas Johnson, Jean Toomer, and Brown, who includes six of his own poems in the timeless anthology.[37]

Next, in 1944, comes one of Brown's more well-known essays—"Count Us In." Considering that the pressure for equal rights in society for African Americans is increasing at this time, Brown's sentiments make historical sense. For Black people in the nation's capital in the 1940s, whether poet or painter, postal worker, government clerk, or schoolteacher, the focus is now on equal justice in the city. Civic equality. How could the nation's capital allow "Jim Crow" life to be perpetuated on so-called citizens just a stone's throw from the government institutions that run the state? When the Second World War ends in 1945 and the many Black Americans who have served in a war for world freedom and returned to their country, the country receives a quick response—the American racial apartheid system must go.

"Count Us In" is included as part of Howard University historian Rayford Logan's equally famous 1944 anthology, *What the Negro Wants*.[38] *What the Negro Wants* is a collection of essays from leading African American thinkers on America's racial caste system. W. E. B. Du Bois is included, as is the historian and editor Rayford Logan's own work. Brown's essay's title exudes his sentiments—"count us in" the American experiment as full citizens, the time has come.

In his contribution to the anthology, an essay, Brown spells out the indignity of how African Americans are still treated while they at the same time remain loyal, hardworking citizens. Brown notes that "advances have been made but the Negro was far behind in opportunity."[39] Using the military as his entry point repeatedly for his discussion, Brown takes apart America's racial apartheid system with meticulous precision.

He writes of being in the South and meeting "on every hand the sense of not belonging." He also is smart to point out that in the South there is a "friendliness" between "many whites and many Negroes." Brown calls this sentimentality "exaggerated" and a "mystical cult." It is not genuine "human attachment" according to Brown, the basis of the "master and underling" legacy of the racist and segregated South.[40]

Brown does not let the North off the hook either. Brown writes that the North is not "blameless." Using the race riots in Detroit as evidence,[41] Brown writes that the South does not have a "monopoly" on "bloodshed and destruction" in America. Brown demands "first class citizenship" everywhere in America for African Americans, North and South. "If America has more than one class of citizenship, it is less than a first class democracy," Brown wrote.[42]

Brown also summarized the path of Black poetry in the essay and how it had embraced political agitation. Brown wrote that Black poetry from 1940 to the mid-1950s went from "public verse" to "private symbolism." He described the poetry as social in nature and again praised his longtime friend and fellow poet Waring Cuney for the work Cuney had done with Josh White in turning poetry into radical protest. Brown described that what Cuney had done was turned "elegiac lyrics to harsh blues."[43]

But Brown's essay is quite more than just part of an anthology. Brown proved again that an African American poet can take the role in society as a public citizen and advocate. Furthermore, the essay is more evidence of Brown pursuing the mission to be embraced in 1922 at Williams College when his professor George Dutton convinced him that his mission in life was to work for his people, African Americans. His essay demonstrates that Brown was quite serious about that life mission, and it was not just empty talk.

LeDroit Park

At this time as well, native Washingtonian Dolores Kendrick was just beginning to begin her life writing literature. Kendrick, born in 1927 in the city, would be named the city's second poet laureate in May 1999. Kendrick once said she was first told she could be a poet when she was a young student at St. Augustine's Catholic High School in the city. Yet, it was after Kendrick departed St. Augustine's and attended Dunbar High School that she really decided her life would be literature. She would become a poet and teacher of literature.

Kendrick firmly credits her teachers for introducing her to literature and pushing her in that direction at both St Augustine's and Dunbar. Kendrick links her path to the life of a poet to public education and the tight African American community where she was raised. She constantly mentions Howard University as important and Miner Teachers College (now known as the University of District Columbia, or UDC) and public schools such as Dunbar and others as the key to education for African Americans. This education is also a key to her development as a writer and poet.

Dolores Kendrick was born September 7, 1927,[44] and earned her bachelor of science in 1949 from Miner Teachers College. She taught English and Poetry in DC public schools and received a master of arts in teaching from Georgetown University in 1970. She also helped to design the curriculum for DC's School Without Walls and served the school as its humanities coordinator for several years. In addition, Kendrick taught for twenty years at Phillips Exeter Academy in New Hampshire.[45]

Kendrick's father was a newspaperman, Ike Kendrick, who owned and published the local newspaper the *Capitol Spotlight* for decades. The paper was a pillar of the African American community in Washington, DC, with a circulation of 50,000 at one point.[46] Ike Kendrick was close friends with Sterling Brown, and the two regularly played tennis together. Delores, though she would not be aware of it until many years later, met Sterling A. Brown when she was just three years old. Her father and Brown had a golf outing, and Kendrick introduced his daughter to Brown at that time. Kendrick later admits she has no recollection of meeting Brown. She does remember meeting him years later and getting to know the elder poet. It is interesting that Kendrick paused when her father suggested she work for his newspaper. But she wanted to write and teach. And so, that is what Dolores Kendrick would eventually do. She would take the same path as her father's friend Sterling Brown.

Kendrick grew up in LeDroit Park. This is the same neighborhood where Paul Laurence Dunbar and his wife, Alice Dunbar, lived briefly at the turn of the century. When Kendrick was a student at Dunbar High School she was on the staff of the school's newspaper, the *Dunbar News Reel*. She also was a member of the Short Story Club at the school and stated that it was her desire to be a novelist after graduation. She graduated from Dunbar in 1945 just as the first generation of Black poets had matured and were professionals in life and work.[47]

Dunbar High School was a dynamic school that did not shy away from literature and the arts. There was high exposure at the school to poetry and prose. The school also always incorporated poetry and literature into its education for the students. Over the years, the school even had a Poetry Club. There was always poetry in the class yearbooks, and each class or at least many of them had a class poem included. The yearbooks also always included the poem "Keep A-Pluggin' Away" by Dunbar, whose title and refrain became the school motto:

Keep A-Pluggin' Away
Perseverance still is king;
Time its sure reward will bring
Work and wait unwavering—
Keep a-pluggin' away.

Keep a-pluggin' away.
From the greatest to the least,
None are from the rule released.
Be though toiler, poet, priest,
Keep a-pluggin' away.[48]
—*Paul Laurence Dunbar*

Dunbar's famous charge to the students who would make the high school named for him the best African American high school in the country for a while was directly applicable to the career of Dolores Kendrick. Kendrick's decision to seek a life in letters did not take form for decades, according to her, even though she was interested in writing and teaching going back to her time at Dunbar High School. Kendrick spent time in poetry venues and remembered reading poetry in a few going back to the 1950s. But Kendrick said she did not get regularly published outside of the tight-knit Washington, DC, poetry community until the 1970s. Kendrick remained close to the heartbeat of the literary action at Howard University and Miner Teachers College, which she attended because she had settled on a teaching career as her professional pursuit in addition to her life in poetry.

Howard University, despite its Black bourgeoisie proclivities, also remained a source of Black poetry in the city in the late 1940s. In 1948 Owen Dodson, another African American writer and poet, came to teach full-time at Howard University. Dodson, originally from New York, would mostly work in the theater department at Howard and with the Howard Players. However, he was a poet who had a collection published before he arrived. He would continue to publish poetry in various publications for the remainder of his professional life.

Paul Breman, the publisher and bibliophile from Holland, would publish Dodson's poetry in his Black Heritage Series in 1970. The collection, *The Confession Stone*, was volume 13 in Breman's series. Breman describes Dodson's poetry output as "rewarding," and Dodson was frequently asked to write poems on commission.[49] While teaching at Howard, Dodson would serve as a mentor to many Black students and writers, but he would make his biggest mark as a playwright at Howard as head of the Drama Department and the Howard Players.

Overall, the focus of African American poetry in the 1940s shifted to the Midwest, with two writers—Gwendolyn Brooks, of Chicago, and Robert Hayden, of Detroit, Michigan—and to the South, with Margaret Walker. Walker won the Yale Prize for Young Poets in 1942. Hayden worked on the Federal Writers' Project when Sterling

Brown was editor of Negro affairs at FWP. Other African American writers of note at the time were Samuel Allen, a good friend of Sterling Brown who wrote and worked out of several locations, and Dudley Randall. Randall, though he was born in Washington, DC, was a Detroit poet and would become a literary institution in that city.

But even with the emergence of Black poets in other parts of the country, Howard University remained a magnet for literary talent. On Friday, February 11, 1949, Langston Hughes, Arna Bontemps, Owen Dodson, and Sterling A. Brown were featured together in a reading at Howard.[50] The reading was held at Rankin Memorial Chapel on campus and was called "An Evening with the Poets." Dodson, a celebrated poet and playwright out of New York, had been teaching at Atlanta University in the South. Howard University had recruited him to teach there, and he had accepted.

The occasion for the reading for Brown, Dodson, Hughes, and Bontemps was Negro History Week, Carter G. Woodson's cause, and to present poetry from Hughes and Bontemps's anthology, *The Poetry of the Negro*. The anthology also featured several other poets from DC, including Georgia Douglas Johnson, Lewis Grandison Alexander, Frank Horne, Beatrice M. Murphy, and Philippe Thoby-Marcelin. All five of these poets were in attendance as well for the event.[51]

Buds of Verse

Though the buildup of poetic energy among African American poets was not guaranteed, the foundational poets continued to keep the magic going in the city. In January 1950 Langston Hughes edited an issue of a literary magazine called *Voices*.[52] Hughes included as many Black poets as he was able. Gwendolyn Brooks, Robert Hayden, Jessie Faucet, and Melvin Tolson were some of the nationally known poets included in the issue. Hughes also included some of his old Washington acquaintances in the issue as well. Waring Cuney, Georgia Douglas Johnson, and the fiction writer Jessie Faucet, who lived and taught in the city, are the most notable writers in the magazine. Cuney's friend and fellow Lincoln University graduate Bruce Wright, who would one day become a well-known city judge in New York City, is also in the issue. Wright published a collection of poetry in 1944 called *From the Shaken Tower*. It would be his only collection published that we know of currently. Hughes, by including Wright, had proven his willingness to spread the literary net.

In addition to Hughes's efforts, many African American poets from the city were published in an anthology out of Argentina, *Dos siglos de poesía norteamericana,* which appeared in 1950.[53] It was not an exclusive anthology publishing only Black poets, but many were included in the book. The editor was Alfredo Casey. Eighteen Black poets are in the anthology, and the poets with Washington, DC, connections are Georgia Douglas Johnson, Waring Cuney, Sterling A. Brown, and Lewis Grandison Alexander. Paul Lawrence Dunbar, Langston Hughes, and Gwendolyn Brooks, among others, also are published in the book. The inclusion of the African American poets in an international anthology of this nature demonstrated the respect Black poets in

America had gained through their dedication to the art in the twentieth century. In addition, Washington core poets Sterling Brown, Waring Cuney, Lewis Grandison Alexander, and Georgia Douglas Johnson had likewise gained great respect for themselves and for the city where they had honed their craft.

One of these poets, Cuney, was paid the ultimate tribute in 1945 when his return from service in World War II was announced in multiple local newspaper accounts. Cuney was said to be back "chock-full of experiences from his experiences in the Pacific." Many letters had been written by and to Cuney while he was away serving, and he was "hungry for news."[54] Cuney had served in the Pacific theater area of the war. Cuney would eventually be interviewed after the war about the experiences of African American soldiers.[55]

He served in Australia and then New Guinea with the 857th Air Corps of Engineers building airstrips "in the South Pacific."[56] Cuney recalled that while in Australia, the Black soldiers faced some "Jim Crow" style racism, and "anti-Negro" stories;[57] it was in that country that they especially experienced open disdain for their presence. Yet the Black soldiers persevered and proved willing and able, so much so that they were sent to New Guinea for more important service during the campaign. The units were the first American troops in New Guinea to serve during the war.

Cuney would continue to publish up until his death in 1976, sometimes struggling financially to continue to write—the fate of many poets. DC's African American poets and the scene that had begun back in the days after Paul Laurence Dunbar left an impact on the city might have been quieter during the 1940s and early 1950s than it had been in the previous two decades, but it still had only just begun as the century made its turn at the halfway point.

7
A Burning Spear

My father graduated from Howard University in 1960. He began attending shortly after the end of his military service in 1951. Wilmer I. Gilmore was born and raised in Baltimore but relocated to Washington, DC, for a career in government. He would marry my mother (Dorothy Pearl) in 1953, and then they both began long careers in civil service in the federal and local governments.

My father always said studying at Howard was amazing. In his 1960 Howard *Bison Yearbook*, in the Liberal Arts section, is a photograph of Professor Sterling A. Brown, the poet and cultural critic. Brown is pictured sitting in a chair reading a book. Brown is listed as a faculty advisor for the School of Liberal Arts. My father took an English course from Brown while a student at Howard like most students who passed through the school during Brown's time teaching.

My father encountered Brown at the height of his profession and talents. Brown was an African American culture giant by this point. Brown was not only teaching and had finished his work with the Federal Writers' Project but was writing about African American literature, the blues, folklore, and many other topics related to the African American experience.

Brown was documenting postwar Black writers and poets. Naturally, he had high praise for his fellow Washingtonian and friend William Waring Cuney. Cuney, according to Brown, during the 1940s and into the '50s, had "turned from elegiac lyrics to harsh blues."[1] Black poets overall, Brown wrote, had moved "from 'public verse' to private symbolism."[2] Others have sought to define the postwar period as it related to Black poets and Black poetry, but it is apparent that the defining theme of this period as far as Black poets are concerned in DC is there is no dominant theme or direction, though some older themes remained strong.

Dr. Arthur Davis, a legendary teacher in his own right at Howard, was also teaching English courses and literature courses at Howard University when Sterling Brown was there. Davis asserted that the protest tradition of the 1920s and 1930s remained in place in the 1940s and 1950s, and that would include Washington. This was so, according to Davis, even though "several . . . outstanding protest poets of the 'Thirties and 'Forties . . . dropped out of the picture as poets."[3]

"One must also remember that the protest tradition was no mere surface fad with the Negro writer," Davis wrote in 1956. The dedication of Black poets to the protest tradition after the war was still about self-respect" and was both "a philosophy of life" and "almost a religious experience."[4] Davis surely was speaking of poets like Sterling Brown and Owen Dodson. Dodson and Brown were both teachers at the "Capstone of Negro education," Howard University.

Lucille Clifton, A. B. Spellman, Amiri Baraka, and Toni Morrison also would be affiliated with Howard University by the 1950s. Morrison would study at Howard, return to teach for a few years, and mentor aspiring scribes. She joined the Writing Club on campus and aspired to write novels.[5] Dodson, the playwright and poet out of New York; Morrison; and Claude Brown, the author of *Manchild in the Promised Land*—all were in the Writing Club that eventually formed at Howard together, according to Myra Sklarew, the local DC poet and longtime professor at American University.[6]

As for the source of their protest for the many Black bards in Washington, at Howard or not, the push for equal rights and the end of Jim Crow life in the city was the goal. It was at the front of the local agenda by Black residents in the capital. It reached its apex in 1953, when the city's downtown eateries were finally integrated after years of protest by locals such as Mary Church Terrell. The case *District of Columbia v. John R. Thompson Co.*, forever known today as the *Thompson's Restaurant's* case, was one of the largest changes in the legalized social order in the city. Five years before, in the three racial covenant cases that came before the US Supreme Court, the High Court held that state enforcement of racial covenants in housing was unconstitutional.[7]

One of the three racial covenant cases before the US Supreme Court at the same time as *Shelley v. Kraemer* was *Hurd v. Hodge*. *Hurd v. Hodge* involved a house located at 116 Bryant Street NW in Washington, DC, just off the Howard University campus.[8] The following year, 1954, would bring the *Brown v. Board of Education* case.[9] As a result of those cases, legalized racial segregation was over in the city, even though racial desegregation in the city would take time.

The litigation again demonstrated the unique political positioning of African Americans in Washington, DC. Political results occurred in the city seemingly always before it occurred in other cities in the country. After and during the Civil War, African fugitives from the bondage of slavery came to the city in droves because it was the first city Lincoln legally emancipated. It made perfect sense that Washington would also be legally integrated much earlier than many other American municipalities as well.

The main effect of racial integration from the US Supreme Court cases in 1953–54 was the city's African American population would no longer be hyperconcentrated in the city's U Street Corridor, the neighborhood where the Black poetry Renaissance had begun. Segregation would continue, but Black families were able to move into other areas of the city. Also, more African Americans, from all over the country, would come there to try to make a life for themselves in the nation's capital.

By the 1950s the city's African American population was over 50 percent.[10] This change had been coming for over a decade. White families began leaving the city en mass at this same time. The metropolitan area was already segregated. Investment in the construction of highways and the suburbanization of the region using federal housing policy perpetuated the change further.[11]

Housing policies perpetuated by the federal government and the real estate industry resulted in African Americans being "trapped in Hitler-like ghetto" situations.[12] One such "ghetto" was described as "a narrow, semicircular slum belt surrounding the Government palaces in the center of the city."[13] But like always, ever since the days of Dunbar and prior to his arrival, the African American population of the city pressed forward and kept making a world they could call their own.

Howard Poets

The poet and intellectual Percy A. Johnston enrolled in Howard University in 1957. Percy Johnston is the bridge from the *Brown* decision to the end of legalized Jim Crow and then the Black Arts Movement (BAM). Johnston and several other important writers did something at Howard that had been done before, but perhaps Johnston and his colleagues did it better than most. They came to be known as the Howard Poets, and they would engage in a period of artistic expression that stands apart for its free thought and lack of ideological thrust. If anything, the Howard Poets' ideology was not to have any one ideology but to allow writers and artists to find their own voice in a time of ever-shifting politics.

According to writer and literary scholar Myra Sklarew, African American poets were not being published much in the 1950s anyway.[14] While Sklarew's statement is anecdotal, her observations are likely accurate. This is the city and community of literature that Percy Johnston and the Howard Poets navigated. There was a level of insulation because they were on the Howard University campus, but they still operated in an underresourced racially segregated literary community.

Johnston was born May 18, 1930, in New York City.[15] He graduated from Dunbar High School in Washington in 1947, worked as a florist, then joined the United States Air Force in 1949.[16] He became a police officer in Dayton, Ohio, and a credit investigator before finally attending Saint Peter's University in New Jersey. He had also worked as a reporter briefly for the *Capital Times* newspaper in Washington, DC.[17] He wanted to write, and he eventually came to Howard University in 1957. At Howard he wrote for the *Hilltop Newspaper*, the school newspaper, and was president of the English Club.

Johnston is the most revered of the Howard Poets and is well published. But there are others. Oswald Govan, Walter DeLegall, Leroy Stone, Joseph White, W. Alfred

Fraser, and Percy Johnston are the original Howard Poets.[18] Dolores Kendrick cites her connection to the Howard Poets and Johnston as critical to her growth as a writer.

"I had a hard time getting anyone to listen to what I wrote," Kendrick said in 2005. "Percy encouraged me, and said, you are a very fine poet, you just stick to what you do."[19] Kendrick also credited Johnston for helping her gain more confidence to get published in various places. Kendrick worked on one of the singular achievements of this period that is associated with the Howard Poets—the journal *Dasein*. While the Howard Poets and the Dasein Poets (Dasein Literary Society, or Dasein), which both emerge in 1959, seem like one and the same, they are separate projects and collectives. The African American literary scholar Winston Napier only lists six poets as the original Howard Poets. The Dasein Poets are the publishing venture that emerged out of the Howard Poets.

Yet *Dasein*, a journal that a group of poets began to publish in the early 1960s, just before the BAM period, is one of the more impressive journals to appear at any point in the twentieth century in DC. This is because it does not have big financing or institutional backing. Johnston, Govan, and others put the journal out themselves. It is a remarkable achievement, and the fact that they produced several issues is testament to their fortitude. According to literary scholars Eben Wood and Aldon Nielsen, Dasein, the poets and their movement, were the product of Sterling A. Brown and Owen Dodson encouraging the poets to act and create the art they wanted to create.[20] In addition, Toni Morrison, who taught briefly at Howard under her real name, Antonia Wofford, also encouraged the writers.

In the first issue of *Dasein*, the artists declare that "the aim of Dasein is to provide an exhibition place of contemporary art in all the media art that can be reduced to the printed page."[21] The advisory board of the journal consists of Owen Dodson, Sterling Brown, Arthur Davis, and Eugene Holmes. Walter DeLegall is the editor, and Johnston is the publisher, with Lance Jeffers, Govan, Stone, Joseph White, and W. Alfred Fraser serving as editors. It is part of a tradition where Black writers and artists unable to find outlets for their literary expressions must create them themselves.

The first issue appears in the wake of the death of Richard Wright, who died suddenly in 1960. Eugene C. Holmes effectively writes a literary eulogy for Wright. Wright, Holmes writes, "blazed like a flame across the literary horizon." Clyde Taylor follows Holmes's tribute with a poem inspired by Wright.

The issue is like many of the issues to come afterward. It is full of poetry and art and, most of all, has no theme or agenda. Poets are allowed to track in any thematic, formal, or informal direction of their choice. Most, if not all, of the notable Howard Poets have work here. Govan, Johnston, DeLegall, and Leroy Stone all are published in issue 1. Owen Dodson, a professor on the faculty at Howard at the time, even has a poem included here, again demonstrating his poetic roots. But Dodson, and others including Dolores Kendrick, are not Howard Poets according to the late literary scholar Winston Napier. He made that clear as someone who was there up close when it happened:

> The *Dasein* movement, it is important to restate, derives from the publishing efforts of the Howard Poets, a venture through which the latter expanded their audience beyond that of the oral readings to a much larger one afforded by the printed page. Hence, the *Dasein* poets existed only as a community in print. In fact, any poet whose works were published in *Dasein* and who was not part of the original six-man reading ensemble is strictly a member of the Dasein grouping (this would include Richard Eberhart, Lance Jeffers and Owen Dodson).[22]

The most famous poem in the first issue of *Dasein* is Lance Jeffers's "my blackness is the beauty of this land." The poem is well anthologized now and became very well known a few years later, when the Black Arts Movement commenced. The poem would eventually be published by Broadside Press in 1970 by Dudley Randall. Jeffers was born and raised in Freemont, Nebraska, November 28, 1919. Jeffers would many years later read in Washington, DC, in E. Ethelbert Miller's Ascension Poetry Reading Series, one of the most important poetry outlets in the history of the city's literary scene.

The poets, the Dasein Poets and the Howard Poets, would not last long, but they were a busy group, energetic and engaged on the campus and in the city. On June 29, 1963, the Dasein Poets were featured at the opening of Open Way Coffee House at 945 K Street NW in the city.[23] Open Way was a gallery and artistic space that offered poetry and visual arts to the public and was framed as a venue that was rooted in unitarian principles.[24] The independent thinking of many of the Dasein Poets would fit comfortably within these deals.

Dasein continued to publish through 1964. In future issues, the Howard Poets continued to publish their work, and the journal regularly published the work of other poets and other artists. By the next set of issues, Dolores Kendrick, the Dunbar High School poet who wanted to be a novelist, was an editor of the journal.

The journal includes artwork by Lois Mailou Jones, of Boston. Jones eventually become an iconic figure in the art world while living right in Washington, DC. Wallace Terry, the chronicler of the African American experience in Vietnam, has writings in the second set of issues.[25] Other notable persons published by *Dasein* include longtime actor Helmar Cooper and visual artist and painter of Washington, DC, Yvonne Pickering.

Of the Howard Poets, Percy Johnston had the most impact as a literary figure. Even with all the work with the Howard Poets and *Dasein*, he would publish several books of his own, poetry and literary criticism.[26] Like all the Howard Poets, Johnston's work was wide in theme and style. His poetry was well structured, and he was writing at a time when the boundaries of what poetry should be were broad. When the Beat poets became popular, Johnston and some of the other Howard poets took notice. Johnston visited one of DC's more well-known Beat poet venues, Coffee and Confusion, when it was briefly a presence in the city.

Coffee and Confusion's life was short. It was the creation of George Washington University student and poet William A. Walker. Walker, whose full name was William Addison Walker, opened the first version of the venue on April 1, 1959. In May 1959, at the time of the heyday of the Howard Poets, Walker was seeking a license to operate Coffee and Confusion at 945 K Street NW.

Dolores Kendrick confirms that it was a spot for poets and that she did visit the venue. Percy Johnston did as well. Brandel France de Bravo, poet and Walker's daughter, confirms that many Black poets read in the space.[27] Walker's efforts, much of the time, were shut down by the local police, but Walker pressed on, and the Beats enjoy a history in the city mostly because of him and the space he provided.

1960s

If the 1950s were a period where Black poetry stalled in terms of published works, the early 1960s saw a resurgence. The Howard Poets would be part of that increased activity but not as a group or anything. Some of the poets, like Percy Johnston and Walter DeLegall, would achieve as individuals. Other African American poets from Washington or writing in the city would make important strides as well. As was the case in some of these achievements, the larger publishing and literary world helped make this happen. The crowning achievement of this period for the Howard Poets was the publication of their anthology *Burning Spear: An Anthology of Afro Saxon Poetry* in 1963.

Burning Spear is a collective statement by these poets. They even call it "the first comprehensive presentation of the word men who were once called the Howard Poets." They describe themselves as "not members of a literary movement in the traditional sense of the word, because they do not have in common any monist about creativity or aesthetics." They fashion themselves as "indifferent to most critics and reviewers—since criticism in America is controlled and written by Euro-Americans."[28]

Many of the Howard Poets and poets associated with Dasein were published a year before in 1962 by Rosey E. Pool in her celebrated anthology *Beyond the Blues.* It was one of several anthologies that would begin to emerge in the 1960s. Pool is one of a few celebrated non–African American figures associated with many of the Washington, DC, poets. Her dedication to showcasing African American poets is noteworthy in a variety of literary circles. *Beyond the Blues* is her singular contribution to the period of Black poetry right before the Black Arts period takes off. Pool, modest in her assessment of her contribution, describes herself as a "Caucasian from Holland" who put together the book just before the 100th anniversary of the "Emancipation from Slavery" was proclaimed.[29]

Many of the poets associated with Washington, DC, Black poetry scenes, past and present, are included by Pool. These comprise Waring Cuney, May Miller, Howard University's Owen Dodson, and the lesser-known Carl Gardner. Of the Howard Poets,

Percy Johnston is included, as is Walter DeLegall, Oswald Govan, Lance Jeffers, and R. Orlando Jackson.

Pool was well respected in circles where the writers were of African descent. If Pool's goal with *Beyond the Blues* was to make a statement, she accomplished her goal, at least according to J. Welfred Holmes, who reviewed the book for the *CLA Journal* in March 1963.[30] Holmes, though his wording is strange at times, wrote that *Beyond the Blues* had "meaning and worth" and was "another facet of the increasing preoccupation of the English speaking world with the life and literature of the world of color."[31] Holmes, who was teaching at the historically Black university Morgan State University at the time, asserted that England had its own challenge of African people entering British society now so the book could become important.[32] DC-based poets A. B. Spellman ("a theft of wishes") and Leroy Stone ("Calypso") are both mentioned in the review specifically for their outstanding work by Holmes.[33]

Pool's love and support of African American poetry continued throughout her professional life, and African American poets with ties to DC were part of it. After the publication of *Beyond the Blues*, she published the anthology *Is ben de nieuwe Neger: gedichten, rijmen, liedjes en dokumenten uit 300 jaar verzet van de Amerikaanse Neger* (I am the New Negro: Poems, rhymes and songs from 300 years of resistance)[34] in 1965 out of Holland. Of the DC poets, Waring Cuney figures most prominently. Sterling Brown is also in the anthology, as is Howard University Drama professor and poet Owen Dodson.

The endurance of the Howard Poets and Dasein Poets is a key period, considering the political and cultural dynamics of the postwar period. They reflect a certain independence, a rebuilding and continuation. Most of them, like Jeffers, Kendrick, Johnston, DeLegall, and Napier, stand out on their own. Scholars continue to search for answers as to what made the group emerge at a time of little definition. Even the Howard University literary critic Stephen Henderson will consider the Dasein Poets and their efforts many years later.[35]

Puzzles

In 1962, Langston Hughes again writes to his longtime friend Waring Cuney. Hughes comes away from the exchange believing that Cuney was a recluse.[36] He tells Arna Bontemps the same. Bontemps has difficulty over the years getting Cuney to respond to letters and requests to publish.[37]

But Cuney is no recluse. He continues to write poetry and songs and to correspond with some people. Marguerite Cartwright, the actress, journalist, and arts supporter, is one such person, along with her husband, Carl, who regularly receives poetry from Cuney.[38] After Cuney's military service, he is writing poetry again and sends poetry to the Cartwrights he has written in 1948. Cuney also hopes to receive some financial support for his writing. In 1952 the American folk singer Burl Ives records a song

Cuney wrote called "This Time Tomorrow." It is the B-side to Ives's hit song "One Hour Ahead of the Posse" released in 1954.[39]

Rosey Pool, the champion of Black poets who published Cuney in *Beyond the Blues*, is in touch with him, as is Paul Breman, the bookseller, bibliophile, and eventual creator of the Heritage Series of Black Poetry. Breman, from Amsterdam (Bussum, a suburb), spent his life in the world of books, publishing and selling.[40] Breman contended that Cuney went a bit quiet at this time to avoid Rosey Pool.[41]

In 1958–61, Cuney sent Breman reams of poetry that Cuney has typed onto notebook paper.[42] It is enough poetry to probably comprise several volumes. Almost all the poems arrived bundled in large envelopes. He even includes some poetry he wrote out in longhand. Some of the writings are poems, some blues and folk songs.

Breman published Cuney in 1960; the collection is called *Puzzles*. Cuney, whose poetry output had diminished in publication but not in production according to Rosey Pool, has never published a collection. *Puzzles*, by many indications, was originally to be called *Beale Street*. In the introduction to *Puzzles*, Breman calls Cuney, "one of America's major poets."[43] Breman firmly believes that if Cuney had been white, his writing career would have been different. He describes the contradiction of Cuney's life as follows: "Because Washington was a town where no Black man was allowed inside a downtown theater, not even in the gallery. Strange to know that a negro, Benjamin Bannaker, played an important role in planning the city. . . . In this city, Waring Cuney was born."[44]

Breman's effort to challenge the racist narrative of African Americans in general is self-evident in his notes to *Puzzles*. "A Negro poet is first of all a human being, subject to the same sensations as all other members of the species. He happens to be a poet. . . . He also happens to be a Negro, and this too, conditions his emotions," Breman also writes.[45]

Breman refers to Cuney also as a poet who makes himself "heard and felt," a poet of "quietness which is no meekness."[46] Most of all, Breman is pleased that finally Cuney will have a collection of poetry that brings together his aesthetics and voice. Cuney's work can now "cease to be scattered through many magazines, from 1925 to the present."[47]

The work itself is typical Cuney. Cuney is writing lyrics of songs, scenes from stories; also, as Breman writes, he is a poet of "pungent anecdotes."[48] Included in the book are drawings by Ru van Rossem. The drawings depict some of Cuney's poems and add a necessary element. Because Cuney is a songwriter seeking to help the reader visualize and feel, the drawings propel the book's overall thrust, the human qualities of the book, and the elusive and fierce emotions.

Waring Cuney's endurance as a poet and songwriter is a credit to his personal devotion to the art. He was born in 1906, the year the poet Paul Laurence Dunbar died in Dayton, Ohio. He was close friends with Sterling Brown and Langston Hughes. He served in World War II. By the time of the Howard Poets, the African American poetry landscape reflected an evolving literary moment. Waring Cuney, who had been writing since he was a teenager, probably should have had a collection or two by 1960, when *Puzzles* was published. His contemporaries and friends Sterling Brown, Langston Hughes, and Arna Bontemps were well published by 1960. This is more reason why *Puzzles*, though not well known, remains a critically important collection of verse. The work of Dasein and the Howard Poets is likewise a guide to the history of race relations in the city and a hint to the African American cultural patterns that would soon emerge.

8

New Schools

I met the poet and cultural mover Gaston Neal in 1993. Neal was a local legend and an unsung national poet by that point. He had been chasing poetry since the late 1950s.

In the late 1950s, the Beat poets (Beatniks) were the talk of the literary world in America. Allen Ginsberg, Gregory Corso, and LeRoi Jones (soon to be Amiri Baraka) were some of the movement's main poets in the 1950s. Gaston Neal and Amiri Baraka connected at this time as well. The movement itself had its roots at Columbia University in the 1940s, as poets in New York revolted against the academic stiffness of poetry.[1] Ginsberg was one of the main ideological movers at the time. Amiri Baraka and Ginsberg would eventually connect on the scene in New York in Greenwich Village. Baraka and Neal became fast friends during the Beat period along with jazz critic and poet A. B. Spellman.[2]

Washington, DC, had a vibrant Beat poetry scene, and many poets across the spectrum remember the scene and what it sought to represent. When Baraka (as LeRoi Jones) was invited to Washington to read at Howard University along with Gregory Corso, Allen Ginsberg, Ray Bresmer, and others, Baraka also connected with his poet friends Gaston Neal, and A. B. Spellman that evening.

Spellman made the trip happen, even though he was in New York at the time. He and Baraka had met as students at Howard University in the 1950s.[3] Baraka had not yet gone to Cuba and become deeply radicalized, but it was still a long time since Spellman and Baraka were fast friends at Howard. Spellman would eventually write the seminal book on jazz criticism, *Four Lives in the Bebop Business*, and during a year of traveling and reading, Spellman launched his career writing jazz criticism.[4]

Years later, both Spellman and Neal became significant poets in DC and close friends for decades. Neal and Spellman are part of that tradition in Washington where African American poets, activists, and cultural workers chose to come to the city for opportunity. Spellman came to the city from New York to attend Howard University.[5] Neal came from Pittsburgh and was in the military at one point, serving as a medic at Walter Reed Hospital. Spellman met Neal in 1956 in New York City.[6]

Regarding the reading at Howard University, Spellman came down to the city with Baraka, along with Corso, Ginsberg, and Bresmer. The Howard University community was already prepared for the reading and a close interaction with the Beatniks. Beat poetry had been the talk of the campus as it had been around the country.

In late 1958 Percy Johnston had written a poem about the Beats and called it "Ode to the Beats." He also organized a forum on the Howard University campus for students to discuss the Beats. The Beats were described by the forum as a "group of artists who endeavor to reject and belittle some of the values of society."[7] Other artists and intellectuals on campus responded to the Beats. Poet Primus St. John, a student at Howard University at the time, commented on the meaning of Beat poets (the Beatniks). St. John said he came away from the forum still not knowing what a Beatnik was in America at the time. "Who was the Beatnik?," he asked in an editorial in *The Hilltop Newspaper*. "Beatnik or beat generation has a public connotation that embodies the eccentric, the juvenile delinquent, the bop, the skid-row bum, the jazz musician, and anyone else who fails to be nonconventional. Can all these people accurately be called "Beat"?[8]

Leroy Stone, another poet at Howard at the time, along with Percy Johnston, also commented on the Beats and the school forum. Stone was impressed by the "diversity of points of view taken by the speakers" regarding the Beats. Stone was disappointed in the views embraced by the students who were insensitive in his view to why individuals had elected to embrace a "Beat" culture that is "self-consciously at odds with some of society's important values."[9]

With all that campus chatter and intellectual exchange on campus, Baraka, Allen Ginsburg, Ray Bresmer, Gregory Corso, and others did descend on the campus and read poetry. Gaston Neal and A. B. Spellman were also there, though they didn't read. Ginsberg called the trip from New York City and the event "the climax of that era of good feeling." Ginsberg considered it a "big big reading" as they were all considered "weirdo celebrities in the newspaper." Howard University in 1959, according to Ginsberg, had been labeled a "bastion of bourgeoise culture" by Baraka.[10]

Spellman recalls that the reading, even though it was at Howard, included a good number of whites in the audience.[11] It was such a big deal for Baraka that he thought enough of the night to write a poem called "One Night Stand" about the whole experience. That poem appears in his first collection, *Preface to a Twenty Volume Suicide Note*.[12]

The reading and the hang occur in March 1959, according to poet and literary critic Aldon Nielsen. Howard University's *Hilltop Newspaper* covers the reading and a photograph of the event.[13] Baraka is at the microphone, and Ginsberg, Corso, and Bresmer sit behind him onstage. Spellman also confirms they went to another spot around the city to read their poetry, which could have been the venue Coffee and Confusion,[14] the short-lived Beat poetry café down on K Street NW.

As for Neal, who was among the group on the trip, it is not known if he was a busy poet at the time of that reading. He was hanging with some of the Beat movement's top poets at the time at least in terms of history. Baraka throughout his life celebrated Neal as the most important unpublished poet in America. It became Baraka's standard introduction of Neal at numerous literary gatherings in Washington. In an essay right before Baraka's death, he describes Neal as "criminally underknown."[15]

By 1964, just a few years later, when he was just thirty, Gaston Neal, the Pittsburgh native, was a poet in DC and trying to organize politically and culturally. He was born in Pittsburgh in 1934 in the Hill District, the neighborhood made famous by the playwright August Wilson in his plays. Neal, in fact, knew August Wilson from Pittsburgh and even encouraged Wilson to take up poetry, which Wilson tried to do before he mastered drama.[16]

But by 1955, well before the Howard reading, Neal was already writing poetry, though little is known about what he wrote and who his influences were. When he was twenty-one, he met the Howard University poet and drama professor Owen Dodson. Dodson was talking with Langston Hughes on the phone long distance, according to Neal. Dodson read Neal's poetry and gave him the encouragement every poet seeks early on. He invited Neal in from a rainstorm, and Neal had a mentor.

It still wasn't a smooth trip ever for Neal to the cultural life in the nation's capital. Neal had dropped out of school in the eighth grade in Pittsburgh because an English teacher discouraged him from the writing life. Neal was not surprised by the teacher's actions either. "There I was a ninth grade dropout from a large city slum. This type of person almost never got involved in the civil rights movement, which was the big thing during my early adult years," Neal told William Raspberry of *The Washington Post* years later.[17] Neal stressed that he wasn't ever part of the movement. His approach was culture. "I decided to try to make my contribution by helping my people to rediscover their cultural heritage."[18]

But it took a long time for Neal to reach this purpose, due to the challenges set before him as a young kid in Pittsburgh. After dropping out, he wound up in reform school. Neal next worked as a plaster helper with his brother. He set his sights on enlisting in the military. His mother gave her permission, as did a local priest. When some assistance also was presented by the Pittsburgh city government, Neal got into the army. Still, it was bittersweet. "The United States was just begging me to get into the Army. Again, when you are oppressed, you are put in that situation," Neal said in 1968.[19] Neal signed up to serve three years but only served two. He was tossed out because he didn't believe in what the army was doing.[20]

After leaving the military, as Neal put it, he "bummed around trying to find myself." He was just twenty years old and, in his words, "hadn't found who I was, what I was." He described the period as "difficult" because in general finding yourself is difficult for any young person. But Neal also made it clear that the task was just that more difficult for young African American men because, as he put it, "no way is made for you."

Neal worked various jobs and traveled around the country from place to place.[21] He spent time in New York, Ohio, and Philadelphia and was always traveling from DC to Pittsburgh and back and forth. He even worked on Capitol Hill, where he learned the inner workings of how the government functions. He said he got "lucky" in obtaining the position. "I was kind of a messenger clerk. And I picked up whole statements from each Congressman and each Senator . . . for a whole year that gave me a whole insight into the working of Congress and of the workings of our legislature—you know, their workings[,] the white folks' government."[22]

When Neal did get serious about writing—after trouble with the criminal justice system, substance abuse, and an extended stay in St. Elizabeths Hospital for psychiatric issues (Neal called it "the madhouse")—he found his way into the world of verse, written and spoken, quickly.[23] In 1964 he read his poetry in Washington, DC, at a big event dubbed "Four Acts for Act: The Organization of the Militants."[24] The local political and educational activist Julius Hobson organized the event. It was held at Ninth and V Street NW in the heart of the city's African American community. The building is WUST Radio Hall, which still stands today but is now called the 9:30 Club.[25]

It is not known what Neal read that night or what happened, but the event was held on November 23, 1964, beginning at 8:30 p.m. John Blair performed folk music and some blues. It was just one year out from the dramatic beginning of the Black Arts Movement (BAM) officially in American cities throughout the "Black Belt," but as with the Black Renaissance of the early twentieth century, change was already underway. If BAM itself was the fire, Gaston Neal was one of its sparks.

In the middle 1960s, Neal became politically active at the same time as the Student Nonviolent Coordinating Committee (SNCC) set up shop in the city. He was a jazz lover, promoter, poetry writer, and community activist. He also fought an addiction to controlled substances for decades. In 1960 Neal was arrested for possession of heroin in the city. Neal was living in the 1900 block of Tenth Street NW at the time.[26]

This is when Neal's personal temptation and demons eventually landed him in St. Elizabeths Hospital. Neal often told the story during his life of being informed when he was committed that the room he was assigned was the same room where Ezra Pound had resided when he was there. Pound was committed to St. Elizabeths during his days as a highly vocal fascist. Pound's residency has become part of the folklore of American poetry. Neal mostly recounted his St. Elizabeths' sojourn in various conversations.

Gaston

By 1965 Neal was a known poet on the Black poetry scene in Washington. Along with Howard University activist Don Freeman, Neal founded the New School of Afro-American Thought right in the heart of the city's most vibrant African American neighborhood. As the city was making its big push for civil rights, home rule, and equality for all citizens in the city, Neal was in the middle of it.

The New School would become an institution where Black poets found a safe space for expression and where art and politics came together for revolutionary activity. When the Black Arts Movement came to Washington, DC, Neal, the poet, and

Freeman, the political activist, drummer, and cultural visionary, provided the perfect landing strip—the New School. "We needed a center where Black artists and potential artists could learn who they are and have it reflected in their work," Neal said. The New School was also created, Neal stated, because though Howard University was a kind of Black cultural center, it was "not acceptable to poor people." Neal's vision was right in line with BAM.[27]

The accepted origin story of the Black Arts Movement is that it was launched when poet Amiri Baraka (LeRoi Jones) established Spirit House (the Black Arts Repertory Theater), the theater company in Harlem, New York. Baraka symbolically had taken his art from Greenwich Village to Harlem. In his 1984 autobiography, Baraka wrote, "When we came up out of the subway, March 1965, cold and clear, Harlem all around us staring down, we felt like pioneers of the new order." He also proudly describes himself and his associates as "back in the homeland to help raise the race." As he also accurately pointed out, "Youth in their fervor know no limitations."[28] This was not much different from what Neal would do at the New School in Washington, DC.

Many other cities with large African American populations were also moving into their own, as Black Arts poet Haki Madhubuti would put it later. Black poets and artists needed to express themselves through the prism of African and African American cultural traditions. They also needed autonomy and control, a clean break from western norms in their art. New Orleans, Detroit, Los Angeles, and many other cities besides New York were part of this shift.

Collectively, BAM was the cultural wing of the African American struggle for self-definition and self-determination in the United States. Larry Neal (no relation to Gaston Neal), a poet and essayist, described the movement as an attempt "to link, in a highly conscious manner, art and politics, to assist in the liberation of black people."[29] Neal (Larry) described it as art (literature in his case) that spoke directly to Black people. Neal (Larry) and others also described the "Black arts" as having its own aesthetics and "cultural tradition."[30]

One of the key moments of BAM was the publication of *Black Fire: An Anthology of African American Writing.* In fact, this anthology defines the era and announces a change in African American literature. It is no accident that there are many African American poets based in Washington, DC, included in the anthology. Some notables are Walter DeLegall, the poet and jazz critic A. B. Spellman (Spellman was not in DC at the time), and Gaston Neal. It is a credit to what Howard poets like DeLegall are doing many years before, that DeLegall is included in an anthology with an overt ideological thrust, even though his writings are not necessarily that kind of writing. DeLegall has attended Howard University and has become a member of the Howard poets and the affiliated collective called the Dasein Poets. His two poems in the book are "Elegy for a Lady" and "Psalm for Sonny Rollins," a praise poem for the jazz saxophonist.[31]

Neal's poems in *Black Fire* are "Today," which would also appear in several other publications during this period, and "Personal Jihad," perhaps his most well-known poem of the period. Neal's activist rage is evident in his self-written biography in the book. As Neal puts it, his goal is to "purge myself of the whiteness within me and link completely with my Black brothers in the struggle to destroy the enemy and rebuild the Black Nation." He also wrote that he was "editing a volume of poetry of my time spent in St. Elizabeths Hospital."[32]

Both Neal and Spellman emerged from the same wellspring of poetry in the 1960s that embraced the aesthetics of the Black Arts Movement. Spellman would not become a fixture in the city until many years later. However, in DC, Neal's New School of Afro-American Thought became the centerpiece of BAM. The school commenced its operations in October 1966 in a storefront building, though it had been functioning already before that time. Neal described the school's purpose as creating awareness and identity in "black people through the arts and humanities."[33] Neal added that he wanted the school to bring all Black people to the "point of realization" that "'yes you are beautiful, and you are beautiful because you are black.'"[34]

One year prior to the opening of the school, Neal had put together an art exhibit right in the Cardozo community. Neal even admits that initially a school wasn't necessarily on his mind or the minds of anyone. They were feeling their way around, trying to figure things out. "It began as the Cardozo Area Art Committee. . . . I was working for that new money that Johnson via Kennedy had put out here in the black community," Neal said. Johnson and Kennedy, according to Neal, were trying to "buy off" some Black people.[35] Neal insisted upon using the war on poverty funds he received on his own terms. It is ironic that the New School of Afro-American Thought would originate through government funds, the same government Neal opposed in so many ways.

Shortly after the successful art exhibit, Neal organized "Three Days of Soul," a music festival right in the same community. Amiri Baraka, Neal's close friend and poetry partner, participated in the festival and in the opening ceremonies for the New School. In addition to Baraka, Sterling Brown participated in the 1966 opening, as did poet Owen Dodson, and Neal's close friend and poet A. B. Spellman.

According to Don Freeman, the festival was impressive.[36] Neal had been able to bring twenty-five different African American music acts to the city to perform over three days.[37] The festival traced the evolution of African American music by showcasing all sorts of music genres. Among the performers was the spoken word group out of New York City known as the Last Poets. It was the success of the festival that convinced Freeman that the African American communities in the city needed a school. They could not just do events and festivals; they needed something more comprehensive.

By the late 1960s, Freeman and Neal had put together an organization and institution that was a key player in the city along with Marion Barry's Pride Inc., the SNCC, Free DC, Julius Hobson's Associated Community Teams, and George Storey's Build Black.[38] Washington, DC, was a "colonized city" according to many African Americans at the time. But it created the perfect atmosphere for unity and organizing politically and through the arts. Considering Neal's focus on art and culture, he was well positioned for this period in the city. He also had the New School, where, among many things, he ran a poetry workshop. "I saw where black people had no place to go. Black people who wanted to do things, learn and black people who wanted to grow in terms of intellectual growth," Neal said.[39] This observation is what led Neal, Don Freeman, and others to begin the New School.

In addition to arts organizing, Neal was writing poetry and reading it. When Langston Hughes died on May 22, 1967, Neal was part of a tribute reading to Hughes in the city.[40] The reading, "Four Decades of Negro Poetry," was appropriate. Forty years prior to Hughes's death, Hughes had come to live in Washington, DC, and had connected with the Black poets of the city. The reading in tribute to Hughes was held at the Sheraton-Carlton Hotel in the city, and the proceeds from the event were donated to Neal's efforts with the Cardozo Area Arts Committee.

In October 1967, Neal's New School celebrated its first anniversary, proving its perseverance under difficult circumstances to deliver African American culture to the people of the city.[41] Neal also published one of his more famous poems in 1967. The poem, entitled "Today," mentioned earlier, would take on a life of its own. It reflects Neal's unique style as a poet and his singular voice rooted in the ordinary.

But in Neal's ever-evolving life, he was arrested on a gun charge in 1968, tried, convicted, and sentenced to ninety days in jail.[42] Yet it would not stop Neal's momentum. It was a small obstacle to overcome, and Neal would endure. The founding of the New School and his writing had given him space and a name. He could grow and evolve; he knew his purpose. His poet "Today" is the best proof that Neal was on the path of his life work.

In the famous anthology *The Black Power Revolt*, published just as the Black Liberation Movement and the Black Arts Movement were accelerating, there are only two poems included.[43] The book is all essays, by writers living and dead pushing the politics. Amiri Baraka, Maulana Ron Karenga, Stokley Carmichael, W. E. B. Du Bois, Marcus Garvey, Floyd B. McKissick, and Malcolm X. Sadly, very few Black women writers are included in the anthology, exposing one of the major flaws of the Black Liberation struggle. This is quite typical of the era. Sexism and patriarchy did not go away just because African American men decided they wanted total freedom. Black women were left to wage a dual struggle within the overall struggle.

One of the women included in *Black Power Revolt* is the Mississippi poet and intellectual Margaret Walker. Her timeless classic poem "For My People" opens the book. The second poem, the poem that acts as the afterword for the book, is Neal's poem "Today." It appears right after Malcolm X's closing essay.

Two years later the poem "Today" would again be published in *The Washington Post*.[44] It was 1969, and the Black struggle for liberation in America was at its most intense moment. Gaston Neal was still a poet and still fighting the good fight in the city. It is Neal's self-penned biography in the *Black Power Revolt* anthology that says it best: "Dead born—1934, reborn '61 with the knowledge of the beauty of my blackness, the unfailingly destiny of my people and me."[45] But the real importance of this late 1960s period is that the African American community overall in the city had become even more cohesive in a sense, despite the patriarchy and the political divisions. The various institutions—cultural, political, and educational—had come together. Howard University and the Black educational players had grown even more into part of the city's literary and political aspirations. It was the beginning of something deeper and more profound.

Elias Rodrigues wrote about the fusion of Black poetics in the city in 2022 in the publication *The Nation*. According to Rodrigues, the period mostly reflects the influence of Sterling Brown. Brown, Rodrigues writes, "mentored students who became key organizers in SNCC as well as those who became noted Black Power activists, including Stokely Carmichael, and Black Arts Movement writers, such as Baraka and Toni Morrison." Brown also mentored Gaston Neal, who, according to Rodrigues, cleverly "used War on Poverty funds to establish the Cardozo Area Arts Committee, which in 1965 started the New School of Afro-American Thought."[46]

Neal was smart and deferential to the traditions he was following. That first event he organized "featured Black artists ranging from the Harlem Renaissance to the Black Arts Movement, from Brown to Baraka."[47] In a sense, Brown was the glue and the force behind the movement of poetry in the city by Black poets but was still actively teaching at Howard and nurturing tomorrow's important literary figures who would matriculate on that campus. It was 1968, and Brown would soon retire from teaching. But he had provided the leadership to the younger poets, especially poets and artists outside accepted literary circles.

Brown's work never stopped, even after Howard. He was too revered by the late 1960s by the young Black poets who had digested *Southern Road*. Howard's bourgeois sensibilities were not supposed to produce Brown's kind of poetry. But perhaps that is why the life of the Black poet in Washington, DC, is quite specific to an experience but also rooted in tradition.

The traditionalists and academics are drawn to what is happening among the people, with their antiwestern approach to art. And the poets with their ear to the lives of ordinary people, the common everyday hardworking souls who make the big cities run, who deliver mail, change beds in hotels, bag and check out groceries, or put out fires, and so on, are intrigued by the movements on academic campuses. African Americans also know by the 1960s that success has to be of their own making in America, as has historically always been the case. This, without a doubt, also includes any achievement in the arts.

9
Dreams

My clearest memory, as a very small boy, of the assassination of the Reverend Dr. Martin Luther King Jr. is of my mother playing the same record album in the days following Dr. King's death. The record was the 1963 March on Washington album with Dr. King's "I Have a Dream" speech and the African American spiritual "We Shall Overcome." Whether she was relaxing, cooking, cleaning, or ironing clothes, tasks she did religiously, the album played that week over and over in our house.

Marita Golden, one of the city's most celebrated literary figures, remembers the assassination of Dr. King as "a declaration of war."[1] According to Golden, the response to the killing of Dr. King was "an angry cry along the streets, using bricks, bottles and torches for its song of sorrow."[2] Stokely Carmichael, of the Student Nonviolent Coordinating Committee (SNCC), was in the city on the night of King's murder. Carmichael, poet Gaston Neal, and others began going door-to-door at the shops in the U Street Corridor, telling shop owners to close their stores because of Dr. King's death.[3]

"If Kennedy had been killed, they'd have done it," Carmichael told the group. At around 9:25 p.m., the first store window on the 14th and U Street Corridor was broken. The riot was on. Gaston Neal, who had put together the New School of Afro-American Thought in 1966 in the heart of the neighborhood, recalls the building where he was living was also burned to the ground. Neal lived in a unit above a store in the U Street Corridor owned by a white shopkeeper. "Y'all burned me out," the poet Karl Carter recalls Neal saying.[4]

Two months later, in June 1968, Robert F. Kennedy, the likely Democratic Party nominee for president of the United States, was murdered in California. My father understood the moment. As Kennedy's funeral train arrived in Washington, DC, for him to lie in state in the US Capitol Rotunda, my father took my brothers and me down to the railroad tracks near our home with hundreds of other locals to pay tribute as Kennedy's train arrived in the city and passed by.

Rebuild

At the same time the city was recovering from the riots, the Drum and Spear Bookstore opened downtown in the city. It was an important event then and now historically.

"There was still tear gas in the air," said Judy Richardson, a member of the SNCC and a co-founder of the store. "You felt it in your nose." Drum and Spear Bookstore officially opens in Washington on June 1, 1968. It is immediately part of the city's cultural, political, and poetry scene.

"Black poetry was central to Drum and Spear," Judy Richardson said, "Gaston Neal, Charlie Cobb . . . Sonia Sanchez."[5] The store was a meeting place for black artists and activists determined to continue the movement against racism in America, according to Richardson. Judy Richardson described it as "expanding an awareness of ourselves and our ability to change the world."[6]

Tony Gittens, a former director of the DC Commission on the Arts and Humanities (DCCAH), was also a founding member, as was Charlie Cobb (Charles E. Cobb Jr.), poet and writer and member of SNCC. Gittens also recalls the store's link to Black poets in the city and notes the presence and work of Gaston Neal to make poetry a big deal at the store. According to newspaper sources, the address was riot central: 2701 14th Street NW, just blocks from where the city exploded only minutes after the post-King assassination melee began. It was—according to descriptions—a "burnt-out shop."[7] *The Washington Post* also referred to the popular cultural meeting ground as a "ghetto bookstore" that had reached out successfully to an "untapped literary mart."[8]

The presence of SNCC was no accident. SNCC had come to Washington, DC, to bring democratic change to the city. Gaston Neal, while not a SNCC member, was politically aligned with them. Neal's recently founded New School of Afro-American Thought was right on the same block as the store. Richardson said Neal's presence was simply part of what we did at Drum and Spear.

The store provided books one would not otherwise find in other stores, specifically books written by Black authors. Marita Golden called the store "an important cultural beacon during the '60s and '70s," and "crucial as a part of the Black arts and consciousness movement."[9] Golden grew up right in the neighborhood where the bookstore opened. Golden also wrote poetry back in 1968 as a student at American University.

Golden said Drum and Spear was "a panorama of genius and endurance"; its wide selection of Black and African books motivated her to write "bristling Black poetry that sizzled on the page."[10] Lurma Rackley, a journalist writing for *Evening Star*, called the Drum and Spear Bookstore a "laboratory of blackness," describing the store's walls as "decorated and covered in moving and colorful paintings by and about black people."[11]

Simba Sana, who would one day become part owner of a very successful Black-owned bookstore chain in the DC area called Karibu Books and who wrote his MA thesis at Howard University on the importance of Black bookstores, devoted commentary and research to Drum and Spear.[12] "The importance of African-centered bookstores, as warehouses of black literature, is directly linked to attacks on black culture by mainstream America," Sana wrote in the thesis. While Drum and Spear only lasted into the 1970s, it forever planted the notion that Black bookstores were wanted and needed in African American communities. They served as community spaces where Black people could "celebrate black culture."[13]

The bookstore was also noteworthy to J. Edgar Hoover's FBI. According to Joshua Clark Davis, "Drum and Spear Bookstore in Washington, DC, seems to have drawn more scrutiny from the Bureau's agents than any other black bookstore" in the country. The fact that it had been "established by veterans of the SNCC, didn't help matters, and the fact that the revolutionary Stokely Carmichael visited the store made it a target of Hoover's COINTELPRO."[14] In addition, plainclothes agents regularly visited the store, and "from 1968 until the store's closing in 1974, the Bureau compiled nearly 500 pages of investigative files on Drum and Spear."[15]

Jonetta Rose Barras, poet and journalist who would also eventually settle into cultural and political life in DC, calls the period after the assassination of Dr. King the "Black Liberation period."[16] The Black Arts Movement (BAM) was intensifying, and the African American poetry scene (not necessarily all the poets) took a distinct direction following the killing of Dr. King. The riots, white flight from Washington, DC, and other factors would lead to the city being officially called "Chocolate City." It was a title young locals such as me adopted proudly.

The political activity intensified in the city, and the cultural expression became sharper for African Americans in 1968 and onward. "Everybody is ready to riot here but the Black man who is supposed to start it," Gaston Neal told the *The Wall Street Journal* back then.[17]

Howard University students occupied the administration building and demanded change and the resignation of the president, James Nabrit, on March 19, 1968.[18] After several days, their demands were met except for the resignation of Nabrit. That fall, November 1968, the "Towards a Black University" conference was organized at the Drum and Spear Bookstore. Sterling Brown, Amiri Baraka, and Sonia Sanchez participated.[19]

The poetry inspired by the politics of the time and BAM kept coming. Gaston Neal continued to perform around the city. He benefited from his friendship with Baraka, Larry Neal, and A. B. Spellman. Between 1968 and 1969, Baraka, Neal (Larry), and Spellman produced a literary music journal called *The Cricket*.[20] While only four issues of *The Cricket* were published, the leading African American artistic intellectuals are in the pages of the journal. Neal appears in issue 2 of the journal with his poem "To Otis," an ode to the late soul singer Otis Redding, who died in a plane crash in December 1967.[21] Other notables included in the four *Cricket* issues are Larry Neal, who would live in DC for several years; Baraka, Stanley Crouch; Sun Ra; and A. B. Spellman. While Spellman did not live in DC until the late 1980s, his connections to Gaston Neal formed an important bond across the miles.

Spellman wrote the "Preface" for the reissue of the journals in 2021. The journal is more about African American music than poetry, but the poets are there writing as well standing tall. As Spellman writes of the journal's thrust: "The cultural nationalism broadcast from the pages of *The Cricket* was youthful, a proto-ideology akin to but younger than the Garveyite movement."[22] It was self-evident now that the younger population was firmly casting aside Dr. King's approach to political struggle.

The African American poets of the city were part of artistic momentum throughout the country in African American literary circles. Bernard W. Bell described the moment when "Afro American art, especially poetry," began to flourish in the mid- to late 1960s, "as the most phenomenal cultural development in the nation" at this time.[23] Bell directly linked the 1960s resurgence to the efforts of the earlier "Renaissance" (Harlem Renaissance) period pushed forth by Alain Locke and others. While the poets of the earlier Renaissance were concerned more with aesthetics and philosophy, the poets of the '60s were "political," according to Bell (quoting Robert Hayden). These Black poets, which included many poets in DC, sought to strip "away the sham of outmoded academic poetic conventions" and challenge "the primacy of Western values," in order "to liberate the minds and voices of many new black poets." [24] It was this kind of artistic thrust that would dominate African American poetry during this time.

The New Black Poetry (1971)

It is challenging to describe life in the city of Washington, DC, in the 1970s in the years after the killing of Dr. King and the riots. According to the official population statistics, the city was 71 percent African American in 1970.[25] I was born and raised into that moment, which has forever shaped how I view the world and the city. It was a moment of great pride, politics, and people for African Americans who lived there at the time. The city was the closest it would ever come to becoming an African city in America. It wasn't "African" as in African traditions, culturally and politically, but it was shaped politically and culturally by persons of African descent who understood the challenges ahead.

In 1975 the funk band Parliament released its album *Chocolate City*, officially giving the city its name and cultural and political history. DC poet Kenneth Carroll described the moment years later:

> When Parliament-Funkadelic founder George Clinton uttered, "What's hap'nin' CC?," on his 1975 album "Chocolate City," he might as well have said, "Watson, come here." Clinton's cool, didactic diatribe, buoyed by five minutes of chitlin-cleaning funk, became the allegory that linked black Washingtonians regardless of caste, class or politics. Even before Clinton put a beat to it, Chocolate City was a metaphorical utopia where black folks' majority status was translated into an assertion of self-consciousness, self-determination and self-confidence.[26]

To Carroll, one of the most important poets the city has ever produced, when Washington became " 'Chocolate City,' [it] was a cultural muscularity flexing itself in images like Gaston Neal and the New School of African American Thought hosting Sun Ra in the middle of 14th Street." But it was also African American theater giant Robert Hooks, Shirley Horn, Buck Hill, and Carter Jefferson with jazz, "Bill Harris on guitar at the Pigfoot," and "Butch Warren on bass anywhere." And, according to Carroll, do not forget go-go music creator, Chuck Brown; the soul crooner Billy Stewart; and Gil Scott-Heron.[27]

Stephen Henderson, a literary critic and professor teaching at Howard University, was one such person who embodied these ideas even though he was not from DC. Yet, his scholarship and work embodied the culture of "Chocolate City." Henderson was a literary critic and teacher, not a poet. He was a mentor to E. Ethelbert Miller and many other writers and artists. In 1971 he published one of the most influential African American literary anthologies ever, *Understanding the New Black Poetry*.[28]

Understanding the New Black Poetry is the kind of anthology that serves as a snapshot of Black poetry at the near end of the twentieth century. Henderson was able to do what few ever could do: give Black poetry in America its own language, life, and culture. By the time of *Understanding the New Black Poetry*, Henderson's reputation was rock solid. In 1969 the University of Wisconsin Press published *The Militant Black Writer in Africa and the United States*,[29] a book Henderson cowrote with Mercer Cook. It is a book of literary criticism that frames the "Black Revolution in terms of the Black writer" at that time. It was also, at the time, the definitive book of literary criticism on Black writing in the late 1960s. Henderson cowrote the book while teaching at Morehouse College in Atlanta.

In *Understanding the New Black Poetry*, Henderson continues this approach. In the anthology, there is also something for everyone. It has a well-crafted scholarly critique of Black poetry in history and in the present. It also places Black poetry in the middle of African and African American history and culture. Black poets stood on their own ground, with their own aesthetics that informed their lives and art. "Black poetry in the United States has been misunderstood, misinterpreted, and undervalued for various reasons—aesthetic, cultural, and political—especially by white critics," Henderson writes at the beginning of his text. This sentiment becomes the mission and passion of the book.

The book is subtitled "Black Speech and Black Music as Poetic References." Henderson splits his long introductory essay into sections titled "Theme," "Structure," and, most important, "Saturation." These three topics form the unique nature of Black poetry and, by default, Black art. As Henderson describes it, "saturation" is "the communication of Blackness in a given situation" and "a sense of fidelity to the observed . . . Black experience." This term, more than the other two, made Henderson's anthology important when it was published and still important today.

In a review of Henderson's book in the *Baltimore Afro-American*, Joseph H. Jenkins has high praise for what Henderson is trying to do in the book, even though he describes it as "an unusual anthology."[30] Jenkins also calls the book a "carefully documented position paper on the black aesthetic" and a book that tells the reader what "black poetry is." Hollie I. West reviewed the book for *The Washington Post.* She identified the inherent politics in the book and Henderson's ideas. Henderson makes clear that he is trying not just to document Black poetry as it is at the time but also to provide context and critical analysis.[31] Barry Beckham, a writer long based in the Washington, DC, area, reviewed the book for *The New York Times.* Beckham describes *Understanding the New Black Poetry* as "provocative" but in a "positive sense." Beckham writes that Henderson's long introductory essay should be "savored" and "utilized."[32]

Because Henderson includes much commentary and support for his thesis, it is almost forgotten that the book is an anthology. Most anthologies have a short introduction followed by pages and pages of poetry. Henderson gives the reader sixty-seven pages of commentary and seventy-two poets. Some Washington voices are included, as well as numerous other Black poets who are associated with the city's poetry scene in some capacity.

Sterling Brown, Owen Dodson, and Jean Toomer are published in *Understanding the New Black Poetry.* The Howard Poets are also here: Oswald Govan, Walter DeLegall, Percy Johnston, and Lance Jeffers. But two poets who would also make their mark in the city are also included. They are Larry Neal and Karl Carter.

Carter and Neal stand out because they are poets of BAM. They were born elsewhere (Carter in New Orleans, raised in Los Angeles, and Neal in New York) but would each live, work, and write in DC and become important contributors to the poetry scene. Carter was a law student at Howard University School of Law when Henderson published two of his poems—"Heroes" and "Roots"—the kind of poetry Henderson focused on in the book. Carter met Henderson and Sterling Brown and was part of the local DC poetry scene and studying law.

"Heroes" is a great poem because it is not preachy or didactic. It uses storytelling to lean into history:

> Places come back like shadow figures upon a darkened stage and bodies lie
> strewn there soaking the ground red with their blood. . .[33]

At Howard, Carter also met the literary critic Mercer Cook, the son of the famed local musician Will Marion Cook. By meeting Cook, Carter connected with León Damas, who was teaching at North Carolina Central University. Carter shared some of his work with Damas via Cook, and soon, *Présence Africaine,* the famed Francophone literary journal out of Paris made famous by George Padmore and others, published Carter.

In Carter's chance encounter with Damas in North Carolina and the poem "Markings: In Memory of Vashti Cook," Mercer Cook's wife remains a fresh memory for Carter:[34]

Markings
(In Memory of Mrs. Vashti Cook)
The day has become
a deflowered jungle
Burned crisp by napalmed years
of expectation
We have no monuments
The ashes mark the spots
where we buried
—ourselves—
Run through by gun wounds
of the day
Shot down when we carried
TV sets into the night
As the slow math of waiting
that quiet rheumatism
of thought
—Prevails—
While the whine of what was
my life has become
a scream.[35]
—*Karl Carter*

Larry Neal's (Neal is unrelated to Gaston Neal) time in Washington, DC, would happen later. While he always had a connection to the city through his friendship with other Black poets, Neal's unofficial arrival occurred in 1969, when *The Washington Post* published part of his Black Arts Movement manifesto. By this time, *Black Fire*, the anthology he edited with Amiri Baraka, had proven to be influential. BAM had also proven to be influential; also, the politics of the time demanded it. Neal said as much in his manifesto: "It is a profound ethical sense that makes the Black artist question a society in which art is one thing and the actions of men another. The Black Arts Movement believes that your ethics and aesthetics are one," Neal wrote in that manifesto. It is a universal statement from Neal.[36]

Larry Neal would eventually move to Washington in the 1970s, where he would write and work in the city. In 1974 Howard University Press published his collection of poems *Hoodoo Hollerin' Bebop Ghosts*. It was the first publication by the press. Neal described the book as his "personal statement," a collection of poems he wrote from 1964 to 1974.

Neal writes in the dust jacket introduction that his poems here are "polemic" and "poetic." The polemic for Neal is the influence of his father, whom he describes as a nationalist and a race man. The poetic is his mother, according to Neal. The poetry is full of Harlem, New York, the unofficial capital of Black America, and music. In a review of the book in 1976, Harry L. Jones praises what Neal tries to do in the book. He is especially impressed with his use of music and his ode to Harlem. "Neal treats Harlem with an affection that rivals Langston Hughes," Jones writes, "but Neal's city is closer to the Harlem of a young Malcolm X rather than Jesse B. Simple." Jones also points out that "music is everywhere" in the book. Coleman Hawkins and Bird (Charlie Parker) are just two legendary musicians Neal works into the verse, but Neal goes deeper, according to Jones. "Neal manages to evoke the lyrical life of an era when music was life, love and death . . . a time of Minton's and the beboppers—Bird, Prez and Mingus—who changed the whole course of jazz music."[37]

In 1976 Neal would become something arts related but altogether different—director of the DCCAH. Chocolate City was making a push to promote the arts and, in turn, to prioritize human ideals. It was, for a dedicated artist like Neal, a sacrifice. His poetry defined BAM in aesthetics—how could that work inside the government?

Gil Scott-Heron, the poet, singer-songwriter and self-proclaimed "bluesologist," also came to DC in the early 1970s. Scott-Heron was raised in Jackson, Tennessee, by his grandmother, but by the 1970s he was in Washington, aka "Chocolate City." Scott-Heron is considered by many to be one of the most important spoken word artists of the twentieth century. While he delivers his politically charged writings through songs, it is still poetry and it becomes a movement in and of itself.

The politics, the culture, and the majority Black population of the city all would appeal to Heron, who wrote poems and songs about social issues and who helped resurrect the spoken word (the oral tradition) in the 1970s. He also was yet another Black poet who came to live and work in the city, just like Dunbar, Hughes, and many others.

"Gil," as he will always be affectionately known, came to the city to teach at Federal City College (FCC) in 1972.[38] He had already created a big reputation for himself, creating musical commentary that defied definitions. One writer called it "revolutionary violence."[39] As proof of Scott-Heron's credibility as a musician and singer-songwriter, but mostly poet, when Howard University's Institute of the Arts and Humanities convened its 1972 tribute to Gwendolyn Brooks, Scott-Heron was part of the program along with poets Lucille Clifton, Mari Evans, Clay Goss, and Dudley Randall.[40]

At FCC, where the school was forging its own artistic traditions and history, the great Trinidadian intellectual, C. L. R. James was also teaching when Scott-Heron was in residence. This is the same university that Dolores Kendrick had attended and embraced fully, though it was known then as Miner Teachers College (known today as the University of the District of Columbia, UDC). The literary scholar Aldon Nielsen remembers taking Gil's writing class at FCC. Though Nielsen admits Gil was away a lot, he has come away from the experience with a positive view.[41] David Nicholson, another local Washington, DC, writer, took Gil's class. Nicholson, the former editor of *Washington Post Book World* and writer, remembers Scott-Heron being away a lot performing on the road.[42]

Scott-Heron's time in DC and his initial rise as an important musician and poet occurred at a time of white backlash in the country. The pursuit of basic civil rights by African Americans ran into the brick wall of neoliberal economics and "property rights for Whites."[43] This became the ideological thrust of his poetry and music. Scott-Heron is considered part of the "Black radical tradition," and his musical and literary offerings were seeking to challenge the frontal assault on the "welfare state" by conservatives and centrist Democrats.[44]

According to Jack Hamilton writing in the journal *Transition* the year of Scott-Heron's death, "Scott-Heron's voice" was "an instrument" and his writings (poetry, commentary, etc.) presented "a vision of America as nightmare."[45] But from the beginning it was always his goal to wake people up and get them to engage with the nightmare.[46]

Scott-Heron would record his album *Winter in America* in a studio just outside Washington, DC, in 1973 at D&B Studios in Silver Spring, Maryland, with his long-time collaborator, Brian Jackson. *Winter in America* is some of Scott-Heron's most impressive jazz spoken word music. Scott-Heron and Jackson would record two other albums in Silver Spring, Maryland, at D&B Studios.[47] Scott-Heron also notes that DC was fertile territory for inspiring songs including "The Bottle," inspired by a man he would observe at a liquor store behind his house just outside the city.[48]

Scott-Heron's recordings and performances would lay the foundation for hip-hop and rap music, which would take over pop culture beginning in 1979.[49] The poet Scott-Heron also inspired poets like Haki Madhubuti, the Last Poets of New York, and Kenneth Carroll of Washington, DC. They all trace their art back to Gil Scott-Heron's early work to a degree. And as it turns out, many African American poets took classes or taught at UDC over the years. David Nicholson, Dolores Kendrick, Jennifer Smith, Kenneth Carroll, and Marita Golden share that connection. Nicholson was part of *Slave Speaks*, an impressive poetry anthology published at the time. The group convened a reading for the publication of the anthology at Howard University in 1975.[50]

Post-Dream

The political activist–poet Gaston Neal returned to the city of Washington at this time of political struggle. For much of his life, Neal has been pushing ahead amid personal challenges. He is, nevertheless, now changed. His more radical, revolutionary approach to art and politics has been tempered in favor of service. And though Neal's appearance in the city in the early 1970s is described as a return, he is never fully gone.

On April 18, 1969, he presented his poetry at Eastern High School. The program, sponsored by American University's Organization of African and Afro-American Studies, was described as a tribute to the Black Arts.[51] Neal would also serve as a poet in residence at Eastern High School, an innovation today that seems normal but back then was quite radical.[52]

Upon his return to the city, Neal's biggest work was being appointed as a long-term consultant to the Corcoran Gallery of Art in 1971. As was noted at the time, "the shouting" of the Black Liberation movement was over; the focus thereafter was on "practical problems."[53] Neal's first effort at the Corcoran—a two-day program of concerts, photography, and posters from the grassroots organization Pride Inc—reflected his new approach.[54]

Pride Inc. was a powerful job-training organization operating in Washington, DC, during the 1960s and 1970s under the direction of Marion Barry, the most significant and influential politician in the city's history. Barry's work with Pride Inc. helped launch his political career and paved the way for the major political change in the city. Neal produced several other programs with the Corcoran Gallery of Art and remained committed to poetry representing the "context of the struggle of black people." Neal continued to work in this vein and repeated the Pride Inc. program in other locations in the city.[55]

Neal's energy and the program's content again reflected the city's emerging politics and culture. Washington, DC, had emerged as a "Black" city in the early 1970s, and everything about it began to reflect the long-sought African American goal of self-determination. Howard University also adopted a similar track of emphasis on Black culture and politics in its literary efforts. While Sterling Brown was in retirement mode as a professor, his influence remained on and off the campus in the city.

In addition, Gaston Neal was a magnet for connecting writers to poetry and the culture and pulse of the city's African American community. One of those writers was Ken Forde, who came to the United States in 1965, when his father left Trinidad for work. Forde's skill was pipefitting, then, but he had higher goals.

"Poetry is my life," Forde said. He still writes today, though he does few reading events. Forde met Gaston Neal at Martin Luther King (MLK) Jr. Library in 1973, when Sterling Brown was honored for his life's work. It began a lifelong connection and friendship that included the poet-lawyer Karl Carter. Other poets who formed the core of Forde's poetry world include Adesanya Alakoye and Ahmos Zu-Bolton, who also arrived in the city. Forde was especially busy in the city during the 1970s and early 1980s with various reading events.

Zu-Bolton's signature publication, the journal *Hoodoo*, would be in full bloom during this period, and Forde would anchor *Hoodoo* no. 7 with his poem "Man from Soweto" for Steve Biko. Biko, a South African Black liberation fighter, was killed in police custody in 1977. Forde's poem was described as "impassioned" in a review of the journal by James Borders published in the journal *Obsidian*.[56]

Ahmos Zu-Bolton would publish thirteen volumes of poetry chapbooks. Zu-Bolton's work is critical to the advancement of Black poetry in DC. Zu-Bolton described his "The Hoo-Doo Black Series" as a "thirteen-volume mini-anthology."[57] The first volume, *Tell Me How Willing Slaves Be*, by Adesanya Alakoye, set the tone from the beginning. In addition to Alakoye, other poets published by Zu-Bolton and connected to the city of Washington at that time were E. Ethelbert Miller, May Miller, and Joanne Jimason.[58]

Zu-Bolton, Forde, Carter, and many of the others again represent the magnetic legacy the city's African American cultural scene has maintained since the nineteenth century. It is that same draw that brought Dunbar, Langston Hughes, and many other poets and cultural workers to the city for short and long residencies.

Ever since the 1920s, the city's African American community "had a rich and diverse creative and expressive culture and social scene" that included "nightclubs and restaurants to social events."[59] Cultural and social gatherings of this nature were just one draw to the city for so many Black people, visitors as well, from all kinds of trades, professions, and disciplines throughout the twentieth century.

By the 1970s this energy became even more obvious, as the majority Black city had maintained that "race-specific cultural and social infrastructure." As the Black population in the city increased, the "number of social and cultural venues founded by and serving African Americans" increased as well.[60] It was something that had been nurtured both intentionally and simply by the passage of time and the movement of Black people as necessary.

10

A Community of Poets

At E. Ethelbert Miller's Ascension Poetry Reading #12 in October 1976, Miller began the program by stating that "Ascension follows Resurrection." Miller's artistic declaration was inspired by the late saxophone player John Coltrane. Miller was channeling 'Trane's 1966 *Ascension* album. That recording is one of 'Trane's later recordings that continues to influence poets and artists today. In his opening remarks, Miller added that "the purpose of the Ascension poetry series was to restore vitality and meaning to our lives."[1]

By October 1976, when that reading was convened at the Folger Shakespeare Library, Ethelbert Miller, poet, and director of the Afro American Resource Center at Howard University, was well on his way to establishing the most important regular poetry reading series in Washington, DC, at the time. According to *The Washington Post*, Miller presented two heavyweight African American poets to the DC audience that night. Jayne Cortez read followed by Ishmael Reed; they are two writers who are part of the American literary canon now and essential reading for anyone trying to understand African American poetry.

Yet, there was a lot more to it than just two Black poets reading at the Folger Shakespeare. It wasn't as if Black poets locally or nationally read regularly at the Folger Shakespeare. It was an institution in Washington but mostly for advancing the western European canon. The library's reading series began in 1970 and has featured African American poets now and then most of that time. However, back when the city was over 70 percent Black, and was known nationally as "Chocolate City," it was not a guarantee that Black poets found the Folger Shakespeare a wanting space. Miller's ability to navigate into such spaces is a credit to his ability to build relationships and alliances in a city with a complex and troubling racial history. Miller credits Leni Spencer, who was directing the Folger series at the time, for partnering with him on poetry events.

Miller was a busy artist when he started his Ascension Series (he was writing and publishing work and had the reading series). He was supporting and befriending other writers. He shared knowledge given to him by other writers and scholars. He also networked and slowly built a cache of great writers and artists whom he studied and made connections with closely even at a distance.

Dolores Kendrick would remark many years later that Ethelbert had the skills to network.[2] It all began in 1968, when Miller came to Washington, DC, from the Bronx, NY, to study at Howard University. In a 2020 essay, Miller described the city that he would become a part of and then help shape the literature of:

> I arrived in Washington, DC in September 1968 when I was 17 years old. I was coming from the South Bronx to attend Howard University, . . . I didn't know what to expect at Howard. Martin Luther King Jr. had been assassinated a few months before. Students at the university had organized a major protest, taking over the administration building and calling for the abolishment of mandatory ROTC and the creation of an African American Studies Department.[3]

The city was Miller's introduction to the South. His parents, he noted, were West Indian Americans, so there were new worlds to experience for Miller. Miller met the longtime Howard University professor Sterling Brown when he and Steve Jones recorded interviews with Brown at his home. By the time of the Ascension Series, Brown was in retirement mode. Miller describes "being around Brown" as "a celebration of Black History Month without a calendar."[4] It is also at this time that Miller met the literary critic Stephen Henderson at Howard University and was mentored by Henderson closely.

Miller and Stephen Henderson met in 1971. Miller, an Afro-American studies major, took classes from Henderson at Howard University and credits Henderson with changing his life. "Henderson's classroom," Miller wrote in 1997, "opened a new window from which I could view the beauty and richness of African American culture."[5] Henderson had great influence over Miller's literary career and the institutions he would forge. Miller became interested in poetry in his second year at Howard University, and that love has never waned judging by his production as a writer and editor of poetry books and anthologies nonstop since 1974. In 1974 he became director of the Afro American Resource Center at Howard and would serve in that post until 2015.

Miller also connected with poetry in the city and had been attending poetry events there back to 1968. In 1968 poets Ebon, Askia Muhammad Touré, and Carolyn Rogers read at All Souls Church in the city's Mount Pleasant neighborhood.[6] Miller would later read some of his own work at All Souls Church around the same time and would read at Dingane's Den in 1973 with Black Arts poets Lance Jeffers and Jayne Cortez. Dingane's Den was located at 2016 18th Street in Northwest DC. Charles and Lillian Green, jazz fans in the city, opened the venue in 1967.

Miller's work also began during his college years when he edited the Howard

University journal *Transition*, which continued for two issues.[7] *Transition* was a journal of necessity at the time (1974) and was, like the Ascension Reading Series, inspired by John Coltrane's album *Ascension*, according to Miller.[8] He also published poetry in Howard University's *The Hilltop Newspaper* in 1972,[9] just before his graduation from the college with a degree in Afro-American studies. Miller was part of the first class of graduates with that major, a direct result of the political occupation of the administration building in 1968 and political change in all of America. It was the launching of a career that "helped to shape" the Black poetry scene and the many poets who helped shape that scene.[10]

Miller was publishing his work not long afterward and then organized the first of 133 Ascension Poetry Reading Series events. It was the right time for African American poetry to stretch its wings in the city more, considering the instant politics at the time. Miller's Ascension Series would fill that need and the want.

In a July 27, 1975, *Washington Post* exposé called "Poetry in Washington," the writer Jack Foley pointed out the lack of one press in the area "devoted to black poets."[11] In a city that was over 70 percent African American, it again spoke to the city's Jim Crow racial history and who controlled the wealth, land, resources, and income flowing through the nation's capital. The DC Commission on the Arts and Humanities did award Ahmos Zu-Bolton, a Louisiana publisher and poet who came to the city, a grant for his BlackSouth Press at this time to publish an anthology (it would be called *Synergy*), but that was it.

As with any city, Washington, DC, possessed many positives for African Americans but also high negatives. The city was in America and America's racial caste system, which touched all aspects of life in the country. If enough opportunities did not present themselves to the Black poets of the city, they had to create their own. Dunbar's experience in his short time in the city was not isolated from this experience either, despite his fame as a poet.

Dunbar worked at the Library of Congress, but there was nothing special about the post he received before he took ill and left the job. In addition, the notable poets who followed Dunbar's example into a life of letters and who were able to give Black poetry in Washington some acclaim, such as May Miller, Georgia Douglas Johnson, William Waring Cuney, and Sterling A. Brown, likewise had to navigate the same racial caste system despite their education and connections.

That system consisted of congressional control over the city historically, redlining and housing discrimination since the 1930s, and neighborhood demolitions in the 1940s and 1950s, followed by "white flight" in the 1960s and 1970s.[12] These public policy decisions by the federal government forever fixed inequality into the city's fabric, and that inequality would extend into opportunity in the arts. The Black poets and activists had to look within and also within the institutions where they were employed in order to forge a poetry community with strength and resolve. Howard University was one such institution where African Americans were able to make use of the resources and their talents.

The Institute for the Arts and Humanities

Dr. Andrew Billingsley, the longtime sociology professor at Howard University, is, according to Miller, responsible for the idea for creation of the Institute for the Arts and Humanities (IAH).[13] Stephen Henderson also played a key role in its advancement, as did Miller and Ahmos Zu-Bolton. Henderson was the founding director of the institute and served in that position for twelve years. Professor Jeanne-Marie Miller, of the Howard University English Department, would act as assistant director. Miller and Ahmos Zu-Bolton would both work at IAH. Miller would serve as a junior research associate, and Sterling Brown was senior advisor to the institute.

Billingsley hired the novelist John Oliver Killens and the Black Arts poet Haki R. Madhubuti to run writers workshops for writers. Madhubuti commuted from Chicago three days a week to teach his classes and was able to impact the poetry scene in Washington, DC, some while he was there. Eventually Black women in the Killens's workshop broke off and formed another workshop called the Free DC Workshop. A. B. Spellman, the poet and jazz studies expert, facilitated that workshop.

Madhubuti, of his time at Howard, described Stephen Henderson as "professional, collegial" and "extended family like."[14] Henderson encouraged Madhubuti to reach beyond the normal boundaries of teaching at a university, and he did so with great joy and energy. He gave poetry readings in Washington and worked with young artists in the city to produce art through a course he created called Toward a New Consciousness. Madhubuti and many of the artists collaborated to produce an album of jazz and spoken word called *Rise, Vision, Comin'* (1973). The group was called the African Liberation Arts Ensemble.[15] To this day, the recordings are tight expressions of poetry and music, making a statement of Black liberation. Reed Tuckson, who is now Dr. Reed Tuckson, the former director of public health for the city of Washington, DC, played drums on the recording. The late and great trumpet player Wallace Roney is part of the recording. Roney was fifteen at the time and attending Duke Ellington School of the Arts. Clarence Seay, another native of DC and graduate of Duke Ellington School of the Arts, played bass.[16] A second album, *Medasi*, would be recorded in 1976.

IAH launched with a flurry of programs in 1973, the first two devoted to two of America's more important poets: Amiri Baraka and Gwendolyn Brooks. The program was held over six days at Howard University, and Henderson was able to lure many of the top African American poets in the United States to the event. Dudley Randall, Haki R. Madhubuti, Clay Goss, Lucille Clifton, Gil Scott-Heron, and Mari Evans all participated. Other participating poets included E. Ethelbert Miller, Lance Jeffers, Johari Amini, and Jayne Cortez. John Oliver Killens, who was teaching at Howard University at the time, participated, as did the legendary cultural critic Addison Gayle.[17]

In the spring of 1974, IAH sponsored an Ascension Poetry Reading. The reading, held at Howard University, featured writers JoAnne Mary McKnight, Clay Goss, Debbie Wood, Amma Khalil, Gwen Holland, Arnell Hammond, Stephanie Stokes, Damani Yero, Corrie Haines, Adesanya Alakoye, and Nehemiah Dixon. Of the writers, Alakoye and Goss were most known by the Black literary community of the city.[18]

Miller's Ascension Series emerged just after the IAH was established. Dr. Billingsley, another big shaper of the institute, always wanted the institute to have a community component, according to Miller. The first reading was held on the campus of Howard University. Future readings would be held at libraries, performance spaces, and museums in the city. The series is a testament to the importance of relationships, cultural, political, or social. Ahmos Zu-Bolton brought a fresh vision to the series as well as working with Miller. Miller describes his relationship with Bolton as "like Marx and Engels" in those days.[19]

"I was fortunate to be around Ahmos Zu Bolton," Miller writes in his 2000 memoir, *Fathering Words: The Making of an African American Writer.*[20] Miller credits Zu-Bolton with connecting him with many writers from a variety of backgrounds. This included May Miller, who was one of DC's most well-known poets by the 1970s. Zu-Bolton, when he came to Washington, DC, was already publishing his journal *Hoodoo. Hoodoo,* a publication of Zu-Bolton's Energy South Press, published the leading African American poets and critics of the day. Writers like Adesanya Alakoye, Pinkie Gordon Lane, Jerry Ward, Dudley Randall, Alice Walker, Ishmael Reed, Alvin Aubert, Audre Lorde, Michael Harper, May Miller, and Lorenzo Thomas. Zu-Bolton, along with Ethelbert Miller, published *Hoodoo* regularly and published the grant-funded anthology *Synergy*, "a collection of 40 poets living and writing in the Washington, DC area." Ethelbert Miller edited the anthology. *Synergy* was more proof of the rich and very busy African American poets and poetry scene in the city.[21]

Eugene Redmond—poet, literary scholar, and archivist from East St. Louis, Illinois—referred to *Synergy* as a "monster" in a letter to Miller. "You and Ahmos have so much energy in addition to being two of the baddest and most beautiful brothers I have had the pleasure to meet," he added.[22] Bolton had started the work he was doing in DeRidder, Louisiana. Bolton also established what he deemed an "UpSouth" office for his operations in DC. Miller was also involved as an associate editor of the press.

The Ascension Series took off like a jet and quickly became very popular into the 1980s. Miller was doing work with Henderson and still directing the Afro American Resource Center on Howard's campus. When IAH convened an African Liberation Day conference in 1974, Miller and Harold Burke videotaped the entire conference.[23]

Miller and Bolton also fought hard to make sure the IAH programs had a wide swath of African American writers, poets, and intellectuals. This is why, according to Miller, Ishmael Reed, Ntozake Shange, and Barbara Smith, the latter a socialist, feminist, and lesbian critic, were included on programs. Miller's Ascension #3, held on the campus of Howard University, was "The Black Women Poets,"[24] featuring Viki Andrews, Aisha, Gwen Holland, Janet Gaillard, Donna Mungen, and the Baltimore-based poet Lucille Clifton, as special guest.

While it might seem like not a big deal to do a poetry reading with all Black women poets, this is the kind of thing the series would try to do: break new ground by providing a safe creative space for artists usually marginalized in the artistic circles dominated by men. Black women in the 1970s were marginalized as human beings, citizens, and artists. The fact that the third reading in the Ascension Series featured an all-Black women lineup sent a message.

Miller did something similar not long after with Ascension #8 (September 4, 1975). Entitled "Songs from our Sisters," it also featured all women poets: Ambrosia Shepherd, Afi-Kai Nache, Sharon Douglas, June Donaldson, Edelin C. Fields, Karen Morgan, Debbie Wood, Brenda Williams, Dahomey, Shirley King, Hazel Robinson, Joanne Jimason, and Zeharaa'a al Mahdi.[25] Ascension #12 featured Ishmael Reed on November 25, 1975. Miller provided a glorious introduction of Reed, something that became one of his trademarks over the years—celebrating the writer: "Since its beginning in 1974, nearly one hundred poets have read on Ascension programs. Some programs have featured 7 or 8 poets, one featured as many as 16. Tonight is the first time we will feature just one," Miller wrote in his introduction.[26]

Reed was well deserving. Introducing Reed as a poet, essayist, novelist, and publisher, Miller told the audience to "let Ishmael Reed put a spell on you" as he brought him up to read. Miller also had Reed read at Ascension #19 the same year. By early 1980 the series had already presented forty-nine readings. The forty-ninth reading featured Calvin Forbes and Gloria Hull (now Akasha Gloria Hull).[27] Forbes was an outstanding poet but despite widespread fame still put time and energy into local community, as a few years later he would be one of the first poets I met when I joined the African American Writers Guild in Washington, DC.

As early as the late 1970s, Miller had an institutional structure as well. Miller was "director" of the Ascension Series. Jonetta Rose Barras, a poet and journalist, was "assistant director." The board of the Ascension Series consisted of the poet and poetry archivist Grace Cavalieri; Howard University professor Stephen Henderson; Alan Austin, a poet and creator of the Black Box Poetry series; Thulani Nkabinde (Davis), a poet and soon multifaceted writer; Octave Stevenson, the public programs director at the city's MLK Jr. Library; and the poet and folklorist Ahmos Zu-Bolton. The fact that the Ascension Series had such an impressive array of individuals on its board is a testament to its serious work. Davis, for example, was featured in Ascension #44. Davis taught high school at Sidwell Friends when she was living in DC. As evidence of Davis's impact in the city, Miller introduced her in a celebratory fashion when Davis read in the series. "Tonight's program is special—because our poet tonight is special. Thulani Davis has meant a lot to Washington. She has been an inspiration to many writers in the city. We quote her poems in telephone conversations. We pack her book when making long trips. We love this woman. . . . We love her wisdom."[28] The reading was held at the Washington Women's Art Center on June 2, 1979. Miller also featured Davis for Ascension #60, the seventh anniversary of the reading series in April 1981.

At the end of the 1970s, it seemed no surprise that the city proclaimed September 28, 1979, E. Ethelbert Miller Day with a full proclamation. The city with a mayor

(Marion Barry) who supported the arts openly had recognized a Black poet. But accolades of this type did not cause Miller to become complacent.

In 1980, when the legendary "Negritude" poet Léopold Senghor was brought to the city and celebrated by Mayor Marion Barry, Miller was part of the celebration along with poets Sterling Brown, May Miller, Ken Forde, Jonetta Barras, Connie Carter, and others.[29] A poetry reading including the above poets was held at the Corcoran Museum in downtown Washington to pay homage to Senghor and his official state visit to the capital city.

In January 1981 Miller appeared on the radio with the poet Grace Cavalieri, the creator of *The Poet and the Poem* radio program.[30] Grace Cavalieri and her program were vital to documenting the history of poetry in the city in general. On January 27, 1982, Miller was a featured poet along with poet/writer Ken Forde at a literary event at the Kennedy Center. The event showcased Caribbean and Caribbean American poets.

Miller also read at the ten-year celebration for the poetry project known as Black Box. The Black Box poetry project was founded in 1972 by ten writers who began recording poets on cassettes. It has been described as an audio literary magazine. The tenth anniversary celebration featured Miller and other local poets—Myra Sklarew, Joanne Jamison, Connie Carter, and Roberto Vargas.[31]

The Ascension Series also kept doing events and offering space to young poets and established voices. In April 1980, Miller brought fifty poets to the Washington Project for the Arts (WPA) for a marathon reading.[32] It was a downpour of poetry in the city to try to force it to pay attention to literature. Ascension #67 took place on November 8, 1982, and featured Alexis DeVeaux and Greg Tate. The reading, held at the Folger Shakespeare for its own reading series, again spoke to the strength of the series.

Tate is especially of note for local African American poets. Though he left the city shortly after his formative years for New York and *The Village Voice*, and the life of one of America's top cultural critics, he was always part of the city. His mother, Florence Tate, a political activist and cultural presence in the city, was also very well known in the nation's capital, as was Tate's younger brother, Brian Tate, a musician. Brian Tate, like his brother Greg, was ambitious. He was a performance poet and formed The Umbra Group in 1983, which sought to combine music, poetry, and artistic expression into one cohesive force. The sole purpose of the group was to be supportive of creative artists.[33]

In March 1987 the Ascension Series devoted an entire week to workshops and readings at Howard University. Darrell Stover, Reuben Jackson, Sharon Bell Mathis, Jonetta Barras, and David Nicholson are some of the African American writers featured during Writers Week at Howard University.[34] By this point, Miller had organized eighty-seven Ascension Readings in just thirteen years.

After those brisk and busy thirteen years, *The Washington Post* published a full feature on Miller's work promoting poets. Elizabeth Kastor described Miller in the feature as "an encyclopedia of idiosyncrasies" and someone who seems to "know everyone."[35] She also wrote about Miller's ability to accomplish things using more subtle approaches. The late Peggy Cooper Cafritz, the founder of Duke Ellington School of the Arts, said that Miller could cross "academic, racial and social lines" and "bring people together."[36]

Michelle, Essex, Wayson . . .

Michelle Parkerson arrived back in DC from college in Philadelphia at this time. Parkerson, born and raised in Washington's Anacostia neighborhood located east of the river, would immediately fall into the local arts scene, including the poetry scene. Parkerson grew up in the Parklands section of Southeast Washington, DC. She attended Anacostia High School and, as a teen, grew up in a proud African American neighborhood in a home full of Black art and culture. Her father was into jazz, and her mother was into Black literature. Both would become influences on Parkerson. Parkerson was also interested in theater early on. In 1971 she appeared in a production of the Back Alley Theater's Political Workshop called *Black Pepper*.[37] The show, a series of improvisational pieces, was presented in August. "I was always a reader," Parkerson recalls. "My mother . . . moved me to read Black writing and poems and all of that . . . she was particularly interested in me reading Black women."[38]

At the time, Parkerson describes the city as "so Black . . . so cultural."[39] Parkerson fell in love with theater as a teenager, and that's when she wrote her first poems. Her career in mastering multiple artistic disciplines was launched. She also was part of the artistic scene in Philadelphia because of her college career at Temple University studying film.

It was 1974, and Black culture in America was at its apex. Parkerson describes what she was immersed in in her hometown as "cultural fermenting" and "incubating." Eventually, Parkerson heard of the writing workshop John Oliver Killens had convened at Howard University at the behest of Stephen Henderson and signed up for it.[40]

It was not long before Parkerson met Ethelbert Miller and began attending his Ascension Series Poetry Readings. She also met Essex Hemphill, an African American gay male poet who would pull Parkerson deeper into the city's artistic circles. Parkerson and Hemphill met at Ascension Reading #9, according to Miller.[41] Parkerson and Hemphill did not waste much time getting started. Both were African American gay artists, the same combination that fed James Baldwin's fiery writings. Parkerson credits Hemphill with setting her on course. "Our sexuality is as important as our cultural identity, so . . . we have to call ourselves gay before they try to slander us," Parkerson said of Hemphill's words to her.[42]

Essex Hemphill was born in Chicago in 1957. He grew up in Washington and attended Frank Ballou Senior High School in the southeast part of the city. Hemphill did attend college at the University of Maryland, but his life was poetry and art. It did not take him long to make his mark. By 1976 he had recorded an audiobook of his poetry while a student at Maryland. Hemphill's readings at the University of Maryland are the stuff of legend today among many poets.

By 1976 he was way ahead of the curve as far as poetic development and aspirations. *Obsidian II,* one of the leading African American literary journals at the time, published several of his poems in its winter 1977 issue.[43] In May 1979 Hemphill was published by one of the leading academic African American– and African-centered journals, *Callaloo.*[44] Hemphill's work was consistently published in many of the leading African American literary journals, and he kept up a healthy schedule of readings.

Hemphill's courage and Parkerson's willingness to also be forward in her expression as an artist are historically important. They brought high energy to a scene that was already full of energy. And Hemphill launched a movement. Most of the gay African American poets of the city's past were not so bold. Parkerson and Hemphill also were multifaceted. Hemphill wrote, performed, and organized; Parkerson did all of that but was also a trained filmmaker who would eventually use film to take poetry and storytelling to new heights in America. Both were busy in the 1970s and into the early 1980s with their art.

The Washington Project for the Arts organized many poetry events during the late 1970s, as did Ethelbert Miller's Ascension Series. WPA, as it is affectionately known, was founded by the late Alice Denney, the longtime arts administrator and arts curator in the city.

Hemphill was featured in the Ascension Series on December 22, 1979, with four other writers: Jocelyn Johnson, Larry O. Frances, Claudia Gibson, and Tracy Conley.[45] His volume of readings remained quite strong in the '70s and into the '80s, when he not only nurtured a local reputation but a growing national reputation.

In October 1978 Parkerson read at the Washington Women's Art Center, another organization and venue that began to offer space for poetry in the city. Barbara Berman was a key figure in establishing a partnership facilitating African American poets and artists' finding another venue where they could perform.

In April 1978 Parkerson also read at DC Creative Space, one of the city's more beloved arts venues at this time.[46] Popularly known as "DC Space," Parkerson read there with the poet and writer Thulani Davis. Thulani Davis was yet another significant writer to come to the city for a spell only to leave and achieve greater heights elsewhere.

The DC Space arts venue hosted many poetry events featuring a new generation of writers and performers like Hemphill, Parkerson, and Davis. It was a favored place for jazz, punk, rock and roll, spoken word, theater, poetry, or a combination of these art forms. Free jazz saxophonist Anthony Braxton played there in 1978. He was the kind of act that could draw enthusiastic crowds to the club. The Ascension Poetry Series held readings there, including an event that lasted all night into the next day. Sun Ra, the jazz legend, called it "the place." I never read at "the place," but I did catch Amiri Baraka there before the venue closed, performing with the bebop drummer Sunny Murray. It represented a particular artistic movement in the city that also included ambitious activity by Black poets who would read just about anywhere that offered a microphone and listeners.

On March 7, 1983, Parkerson and Hemphill presented one of their important performances together at the Washington Project for the Arts. The performance, *Murder on Glass*, encompassed the kind of art Parkerson and Hemphill would pursue together and with others in the city where their impact had only just begun.

Hemphill also collaborated regularly with Wayson Jones, a formidable artist in his own right. Jones graduated from the University of Maryland in 1980. By the mid-1980s he was performing in the area at various places including DC Space and the ENIKAlley Coffeehouse. His gigs with Hemphill grew in stature as the local poetry scene intensified. In March 1986 Jones and Hemphill performed a jazz and poetry set at the University of Maryland's Nyumburu Cultural Center.[47] Otis Williams, a blues poet who had attended nearby Morgan State University in Baltimore, was director of the center and had energized cultural life for Black students there. In April 1986 Hemphill and Jones performed in a series called "Four Evenings of Music, Poetry, and Disruption" at DC Space. Jones played various instruments and provided vocals and sound; Hemphill read his work.[48]

Jones also performed with Hemphill the night of the famous Mayor's Arts Awards controversy in DC. The event was held September 28, 1987, and Hemphill and Jones read a poem called "Family Jewels" about a Black man unable to hail a taxi in the city. They were asked by a member of the arts commission not to read the poem because it contained the word "corruption," according to news accounts. While Mayor Marion Barry's administration had trouble with corruption during his time in office, the request seemed odd, and it was then. Hemphill and Jones, true artists, did not waver. "Family Jewels" was read as is with the word "corruption." Hemphill was asked to censor it right after it was read, and the show continued.[49]

Jones and Hemphill were called "explosive artists" right after the incident; it only increased their reputations as dedicated to the art they were creating. Parkerson, Jones, and Hemphill were able to tour to other cities because of their brash but honest spoken word performance art.[50] An indication of their growing popularity and the audience they had created was the release of the film *Looking for Langston* in 1989.

The film, a creation of Isaac Julien, was highly controversial when released because the Langston Hughes's estate disapproved and made sure Hughes's work did not appear in the film. The film explores Black sexuality and Hughes's sexuality, even though at the time Hughes's sexuality was unclear (and remains so). Parkerson, Jones, and Hemphill performed at the release for the film in December 1989. Jones and Hemphill are part of the film itself.[51]

Poets Across Town (1976–1977)

In the '70s in the city, as the Ascension Series was getting started, African American poets were able to get published outside of their traditional circles and outlets in a few places. It was again alliances that helped this to happen. Two anthologies are noteworthy: The first was published in 1977 and is called *City Celebration 1976: Poetry*

Anthology.[52] The anthology was put together to commemorate the nation's bicentennial. It is mostly the work of Octave Stevenson, editor, Language and Literature Division, of the DC Public Library system (along with Peter H. Share—DC officer of Heritage Programs, for the bicentennial).

Stevenson played an important role in poetry in the city through his partnership with Ethelbert Miller and the Ascension Poetry Series. He provided space for poetry events and exposure. Stevenson also ran a reading series called Poets in Person through the library to some great success. Stevenson worked not only with the Ascension Reading Series but also with Jonetta Barras-Abney (Jonetta Barras), who directed the Institute for the Preservation of African American Writing, to present the Poets in Person series at the library. Karl Carter, Jonetta Barras, Garth Tate (Tate would make a big impact in the city in the 1980s), Njeri Nuru, and many others would read in the Poets in Person series.

Stevenson's anthology, *City Celebration 1976* is full of many of Washington, DC's more celebrated non-Black poets from the twentieth century: Ed Cox, Grace Cavalieri, Roland Flint, Ann Darr, Linda Pastan, Rod Jellema, and Karren L. Alenier. Stevenson also includes several Black poets from the Washington, DC, area in the anthology. Just as with J. C. Byars in 1928 in the anthology *Black and White*, the inclusion of the Black poets is significant enough to seem intentional. Sterling Brown, May Miller, Ethelbert Miller, and Ahmos Zu-Bolton II are included but also Dolores Kendrick, who was just getting started at the time. Karl Carter, who emerged during the Black Arts period with a distinctive voice and command of language, has a poem in the publication, as do Jonetta Barras, Ambrosia Shepherd, and Essex Hemphill. Two years later, in 1979, Stevenson would produce another anthology that sought to have reach and depth of voices. Stevenson's second anthology in three years is called *The Poet Upstairs*.[53]

The range of poets in *The Poet Upstairs* is expansive. The poets in the *City Celebration* anthology are all here, but Stevenson adds more. There are 111 poets with verse published in *The Poet Upstairs*. The poet Ken Forde is included in the anthology, as is Joanne Jimason. Both Forde and Jimason would read in Ethelbert Miller's Ascension Series and were very active on the DC poetry scene during this hot time. A review of *The Poet Upstairs* also captures the flavor of the city's literary scene.[54]

F. C. Rosenberger, who edited an anthology called *Washington and the Poet*, describes *The Poet Upstairs* as a "big, generous, inclusive collection." Rosenberger notes that the city has an active poetry scene but, really, "several communities of poets—and several hermits—with many public readings and small press publications." Rosenberger's description of the city is at least partly correct. There are poetry events and venues seemingly everywhere. Some of it is because it is the nation's capital, and some of it is the determination of the poets and those who support poetry.[55]

As an example, in the 1970s numerous Black poets were occasionally invited to the city to read poetry at well-funded institutionally based venues. Sam Allen read at the Library of Congress (November 1972) and the Textile Museum (September 1973), and Michael S. Harper was featured at the Folger Shakespeare Library Poetry Series

(May 1973).[56] However, these were rare occurrences and noteworthy because by the 1970s, the city was over 70 percent African American. Nevertheless, very few Black poets locally or nationally graced the more monied arts venues in the city.

Another publication that emerged at this time that proved to be quite important is Richard Peabody's *Gargoyle Magazine*. It began publishing in 1976, and unlike Stevenson's two efforts, *Gargoyle* was a continuing publication. *Gargoyle* also had as its overall mission to publish writers who were not getting published.

In Washington, the city that lacked independent presses for Black writers, a segregated city where the art was also segregated in resources and location much too often, *Gargoyle* would become a steady source of validation for African American writers. At the beginning, there were Peabody, Russell Cox, and Paul Pasquarella all as editors, but Peabody has been the editor all alone for most of the publication's long life. Peabody was a local and graduated from American University. His love of writing and books is intense and measured. He met Ethelbert Miller early on and published him, Essex Hemphill, and many others. Miller, in fact, is one of the first writers to submit to Peabody's *Gargoyle* when he sent Peabody poems in 1976.[57]

In publishing all sorts of writers in *Gargoyle*, he knew what he was looking for, whether poetry, fiction, or nonfiction. Many African American writers were published by *Gargoyle*.[58] Peabody also produced multiple versions of *Gargoyle* in cassette form, giving Black poets and other poets another forum to present their work.[59] While *Gargoyle* went on hiatus in the 1990s, it returned in 1997 and has continued to publish ever since.

Nethula

Officially called the *Nethula Journal of Contemporary Art and Literature, Nethula* was an Essex Hemphill project along with Kathy Elaine Anderson, another local African American poet. While Hemphill and those in his immediate circle were publishing poetry in many well-respected journals, Hemphill, Anderson, and others were establishing *Nethula*.

By 1977 the journal was established and planned, and work was solicited for publication. Kathy Elaine Anderson was editor, Hemphill its publisher. Many other writers and artists contributed to the rise of *Nethula*. Elbert Robeson, Ahmos Zu-Bolton, Jonetta Barras-Abney, Herman Piper, Arnette Holloway, and Sterling A. Brown all had some involvement with *Nethula* in the early years.[60] *Nethula* was finally incorporated in January 1982, but it had put out issues by then.

"Nethula was born out of the realization that the outlets that exist for Black writers are small in number," Hemphill writes in the first issue.[61] This is consistent with the city's arts scene. While Black poetry enjoyed a hot period in the early 1960s to the mid-1970s, it slowed down some in the 1980s. *Nethula* was born of that moment. In the first issue, local poets, Ken Forde, Gail Melinda Shaw, and Patrice Wilson have work presented. The first issue was celebrated with a reception at the Savile Bookstore in the Georgetown neighborhood of the city. Approximately "150 local literary connoisseurs" attended the event. Ken Forde, Michael Blum, and Patrice Wilson read. Essex Hemphill's vision of a literary journal serving African American and other Third World writers was launched.[62]

Alvin Aubert, Yusef Komunyakaa, Mwatabu Okantah, and Kathy Anderson also have work included in the first issue. Other writers *Nethula* published during its time include Langston Hughes, Connie Carter, Michelle Parkerson, and Carol Olivia Herron. Joanne Jimason and Eloise Greenfield, the children's book writer, worked for the journal, as did the soon-to-be legendary *Village Voice* critic Greg Tate. Tate reviewed books.

Nethula held readings to promote the journals. Ethelbert Miller read on the *Nethula* reading series in 1980 with Rosemary Mealy. Others who read on the *Nethula* Poetry series were Michael Weaver, Patrice Wilson, Alexis DeVeaux, Gloria Naylor, Michelle Parkerson, Theresa Ford, Kongnyuy Jumbam, and Carol Olivia Herron.

Hemphill sought resources and allies all over the city to advance the publication. *Nethula* applied for grants and solicited subscriptions and donations. Hemphill even wrote the city's public school offices seeking to use abandoned school buildings for public programs.[63] While Hemphill's role diminished in 1983, the journal continued publishing until 1985.

Jonetta Barras

It was also during this period that Jonetta Barras (she went by the name Jonetta Rose Barras-Abney at the time) appeared on the DC poetry scene. Barras, originally from New Orleans, came to the city of Washington from San Francisco. She became a poet in high school and is still a poet, even though she is much more known as a journalist in DC. Her literary path is unique but like that of other poets who came to the city.

"I came to DC from San Francisco to work as a community organizer for the Movement for Economic Justice (MEJ), an organization begun by George Wiley who also founded the National Welfare Rights Organization," Barras wrote of her journey to the DC poetry scene.[64] Barras continued to work for MEJ even while pregnant but also continued to chase poetry. Barras eventually met Ethelbert Miller and participated in one of his readings at Mr. Henry's, a popular restaurant/jazz club. She kept doing readings after that at just about any and every venue in town. She attended the John Killens writing workshop on the campus of Howard University and broke off to join another workshop—the Free DC: The Writing Workshop. The Free DC Workshop was started by poet and visual artist Sheila Crider and produced the anthology *Free DC (The Writers Workshop)*.[65]

The anthology included visual art by Mark Montgomery and writings from Barras (as Jonetta Rose Barras-Abney), Crider, Greg S. Tate, Kwame (Samuel L. Johnson III), Gladys Lee, Calvin Reid, RSED (R. Susan E. Dorsey), Askia Muhammed, Mark Montgomery, and Sandra Turner Bond. A. B. Spellman, the facilitator of the workshop, said that the workshop began when he was approached by Crider to critique her writings. Crider then brought the other writers into the fold, and the workshop began at Louise and Vernard Gray's Miya Gallery in Washington, DC, at 1120 Seventh Street NW. The workshop eventually moved to Howard University. Spellman described the poets as "well hatched" when he became involved, writers who produced "lines that jump off the page."

In 1976 Jonetta Barras became part of an organization in the city known as The Black Literary Artists of the Creative Kingdom. The group organized a reading in November 1976 at the Miya Gallery in downtown DC.[66] During the late 1970s and 1980s, Barras participated in many readings in the city. Barras read at MLK Jr. Library in May 1979,[67] and in June 1979 her organization, the Institute for the Preservation of African American Writing, presented poets Greg Tate and Michelle Parkerson in a performance called "Live in Poem."[68] Barras in addition began to collaborate and work with Ethelbert Miller to present readings while also presenting her own readings. She was fully immersed in the city's poetry scene, and, most important, she helped the scene evolve by promoting poets. Barras published consistently in leading African American journals including *Obsidian II* and *The Black Scholar*. Barras has fond memories of the time and the people she met. "I think all poets are important," she says. She names many important poets who stretch across the decades and who have made a difference: Ahmos Zu-Bolton. Ethelbert Miller. Kenneth Carroll, May Miller, Dolores Kendrick. Sterling Brown.

She describes her experience as a poet in Washington during the days of "Chocolate City" as special. Judging by her impressive list of poetry credits, you would have to conclude Barras was energized. Barras is published in many of the local anthologies highlighting DC poets such as Stevenson's *The Poet Upstairs* and Kim Roberts's *Full Moon on K Street* (Plan B Press, 2010). Yet she has also achieved national recognition in Ahmos Zu-Bolton's journal, *Hoodoo*. "It was magical," she said of those days; "maybe it still is. . . . DC has one of the richest literary histories and scenes in the country."[69]

11

The Professor and the Poetry

On November 21, 1976, Sterling A. Brown, the poet and public scholar, was honored with a tribute program by his city. It would be the first of many tributes in his post-teaching life.[1] The poetry consultant to the Library of Congress at the time (1976–78), the Detroit poet Robert Hayden, appeared and introduced Brown to an audience that included scholars, poets, actors, and others. Hayden served as honorary chairman for the Sterling A. Brown tribute. Walter E. Washington, mayor of the city, sent written remarks. Larry Neal, the poet and one of Brown's mentees, read the remarks. May Miller, the poet and playwright, was there representing herself and came to praise her lifelong friend. León Damas, a Howard professor, saluted Brown for influencing the "Negritude" poets who found Brown's work comforting.

Alan Lomax, the celebrated ethnologist, spoke, as did W. Montague Cobb, of the NAACP. DC poet A. B. Spellman read poetry, and Ossie Davis and Ruby Dee appeared for the program to hail Black America's cultural voice. Visionary blues singer Big Chief Ellis performed, and William Raspberry, the *Washington Post* opinion writer, was present. Few people could have drawn a cross section of the Black world from all over, from all walks of life and professional backgrounds. Brown, emotional but happy, obliged the audience with a reading of his more famous works "Strong Men," "Old Lem," and "Ma Rainey."

Then, on May 1, 1979, Mayor Marion Barry declared Sterling A. Brown Day in the city. Barry, a champion of the arts in the city, would make sure Brown got his due. Brown was his familiar charismatic self. *The Washington Post* devoted a column to Brown on its commentary page. "He is the last in the line of great writers who came to prominence during the Harlem Renaissance," the *Post* wrote at the time. "Mr. Brown has always seen literature as a popular art—not a puzzle," the commentary added. "His poems are stories, work songs, and the blues—simple but rich and various depictions of Black American life."[2] "I know Barry . . . I knew him when he was a militant when the police were arresting him every day," Brown told the attendees.[3]

Over 300 people turned out for the Brown's fete, including standout African American poets like Michael Harper and political activists like Charlie Cobb, one of the seminal political figures in the city in the 1960s. Brown had mentored them all—the militant political activists and the poets who sought to emulate his example as a man of intellectual excellence. "I've been rediscovered, reinstituted, regenerated, and recovered," Brown said. Of Howard University, he stated: "I was hired at Howard, I was fired at Howard, rehired, and retired."[4]

One of the best tributes for Brown as he was finishing up at Howard University was written by Dr. Stephen E. Henderson, the Howard University literary critic and author of *Understanding the New Black Poetry*. Henderson's portrait of his friend Sterling Brown would appear in *Ebony* magazine in October 1976. It centered on Brown's return to teach at Howard after Brown's retirement. According to Henderson, with the "changing intellectual climate brought on by the ferment of the 60s, institutions have begun to catch up" with Brown. Brown was almost lured away to Vassar at the time. But Brown stayed at Howard. According to Henderson, Brown "learned to live with and has chosen to resolve" his life "through the excellence of his mind and his art and his dedication to his people."[5]

In the 1970s, as Brown's post-Howard life began to take shape, his good friend William Waring Cuney published his last book, *Storefront Church*. It was published in bibliophile Paul Breman's Black Heritage Series in 1973.[6] The book represents the kind of work Cuney had been writing since high school in DC. In June 1976, just three years later, Cuney died in New York City.

According to Paul Breman, Cuney regularly sent poems to him over the years. From 1958 to 1962 and then later in the early 1970s, Cuney sent him package after package of poetry.[7] Some of the writings were poems or little anecdotes, while some of the writings were songs. Cuney was at his best when the two forms—songwriting and poetry—came together. He was still also concerned with the ordinary person in society. Cuney also sent over 100 pages of poetry to his friends Marguerite and Carl Cartwright over the years.[8] Rosey Pool, the editor of the popular anthology *Beyond the Blues*, also received a substantial cache of poetry from Cuney over the years, according to her papers collected at the University of Sussex in England.[9]

Cuney had kept in touch with his friend Sterling Brown in Washington, DC, via letters, postcards, and occasional news clippings, usually about music or literature. Cuney always asked Brown about his beloved wife, Daisy, in these exchanges. In 1973 Brown updated the anthology *The Negro Caravan* and contacted Cuney about submitting poems. Cuney sent back a bunch of poetry to Brown in DC. "Dear old friend," Brown replied on the same envelope. "Thanks for your occasional notes. As senior editor of *New Negro Caravan*, soon to be published, I can tell you we definitely intend [on] using ten of your poems starting with 'No Images' including 'My Lord What A Morning,'" Brown concluded his response to his friend: "You have never received your just and very credits [*sic*] . . . Sterling A. Brown."[10]

The last mail exchange was in February 1975 between Brown and Cuney. Cuney wrote to Brown about Jimmie Daniels and Helen Humes, music stars from the Harlem Renaissance.[11] Humes had been a hot singer in the 1920s and 1930s and sung in the Count Basie Orchestra. For two poets who made it their life's work to use Black music to advance culture and art, it is an appropriate coda to their lifelong friendship.

At the time of his death, Cuney was engaged to be married. According to newspaper accounts, his fiancée, Adeline Norris, passed away on Thursday, December 11, 2008, in Madison, Wisconsin. Cuney was listed as her fiancé in Norris's obituary. She was born on June 14, 1913, in Montana and raised in Wisconsin, where she would attend school and then nursing school. Eventually, Norris would serve as a nurse in New York City at a hospital on Roosevelt Island.[12]

The Collected Poems of Sterling A. Brown was published in 1981. The book put an exclamation point on the career of the city's most important poet. The poet whose mother read him Paul Laurence Dunbar's work and who wanted to become a servant to his people, had come full circle. The book was published by the newly created National Poetry Series. The series was created in 1978 by way of the cooperation of poets and publishers. The new series was started to subsidize "publication of several books a year, to get the major New York houses back in the business of publishing poetry."[13] The poet Michael P. Harper selected Sterling A. Brown's collected poems for publication.

"The publication of Sterling Brown's *Collected Poems* is an historical event, and it is also a personal triumph, another instance of Brown's 'jumping the gap of the generations,' for his poems have always been very demanding on the senses, and on the intellect; though he has never been a poet of fashion,"[14] Harper wrote in the preface for the book back in 1979. One triumph of the book is that Brown's second collection (*Hiding Place*), rejected for publication by major publishers in the 1930s, is included in full.

One of Brown's good friends, and contemporary poet, Sam Allen (Samuel Allen), also had high praise for the book. "The body of Brown's work examines with [an] unblinking stare the historic oppression of black humanity in this country. It is an uncompromising portrayal, and, unlike that of some of his contemporaries, without the consolation of an underlying sense of religious purpose," Allen wrote.[15]

The book's publication was also a reminder that Brown had been ignored mostly after his monumental, game-changing tome *Southern Road*. Perhaps it was because the Great Depression happened, but that is doubtful. "Nobody—not even Sterling Brown—can say what poems might have been written if his early efforts had received a bare minimum of the encouragement they clearly deserved."[16] But his moment had come now, and he was forever recognized for his dedication to his craft, his people, and his vision of Black American life. "Brown's poems are full of pain and sorrow . . . but the overall feeling that emerges is joy: joy first of all in people's resilience, their ability to endure and persevere, and wait for better times."[17]

Many years later, *The Collected Poems of Sterling Brown* was republished just as Brown's reputation was rising even more. There had been countless tributes by this point, and poets across the country and the world paid homage to the artistic life he had led during the twentieth century. It is again the ultimate tribute to Brown and what he represented as a scholar, poet, academic, and human being comfortable in any setting.

Northwestern University Press published the book, and not only was Michael Harper's original introduction included, but poet Cornelius Eady penned a new introduction to update to the literary world the importance of Sterling A. Brown. "The art of Brown is the art of a poet who refuses to blink," Eady wrote. "In his poems, as you will read, black folk are allowed to be, so the warts of a people are allowed to cohabit with the heroic." Eady added: "How do you live black, knowing that at any time you can be killed for being black? That question is at the core of Brown's poetry, which still works as a revelation."[18]

Eady's willingness to place Brown's work in contemporary context is clear. The African American experience has changed, but in many ways it has not. Brown's focus always on the ordinary person in his poetry makes big worldly issues accessible for everyone while also maintaining important levels of artistic excellence.

The Poets and Their Poetry

In January 1970 the Folger Shakespeare Library commenced a new poetry reading series in the city. The series was held on Thursdays and Sundays. It got off with much momentum. Lucille Clifton, the former Howard University student and poet in residence in Baltimore at Coppin State University at one point, read on February 8, 1970.[19]

It was an audacious beginning, as the Folger was mostly not strongly connected with the majority African American city culturally and politically at the time. Considering that Sterling Brown, perhaps the most important African American poet in America, was teaching just across town at Howard University, the new series presented new opportunities for connections. Few poets could straddle the academic world and the ordinary world of people and their daily lives of work and life like Brown. Brown would read in the series on March 9, 1982.

E. Ethelbert Miller was important to the new Folger Poetry series. The lack of many poets of African descent as readers in the series had been evident from the beginning. White residents were leaving the city by 1970 or had already departed. African Americans were also leaving, as the quality of life deteriorated after the 1968 riots. The city was majority Black and was administered by African Americans, and revenue to run a major city was diminishing.

The Folger series went forward and is still in operation today, much to its credit. It was started to "fill a need" for "working poets" and poets of "all levels" could get together, according to the Folger. In year 2 of the series, former Howard University student Primus St. John was among the readers on February 21, 1971.[20] The series continued, and by the mid-1970s the Folger was considered one of several venues that finally led someone to declare that DC had a real poetry scene.

"Bards can be found everywhere," Mary Anne Dalton wrote in the *Evening Star* newspaper. For example, Dalton also recounted the moment when Howard University's Clay Goss, a playwright and poet, stood in the middle of Farragut Square downtown in the city and recited a poem. "He stationed himself among the orange zinnias and in a voice to mute a Metrobus, began 'Remembering Rhythm and Blues.' "[21]

Goss was part of the National Park Service's Poets in the Park program along with Deidra Baldwin. Many other poets would participate, though it is hard to conclude that this made the city a vibrant poetry scene suddenly. Poetry had been happening in the city for quite some time. This was an acknowledgment that the institutions alone didn't own poetry; the people did, according to the Library of Congress at the time.[22] This was the time of Miller's Ascension Series, the *Black Box* cassette poetry magazine, and WOOK AM radio's Sunday poetry series. Poetry was happening and especially so among African American poets.

Books and publications finally began to come despite little support from the city or access to resources that institutional poets often received. There had been books written before by poets in Washington, DC, but African American poets found the opportunities lacking, mostly, except for the more well-known writers. Even Sterling Brown had only published one volume of poetry over his career by the 1970s, and Beacon Press had published that in Massachusetts. Jack Foley's famous assessment of the city's literary scene was accurate. In a city with a majority Black population—full of Black poets, venues, educational outlets, and resources—somehow Black poets rarely, if ever, got books of poems published.

In the city there were plenty of opportunities to read one's poetry, and there were anthologies where some Black poets could publish a poem here and there, but entire collections were quite rare. But the energy created by the poets and the need for artistic expression made books inevitable. Ethelbert Miller was one of the leaders of the pack in the 1970s. His books/collections initially included *Andromeda* (1974), and *The Land of Smiles and the Land of No Smiles* (1974). In 1978 the Washington Writers' Publishing House published *Migrant Worker*, Miller's third collection, and in 1982 his fourth collection, *Season of Hunger, Cry of Rain*, was published by Lotus Press, out of Detroit, Michigan.[23]

Miller wasn't alone in pushing boundaries in the literary world. Michelle Parkerson, who was making films then, published her first book, *Waiting Rooms*. One of her most acclaimed films, . . . *But Then, She's Betty Carter*, was completed in 1980. Parkerson's art from this point forward would rarely not include film and/or performance.

Of course, at this time, May Miller, now in her seventies, was still writing poetry and producing poetry regularly, including collections. Her career began when she was a young girl. She was a literary ambassador of African American poetry in the city. She did not stop publishing or writing. Her 1975 collection, *Dust of Uncertain Journey*, was published by Lotus Press. Robert Hayden described Miller's work as "quiet strength" and "lyric intensity" and "a poet of humane vision." The Louisiana poet

Pinkie Gordon Lane hailed Miller as a "poet with a worldview."[24] *Dust of an Uncertain Journey* was the third year that Miller had published a book.

Dolores Kendrick also published one of her volumes of poetry at this time. Again, Paul Breman was publishing an African American poet from Washington, DC. Her book in Breman's Black Heritage Series was called *Through the Ceiling*. Kendrick was very thankful to Breman for publishing her collection. It was one of the last books Breman published in the series. Kendrick was quite grateful that she and Breman connected.

"Nothing can diminish the contribution Paul Breman has made," Kendrick said years ago. "He was out there by himself, publishing this important African American poetry."[25] Breman is a key figure in Black literature during a period of political volatility. When Breman began publishing, Black poetry was not necessarily following the world's political events. Yet, by the time he finished the series, he had published writers who did embrace politics overtly and other writers who wrote honestly.

The output of African American poetry at this time was heavy. It reflected the city's legacy of African American poetry, and the support poets received from other poets. Some of the poets and titles at this time include *Tell Me How Willing Slaves Be*, by Adesanya Alakoye; *Dawn*, by Jonetta Barras-Abney; *Hoodoo Hollerin' Bebop Ghosts*, by Larry Neal (1974); *From the Inner City*, by Wendy Johns (1975); *Black Rap and Rhyme*, by Ambrosia Shepherd (1975); *Hoochie Coochie Man*, by Otis Williams (1976); *Among the Living Dead*, by Carl Shears; and *The Last Ride of Wild Bill*, by Sterling A Brown (1974). There were many other poetry chapbooks and broadsides published, but nearly all of them were published by small independent publishers, usually locally. Many of the publications were self-published. This trend again reflected the lack of resources to properly publish the many Black poets who were writing at the time in the city. It did not stop the poetry from being written and produced and read all over the city.

By this time, there was a momentum now. Black culture including poetry in the city was expected, and though the more radical politics of the 1960s by African Americans had given way to pragmatic, progressive politics, the time remained important. The city's Black activists were pushing successfully for voting rights for residents of the city and for home rule by them.[26] Decades earlier the poet Sterling A. Brown, who was teaching at Howard and serving as an editor for the Federal Writers' Project, wrote that the "Negro in Washington has no voice in government, is economically proscribed, and segregated nearly as rigidly as in southern cities he condemns."[27] By the mid-1970s, Black residents, a majority now, had obtained voting rights and home rule for the city's residents.[28] The Black poetry scene, a witness to this political achievement, remained vigorous and connected even as whites left the city in droves. The future of the city was uncertain economically, but not Black poetry. It was as strong as ever even as it mostly pushed forward on its own.

12

Corners and Performers

According to Darrell Stover, a Washington, DC, native who grew up in nearby Prince George's County, "people heard me before they saw me read poetry."[1] Stover, who was writing poetry by his early teens, was referring to another phenomenon of American poetry called Dial-A-Poem. Dial-A-Poem allowed poets to be heard on the airwaves around the Washington area.[2] WPFW-FM 89.3 radio sponsored Dial-A-Poem by at least the mid- to late 1970s. While it did not originate in the DC area, it eventually found its way to the city, and Stover recalls sharing his work over the airwaves with the people.[3] Poets could call in and recite their poems, providing them with an immediate audience and connection.

Stover began publishing poetry in the school's *The Black Explosion Newspaper* when he was a student at the University of Maryland. He also connected with Otis Williams, a senior poet and director of the University of Maryland's Nyumburu Cultural Center on the campus. Williams brought all kinds of poetry and cultural programs to the university, including some of the leading Black poets of the day from around the country. Williams's work impressed Ethelbert Miller and Ahmos Zu-Bolton, who had launched their own community poetry programming in the early 1970s. Stover connecting with Williams was no surprise either.

In 1972 as a young teen, Stover bought a used copy of *Black Fire*, the seminal anthology of the Black Arts Movement (BAM). The book, the creation of poets Amiri Baraka and Larry Neal, deeply impacted the world of Black poetry in America and still does today.

"It lit a fire under me," Stover said of the book.[4] Like many poets in the DC area, Stover would also forge a close bond with the book's coeditor, Amiri Baraka, from afar (Baraka lived and worked in Newark, New Jersey). But poetry was a big part of Stover's life afterward. He would study science in college, but he continued to also stay faithful to poetry.

Right before Stover became central to the Washington, DC, Black poetry scene, Larry Neal, *Black Fire*'s coeditor, came to the city. Neal had direct and strong connections to Sterling Brown like most Black poets in Washington. Neal had moved there and eventually came to direct the DC Commission on the Arts and Humanities (DCCAH). Neal tried to promote the arts and provide artists with monetary support for their work.

When Neal assumed the post of director of DCCAH, he noted: "What is life without art and ideas? Government can help take art to people." Neal, channeling the WPA from the Great Depression, spoke to history. Neal served as DCCAH from 1976 to 1979. As for the art part, Neal spoke to that question in the *Washington Post* in 1969: "It is a profound ethical sense that makes the Black artist question a society in which art is one thing and the actions of men another. The Black Arts Movement believes that your ethics and your aesthetics are one."[5]

Even though Neal's statement is grounded in BAM ideals, his statement has universal appeal. But support for art during Larry Neal's time running the commission was weak financially. The federal government slashed the arts commission budget when Neal was in charge. And Neal was also no bureaucrat; he was a writer and artist.

Tragically, Neal died suddenly in 1981 of a heart attack. Upon his sudden death, the city celebrated his literature and his sacrifice to the arts with an adoring tribute. The city also convened several literary conferences in his honor and established annual literary awards in his name. At the second Larry Neal Writers Conference, held in 1983, Baraka described Larry Neal as the "spiritual leader" of the Black Arts Movement and an artist "who wanted to make revolution."[6] The awards are still presented annually by the agency Neal once directed—DCCAH. This is the literary world that Darrell Stover found waiting in DC in the 1980s.

At the University of Maryland, Stover got deeper into the art form. He then encountered Essex Hemphill, who was also making his way in the world of poetry. Stover describes Hemphill's readings at Maryland as legendary.[7] Stover became a key part of the larger Washington, DC, poetry scene after college. He took writing workshops at the Institute for Policy Studies and attended various poetry events in the city. He met Garth Tate, who would lead one of the city's more vibrant poetry collectives—Station to Station. The decades of poetry in the city were coming together.

Tate, like Stover, began to make his mark in the city. Tate helped promote *Nethula Journal* in the late 1970s and early 1980s and began performing his own poetry. Tate's first performance group was called Starving Artists Still Alive.[8] Not long afterward, Tate formed the poetry performance collective Station to Station with several other poets. Station to Station was a community of like-minded poets. It evolved into a performance group.

"We were critiquing our work and decided why not present it. . . . We didn't want to just stand at a podium and read, like most poets, so we opted for performance," Tate said in 1982.[9] Tate and the other poets evolved into Station to Station. Station to Station was quite formidable in the city of Washington. It continued the traditions advanced by so many other Black poets in the city and other poets in search of an audience and fellowship. Tate, who was a Black gay male poet, also proved to be an essential creative artist in his own right.

In November 1984 Garth Tate, through Station to Station, organized a two-day poetry forum called Poetry Free For All? The event was held partly at DC Creative Space for performances but also at other venues where panels on poetry were convened. The event was ahead of its time. It was described as a forum where poets would gather without regard to "race, gender, sexual orientation, physical disability, ethnicity, or creed."[10] The panelists and poets reflected that diversity. The panelists included Ethelbert Miller, Michelle Parkerson, and Claudia Tate. The poets were also impressive: Gideon Ferebee, Essex Hemphill, and Calvin Forbes.

A year after Garth Tate's forum, Tate asked Darrell Stover to join his performance collective Station to Station. Stover joining the group reflects his dedication to the DC poetry scene and his reputation among performance poets. Station to Station would continue to perform, share each other's work, and organize forums on Black poetry throughout the 1980s. Stover joined but also set his own path at the same time as a poet and performance poet. One of his most important early initiatives was called A Poet on Every Corner.

This project would be partly made possible by collaborating with the African American Writers Guild (AAWG), another organization that emerged in the late 1980s to bring Black artists and writers together. The Guild, as the organization came to be known, was started by the Washington, DC, writer Marita Golden.

Golden is a child of Washington, DC. She had been involved in the DC writer's scene back during the days of the 1968 riots and the establishment of Drum and Spear Bookstore that same year. By the late 1980s Golden was living back in DC and publishing her first few books, including a memoir, *Migrations of the Heart*, and a novel, *A Woman's Place*.

But starting the AAWG with many other locals at the time, like poet Calvin Forbes, bibliophile Clyde McElvene, Diane Simpkins, and Cuthbert "Tuffy" Simpkins, was part of the institution building wing of Black DC. Black writers did not have enough publishing opportunities or safe spaces to create fellowship. Golden created an important one for the period.

The Guild held regular meetings at the homes of members or local libraries. It published a regular newsletter called *Word Up*. The Guild sponsored readings by national and local authors and occasionally held a potluck for a few of the very well-known writers such as Ishmael Reed.

Darrell Stover partnered with the Guild for his first of many Poet on Every Corner events. The Poet on Every Corner project likely would have happened anyway, even without the partnership, though having more writers and artists involved makes it even better. Stover's idea also stemmed from his relationship with Otis Williams of the University of Maryland, who believed in taking poetry to the people.

"We need to do public events and then do them in the community" is how Stover described Otis Williams's charge to him when he was a student at the University of Maryland. So he did, and he recruited several other poets to join the celebration. The first Poet on Every Corner occurred on January 9, 1987, and celebrated Rev. Dr. Martin Luther King Jr at the city's Martin Luther King Jr. Public Memorial Library.[11]

The roster of poets who read that day outside on the corners and then inside the library was impressive and quite long: Kenneth Carroll, Otis Williams, Askia Muhammad, Alaivc Moseley, Jemela Mwelu, Traci Abena Hill, June Collins, Garth Tate, Sybil Robert, Charles Blackwell, Foodhead (Harold Finley Jr.), Valerie Russell, B. Wright, Steve Monroe, Jaren Hailey Yemi Bates, Darla Davenport-Powell, Akindele Akinde, Lee Brown, g.r. adams, Darrell Stover, Jeanean Gibbs, Reuben Jackson, Jacquie Jones, Mphela Makogba, Lasana James, Muhammad Abdullah Ali, Theresa Ford, Jackie Jones-Minerva, and others.[12]

The Guild and Stover convened another Poet on Every Corner in August 1987 downtown outside the historic Frank D. Reeves Municipal Building. The event was held to "strengthen ties between writers and the community" or bring "poetry to the people."[13] Stover followed those Poet on Every Corner events with another such event on the issue of South Africa. At the time, racial apartheid in South Africa was a big political issue in the United States, especially among African American poets, artists, and radicals.

Stover's event on July 17, 1988, began in Lafayette Park across from the White House. Poets who attended met up at the South African Embassy to read outside that location.[14] Another Poet on Every Corner followed on November 12, 1988. This reading, held in the city's Mount Pleasant neighborhood, featured another large list of locals.[15]

Not long after this flurry of poetry readings, Stover formed a performance poetry ensemble known as The Spoken Word. Kenneth Carroll was an original member as well. At the time, in the late 1980s, various musical, historical, and cultural influences had been pushing African American poets in this direction. Gil Scott-Heron's heyday had been the 1970s. Haki Madhubuti taught at Howard University in the 1970s and had recorded a spoken word album. The Spoken Word was in that tradition.

The poets Caprese Jackson, Joy Jones, Leslie Nia Lewis, and Lansana Mack were also members of The Spoken Word.[16] Drummers began performing with The Spoken Word: Butch Jackson, Lansana Mack, and Doc Powell were three notables.[17] The Spoken Word performed at Kwanzaa celebrations, festivals, and literary venues in and around the city. They also began to get invited out of the city to perform as well. And with "spoken word" poetry presentations becoming bigger and bigger locally and nationally, what The Spoken Word offered was timely and a welcome sound. In 1993 the group released a book, *Bad Beats, Sacred Rhythms*.[18] The book included an audio CD with the poets reading their poetry.

When Reuben Jackson died in 2024, many people, poets, artists, musicians, and intellectuals finally understood his impact and excellence as a poet, writer, and archivist. His memorial service was live streamed on YouTube and social media, with many poets and cultural players in Washington, DC, paying him tribute for his life in letters and music, especially jazz.

Jackson, born in Augusta, Georgia, but raised in Washington, DC, also was a rising star on the Washington, DC, poetry scene in the early 1980s, as the number of venues offering poetry proliferated. Jackson had emerged before the spoken word scene in the city got busy and hot. He was the first poet I saw read in the city at a venue. I knew when I saw Jackson read and present himself as a poet with a particular voice and style that I wanted to one day develop into that kind of poet.

Jackson, a child of the city's public schools and an intense music lover, graduated from Goddard College in Vermont. Upon his return to DC, he slowly slid into the local poetry scene. Jackson, onstage, was comedic, sensitive, and brilliant all in one sentence. He was shy initially, attending readings and then occasionally reading his work. He attended his first reading in 1980 at the DC Space, he said, and then eased into the scene as a more confident voice by 1982. His work sung with honesty and a flair for the unique.[19]

He could listen to and discuss Jimi Hendrix equally as well as Frank Sinatra and Frank Zappa. He loved Duke Ellington but was comfortable embracing the "Duke of Earl" as well. Jackson spent years working at the Smithsonian as an archivist at the Duke Ellington collection, and in 1990 he published his first book, *fingering the keys,* on Gut Punch Press.[20]

It was a tour de force, and like the individual poems he had published, it was a favorite of young poets in the city who were just getting started and trying to find their own voices. *Fingering the keys* won the Columbia Book Prize in 1992, a local award that recognized the year's most outstanding book published locally. In his very humble ways, Jackson just kept doing what he had always done: writing great works of art. In addition to poetry, he penned music and book reviews. There was a time in the city when his byline was weekly he was writing so much journalism.

When Ethelbert Miller convened Ascension #94 in April 1989, Reuben Jackson was one of the featured readers. This presence demonstrated the growth of his reputation in the city as a favorite poet. In addition to Jackson, Darrell Stover was featured, as were Deidre Cross, C. Moon, Kenneth Carroll, Jacquie Jones, Peter J. Harris, and Lynelle Johnson. Miller's Ascension Reading Series was fifteen years old and had provided ninety-four poetry readings by then. The roster of readers demonstrated the strength of the series. An Ascension Reading was always a place to catch up. It was where you realized how lucky you were to be a poet in Washington, DC, and even more an African American poet.

After Winter

When Reuben Jackson was polishing his chops as a young voice among many in the 1980s, the city was losing its greatest poet—Sterling A. Brown. Brown had died just three months before the fifteenth anniversary of Ethelbert Miller's Ascension series. Brown had become a literary institution in the decade preceding his death.

On May 11, 1984, Sterling A. Brown was named the city's first poet laureate. Brown, eighty-three at the time, would live out his remaining days with that title. He had received just about every accolade a race man could receive. "It's important to me that something I said resounded and reached certain ears," Brown said.[21]

And then, the following year, in 1985, Haile Gerima, the filmmaker and Howard University professor of film studies, completed a film about Brown called *After Winter.* It was the most authentic tribute to Brown out of all the tributes Brown received during his life. Gerima had never heard of Sterling Brown when he decided to do the film, even though Brown was a literary icon in the city and had taught at Howard University for decades. "I only knew about Sterling because he wrote about 'Imitation of Life.' . . . Nobody I know ever wrote that much on Black film. I read this thing on 'Imitation of Life,' and I didn't even know he was a poet or at Howard."[22]

Gerima said he met Brown at a gathering at Dr. Fletcher Johnson's house. "There was an old man, with a pipe, in front of a fireplace, on a rocking chair." Gerima introduced himself and noted to Brown his admiration for his criticism and his career at Howard University not conforming to the easy status quo.

Gerima and his filmmaker wife and partner, Shirikiana Gerima, then began to go by Brown's house for Brown's famous gatherings of intellectual talk, Black history, and music. Brown always made it all connect. Gerima was so inspired that he proposed to Howard University to do a film called *Around the Fire.* It would include Sterling Brown and would focus on the relationship between elders and young people, in particular, students. Gerima called it an "African concept." He wanted Brown to be filmed around a fire talking to young people, doing what he had been doing for fifty years by then. The film was rejected by the university, according to Gerima. Howard did not hold Brown in high regard despite the attention he brought to the school.

When Howard University did not provide Gerima with any support, he used his class along with his own resources to film Brown. He organized his students into rotating crews to film Brown in various places, including Brown's office.[23] Gerima's *After Winter* is now a timeless work of art about a man and poet who is a timeless artist. The Black poets of DC who saw Brown as their literary superhero and cultural guide absolutely know from watching the sixty-minute film how fortunate they were or have been able to experience the life and work of Sterling A. Brown upon viewing the film.

Alive and Well and Living

When I returned to Washington after college, the first person I spoke to about wanting to be a poet was my father. He didn't waiver or hesitate. He encouraged me to pursue my art. He just added that I would have to figure out how to pay my rent. In a few days, he handed me a list of names. One of his fraternity brothers, Lewis Thompson (Kappa Alpha Psi), had compiled a list of contacts for me to seek out in the city. The first contact was Gwendolyn Brooks, poetry consultant to the Library of Congress; the second was the Writer's Center in Bethesda, Maryland; and the third was E. Ethelbert Miller of Howard University. I immediately sought to find these resources and make use of them all.

But for the fact that Gwendolyn Brooks had come to DC and had been the poetry consultant to the Library of Congress for a year, my own space in the Black poetry scene in Washington would have been different. Yet by the time I returned from college, Brooks's time in that position was over. She had served from 1985 to 1986. She was the second African American consultant chosen for the post; Robert Hayden had been the first. The post today is known as the poet laureate of the United States. I had missed her celebrated period of service.

In a short interview film completed in Washington, DC, about Gwendolyn Brooks completed while she was poetry consultant, Ethelbert Miller asks her about the day she found out she won the Pulitzer Prize, the first African American, in fact, to win the coveted award.[24] Brooks, in her humble and colorful way, advises Miller that when she won, the power had been out in their apartment.[25] The committee did eventually call and advised Brooks she would win the prize, and the next day when the press arrived to cover the moment, the power, she said, was suddenly restored.

The interview, one of the key archival gems in the film Brooks left behind to the city, also discusses her career, the question of writing for Black people, her family, and how the Black community can support its writers in the future. It is, to a certain extent, an ideal summation of her life and work as she talked of her own long and arduous journey to become a poet. Yet, most of all, the film shows Mrs. Brooks, as she has been described by nearly everyone I know who interacted with her: humble, gracious, and honest, but also quite adept at language, and colorful in every way.

The film, and other sources, demonstrate that Brooks was part of the city's literary pulse during her time here. She did not disappear into the federal apparatus that made her time here possible. She gave a reading during Black History Month (February 5, 1986) at Martin Luther King Jr. Library downtown in the city. She came to town by rail each Monday and would stay through Tuesday, choosing to continue to reside in her South Side Chicago home. She started a noontime reading series at the Library of Congress, where poets were invited to read their work and lunch would be served. Her own first reading in the city, something typical now when a poet laureate is installed, was September 30, 1985, at the Library of Congress in the Coolidge Auditorium.[26]

Brooks spent each Monday and Tuesday in the city at her post as poetry consultant, using the time for "oral interviews, exhibition lunches, evenings with Black and Hispanic poets and exchanges with critics."[27] This is likely why Brooks's time in the city is memorable to so many poets, especially African American poets.

Demonstrating her commitment right away to young poets in the city, Brooks read at the Discovery Theater at the Smithsonian Museum in DC in March 1986. She also kept a regular reading schedule at the Library of Congress during her tenure and brought in other writers to read, whom she would introduce and celebrate. In April 1986 she read at Georgetown University, in the city, and later that month she gave a lecture at nearby Hood College in Frederick, Maryland (about forty miles outside Washington, DC) on books.[28] She also read in nearby Baltimore at the Community College there and was featured in *The Baltimore Sun* newspaper.

In May 1986, as is customary for the poet laureate, Brooks gave a lecture at the Library of Congress. The title of her lecture: "The Day of the Gwendolyn." It seems almost uncharacteristic of her humble style to call it such. Yet considering the force she became on the literary scene in Washington, it hardly matters.

Gwendolyn Brooks was the first black woman to serve as poetry consultant to the Library of Congress and the last one. According to the DC poet Darrell Stover, regarding Brooks's time in the area, she was "like a burst of spring on the Washington Metropolitan poetry scene" when she was here. This metaphor is Stover's epigraph to his poem, "Oh! And All This," a poem inspired by Brooks's presence in the city.

Oh! And All This
Brown-oranges
Red
Yellow-greens
Laying lightly in view. . .

the poem begins. You get the feeling Stover is writing that Brooks planted some seeds here that will be long lasting.[29]

Over the years, I have had many conversations with Stover and others regarding when Gwendolyn Brooks was poetry consultant to the Library Congress in Washington, DC, and was right downtown. Stover once told me of the time at the University of Maryland, College Park, just outside the city, that Brooks gave a poetry reading memorable for not just the reading but also how Mrs. Brooks was treated with so much respect.

Dr. Joyce Ann Joyce, the literary scholar and critic teaching at the University of Maryland, set up the reading.[30] In addition, Dr. Joyce arranged for University of Maryland basketball star Len Bias to come to the reading and present Gwendolyn Brooks with flowers. Bias, who by the spring 1986 was a national basketball superstar, appeared at the reading and presented Brooks humbly with yellow roses.[31] Bias had been at the school's end-of-year basketball banquet but slipped out just to present the flowers. The small gesture had been that important. It was a testament to how many felt of Gwendolyn Brooks and what she meant to Black people.

In October 1988 Ethelbert Miller invited me to read on his Ascension Series, Ascension #92.[32] My fellow readers that night are noteworthy—Debra Garner, a fine poet, who had already published a collection of poetry, and Helen Elaine Lee, a fiction writer—both of whom graciously shared literary space with me that evening. Lee has now published three novels: *The Serpent's Gift* (Atheneum Publishers, 1994), *Water Marked* (Scribner Books, 1999) and *Pomegranate* (Atria Books, 2023). Garner continued to write for years and publish, and like some other African American poets she became a minister of the Gospel.

My parents came to the reading, as did the many poets of Washington, DC, who were part of the city's poetry scene at the time: Kenneth Carroll. Darrell Stover. Peter Harris. Jacquie Jones. And many others. I always hated to speak in public, but I did it. And just as I was about to leave the reading afterward, an African American woman came up to me and introduced herself.

"Hello," she said, "my name is Junette Pinkney. I loved your poetry. Would you like to meet Gwendolyn Brooks and Haki Madhubuti?"

My knees buckled.

Two nights after Ascension #92, I met Gwendolyn Brooks and Haki Madhubuti. Pinkney, a media producer, and the organizer of a fundraiser for Third World Press's twentieth anniversary that evening, arranged the meeting.

"You are a poet," Madhubuti would say after I showed him some of my poetry before the scheduled event. "I will call you up during the evening . . . come up and read a few of your poems." I was astonished.

Two of the poets I respected more than most in the world had become part of my personal poetry journey that fast. I immediately felt a sense of community about what had happened. I understood now how tight-knit and cohesive the African American poetry world was in the country and in the city. It was only because my father had given me Ethelbert Miller's name that I was standing there talking to Madhubuti. It was only because of Howard University, as well, the college my father had attended. It made me feel as if I had become part of something much bigger, something that had been nurtured out of love and respect for writing and humanity.

Not long into the program that evening, Haki Madhubuti, the poet and publisher at Third World Press, did in fact summon me to the podium to read before a captive audience of the best of the DC African American artistic and intellectual community. Gwendolyn Brooks was sitting right up front smiling, listening to my poetry. Frances Cress Welsing, the late psychologist who had written extensively on race and mental health over the years, was also sitting right up front. Jeff Donaldson, the legendary visual artist from Chicago and the BAM period, was there, as were countless other Black artists and poets I would soon get to know.

The program went well. It was, most of all, like many poetry events in the city: jam-packed. Peter J. Harris, a Washington, DC, poet a little older than me, was there. We became friends that night. The legendary DC-based photojournalist Roy Lewis was everywhere snapping photos. Haki and I started a long-distance mentorship that would eventually lead to the publication of my first book, *elvis presley is alive and well and living in harlem,* in 1993. Ethelbert Miller was there. I was officially a member of DC's African American poetry scene. The one that could trace its roots at the very least back to the arrival of Paul Laurence Dunbar's residence at the turn of the century.

13
Something Else

As the 1980s progressed, there was an uptick in the poetry books published by African American writers in Washington, DC. The city was 70 percent African American at the time. The resources devoted to Black poetry and Black poets and to perhaps assist them in creating their art did not reflect those numbers. The African American poets in the city knew this very well, so they did what they could to promote their work and to publish. They sought all available outlets. The books that did come to life in a variety of ways continue to reflect a certain excellence and pride by the many poets who found their safe space here.

In 1988 at the same time I entered the scene, Maxine Clair, formerly employed at Children's Hospital in Washington, DC, had her first book of poems published, entitled *Coping with Gravity*. Clair, formerly of Kansas, had a new career now; she was a poet and eventually a writer in multiple genres. Clair obtained a master of fine arts (MFA) degree from American University completing a collection of poetry called "Reincarnation" in 1984.[1] Clair went on to teach at George Washington University. She published a collection of short stories, *Rattlebone*, and a novel, *October Suite*. But her entry in the world of literature began with her very memorable collection *Coping with Gravity*.

The book was published in June 1988 by the Washington Writers' Publishing House, or WWPH. There is some importance here because Clair is African American. It suggested that some African American writers in the city could find opportunity. It harkened back to the days of J. C. Byars's 1928 anthology, *Black and White*. Clair had already been reading around the city by the time *Coping with Gravity* dropped into the world. In August or September 1987, she read at the Folger Shakespeare Library's Midday Muse reading series along with Maxine Combs.[2]

In October 1987 the poetry collective Station to Station, a group established by the performance poet Garth Tate, featured Clair on one of their programs at Javarama.[3] Clair also read in December of that year through the American University's writing program and reading series.[4] She taught at American University and Duke Ellington School of the Arts and published in many noteworthy journals including *Folio*,

Callaloo, and Richard Peabody's *Gargoyle*.[5] The Folger Shakespeare Library and the publisher of *Coping with Gravity* held a publishing release party for Clair.

Two years before Clair's *Coping with Gravity* was published, E. Ethelbert Miller's *where are all the love poems for dictators?* was published by Open Hand Publishing. It is one of the more remarkable collections of poetry that had begun to appear in the late 1980s in DC written by a Black poet. With his steady record of publishing, organizing programs, and assisting writers, Miller was busy. This was his fifth collection of verse in just twelve years. Miller's fifth collection showed growth aesthetically and politically. His work, as it would always seem to be over the years, was an outgrowth of his personal interactions with his community. The collection is full of love poetry and poetry about Central America, an issue that was a big deal in DC at the time. The title *where are all the love poems for dictators?* is Miller's personal statement of quiet protest.

Of the book, Gwendolyn Brooks wrote: "Ethelbert Miller is one of the most significant and influential poets of our time."[6] Ntozake Shange wrote that "Ethelbert Miller conjures the smoke and fire we associate with love and politics. The versatile coming together of opposites." And Ariel Dorfman, the Chilean poet, described the book as a "fit answer to a world where violence threatens to drive us all mad." The Reagan administration's decision to expand imperial activities in El Salvador and other Central American countries inspired poets and artists to speak to their living times. This included African American poets in Washington.

Kwelismith, a local poet and performer, was another scribe who took on the politics of Reagan with force and beauty rooted in African American artistic traditions. Kwelismith was born and raised in Cincinnati, Ohio, and graduated from the Cincinnati Conservatory of Music. The mother of two, she also obtained a master's degree in psychology. Her poetic life in Washington, DC, combines music, poetry, performance, and dance. Grace Cavalieri describes her as a "national treasure."[7]

In the Reagan era, she was a welcome voice in the city, challenging the insidious hate and division broadcast from an administration that had contempt for the poor and people of color. In April 1986 she presented what became one of her trademarks: the one-woman show. At the Bethune-Cookman University Museum Archives, her mixed genre show was *No Place for a Soft Black Woman.*

Her 1989 collection, *Slavesong*, took on the administration directly and indirectly on its imperial designs and its exportation of violence globally.[8] Before the book's publication, Kwelismith performed everywhere in the city. She provided her multigenre shows at DC Space and participated in events sponsored by Martin Luther King Jr. Library.[9] By 1991 even though Kwelismith was very popular locally and nationally in art circles, she was awarded an Emerging Artist Award by the Mayor's Arts Awards.[10]

Essex Hemphill also published books during this period. His own books are less known than the anthologies he would eventually bring into creation. But Hemphill was busy writing. In 1985 his collection *Earth Life* was published and that was followed up quickly with *Conditions* in 1986. Then came *Ceremonies*, a book of poetry and prose. And Hemphill's art had to speak because of the Reagan administration's failure to address the growing AIDS and HIV crisis in America. AIDS was taking the lives of many gay artists during this period, and the government barely could utter the word "AIDS," nor could it respond appropriately to a crisis affecting the entire nation. Yet, because many of the early victims were gay men, the disease did not get enough attention.[11] Hemphill would eventually succumb to the disease in 1995, cutting an amazing career well short of its artistic journey.

The arrival of these many books and performances by poets represented the rising significance of artistic expression of African Americans in the DC area. It was a culmination of years of cultural evolution and determination by artists with minimal resources to produce art of meaning. It was the endurance of the tradition forged decades earlier by writers like Georgia Douglas Johnson but also the oral tradition rooted in African American culture and history. Artists like Kwelismith, Essex Hemphill, and Sterling Brown each were talented scribes on the page and compelling onstage. The local spoken word scene reflected this duality.

The fact that the African American poets were rooted in performance, in bringing the art to life in the moment, as well as on the page, is a tradition that cannot be ignored. Professor Marcellus Blount called certain manifestations "the preacherly text."[12] Blount particularly identified Dunbar as rooting his writing in a Black vernacular tradition. In marrying the text to the performance, poets used all kinds of mediums: rhythm, rhyme, "a back beat," or "musical accompaniment."[13] This would never cease in the DC African American poetry community. Other poets, like Peggy Abena Disroe and Rabia Rayford, would also forge ahead in this line of expression into the 1990s using the oral tradition almost exclusively to present their personal literature as opposed to written words in collections of poetry. Considering all the history they each stood upon, it was natural.

All of this artistic work in the city and around the country also could be seen in the early work of poets Reuben Jackson, Brian Tate, Silvana Straw, and others. They were part of the national movement waiting to launch.

Brian Tate (not related to Garth Tate but the brother of the late cultural critic and poet Greg Tate)—a musician, events promoter, and spoken word poet—had multiple groups of artistic expression, including the Umbra Group and the Sabotage Poets. Jackson and Straw, who were part of the Sabotage Poets, and other Tate incarnations, performed regularly in Tate's collectives and on their own. Straw, who is not African American (Straw is Italian American from the DC suburbs originally), was a regular at all kinds of venues regardless of the racial makeup of the poets and audience.

The arts venue DC Space was a favored outlet for arts performers, including Jackson, Tate, and Straw. Jackson was beginning to read more as was Tate, and "space" was the "place" back then as local poets who remember still will say. Tate and Straw met as students at American University and reflected the growing diversity of the spoken word scene in the city thirty years after the end of legalized segregation in DC.

The 1980s were also when the poet May Miller (Sullivan) received even more love and attention from her city. Of the Black poets of very long ago, the original giants, Sterling Brown, William Waring Cuney, Georgia Douglas Johnson, and Jean Toomer, Miller (no relation to Ethelbert Miller) held the baton to the end to deliver to the next generation.

Miller, described by poet Ahmos Zu-Bolton as a "poet of craft and traditional images,"[14] is the city's direct link back to the days when Paul Laurence Dunbar is part of the city's culture. For Zu-Bolton at this time, while he feels that some of Miller's poetry does not measure up, much of it does meet his standards. Miller, in the late 1970s, according to Zu-Bolton, is "still growing, in search of a language not powered by the passions of our times, rather, spirited by the dreams of ages."[15]

Critic Shantee Woodards described the period for Miller as a "resurgence of celebrity."[16] Right before the 1980s, Miller read poetry at the inauguration of President Jimmy Carter in 1977, and her writing production accelerated. *The Washington Post* published a feature on Miller by local writer Patricia Gaines-Carter. It was "May Miller's turn," according to Carter. Miller was eighty-seven at the time and for seventy years had been writing, teaching, reading, and publishing in the city where she had been born. May Miller, according to Gaines-Carter, is a "link across age, time, and race" and "a willing bridge for any reader or listener willing to cross."[17] Marita Golden referred to Miller at the time as a symbol of "endurance and resilience."[18] Her poems kept appearing too.

In 1983 there was the collection *The Ransomed Wait* published by Lotus Press. Beth Brown, in reviewing *The Ransomed Wait*, described Miller's language as "ponderous and studied."[19] In 1989 Lotus Press also published her *Collected Poems*. Miller had witnessed it all in the city: the politics, the cultural changes, desegregation, the rise of Black poetry in the city.

All through this time, Miller maintained her image and her voice as a Black woman writer and citizen who, most of all, devoted her art to humanity. As Zu-Bolton also wrote of the Black woman poet he admired perhaps more than any other, Miller was about "the journey" in her poetry and not necessarily "the discovery."[20]

The Agitators

May Miller and Sterling A. Brown, DC local scribes, passed their legacy on to Kenneth Carroll, more than any other literary figure. Carroll, born and bred in the city, was a recipient of their baton, even though he was not from the Black literati or the striver class of African Americans in the city like Brown and Miller. Carroll did not attend Dunbar High School or Howard University either. Perhaps, it is evidence of great progress that Carroll, from a working-class family, was reading Brown, Miller, and Dunbar as he came up in the world.

Where the poets, artists, and people of Brown's time were concerned with basic rights, Carroll and many of the emerging poets in the city were more focused on the bigger picture: economic justice, human rights, and the entire African diaspora if necessary. Self-determination for African Americans in these United States was the goal for Carroll's generation of poets.

Some of these artistic values emerged in the 1960s but not to the extent that they would emerge in the post-civil-rights protest period. Kenneth Carroll and many of the poets of his era in the city had witnessed the success of the civil rights period, and now they wanted to finish the job of total freedom and equality for African Americans. When Ronald Reagan was elected president in 1980, it was an insult and yet another reason for activists to raise their voices more poignantly and louder.

"A national progressive commitment to civil rights stopped in 1980," Professor Alphine W. Jefferson wrote in the journal *The Black Scholar* in 1986.[21] The goal of the Reagan administration, among many, was to "roll back the hard won, though limited rights" obtained by the nation's most oppressed minority group (African Americans). Jefferson referred to the time as a time of "indifferent attitudes."[22]

Carroll's generation of poets in DC were well prepared for the political and artistic struggles to come. The Black Arts Movement in the 1960s prepared the emerging Black writers of the 1970s who, in turn, set the stage for the poets and writers who would emerge into the 1980s and beyond. Toni Morrison and Alice Walker both emerged in the 1970s and into the 1980s, and these were the kinds of writers Carroll and his colleagues in the city were reading and observing.

I saw Carroll read for the first time in the city at Market Gallery in Northeast Washington in 1988. It was a popular spot for poets and artists in the city. I came to see Carroll perform that day for the same reason that Carroll had come to my reading at MLK Jr. Library: the love of poetry and the hope to connect with other Black poets. It was a reading that would forever change my view of the possibilities of poetry. Carroll was a humanitarian as well, but like Sterling Brown he did not mince words in his poetry. Also like Brown, Carroll did not mind burning bridges on principle.

Carroll grew up in a tight-knit African American family in public housing. He would graduate from McKinley Technology High School and would eventually take classes at the University of the District of Columbia (UDC). He had begun writing by the fourth grade and would never stop. He was a confident public speaker and performer. He seemed to not fret when onstage and loved the banter of performance spaces. He also loved people, especially young people, and no matter what, it always seemed as if he would be doing something to help young people see the way forward. Carroll's self-education as a poet and writer was also his greatest strength. That and his diligent reading habits.

"I spent many days reading my parent's collection at home and the poetry section at Woodridge Library," he wrote many years ago in a curated exhibit at the Charles Sumner School Museum and Archives. By the time Carroll entered McKinley Tech High School, reading and music were his dual loves, and his poetry and writing reflected this influence.[23]

Carroll studied all kinds of writers as he developed his own writing style. He borrowed bits and pieces from as many as he could. It was his gumbo and his experience of growing up in DC during its intense "Chocolate City" period. He was full of pride and love for Black people, especially the ordinary Black person. The mothers, the fathers, the children. The beauticians at hair salons. The young and old men cutting hair at barbershops. The neighborhoods where Black people struggled forward successfully and unsuccessfully. His art reflected a certain independence and fearlessness.

When I finally saw him read his poetry not long after my reading in Ethelbert Miller's Ascension Series, he did not disappoint. He also had a twist. He performed his poetry with a saxophone player, Warrior Richardson. This impressed me even more. This was the oral tradition that had become more and more important to poetry in the modern era. But Carroll didn't hesitate to learn from those who came before him like Gil Scott-Heron, who had turned music and poetry into its own type of art. I knew I wasn't ready to try such a move, but Carroll looked quite easy in the space.

Carroll and Richardson, in fact, were somewhat in demand around the city in certain circles. It was a soft ode to what other poets had already done or were doing. Carroll and Richardson's group was called By Any Means Necessary, and they even briefly produced an animated graphic print magazine full of Carroll's poetry and Richardson's drawings. It was another level altogether artistically. The first and only issue of *Omowale* appeared in January 1989.

But Carroll's penchant for going his own way and fashioning his work with a built-in cultural and political thrust had only just begun. He would soon publish several successful chapbooks and would become a new engine for Black poetry in the city. He was, in a sense, an institution within himself and began to be able to network and reach beyond the African American poetry community in the same way Ethelbert Miller had been able to do for so many years.

Some of his chapbooks include *Never Piss Off a Poet, Anti-War Poems,* and *Something for My Sisters.* He also became a clearinghouse for opportunities for poets in Washington, DC, for readings, fellowships, grants, and chances to publish in journals and anthologies. He was always one step ahead and always getting to know the players on the DC poetry scene.

He was a member of Darrell Stover's The Spoken Word (he is still an official member, though the group doesn't perform much anymore), with the occasional performance, but back then he had his own goals as well—publish and take the word to the masses. In the late 1980s and early 1990s, he became president of the African American Writers Guild and really began to make his mark by linking writers together through networking and public events. Black poets came to him to connect just as they still sought out Ethelbert Miller up at Howard University. Carroll also wrote fiction, plays, and essays and was not afraid to involve himself in the organizational struggles to take art to the less fortunate.

He was politically involved as well, and that was where we also had a meeting of the minds. In addition to his literary disputes and working with young people and poets, Carroll supported local resistance to apartheid in South Africa and racism in general. I was interested in these issues. I was sure I had found someone I could learn from when I met Carroll. Even though we had different socioeconomic backgrounds, we were both from Washington, DC, and read many of the same books. He also had leadership qualities and a lifestyle that exuded a level of respect for ordinary people.

One of the most interesting outings with Kenneth Carroll was when the poet Amiri Baraka came to town to read his poetry at Georgetown University. Carroll referred to Amiri Baraka, as "Baraka" like he knew him personally. Baraka was a key figure in Black poetry before, during, and after the founding of the Black Arts poetry school. The reading was a scheduled literary tour by the Nicaraguan poet Ernesto Cardenal.

Cardenal was also a Catholic priest who was involved in the historic liberation movements in his home country.[24] However, because US relations with Nicaragua were so strained, Cardenal could not obtain a visa to gain entry to the United States. Baraka appeared alone at Georgetown University and read his own and Cardenal's work. Baraka spent half of his reading trashing the US government for their decision to deny Cardenal's visa request.

I learned much that night about protest and the role of the poet in a society. Baraka was the human embodiment of this ideal. And yet, as I would learn, so was Kenneth Carroll. It again fit neatly into the narrative where the Black Arts poets and artists passed their ideals down to Black poets to come like Carroll and many others across the country.

Poet Jennifer E. Smith (1961–2012) also emerged at this time, and she and Carroll soon coordinated readings and poetry activities in their own spaces. It only made sense that they would connect, as their politics and commitment to the art was unwavering. While the Black poets in DC were very cohesive, they also had their circles within the circle. Jennifer Smith was her own circle.

Smith was born and raised in Washington, DC, and graduated from Theodore Roosevelt High School. She also graduated from the UDC and became the poetry coordinator for the college's poetry reading series. The poetry gatherings she organized in various parts of the city provided a safe space for many African American poets. Kenneth Carroll, Michelle Bond, Darryl Holmes, Izora Irby, and Edwin Drew are some of the poets who read at Smith's readings. Bond and Irby were DC poets constantly on the scene in the early 1990s along with Smith. Bond found her way to the city's scene at the UDC, where Smith regularly organized events.

In the early 1990s Jennifer founded and published a local bimonthly newspaper—the *Black Arts Bulletin*—featuring Chocolate City's most talented writers, poets, and artists and spotlighting local cultural happenings. She was a staple in the DC poetry scene, where she would turn her art into the spoken word and political action. A born writer and profound thinker, Smith deeply respected her (our) ancestors, inspiring her to continue channeling her emotions and powerful feelings. A fearless advocate for marginalized Black populations in DC and beyond—prisoners, seniors, and young adults—she navigated systems and red tape on their behalf, often challenging the norm.[25]

Smith's poetry and short stories appeared in many publications, including *Still Lifting, Still Climbing: African American Women's Contemporary Activism, Obsidian II, African American Review, The Griot, Port Of Harlem, Nommo, Catalyst, Black American Literature Forum, Appalachian Heritage, ColorLines, Black Renaissance / Renaissance Noire,* and *Essence.* Jennifer received several awards for her writing, including a prestigious Ragdale Foundation Residency. Some of her most notable published anthologies of poetry and writings include *DC Jazz & Blues* and *Sistahwords: Poetry and Prose.*[26]

It appears that as far back as 1985, Smith's writings were regularly published in many of the leading literary journals still active today. The August 1985 issue of *Black American Literature Forum* (now *African American Review*) published Smith's poem "Preceding Our Arrival." In addition to Smith, many of Black America's leading younger poets of those days were also included in that issue—Wanda Coleman, Opal P. Moore, Herbert Woodward Martin, Lenard Moore, and Essex Hemphill.[27]

But if one thing also distinguished Jennifer Smith from some other poets during this period, it was her willingness to be directly engaged politically, which had become a task poets in DC had been willing to embrace back to the 1960s. She not only wrote about the issues but took her ideas to the state and challenged what they were doing. In Philadelphia, Smith directly confronted the mayor, Wilson Goode, over the 1985 bombing of African Americans of the MOVE organization.

Smith wrote a poem about the experience of confronting Mayor Wilson Goode after the annual Celebration of Black Writing Conference one year. Many of us attended the conference and witnessed Smith's act of dissent. Smith committed her protest to poetry later:

For All the "They Think They Conscious" Writers Who Applauded Wilson Goode at a Conference Celebrating Black Writing

is this aaanotha MOVE poem?
anotha poem to be read at readings/
publication parties to be marketed
to brothers/sisters who think
cultural aesthetic the correct/only
response to white oppression?

is this aaanotha MOVE poem
for anotha book of poetry/essays/
documentaries to be sold for profit?

yes, there is money to be made off
the torching of them dreadhead
back to nature niggers over
there on osage avenue
by bourgeoise negroes pim
ping the continent pim
ping the cause

ask any bookseller
ask any philly tourguide

or is this a poem to cause you to squirm
in yo seat/strip you naked/shame you/
skin you to the bone/gut your spirit/
make you slam yo soul up against the wall
ask yourself where the hell you were
on May 13, 1985 when 14 black
men women children were eaten by flame
in a house C-4 bombed by the state police?

or is this a poem written to say
"oh, isn't it a shame"
aaanotha poem demanding
    no retribution
    no justice for
birdie & ramona africa?

no, this ain't just aaanotha MOVE poem
to be politely digested with reception/
handshakes/autographs to follow

no, this poem is free is a free MOVE poem
whether you ask for it or not.[28]
—*Jennifer E. Smith*

Smith's poem is inspired by the bombing that occurred on May 13, 1985. With the approval of Mayor Wilson Goode, the police dropped "a C-4 bomb on the home of the MOVE organization, killing eleven people—including five children—and wiping out 61 homes in two city blocks." John Africa, leader of the MOVE organization, was killed.[29] The organization was focused mostly on political and social activism related to racism and environmental causes.

Smith, before she died in 2012, also became a vocal advocate for women and individuals who were incarcerated, and she sought to assist organizations that were trying to stop gun violence in the city. She was especially vocal and aggressive in addressing the issue of conditions in the incarceration of individuals in Supermax prisons in the state of Maryland. Kenneth Carroll published a poem called "Supermax" in 1997 dedicated to the poet Jennifer E. Smith.[30]

14
A Capital of Black Poetry

In a long feature on the Washington, DC, poetry scene written by Ta-Nehisi Coates for the *Washington City Paper* in 1996, Coates explored the details of the rising tide of poets and spoken word artists who gathered somewhere to express themselves just about every day and night. While Coates's article resulted in a debate among African American poets regarding the quality of the expression, it remains a healthy exchange. If anything, it made the poets and artists all the better and dedicated, at least those poets who took their lives and work as artists very seriously. "I wouldn't wanna be reading every week," I said back then. "I wanna be writing every week . . . my goal is to get published . . . I didn't get in it for some spoken word."[1]

Kenneth Carroll was also quoted in Coates's article. Carroll concluded that some of the work heard in the spoken word venues had "little to do with actual literature." He added that when he became a poet, he read at open mics to strengthen his work. According to Carroll, poets wanted "to be published somewhere." Once the goal shifted to just being heard, the quality of the work changed. Carroll is also famous for describing poetry slams as the "most unliterary of literary events." I laughed when I read that because it was a response with a purpose.

I totally understood what Carroll was saying, which is why I laughed. If you compare Carroll's description to the literary critic Harold Bloom's description of "slam poetry" as "the death of art,"[2] Carroll's description is kinder and worth a chuckle or two. But anyone even loosely knowledgeable about Slam poetry will understand Carroll's statement. Bloom not so much.

All the poetry at Slam events was not bad poetry. In fact, much of it was very good, and some of the leading Slam poets (spoken word poets), like Jeffrey McDaniel, Patricia Smith, and Joel Dias-Porter, are very good poets today and are well respected. They were good poets back then. McDaniel and Smith have now enjoyed long careers as poets and performance artists, but they are academics who have taught at some of the best creative writing programs in the country. I did get into poetry to be published and to produce art, but I also grew into the spoken word part of it as well. I find them equally important in the modern era.

Carroll's point is really that Slam events themselves and spoken word events were and are a response to more formal poetry or academic poetry, which was somewhat of a restricted area for most poets writing. American poetry was institutionalized and removed from the people and the various communities across the country, and perhaps it had lost its historical and cultural importance. People had come to believe that the only good poets had to be dead for a few centuries. Slam poetry and spoken word events challenged that notion.

Writer Carly (Frankie) Laird's 2018 article "A Poetry of Embodiment: Queering the Canon With Slam"[3] expands upon that original analysis. According to Laird, "poets of the academy continue to hold their works on a pedestal that alienates the everyday individual and, as a result, poetry no longer tells their stories." She added that "an entire facet of human existence is lost because the stories of those living on the margins are continually ignored and silenced."[4] This was the sentiment at the time Slam events and spoken word poetry began to take off. There was the prevalent feeling that the academy had turned its back on the readers that led to Slam poetry and the expansion of poetry into more spoken word.

In the 1990s in Washington, DC, the spoken word scene was real and authentic. It was powerful and cultural, often bringing the city's poets together. Reading spaces like 8Rock, 15 Minutes Club, the Black Cat, and It's Your Mug, as well as IOTA Poetry Cafe in Virginia, and all the others just served as a testing ground for their voices. Black poets always found themselves welcome at these events to share their art, even if most of the city's academic spaces rarely provided opportunities.

But then, there were the Black poetry anthologies and regular publications that were also highly cherished and began to proliferate in the United States. As much as spoken word outlets multiplied, opportunities to get published by big publishers and small presses also increased. This relationship of the page and the stage was quite important for African American poets in DC, considering opportunities to publish a full volume of one's own work remained weak in the '90s.

By the 1990s Ethelbert Miller had been nurturing Black poets for years in the city. He steered Black poets to journals like *Black American Literature Forum*, *Obsidian II*, and *Callaloo*, for publishing credits. And in 1994 he edited a major anthology for Black poets, *In Search of Color Everywhere: A Collection of African American Poetry*. For local African American poets, inclusion in the anthology with major Black writers stretching back centuries and decades was a big deal. The anthology is still popular today and was released in the heyday of the beginning of the Slam poetry scene.

"African American poetry is a vehicle, a bridge, a device by which history and values are conveyed from one generation to the next," Miller wrote in the dust jacket for the book. He called his project a "poetic chronicle of the African American experience and the making of America."[5]

Sterling Brown, William Waring Cuney, Jean Toomer, Georgia Douglas Johnson, May Miller—poets associated with the original development of African American poetry in DC—are all included in *In Search of Color Everywhere*. Ahmos Zu-Bolton,

Jonetta Barras, Calvin Forbes, Thulani Davis, Garth Tate, A. B. Spellman, Larry Neal, Michelle Parkerson, Adesanya Alakoye, Peter J. Harris, and Gil Scott-Heron also have poems in the book.

While many of these poets were not born and raised in the city, all of them lived and wrote in the city at some point and most of them contributed to the growth of Black poetry locally. *In Search of Color Everywhere* ultimately gave new and up-and-coming Black DC writers an audience in 1994. Kenneth Carroll, Jacquie Jones, Reuben Jackson, Elizabeth Alexander, and Natasha Tarpley all have poetry accepted by Miller into an anthology of great importance at the time.

Lorenzo Thomas, the poet and scholar, wrote of the book that Miller has sought to convey as a "community . . . maintained by poetry—whether transmitted orally, in classrooms, or books." The publication is "editorial focus-indebted . . . to some of the concepts of Sterling A. Brown, and perhaps to a nostalgic view of what functions as the center of African American life."[6] Miller's *In Search of Color Everywhere* was awarded the PEN Oakland Josephine Miles Award in 1994.

Elizabeth Alexander is responsible for the title of Miller's anthology. It was, for Alexander—at the beginning of what has been a remarkable career as a poet, writer, scholar, professor, and philanthropist—an astute contribution. Alexander, born in New York City, was raised in Washington, DC. She has published multiple volumes of poetry and nonfiction and served as a professor of African American studies at Yale University. She now heads the Mellon Foundation.

The same year *In Search of Color Everywhere* was published, Little, Brown and Company published *Every Shut Eye Ain't Asleep: An Anthology of Poetry by African Americans Since 1945*. Michael S. Harper, the critically acclaimed poet, and Anthony Walton, the writer-poet, edited the book. *Every Good Shut Eye Ain't Asleep*'s focus on post–World War II African American poets was a snapshot of Black poetry in America at a certain point in time. It did include Black poets from Washington, DC, but not too many. Reuben Jackson, Elizabeth Alexander, and Dolores Kendrick are the only three poets included with direct connections to the city, though others spent time in the city teaching. In any event, African American critic and literature professor Rudolph P. Byrd declared that the book will be "an anthology of enduring significance and relevance."[7]

Byrd also notes that the publication of the anthology exposes the exclusionary nature of American poetry at the end of the twentieth century. Anthologies edited by Euro-American poets (Donald Hall and Mark Strand) at the same time barely include any of the thirty-five poets in *Every Good Shut Eye*, according to Byrd. Byrd describes this as "the most malign and insulting influence upon African American poets."[8] To their credit, Walton and Harper dedicate the book to Sterling A. Brown, the DC literary and cultural giant and champion of African American life.

But the anthology in the early 1990s that spoke strongest to the state of African American poetry in Washington is Alan Spears's 1993 anthology, *Fast Talk, Full Volume: An*

Anthology of Contemporary African American Poetry. In a sense, Spears's anthology is one of the most chance-taking anthologies published in the 1990s. It is the book that best represents where African American poetry was heading in the early 1990s, especially so in the city of Washington, DC. It is notable that Gut Punch Press, a small independent publisher out of the DC area, published the book. Derrick Hsu ran Gut Punch Press for years and while the press did not publish many books regularly, when it did publish, the books were very notable.

Spears, an African American and a poet on the Washington DC, poetry scene, read on Ascension #107, Ethelbert Miller's continuing venue for poets to find their voice or expand it. He read that day (August 15, 1992) with Meri Nana-Ama Danquah.[9] Danquah, who was writing poetry in those days, would branch out in the years that followed into memoirs, nonfiction, and other genres. Her memoir *Willow Weep For Me* was one of the first to offer a personal story and insight into depression in the African American community. Spears included Danquah in *Fast Talk, Full Volume.*

Spears, when he was completing the anthology, was thinking about the book's place in literary history. In a letter to Ethelbert Miller in 1991, he asks Miller for "a more detailed picture of where *Fast Talk, Full Volume* fits into the continuum of Black artistic expression." Spears must have known he was onto something with the book. The book likely should have been published by a major American publisher, considering it sought to fuse the various strains of expression sweeping America at the time. The anthology includes spoken word artists, performers, poets dedicated to hip-hop, and traditional poets but also post–Black Arts Movement scribes who wanted to keep the spirit of that era alive and well.

"Many of us are newcomers," Spears wrote in the foreword to the anthology. "So be prepared to experience a breadth of style, technique, execution, and even a few imperfections as we strive towards establishing our voices."[10] The book is that exactly. Spears's decision to publish local poets en masse and some from outside makes it one of the most unique anthologies ever.

Toni Blackman, hip-hop artist and poet, is included in the anthology, as are Kenneth Carroll, Darrell Stover, Reuben Jackson, Kim Taylor, Natasha Tarpley, and Yao Hoke Glover. But then there are performance poets like Michelle Parkerson, Kweli--smith, and Rabia Rayford. Spears also anchors the book with other powerful women voices—Jennifer E. Smith, Michelle Clinton, Meri Nana-Ama Danquah, and Wanda Coleman. It was a mixture of Washington, DC, area poets and West Coast poets. Spears claims in the book's introduction that he has no agenda or purpose and writes that the book proves Black poetry is not monolithic.

The book received some good reviews, but there was at least one review that exposes some of the deeply entrenched racism and western bias that did exist at the time toward Black poetry. Because *Fast Talk, Full Volume* took chances to present poetry of the moment with a focus on performance artists and the poetry being presented in open mics and Slam events, it got criticized with terrible specificity for its adherence to the modern.

Poet Fred Chappelle had some praise for Spears's anthology, but mostly he shortchanges it, comparing it to "blather from AM radio." According to Chappelle, "almost all of the poems are written at the top of the voice."[11]

But this is the strength of the book and, most important, the point of the book. It was not going to follow the path of most anthologies. The country had entered a moment, a spoken word moment. Spears was a poet on the DC spoken word scene at the time, and he understood what was happening nationally and locally regarding poetry.

African American poetry likewise was taking on new influences and was loud and boisterous, proud, and not really concerned with the stiffness of western forms or academic allegiance. Black poetry wanted to break free in the anthology and it did, and there is no ideological construct either like during BAM.

The book's clever title and unique alignment resulted in several spirited readings for the book. Irina's Cafe in Baltimore hosted a reading for the book with Spears, Kenneth Carroll, me, and Melvin Lewis participating in the reading. Olsson's Books downtown in Washington also hosted a reading for the anthology, where Michelle Parkerson read along with Spears and a few others.

The appearance of multiple anthologies by African American poets in such a short space of time back in the 1990s was evidence that Black poetry was very much alive and evolving. Other anthologies that are published just in the space of the early 1990s are *Testimony: Young African-Americans on Self-Discovery and Black Identity* and *In the Tradition: An Anthology of Young Black Writers.*[12] These books, while more narrowly focused, also feature DC Black poets.

In the Tradition features two remarkable poets both from Washington, DC—Thomas Sayers Ellis and Elizabeth Alexander. Trasi Johnson, born in Washington, DC, and Kimberly Ann Collins, who would come to live and work there years later, also are featured in the anthology. Esther Iverem, a journalist and graduate of Columbia, is also published in *In the Tradition*. Iverem would settle into the city as a journalist, radio host, and poet.

Testimony, edited by poet and children's book writer, Natasha Tarpley, is likewise an anthology of young writers. It does feature some notable African American writers associated with DC when it is released, including Yona Harvey, Jelani Cobb, and Ta-Nehisi Coates.

In 1995 another call for submissions of poetry arrived in the city from Keith Gilyard, poet, scholar, and professor of English at Penn State University (Gilyard was working at Syracuse University at the time). Gilyard's anthology, published in 1997, is called *Spirit and Flame: An Anthology of Contemporary African American Poetry*. Gilyard, throughout his career, straddled the worlds of poet, scholar, critic, and educator, producing books, articles, and research on a wide array of topics all-encompassing of some aspect of human literacy and writing. It was quite amazing that he was able to reach out to communities of Black poets outside of academia and find poets whose work he could present. Gilyard's quite unique anthology includes Kenneth Carroll,

Ethelbert Miller, and two other exceptional poets who were writing and working the DC poetry scene at the time—Valerie Jean and A. Van Jordan.

In 1996 Clarence Major, the poet, painter, novelist, and writer, edited the anthology *The Garden Thrives: Twentieth Century African American Poetry* (Harpers Perennial, 1996). Several DC Black poets are included. Reuben Jackson, E., Sterling A. Brown, Dolores Kendrick, Elizabeth Alexander, Thomas Sayers Ellis, and Essex Hemphill all have poetry included in the book. The consistent publication of books demonstrated how active poetry overall had become by the mid-1990s nationally and in the city. Spoken word / Slam poetry and hip-hop had energized poetry. This could not be denied.

Dr. Howard Ramsby II, distinguished research professor at Southern Illinois University, contrasts this increase in activity with the prior ten years, which he contends lacked a lot of publishing opportunities for African American writers. This would also apply to Black poets in Washington. The poetry scene I entered in the late 1980s was different from the poetry scene of the 1990s. There were just more chances to be published in the early to late 1990s. Ramsby notes that there are a few reasons for lack of poetry publishing opportunities from approximately 1977 to 1987.[13]

One theory with some credibility is in April 1976, *Black World / Negro Digest* magazine ceased publication. *Black World / Negro Digest* had been a special publication for Black artists and readers since 1942 in several different germinations. It was published by John H. Johnson's Johnson Publishing, the same company that published *Ebony* and *Jet. Negro Digest / Black World* was the more intellectual arm of Johnson's publishing catalog.

The magazine featured poetry, fiction, interviews, music, art, dance, and Black culture in all its glory. There were political essays and criticism as well as of books and art. Many of the Black poets from DC wrote for *Black World / Negro Digest,* including Sterling Brown and May Miller. The claim that African American publishing declined after the publication ended in 1976 is credible. The magazine was an important means of communication in the Black community of America and especially the intellectual community.

Novelist Toni Morrison, once an editor at Random House, famously declared in 1981 at Columbia University that "there will be no renaissance of third world literature."[14] The "established publishers," according to Morrison, would not publish much of it because the poetry, fiction, and nonfiction, "don't earn out," meaning "they are not profitable."[15] Morrison was not talking about just Black literature but all literature. Black writers naturally were a bigger casualty of this downturn. This is also consistent with Ramsby's theory.

Another reason for the decline could be the Reagan administration and how arts funding changed during this period. It did. Arts funding was already poor prior to Reagan's arrival in 1981; Reagan simply pushed back against the government-funded arts even more.[16] Initially, Reagan's proposed cuts were massive, as high as 50 percent in his first budget proposal.[17] While this is not absolute proof of reasons or "a" reason, there is little doubt that publications featuring African American poets seemed to decline during the 1980s, only to gain their momentum again in the 1990s.

Radios and Cameras

Maryland Poet Laureate emeritus Grace Cavalieri has provided Washington, DC, with almost fifty years of recorded poetry via radio and digitized recordings of radio programs at the Library of Congress. Cavalieri, Italian American but the daughter of a Jewish father from Italy (Angelo) and Italian mother (Annette), has recorded more than 2,000 of these programs over that time,[18] and a significant number of the poets are Black poets from Washington or living and writing in the city.

Her *The Poet and the Poem* radio program on WPFW-FM 89.3 was a welcome surprise on the DC metropolitan airwaves when it began. Cavalieri did interviews with poets. Poets would read poetry and then answer her questions. Cavalieri is one of the original founders of WPFW-FM, a Pacifica Foundation radio station. *The Poet and the Poem* was on WPFW for twenty years—1977–97—with Cavalieri as the host. Even though the program stopped airing on live radio, Cavalieri has continued to record poets in the same format through the Library of Congress.

Both May Miller and Sterling Brown were recorded by Miller for *The Poet and the Poem*, as was a legion of other poets who lived and worked in the city.[19] Cavalieri's program began the same way with each poet. Miles Davis's music would play in the background, and then Cavalieri's voice would ease in and introduce the poet she had invited into her space.

> This is *The Poet and the Poem*, and I am Grace Cavalieri.

This would be followed by the name of her guest, who would always be invited to read a poem.

The WHUR-FM 96.3 midnight radio program on poetry called *Spoken Word at Joe's Place* also captured poetry in America as it was happening with living, breathing poets. But considering that *Joe's Place* happened at WHUR radio on the campus of Howard University, it is no accident that Black poets were the thrust of the show's weekly magic.

Joe's Place was the brainchild of two Washington, DC, media titans—Kimberly Washington and Joe Gorham. Gorham, a longtime radio personality in the DC area and elsewhere, and Washington, his producer for the show, provided a unique space for Black poets at a unique time that was almost a community space in the air. It was not unusual for poets who were not the featured guest for the program to show up at the radio station and sit in and watch the featured poet be interviewed by Joe Gorham.

This is because while the poets and their poetry were the focus of the show, the star on some level was Gorham.

Gorham, like many of the poets he interviewed, was born and raised in Washington, DC, in 1952. He graduated from Theodore Roosevelt High School. He also graduated from the University of the District of Columbia. By 1979 he was working at WHUR radio as a technician but was soon on the air hosting all kinds of programs. He would host WHUR's most famous program ever, Melvin Lindsey's *The Quiet Storm*, as the weekend host. The *Quiet Storm* was five hours of slow, relaxing love music in the evening beginning at 7:00 p.m. and lasting until midnight. Lindsey, the show's host, is a legend in the city and on national radio. His *Quiet Storm* has spread across the country since then, with Black radio stations all over adopting the format.[20]

Gorham, however, settled into the midnight hour on WHUR. Usually, Gorham would feature an artist at midnight and play their music into the night. He might feature the funk band Zapp or Roy Ayers, the jazz funk band leader and vibraphonist, as the focus of the music. Eventually, he began doing *Spoken Word at Joe's Place.* Washington,[21] a long supporter of poetry and art in the city and a radio person as well, served as a producer. WHUR noted that Gorham's *Joe's Place* was an attempt by the station to "support the arts community."

Poets from across the country appeared on *Spoken Word at Joe's Place*, but the local poets, especially African American poets, found the show a unique safe space for their poetic expression.

"Joe was the epitome of a radio guy," radio promoter Darryll Brooks said when Gorham died in 2022. "He was innovative and did things that were new and creative like developing and hosting a spoken word program. He was committed to helping local artists gain greater notoriety."[22] Poet and literature professor Randall Horton recalled being on the show with Howard University poet and creative writing professor Tony Medina.

"We would go to talk about poems, read our poems, discuss books . . . that was a cool experience, man. I don't know if I've seen another model like that in the United States, I'm sure there is. Or was. But that one right there seemed to be special," Horton said.[23]

Every significant and well-known, national, or just local Black poet or spoken word artist was given the microphone by Joe Gorham at some point. And the show almost always the same. Joe's vibrantly cool voice, with a soulful accompaniment, would announce to the city his work of art that presented art:

> The words we speak, convey a wide array or range of thought, opinion, emotion, and observation we all deal with on a day to day basis, and sometimes these words are written as a way to purge to paper, poetic thoughts and descriptions for humanity to speak on for generations to come . . . So this morning by way of mouth, we give you the poets who give these writings breath and flight . . . Welcome to Joe's Place.[24]

That was how the moment began on *Joe's Place*. It was a strong and important institution in the city, as the spoken word scene locally and the one across the country rose in stature.[25]

Poetry among African American poets and artists also found a partnership with film in the 1990s. Eugene Wooden, a filmmaker born and raised in Harrisburg, Pennsylvania, created one of the more enduring marriages between poetry and moving pictures in his 1995 award-winning film *Voices Against Violence*, which captured the moment.

The film is right out of the city's social fabric. As the city's spoken word scene grew stronger, Washington and its African American communities found themselves engulfed in the deluge of random violence. The violence began about the same time that crack cocaine showed up on the streets. Substance abuse and narcotics trafficking have always been a part of twentieth-century Washington, DC, but the late 1980s and 1990s had unprecedented activity. It was, by far, the most violent period in the city's history. The number of homicides was astonishing from year to year. In 1988 the city recorded 372 homicides. The following year, 1989, that total was matched on October 30, 1989. For the year, there were 438 homicides.[26] In January 1990, the next year, there were fifty-two homicides during that one month.[27] Eventually, the city became the most violent per capita in the country and was declared the "Murder Capital" two years in a row.

Considering most of the killings occurred in African American communities, Black poets wrote about the deaths. Wooden, who worked at PBS at the time, joined the two mediums: the spoken word and film (moving pictures).

"I just gave those who had no access to the camera a chance to speak," Wooden said.[28]

Wooden's film created quite a buzz in the city's cinematic arts circles and among poets, especially African American poets. The *Washington Post* described the film as one "in which emotional repercussions of inner city violence are explored through song and poetry."[29] The film was made gradually and in segments.

Wooden met Kenneth Carroll, the poet at the 8Rock Cultural Arts Center in Anacostia, and soon the idea for a full documentary on the subject was hatched. Joel Dias-Porter not only wrote poetry for the film and appeared in it but also helped with the creation of the film. He helped Wooden coordinate pieces for the shoots. Kenneth Carroll's poetry and voice can be heard all throughout the film, especially in one of the vignettes called "Lil Sonny," a poem about the death of a young African American boy through gun violence. "Lil Sonny" received a Rosebud Award in 1994.[30]

The film is a series of vignettes based around the poetry, spoken word, vocals, and the stark, black-and-white reality of a city and its African American communities reeling from violence. Dias-Porter recites his poem "Letter Found in a Purse on the Subway" in the film. Other poets in the film include Toni Blackman, the hip-hop MC, poet, and cultural ambassador. Ayanna Gregory, the singer and daughter of the late

Dick Gregory, sings in the film. Wooden also included one of my poems, "black on black homicide," in the film.

There are hip-hop/rap segments where local rap duo Poor Excuses have their say about the violence along with hip-hop artist Sub-Z (Terence Nicholson).[31] These are the voices of the hip-hop generation that bring clarity and authenticity to the production. *Voices* would win the Rosebud Award in 1995 and be shown at Filmfest DC. Michelle Parkerson's documentary about the African American revolutionary lesbian poet Audre Lorde, *A Litany of Survival*, was screened at the same festival that year. It seemed appropriate for film and poetry in the city to match up in this way.

Then there was the film *Slam*, the artistic vision of Marc Levin and starring New York poet Saul Williams. *Slam*'s film crew and creative impulse arrived in the city in the heyday of the nation's spoken word / Slam movement. Washington, DC, a city of poets, and especially Black poets, was ready and mostly because that is what the city was each day and night back then—a place where poetry was shared and respected, and was just part of the social culture.

In DC, where the film was shot at least in part, the African American poetry community had a close and personal view of the film. The star of the film, Saul Williams, was already a rising spoken word star in the world of American poetry. I met Saul in New York City at a Black Writers Conference at Medgar Evers College via Joel Dias-Porter. Our poetry collective 8Rock (I, Dias-Porter, Kenneth Carroll, and Judy Cohall) was performing along with a legion of other Black poets at Medgar Evers College for its annual Black Writers Conference. Saul stood out at the conference when he did his reading mostly because he was much different from most of the poets who read their work. When Saul came to Washington later to shoot the film, it was the same: You noticed him.

Many local Black poets wound up in the film by just the fact that the *Slam* crew came to the readings and filmed. Levin shot the film in a cinema verité style and admitted that the film didn't have a hard script structure. It kind of was like some of the poetry performances it was trying to capture—improvisational, impulsive in the moment.

Joel Dias-Porter (DJ Renegade) has a small role in the film and helped the crew scout locations where to shoot scenes. Imani Tolliver, a local poet from California who was studying at Howard University, held a birthday party reception at her house that became a scene in the film. Toni Asante Lightfoot, Brandon Johnson, Holly Bass, and Ta-Nehisi Coates also appear in the film. The city's jail (DC Jail) was a setting for scenes. The former mayor of the city, Marion Barry, the militant former chairman of the Student Nonviolent Coordinating Committee (SNCC), a man counseled and praised by poet Sterling A. Brown, had a part in the film as a judge. It was, in some ways, a triumph for the city's Black poetry scene and the city's forgotten and neglected Black communities. While that might seem like political speculation, it isn't. Levin, the film's director, is seeking to make a statement with the film.

Levin was in DC anyway and sometimes in DC Jail shooting a documentary called *Thug Life*. It is a film about the jailing of Black youth in Washington, DC. Levin describes the city as a "tale of two cities," one city is the federal city, the nation's capital, and the other is the African American city, the one where many young African American boys and men are in prison or on parole.[32]

Thug Life becomes Levin's entry point to access the city's main correctional facility and the path to tell the story of Ray Joshua (played by Saul Williams), a narcotics dealer who finds his poetic voice in prison. Levin admits *Slam* had no script, but that was the plan. Saul Williams, the lead in the film, was fine with it, as was costar Sonja Sohn. Though it was risky, that is why the film works. The film, which grabbed the attention of many African American poets in the city when it was made, won the Grand Jury Prize at Sundance in 1998. It also picked up the Caméra D'Or at the Cannes Film Festival in 1998.

The national success of *Slam* and the local success of Eugene Wooden's *Voices Against Violence* proved that the 1990s were a fertile period for poetry in America, orally but, most important, visually. Something was happening.

Bob Holman's documentary poetry project *The United States of Poetry* also was released in the 1990s, proving even more so, the endurance of the art in a different format. It was a well-funded major project for public consumption and built for public television. The project, as one might expect, did not include any Washington, DC, poets. It was a subtle slight, considering at the time the city had one of the best spoken word scenes in the nation and many well-known working poets, such as Kenneth Carroll, Silvana Straw, Jose Padua, Joel Dias-Porter, and Reuben Jackson.

The answer to Holman's snub of poets from DC, and especially Black poets at perhaps one of the richest moments for poetry in the city, was David Kehinde Chaytor's 2001 film *Rhythm, Rhyme & Life: Spoken Word and the Oral Tradition.*[33] Chaytor, a filmmaker, was living in Washington in the late 1990s and early 2000s when he discovered the rich spoken word scene in the city involving African American poets. Chaytor got to work.

Chaytor, originally from Sierra Leone, came across Black poetry while living in the DC area and immediately saw and heard the connections to Africa, especially the "Negritude" movement. Chaytor was an aspiring filmmaker, as he had already learned the craft at Northern Illinois University. His access to the Black poetry scene was perfect for him. Chaytor told journalist Natalie Hopkinson in a profile for his film for the *Washington Post* that he had been "looking for a topic to do a documentary."[34] To have access to the scene in Washington, DC, he said, was "just wonderful to me."

Chaytor's film, while not likely its intent, serves as a definitive statement on the cultural poetics that were prominent in the city at the time among African American poets. Chaytor's film includes comments and performance slips from local DC poets Joel Dias-Porter, Toni Blackman, and Kwame Alexander. Toni Asante Lightfoot, of It's Your Mug, is likewise in the documentary.

Chaytor does a very good of showing the historical ties behind the spoken word scene that arose among Black poets in the 1990s and West African traditions. As poets, Joel Dias-Porter notes in the film, this is where many African Americans trace their cultural lineage anyway. Dolores Kendrick, the poet laureate (named in 1999) of the District of Columbia when the documentary was filmed, called the "resurgence" of Black poets reading and writing in the city "enlightening."

Toni Blackman, at the time still connected strongly with the city, believed in respecting the entertainment components of the Black poetry scene. "It is important for us to allow art to function and to allow it to be part of our daily lives," Blackman said. Chaytor's camera captures all aspects of the scene. Chaytor talks to and films poet-performers (Toni Blackman, Sistah Joy Alford, Raquel Brown, Kwame Alexander, Denise Johnson, Eric Webb, Joy Jones) but also poets who host venues, such as Matthew Payne (The Movement) at Bar Nun and Raquel Brown of Mango's.[35]

The film takes you to local DC spoken word hot spots like Takoma Station, Bar Nun, and Sankofa Books and Films.[36] While not as well known as other spoken word films at the time, Chaytor's offering is a thread that connects time and culture, an underrated piece of reportage that documents Black poetry in Washington, DC.

15
Pockets

In DC–based journalist Natalie Hopkinson's cultural memoir of a culture, *Go-Go Live: The Musical Life and Death of a Chocolate City*, Hopkinson wrote that a city like Washington, DC, a "chocolate city," provided a " 'counterdiscourse,' an alternate view of everything from history to politics."[1] DC, in Hopkinson's take, is "America's original sin," the policy-driven and deeply rooted social construct that "began with slavery and lived on through segregation."[2]

The music and culture Hopkinson is referring to, created seemingly in a haste by the locals, namely, the musician and entertainer Chuck Brown, is called go-go. But go-go is not just the music and culture; it is a place, a moment, it happens in a blink, almost everywhere, and because it was created, poetry in the city from Black poets, and art, in general, were all the better. Washington poet Thomas Sayers Ellis single-handedly made this so and encouraged many other local poets to embrace their city and metro area and make them live forever like Storyville in New Orleans still lives today, even though it no longer exists. Ellis gave go-go music a spokesperson via verse, and others through various artistic disciplines have heeded the call.

Ellis graduated from the high school that bears poet Paul Laurence Dunbar's name, as did so many of DC's notable literary figures. By the time he was a young man, he was a musician, artist, and a regular patron of the go-go music and cultural scene in the city. His book *The Maverick Room*, a collection named for one of the most famous go-go venues in the early history of that music scene, is an ode to a time, place, and life. It is a tiny piece of "Chocolate City" and a larger piece of the city Ellis grew up in.

American University Literature Professor Keith D. Leonard posits that Ellis, by embracing go-go music as his poetic muse, has derived an "alternative literary-cultural historiography predicated on the principles of formal repetition, rigorously self-conscious attention to cultural form, conceptions of time as nonlinear, and a notion of blackness as dissident creativity."[3] Ellis, while seeking a certain freedom and uniqueness in his art, has done specifically what the artists of the Black Arts Movement did: he, as Leonard also noted, articulated "the cultural heritage and sometimes . . . political dissidence as the ground of aesthetic self-assertion."[4]

Go-go music's connection to poetry is intrinsic. It was created by Chuck Brown as far as anyone can tell, and the form's dominant characteristic besides the percussive funk is the ongoing oral sermon that engages the audience over the rhythms. Ellis, the poet, called this the "Baptist Beat" by way of one of his poems.

Brown's 1978 recording "Bustin' Loose," a party tune that seemingly goes on forever, is often called the moment the music was birthed. This is so, even though that famous song was already considered a big hit in the go-go clubs in the city by the time Brown released it on wax and the musical movement was official.

Ellis's poetry and aesthetics and that of other poets embrace the culture and are steeped in the meanings behind the politics and intelligence that gave birth to the music. His verse is the ethnography of the people who fought to make the music and to preserve it and, oftentimes, died making it:

> It [Washington, DC] was one of the best spots for youth to gather to hear Go-Go and, as I said, the first place I saw a person shot to death, in the same room, and that stayed with me. Post-Watergate, pre-Rapper's Delight, so the hearing, the falling, and the running-all became a part of the content and groove of what I would carry with me into my own aesthetic scaffolding. It also becomes a metaphor for what I think the energy, the tension, the struggle between local and federal Washington are. The nation's capital and all of its capital versus the District of Columbia and its local lack of capital. The District, Dee Cee, and its empty pockets.[5]

Ellis is also largely responsible for the Dark Room Collective, another important moment in African American literature in the Americas. The Dark Room Collective was formed in 1988 in Cambridge, Massachusetts. According to the now-familiar story, the death of James Baldwin in 1987 was the impetus for forming the group and the Dark Room Reading Series. Ellis and the poet-teacher Sharan Strange were the prime movers. The Dark Room Collective was a group of African American poets associated with Ivy League schools who sought community. They also wanted to pay tribute and homage to the Black writers who paved the way for them. They shared their work. They began reading around the country in 1990. Ethelbert Miller brought the collective to Washington, DC, in 1990 for Ascension Reading #101.[6]

8Rock

At the same time that the Dark Room Collective was finding its poetic wings, artists and community organizers had similar ideas in DC. One of those ideas, which has had a long-lasting cultural impact in the city, is called 8Rock.

According to lawyer and cultural activist Peter Clare, the brains behind the 8Rock Cultural Center in Southeast Washington, DC, in the early 1990s were poets Kenneth Carroll, Judy Cohall, Jacquie Jones, and himself.[7] Clare, a community development specialist and Black culture afficionado, thought about something like 8Rock when he and Judy Cohall organized some community cultural events right in the home they shared. The get-togethers, according to Clare, were in the same spirit of the literary salons from the 1920s and 1930s organized by the poet Georgia Douglas Johnson. Clare and Cohall would have food and drink and would invite poets and other artists to their home to talk politics and culture, watch film, and listen to poetry and music. The events were so successful, according to Clare, the pivot to move the events outside a house was a no-brainer. He describes what he and Cohall wanted to do as a "fantasy like the Harlem Renaissance."[8]

Clare also admitted being influenced by writer Trey Ellis's idea known as "The New Black Aesthetic."[9] "NBA" as Ellis nicknamed his theory, was highly underdeveloped and difficult to understand, but it did give many Black artists enough time to pause to consider what was going on in the early 1990s. Ellis saw rap music, Black rock, filmmaking, drama, and many other art forms creating their own legacy for the future. Ellis explained it as "black artists . . . feeling misunderstood by both the black worlds and the white," as well as "young blacks getting back into jazz and the blues" but also being seen at "punk concerts."[10] They could be fans of "Jim Morrison and Toni Morrison" but also the conservative jazz of the Marsalis family.

It is hard for me determine whether the 8Rock Cultural Arts Center fit into Ellis's thinking. 8Rock started something in Washington that probably has yet to end. It is much like what began after Dunbar's residency, where May Miller's father and others formed the Black cultural meeting club called MuSoLit. But 8Rock wasn't elitist or exclusionary like MuSoLit. It was open, and it had to be open because of the tough times. It also had components of the Georgia Douglas Johnson salons that began in the 1920s.

8Rock met the moment. The city, especially the impoverished community where 8Rock was located, needed hope and it needed art. 8Rock brought both. When Clare began trying to make 8Rock happen, funders sought to talk him out of putting the center in Southeast Washington, DC. They were against it, according to Clare. But the audacity of Black artists and visionaries with no money and a scattered sense of what they were going to do at the center known as the 8Rock Cultural Center was the strength of the place and movement. The movement exuded a sense of freedom and control.

Clare worked for a nonprofit known as the ARCH Development Corporation at the time and gives them big credit for helping make 8Rock come to life. Art needed a space, and ARCH provided it. Black people in America felt powerless to a degree as the Reagan-Bush years became a time of tax cuts for the wealthy, a full ideological assault on America's social programs, and a rise in racism. It was also a time of violence and drug abuse in the city. The city would become the "Murder Capital" of the United States. There were so many homicides in the city that it had more murders per capita than any other city in 1991 and 1992. Black poets had much to say about it all, as did filmmakers, hip-hop artists, visual artists, and all sorts of other artists.

"8 Rock," a term coined by Zora Neale Hurston, means "real Black person." That said it all. Clare describes the first year as amazing. "Music, literature, poetry, plays," Clare said, "all of it was happening that year."[11] 8Rock also had access to some resources through its relationship with ARCH. In addition, Clare gives Kenneth Carroll much credit for being able to connect people to other people who would come together at 8Rock.

8Rock's first big event was an appearance by the actor Avery Brooks. Jacquie Jones, the late poet and editor of the periodical *Black Film Review*, helped arrange for Brooks to appear.[12] The event featuring Brooks was billed as a silent auction and held on July 9, 1992. Brooks delivered an inspiring speech in front of the storefront cultural center that sat right on Martin Luther King Jr. Avenue in Southeast Washington, DC. The block where the cultural center was located was lined with boarded-up storefronts. Crime was rampant in the community, and there was little investment by the government or the business sector there.[13]

But 8Rock opened that week and was open from Thursday to Sunday each week with programming: poetry, film, hip-hop music, rappers, discussion, and community. It was an empty storefront in a bombed-out community that was refurbished and clean. The walls occasionally had art and when there were events, it was packed to the hilt. There were writing workshops, jazz performances, theater productions, and recorded shows and performances. Toni Blackman, the poet and hip-hop artist, had formed her Freestyle Union by then and held events at the spot.

Kenneth Carroll made sure poets knew to come to the space and read their poetry with or without a house band that was always there. It didn't take me long to visit, and when I did I met more poets I had never met before, including Yao Hoke Glover (Brother Yao), who was not only writing and reading poetry back then but was also selling African American books inside the space. The small table of books and African cultural items Glover was selling would become part of his early life's work later as a full time bookseller.

8Rock did have a double challenge when it opened, which is probably why it was unable to sustain itself. For one, it was in Southeast Washington, and the neighborhood was severely economically challenged. In addition, there had been so few cultural outlets in the community for so long, even the locals didn't understand what was going on at the time. And finally, to survive, 8Rock had to lure arts and an audience from other parts of the city. As the late David Mills wrote at the time of his feature on the center, people must "cross a psychic bridge as well as a physical one"[14] to arrive at and participate in what 8Rock was trying to do. Clare also recalls submitting forty grant applications for financial support from private foundations and getting no responses. It was obvious that despite the groundbreaking cultural work going on at 8Rock, no one was ready to get on board. Jacquie Jones looked at 8Rock as a can't-lose proposition.

And cross the bridge people and artists did for a little while. Kenneth Carroll's regular poetry events were very popular. 8Rock always had live music, and the microphone was available to anyone and everyone who wanted to bear their soul. There was a live band every Sunday night as well. Carroll was also apt to offer the stage to many poets looking for their first bite of oral expression.

According to Carroll, Jacquie Jones was responsible for much of the programming. Jones was editor of the *Black Film Review* and was well connected to the arts community in various circles. These ties enabled her to always be able to put together events. On a regular basis burgeoning hip-hop artists held their CD release parties at 8Rock, and go-go bands used the space for their live shows. There were hip-hop groups such as X Clan, Michael Franti, and the Disposable Heroes of Hiphoprisy along with films and film discussions.

8Rock, for a short moment, did exactly what its founders wanted it to do: It provided alternative culture and culture in general to the city's neglected Southeast communities. Its programs were varied and interesting. In December 1993, it presented a program on African American cinema called "Gangsta Mack Cinema: Perpetuating Negative Images or Expanding Opportunities?" Filmmakers and Black cinema experts Ada Babino, Bruce Brown, Thomas Poole, Tim Wilson, and *Black Film Review* editor Leasa Farrar-Frazer (Jones's successor) served as panelists for the program.[15]

The regular events were mostly rooted in Toni Blackman's hip-hop Daughters of the Cipher, though her Freestyle Union events were also very popular at 8Rock and usually jam-packed. Hopeful rap stars in the making and young people interested in hip-hop culture packed the space regularly. If you stepped out of "the Cipher," the windows of 8Rock would be steamed up. Blackman also considered it all a teaching moment, a chance to pass culture and respect. This was the essence of the mission of the 8Rock Cultural Arts Center. "When new members come into the group, before we work with them, we explain our belief that poetry is the foundation for the creation of rap. . . . Our credo is "Poetry is to rap as sun is to light." Rap is a combination of the oral and the written," Blackman said.[16] Looking back at all the programming and various poets and artists who came to 8Rock, Carroll attributes much of the credit for 8Rock's programming to the late Jacquie Jones, poet and filmmaker.[17]

"Jacquie did most of the events. She also did most of the publicity for the programs."[18] Jones wrote poetry, but eventually she took over as editor of *Black Film Review* once run by writer David Nicholson. Her connections to the world of African American film enabled her to bring in several important film industry players to 8Rock. This in turn helped anchor and propel all the programs, including the work of the African American poets in the city like Carroll. Carroll looks back on 8Rock as high-risk but very groundbreaking. That was the "allure" of the center as far as he was concerned.

"You are going to get something different here," he said; the message was to the community. "And the difference is what made the difference. People had to come over to Ward 8 to a whole different world." According to Carroll and Clare, 8Rock was a great plan. "To use art to revitalize a whole area" is how they both describe the moment. "There was nothing like it at the time anywhere in the city."[19]

8Rock also inspired a spoken word poetry group. Kenneth Carroll, who was a member of the Spoken Word and had his own group By Any Means Necessary, proposed that I, Joel Dias-Porter, and Judy Cohall form our own poetry-music collective called The 8Rock Collective. It didn't take long for all of us to agree and to start doing paid performances in and around the DC area. This was more evidence that something was happening in the city that hadn't happened in quite a while among the poets. Or it likely can be said that while much of what we were doing wasn't new and had been done before, what was happening regarding poetry in the city and spoken word had never reached this level of energy.

Without trying very hard, The 8Rock Collective was invited to perform its poetry at the Smithsonian; Medgar Evers College; Central Connecticut College; the Aldrich Contemporary Art Museum in Ridgefield, Connecticut; University of Maryland, Baltimore County; American University; and at Dance Place via the Washington Project for the Arts.

If there is something important about cultural centers, it is that they plant seeds and spread their philosophy and purpose. A cultural center like 8Rock in the community is also important politically and for holding a community together on some level. As "the integrationist objectives of civil rights activists waned in the mid-1960s, many in the black community became drawn to militancy and autonomy."[20] This approach had direct links to BAM of the 1960s and the Black Power movement of Stokely Carmichael. 8Rock didn't fully fit that mode, but it contained much of this ideal.[21]

One of the direct offshoots of 8Rock that became important as well was It's Your Mug. It's Your Mug's run was shorter than 8Rock's, but it was equally as important. It was also more writing salon and workshop than a full-blown community cultural center like 8Rock. That was fine for the moment. It was the creation of Toni Asante Lightfoot (Patricia Harvey).

Harvey read poetry once right after church in the 8Rock Cultural Arts Center. She was dressed for church, and she even invoked Jesus in one of her poems. It was the kind of thing that happened at Kenneth Carroll's regular open poetry readings at 8Rock.

Perhaps a year or so later, or less, Toni Lightfoot (to use her professional stage name) had organized her own regular poetry reading series at the coffee shop called It's Your Mug on P Street in the city's Georgetown neighborhood. The readings were held every Tuesday night. It's Your Mug looked fancy from the outside sitting among old brick rowhouses in the city's most storied community that was once African American decades before. On the inside, it looked like a coffee shop and had places to sit, snack, read, and think. It was like many coffee shops that had begun to open all over America at this time, but this one had Black poets and Black poetry.

As she is most popularly known, Toni Asante Lightfoot has immersed herself in poetry since the 1990s. She was born and raised in Washington, DC. Lightfoot said she "started hosting poetry readings at George Washington University, in the 1991–92 school year, as part of the Black Student Union."[22] She then hosted "poetry readings at

Howard University as part of Ubiquity, Inc." and began attending readings at "8 Rock, the 15 Minutes Club, and then started hosting a poetry night at Soul Brothers Pizza on 14th St NW near U St in March of 1992."[23]

The poet Joel Dias-Porter remembers Lightfoot and the beginning of Soul Brothers Pizza. He recalls the venue creating a buzz in the U Street Corridor. But Soul Brothers Pizza closed in December 1993 after a very short stint. Lightfoot started her Tuesday night poetry at It's Your Mug in February 1994. While Lightfoot likes to say that the point of "The Mug" was to have a good time, it was in the end a serious venue and source of good poetry. It did arise during America's "spoken word" renaissance.[24]

Lightfoot believed that much of the popularity of It's Your Mug was because of a "lack of outlets that allow people to talk about and deal with important issues."[25] She called it a "defiance of silence," or "the defiance of the idea that we all must think alike, be alike, act alike."[26] Countless poets around the country, poets who are now enjoying great careers, all recall coming to "The Mug" at least once or twice. Others came because they wanted to become better poets. Still, there were also the participants who were serious about the poetry and the social. It surely began as a fun night of spoken word poetry, but it soon became so well known and so inviting, it became something else entirely.

Nationally known poets Ahmaud Jamal Johnson and Douglas Kearney were Howard students during those years who were lured out to "The Mug." Johnson and Kearney are now award-winning poets on the national scene.

Yona Harvey and Ta-Nehisi Coates were part of the scene at "The Mug." Both were students at Howard University when they ventured into the city. Coates, as he would admit, came to "The Mug" to get connected to the African American poetry scene. Coates and Harvey impressed the audience with their first encounters even though they were younger than most of the poets who read at "The Mug." When Coates was a summer staff writer at the *Washington City Paper* in 1996, he wrote about the significance of venues like It's Your Mug to the local African American poetry scene. " 'It's Your Mug' is part of a larger movement that has swept the country over the past decade. In the form of poetry slams, featured poets, and open mikes, performance poetry has dramatically altered the cultural landscape. You can see poets singing, dancing, jumping, crying—all of it—during a reading," he wrote in an August 2, 1996, feature on spoken word poetry in the city.[27]

Brandon Johnson describes what came together at It's Your Mug as like family. As many poets, the cafe and reading night on Tuesday were conveyed to Johnson by word of mouth. This was 1994 according to Johnson. He came and read poetry and never stopped coming for two years. Johnson had been writing before he came to It's Your Mug and attending poetry events, but It's Your Mug "changed his life" he said. "In 1994 when I walked into 'It's Your Mug.' I was done. It changed my life. I dropped other schedule conflicts and never looked back. Until that time, I hadn't even written much poetry, but the people I met served as encouragement to write and get better."[28]

Johnson would become a fully engaged poet. He came for the readings and the workshops, fully devoting himself to what the spot offered, and offering all that he had to give. He would participate in poetry readings locally and nationally and get published in anthologies and journals. He had several books published, including *Man Burns Ant* (1995), *The Strangers Between* (1999), *The Black Rooster Social Inn: This Is the Place* (coauthor) (1997), and *Love's Skin* (2006).

Fred Joiner, a poet and curator of poetry, attended one of the last readings at It's Your Mug. Joiner, born in Philadelphia, came to live in Washington, DC, in 1993 and attended American University. He quickly connected with the city's vibrant poetry scene. Joiner eventually became involved with a venue called the American Poetry Museum. While a student at American University, one of his professors, Myra Sklarew, the well-known DC poet and teacher, "mentioned the Howard Poets and the Open Mic scene on U Street" to Joiner. "I . . . started frequenting those spaces, Mango's, BAR NUN, State of the Union, Kaffa House, etc. I kept informed about different readings and events from the City Paper."[29]

The last actual official reading at It's Your Mug featured the poet Peter J. Harris. Harris, who had published many of the regular poets at It's Your Mug, in his journal *The Drumming Between Us*, was the apt last act for a venue that made its mark in Washington poetry. Harris, a local-born Washington, DC, poet who now lived elsewhere, had been giving energy to the local scene from miles away. The last featured event was entitled "I Want You." It was a love letter to a poetry venue that has not vanished from the memory of anyone who ever stepped into its magic.

It's Your Mug, or "The Mug," also produced a spoken word performance collective. The group was called Modern Urban Griots (acronym MUG). Poets Tony Asante Lightfoot, Brandon Johnson, Holly Bass, Ernesto Mercer, Joel Dias-Porter, Twain Dooley, Hayes Davis, Jane Alberdeston Coralin, and Lori Tsang were all members of the group. Modern Urban Griots was very successful. They were able to land not only local gigs in the DC area but also out-of-town events.

Many of MUG's members also had their own poetry lives to nurture. Ernesto Mercer was a member, and after "The Mug" closed, he started his own poetry series at a downtown venue called Kaffa House in the city's U Street Corridor. The seeds that 8Rock planted from the other institutions that preceded it continued to grow. Mercer consistently published poetry before and after "The Mug," including chapbook *Gunpower + A Match* in 2011. He continued to conduct his literary pursuits while he was studying to complete an apprenticeship to become a Mayombe priest while also working full-time.[30]

Holly Bass, also a member, would pivot to a career as a multimedia artist. Bass has published poetry, journalism, and cultural criticism and combined dance, spoken word, and singing into her own unique art. Her work with the DC Hip Hop Theater Festival is particularly noteworthy. Jane Alberdeston Coralin would obtain a PhD, continue to write, and teach in her native Puerto Rico. Hayes Davis would continue as a poet but also teach poetry to high school students after obtaining an MFA. Twain Dooley, likewise, continued to write and perform around the city and organize events that promoted spoken word poetry events. He would host a poetry reading series at Busboys and Poets downtown for years and is still active as a host.

Also, out of the It's Your Mug experience, the poetry group Collective Voices was born in 1995. According to Joy Alford (Sistah Joy), the African American women's group was formed because the voices of her "generation were absent" from the poetry venues in the city.[31] Alford, Carolyn Joyner, and Angela Turnbull were a familiar performance literary trio in DC and in Prince George's County in the 1990s. All three pursued poetry in the group but also as individual poets. Alford has published several volumes of poetry, including *Lord I'm Dancin' as Fast As I Can, From Pain to Empowerment,* and *This Garden Called Life.* Alford has served as poet laureate of Prince George's County. Boykin (Turnbull) published poetry in various places and eventually became president of the African American Writers Guild.

Joyner was widely published and continues to remain active. Her work has been published in *Obsidian,* and the anthologies *Gathering Ground, Revise the Psalm, 360 Degrees: A Revolution of Black Poets,* and *Beyond the Frontier: African-American Poetry for the 21st Century.* She has a master of arts degree in creative writing from Johns Hopkins University.

In 1996 the original trio—Joyner, Boykin-Turnbull, and Alford—started a regular poetry reading paying tribute to the Reverend Dr. Martin Luther King Jr. It was held at the MLK Jr. Library downtown in the city.[32] The group also regularly paid tribute to other poets by reading their work and their writings.[33]

16
This Is Poetry

When Howard University Literature professor and literary critic Stephen Henderson died in 1997, his intellectual legacy among literary critics and poets was secure. Henderson's literary life was a series of cultural home runs. He had written the definitive book of criticism on African American poetry *Understanding the New Black Poetry* in 1977 but also, with Mercer Cook, had written *The Militant Black Writer in Africa and the United States*. E. Ethelbert Miller organized a symposium focusing on his work two years before his death.

The program, "In Search of Blueprints: The Making of an African American Literary Critic," was co-sponsored by the Smithsonian (National Museum of American History) and Howard University (Afro American Resource Center). Miller served as chair of the two-day event.[1] Henderson, who was ailing by this time, did attend the symposium. The symposium easily made the case that Henderson was the most important African American literary critic up until that time.

Henderson was described during his life and scholarly work as "not an intimidating person" but "a very engaging man" who "inspired a wonderment."[2] Most of all, he exuded a certain energy and passion that most agree constituted "the black aesthetic,"[3] or a way of expression and living and an appreciation without even thinking of one's culture. His work at Howard University's Institute for the Arts and Humanities was especially celebrated. Henderson always believed in the continuance nature of Black poetry. He didn't separate the poetry out so much into these widely divergent periods, though he always respected what various poetry circles were doing.

Black poetry, for Henderson, was music, the blues especially, which led him to label "the blues as Black poetry" in 1977.[4] For Henderson, Black poetry was part of the survival of Black people in America. This diligent and persistent use of poetry as a medium of survival and even successful protest was no different to Henderson than Alex Haley's famous book *Roots: The Saga of an American Family*. Henderson labels *Roots* in discussing Black poetry as "no isolated phenomenon."[5] "It is," to Henderson, "a commercial but still a brave strategy to jolt the American public into a confrontation with the central contradiction in our history—the fact of slavery, segregation and racism in 'the land of the free.' "[6] Thus, his reference to the blues as Black poetry, and the music.

That continuation, for Henderson, even though there were differences with Black poetry, can be traced back as far as Lucy Terry up until Dunbar and then onward to Langston Hughes, Georgia Douglas Johnson, Sterling A. Brown, Owen Dodson, Gwendolyn Brooks, and then the modern Black bards he encountered—poets like Don L. Lee (Haki Madhubuti).[7] Anyone who attended Miller's two-day tribute to Henderson came away understanding these concepts more deeply. The Black poets who read in tribute to Henderson—Sonia Sanchez, Ahmos Zu-Bolton, Pinkie Gordon Lane, and others—reflected that continuation of the Black poetic tradition that Henderson asserted was firmly in place and in place for a purpose.

But Henderson's use of the blues is not confined to Black poets we know or obvious expressions of verse. Henderson's critique of African American literature was also concerned with African Americans he and others call "Black and Unknown bards," the individuals who are caretakers of the culture with their songs, ballads, spirituals, sermons, and other expressions of the African American experience.[8]

"Not only must one study the history and the sociology of the blues, but one must also consider the blues as part of a 'universe' of Black poetry/art/culture, that has its own characteristic expression, its own function, its own dynamics, its own centers of gravity," Henderson wrote of his concept. "Unless this is done, any study of the poetry is likely to be essentially superficial and condescending."[9]

Kenneth Carroll's long-awaited full collection of poetry was released in 1997, at the same time as Henderson's moment. Carroll was not a literary critic, but his influence is as impactful in the city of Washington, DC, as Henderson's was on the campus of Howard University. The relationship the city of Black poets had with the Capstone of African American education and vice versa guaranteed that Carroll and Henderson would both have impact across the local Black poetry scene.

Carroll is the kind of poet and cultural worker Henderson was speaking of when he sought to explain fully the importance of Black poetry over the centuries in America. Carroll had been published in chapbook form and published chapbooks of his own, but his 1997 book was the full treatment by a small press that seemed to have been coming for nearly a decade. It wasn't as if he didn't have enough verse to make a collection either.

The collection, *So What! For the White Dude Who Said This Ain't Poetry*, was published by Bunny and Crocodile Press. Bunny and Crocodile was a press established by Grace Cavalieri, the host of the popular Washington-based poetry program *The Poet and the Poem*. Cavalieri's radio-based program had been providing Carroll with a venue to read for years. The title is taken from the famous Miles Davis song "So What" but is also inspired by a conversation Carroll had with a literary detractor he encountered at an Institute for Policy Studies event. Carroll read his poetry and afterward was told by the individual in the audience that his poetry wasn't poetry, because of its overt politics. Carroll briefly debated him and then wrote a poem that has become one of his signature moments of artistic expression.

The collection is full of some of his more well-known work and lesser-known poems that do more to tell the reader who Carroll is and why he is the person he is. Poems about his family ties to Upper Marlboro, a distant suburb in southern Maryland outside of DC, are one example. There are family poems ("Blues," "Suite for Daddy," and "Poem for Thomas at 10"), political commentary ("Requiem for Lil Sonny"), and poems of great humor and meaning ("The Domino Theory" and "Dolomite Meets George Bush").[10]

Carroll, on the page, is an unapologetic dissenter. People matter to him mostly but not bureaucrats or famous people who made a mess of their lives. Carroll has written some powerful poems, some of which echo Michael Harper's "concern" over "history," one reviewer wrote of Carroll's poetry in 1997. "The poignancy with which Carroll unerringly sees our human condition is one which we must continually face and answer over and over again."[11]

In addition to the historical traditions and influences soaked into the DNA of the African American poetry scene in DC, like those of Kenneth Carroll and the late Stephen Henderson, you cannot understand African American poetry's evolution in the city without understanding hip-hop music and culture, go-go music and the local DC culture, and the national spoken word / Slam movement of the 1980s and 1990s. These three influences each served a purpose in the 1980s, 1990s, and onward among Black poets of the city.

Slam poetry, a national phenomenon by the 1990s and part of the spoken word poetry scene in the country, is attributable to Marc Smith, a Chicago poet and construction worker. Smith, frustrated like many with the stale academic world of poetry, started an open mic night in Chicago in 1984.[12] By 1986 Smith had created a poetry contest called the Poetry Slam to rejuvenate the art form. According to John Gehring, the Slam was born at the Green Mill Tavern, a former "speakeasy" where Al Capone once hung out in his glory days.[13] The poet who survived the judging of their poetry by usually random judges even received a cash prize.

In DC, one of the early hot spots for spoken word events in the city was the 15 Minutes Club. In a 1993 feature on the DC poetry slam scene, the 15 Minutes Club is described as "funky" and "dark."[14] Usually, alcohol was served, but at some venues the opposite was true—no alcohol, but there was coffee and espresso. The Slam itself, though capable of delivering magical moments in spoken verse, usually delivered self-centered poetry. But that was the point. Poetry had become so inundated with academic rules, it spoke to no one outside the academy. The slams at the 15 Minutes Club were organized by poet Art Schuhart, who, in those days, referred to poetry as a "monster."[15] In Washington poets flocked to poetry Slams and then open mic nights at various locations. Black poets in the city stepped into these spaces as well very regularly.

The District of Columbia Arts Center (DCAC) also convened spoken word events at this time, usually led by poet Silvana Straw. As far back as 1991, poetry slam events were held at the arts center, providing a different vibe from the seedy club atmosphere of some outlets. Poet Silvana Straw organized most of the events at DCAC that included a diverse number of poets across the city's demographics. Black poets found the space very welcoming.

Other spoken word spots that convened poetry slams were the Black Cat in downtown Washington and Planet X in College Park, Maryland. Jeffrey McDaniel and Silvana Straw would curate a spoken word reading series at the Black Cat from 1994 to 1996, and they also pulled in many of the city's more active Black poets with little hesitation.

Andy Fogle, a poet and creative writing teacher today, became involved in the Washington, DC, spoken word scene at age eighteen. "I was there almost every Monday night for slams and open mics," Fogle said of the early days of the 15 Minutes Club. "I had this . . . real world arts thing happening by age 19, only the beginning of which I got back in high school with a few teachers and punk shows in Norfolk and Portsmouth."[16] Fogle, the author of multiple volumes of poetry today, also read at DCAC. He would not only read as a poet but would also later teach poetry workshops to young people in the city.

Jeffrey McDaniel, a native of Philadelphia who was studying for the MFA degree in creative writing at nearby George Mason University at the time, also embraced the spoken word / Slam movement with energy. He immediately connected with Joel Dias-Porter (DJ Renegade) and Kenneth Carroll. In addition to Carroll and Dias-Porter, McDaniel became fast friends on the scene with Jose Padua, Silvana Straw, Richard Peabody, and Quique Avilés.[17] The city's poetry scene had academics who didn't care for the academy and street poets who would eventually be in demand in academia.

The first poet I saw in Washington, DC, who formerly announced that he was about to perform a "hip hop" poem was Kwame Alexander. Alexander, an award-winning writer today (he won an Emmy for Outstanding Young Teen Series in 2023 for *The Crossover*), read a poem and immediately I knew that what I heard and saw was different. He wasn't rapping or rhyming in his poem, but he was creating a hip-hop sensibility in his performance. It was familiar to what one heard from rappers on wax, but it was still poetry and performance. Today, Alexander's moment is distant but is revelatory for me. It was an aesthetic rooted in hip-hop music and culture that I was familiar with because I had heard the music from its beginning days.

A music and cultural force out of the Bronx in New York City in 1973, hip-hop began at "dance parties and in public parks" when "deejays played records on turntables and then transformed these songs by emphasizing, looping, or repeating the parts audiences enjoyed (i.e., the breaks) and disregarding the rest."[18] Some of its major aesthetics relate to other art forms on some level: sampling, layering, rhythm, parody, and irony.[19] Poetry and spoken word, in using hip-hop culture and music, also uses "sound, image, vision, and wordplay" in its expressions.[20]

Alexander—whose 1995 collection of poems, *Just Us: Poems and Counterpoems 1986–1995*, is one of the best examples of the writing style he nurtured over the years—has maintained that connection with hip-hop and poetry throughout his career no matter the genre. He published two anthologies through his own publishing company, the Alexander Publishing Group, which also embrace the music, culture, and politics of the art form. *Tough Love: Kwame Alexander Remembers Tupac*, a collection of writings and reflections about the hip-hop superstar Tupac Shakur, was published in 1996, and a poetry anthology, *360 Degrees: A Revolution of Black Poets*, appeared in 1998.

360 Degrees was edited by the New Orleans poet Kalamu ya Salaam and Alexander. The book was released with two days of programming in Baltimore at the Baltimore Museum of Art, followed by another day of panels and readings at the University of Maryland, College Park. The book was impressive, and some of the DC area's finest poets at the time are part of it, including Alexander, Toni Blackman, Thomas Sayers Ellis, Peter J. Harris, Laini Mataka, E. Ethelbert Miller, and Joel Dias-Porter (DJ Renegade), Black Arts Movement scribes Sonia Sanchez and Haki Madhubuti, as well as newer poets from the spoken word, such as Nadir Lasana Bomani, and Roger Bonair-Agard. As the book noted at the time, "at poetry slams, in coffee houses and cafes, on spoken word CDs, and even featured in Hollywood movies, a new and exciting renaissance of Black poetry is emerging out of the oral tradition of African American culture."[21] This is an apt description of what the book represents.

Joel Dias-Porter (DJ Renegade), included in Alexander's *360 Degrees*, is one of the more notable poets who was part of the project and who was in DC at the time. Hip-hop was key to Dias-Porter's art, though from the beginning his focus was also on the writing and the poetry.

Originally from Pittsburgh, Dias-Porter joined the air force after high school and eventually was stationed in the DC area. His love of hip-hop music was immediate, and after leaving the air force, he became a DJ on the DC club scene. A voracious reader and self-described guerilla intellectual, Dias-Porter took a different tack in his approach to hip-hop and poetry. He had been a DJ at the East Side Club in DC and already had a name—DJ Renegade.

Poetry already intrigued him, though he didn't begin to think about it seriously until after he left the world of "spinning records." In 1991 he cowrote a hip-hop club tune called "Pressed Against the Glass" with local DC hip-hop star, DJ Kool.[22] The song/poem "changed my life," Dias-Porter said.[23]

Dias-Porter was also on the Malcolm X Committee in Southeast Washington, DC, when he met the poet Kenneth Carroll. He had already encountered Carroll from a distance by reading his poetry in Carroll's book *Never Piss Off a Poet*. A neighbor of Dias-Porter's had loaned him the book in passing. Dias-Porter could not put the book down. Dias-Porter was impressed with Carroll's raw sensitivity in his writing and his care for people, especially African Americans.[24] When he saw Carroll perform with a group of musicians, he knew that was his path as well. Dias-Porter also had another ingredient—hip-hop. Where Carroll used the funk of George Clinton to push at the edges of poetry, Dias-Porter used hip-hop.

Not long after checking out Carroll's dedication to the art form, Dias-Porter gave his time over to poetry and ideas. He spent years living at the Community for Creative Nonviolence Homeless Shelter (Mitch Snyder Shelter) studying and then finding his own way into the poetry scene. Dias-Porter said that he began reading at venues, mostly with Carroll. Carroll would attend, and Dias-Porter would read as well.[25]

Until he had met Carroll he did not know much about the city's poetry scene. He also began to do poetry slams. Darrell Stover and his ensemble, The Spoken Word, came to his attention, as did spoken word poets like Silvana Straw. Straw was Washington, DC's Original Poetry Slam champion in 1993 and regularly read at the 15 Minutes Club and other venues.

Dias-Porter's strength as a poet originates with his ability to combine largely self-taught technical skills with street slang, hip rhythms, and strong cultural references. He would eventually conduct workshops and teach creative writing to young people in public schools. He would give the students some hip-hop as an entry point into writing. He would become a fixture on the Slam circuit in the United States and one of the leading spoken word artists as well.

Jelani Cobb, the New Yorker writer, dean of the Columbia School of Journalism, and author of a feature on Dias-Porter in September 1996 in the *Washington City Paper* on Dias-Porter's quest to win the National Poetry Slam championship, described him like this back then: "He does not look like a Joel. He looks every inch a Renegade: visage punched up by a missing front, overworn shorts, and stubble aspiring to become a beard. He is the ex-homeless, ex-DJ, coulda-been-top-dog-on-the-slam-poetry-food-chain who is now lying in wait for a chance to artistically make good."[26]

Dias-Porter was being himself. He livened up the scene. There were plenty of good poetry and poets living and writing in Washington, DC, but there were few like Dias-Porter. His poem "21 Blackjacks" is an example of hip-hop music bleeding into traditional poetry:

21 Blackjacks
21 Black Jacks cooling in a row
21 Black Jacks clocking big dough
21 Black Jacks slinging cocaine
21 Black Jacks hip to hop Jane
21 Black Jacks 40 oz. high
21 Black Jacks let lead fly
21 Black Jacks' beepers go beep
21 Black Jacks six feet deep.[27]
—*Joel Dias-Porter*

Dias-Porter describes the poem as a riff off Gwendolyn Brooks's very famous poem "We Real Cool," another poem about the difficult urban existence for young African Americans. His poem doesn't borrow or sample from Brooks in the hip-hop aesthetic tradition, but it does channel her famous poem. Dias-Porter published multiple chapbooks as he rose on the DC poetry scene. *Slumsong: The Art of Drumming*, *21 Blackjacks*, and *Song for Sarasvati* are three of his early chapbooks. But he had only just gotten started in the 1990s.

Dias-Porter's approach to poetry is comparable to the approach by Toni Blackman, though it wasn't as if the two poets were comparing notes. Blackman's approach is different from Dias-Porter's but also similar. Blackman, as always, was sure to champion Black women.

Blackman was born in Pittsburg, California, "a steel mill town in the San Francisco Bay Area."[28] She was writing poetry by age eight and then memorizing the poetry of Nikki Giovanni and Ntozake Shange. In high school, she was "popping and breaking."[29] She came to DC to attend Howard University and graduated in 1991. In 1992 she was performing her unique brand of hip-hop poetry performance in New York, London, Philadelphia, and other places under a group she had formed called the Hip Hop Arts Movement. She joined a local chapter of Afrika Bambaataa's Zulu Nation, and things took off there. She eventually formed Freestyle Union, "a community of artists who use the medium of Hip hop to promote social responsibility." Blackman's strongest thrust in her art back then and now is to reject the "violence, misogyny and conspicuous consumption of mainstream rap and hip hop."[30]

The first time I heard her read a poem reflected her stand against misogyny and violence against women. Blackman read a poem called "For the Brothers Who Chant the Pussy Song" that spoke loud and true about the poison of misogyny in society. Blackman gained instant credibility. Out of Freestyle Union, Blackman also formed Daughters of the Cipher, where she carried her work further, handing off the Hip Hop Arts Movement to others to continue at a downtown venue called Kaffa House.[31] Kaffa House was the setting for spoken word events, open mics, poetry readings, and hip-hop. It became one of the city's hot spots for the oral culture that had come to dominate the arts scene in the 1990s. Blackman eventually developed a high school course called Hip Hop 101 for high school students that she taught for years.[32]

"I'm an MC and a poet and hip-hop artist . . . who does things and I believe that hip-hop can be used to change our world and make it a better place,"[33] she often says at her performances. Her presence in Washington on the African American poetry scene reflected this manifesto when she was living in the city in the 1990s. Kwame Alexander knew Blackman was a force in the city. He became involved with Blackman as well through the Hip Hop Arts Movement.

Another poet who brought strong hip-hop influences on the scene was Yaphet Brinson, another student who studied at Howard University and was mentored by Ethelbert

Miller while he was there. Brinson was one of DC's brightest lights on the poetry and spoken word scene, among many, and aspired to go into publishing. He was working in a space all his own, combining poetry, hip-hop, visual arts, punk, politics, and a slick sensitivity that allowed him to stand out in a very talented, crowded community of Black poets writing and hustling in the city. He was originally from New York City and New Jersey and by 1995 was getting published in notable journals such as *Obsidian II*.[34] He would also get published in Eugene Redmond's *Drumvoices* journal.

The poet Hoke S. (Brother Yao) Glover III describes Brinson's work most accurately as surreal but also "highly refined."[35] Brinson designed his own collection of poetry, *Different Dementions* (Double Negatives Press, 1993), and helped others design self-published chapbooks and journals. He was part of a fearless generation of young Black poets who emerged in the city and in America during the early hip-hop era.

Gayle Danley, an accomplished writer but also a spoken word artist, emerged as well during this time on the national spoken word scene, with Washington, DC, as her base of operations. In 1994–95, she became National Slam Poetry champion in Asheville, North Carolina. By early 1995 she had already made the decision to move to DC and to reach out to Ethelbert Miller at Howard as she made the transition. Danley, a graduate of Howard University from Atlanta, Georgia, again made the connection between Howard and Black poetry in the city when she wrote Miller. "I'm so grateful I attended a university that made me look at myself, and appreciate what I saw," Danley told Miller. Danley's writings and her pivot into the world of literature and spoken word "was a long time coming," she also admitted.[36]

In 1996 Danley was the International Slam Poetry champion as she continued to keep a busy schedule of readings and teaching opportunities in the DC area. "I love how slam poetry is tearing down the walls between ordinary people and words. Gone are the days where only the elite get to call themselves 'poets,' Danley wrote in an artist statement years ago.[37] On a certain level, Danley is explaining the entire purpose behind spoken word and Slam poetry. This is why she not only became a spoken word superstar but was easily able to shift into teaching.

Danley, as evidenced by her poetry chapbook in 1997, *Passionate: poems you can feel*, was more than just a poet. She was a theatrical artist, an improviser. As that book states on the book jacket: "Gayle has touched the lives of thousands through her poetry performance and workshops called "Soul Sessions."[38] Her mixture of love, politics, art, and spoken words was unique even for a well-developed poetry scene like Washington, DC.

17

The Poetry Life

In 1893, in Washington, DC, James Malone, a Black poet, made a name for himself on the streets of the city. Malone read his works around the city and sold pamphlets of his poetry to the locals. Malone described what he was doing as elevating "the medium of poetic literature." For a short time, he was known by the local people who saw him daily as the poet laureate of the city.[1]

Over the last twenty-five years, another street orator, Howard Sims, aka "Face," has served a similar role. Sims read and frequented all the downtown venues for poetry in DC. He also, from time to time, was able to sell CDs of poetry. He was a constant presence and has been for nearly thirty years.

Face was able to make a name for himself in the city as a spoken word poet because the city consistently for the last thirty-plus years has had spaces for poetry nearly every night of the week for those who want to or need to, rock the mic. By the mid- to late 1990s, even though the celebrated venues 8Rock and It's Your Mug were no more, the poetic energy among African American poets remained high. Raquel Brown, another local poet, had taken over hosting duties for Toni Asante Lightfoot at another venue called Mango's. Mango's was located right in the heart and soul of Black Washington, historically on Fourteenth Street. "This is like church for people," Brown described Mango's: "A lot of times I come out just to maintain that. . . . There's love here. I need them to kick it the way they do."[2]

By 2000 Brown and her daughter, Jordan, were the hosts of the Tuesday night open mics. Brown's audience reflected the city's history of Black poetry. Some of the poets were from Howard University; others were poets who just hung out in the U Street Corridor reading and writing. Still, the DC suburbs, especially Prince George's County, provided even more poets. It is up for debate how Mango's compares to the many other poetry venues that regularly gave readings during the late 1990s and early 2000s. But there is no question, Mango's was an important outlet. It was the closing of Mango's that motivated Andy Shallal, the restauranter and progressive politico, to open a very popular venue on the same block as Mango's, called Busboys and Poets, just a few years later.[3]

Down the street from Mango's were Bar Nun, Kaffa House, and Republican Gardens. If a venue had space and a microphone, poets would come. Matthew Payne, a poet and cultural organizer, hosted the literary and spoken word action nights at Bar Nun with his group the Movement Sessions. Ernesto Mercer started the Afroche readings at Kaffa House, just down the block from Bar Nun. The city had so many spoken word venues downtown it was like Hay-on-Wye on the island of Wales, only instead of bookstores like in Wales, DC had spoken word venues. The importance of these stages to the continuance of the legacy ignited in the days of Paul Laurence Dunbar remains important.

According to educator Anne Hass Dyson, the appeal of spoken word can be found in its very situatedness in, and thus its relevance to, the overlooked, the unheard, and the uncomfortably common place—the daily "mess."[4]

Bookstores likewise in the city provided a stage and microphone for poets, as the African American poetry scene evolved and grew more vibrant in the 1960s onward. While Drum and Spear has already been mentioned, there are other book outlets of note that provided space for poets. Vertigo Books, a bookstore that anchored the city's poetry voices many times, is at the top of the list.

Bridget and Todd Warren, two longtime booksellers, made Vertigo Books work in a busy part of downtown Washington, DC. They took a risk down where the rent was high and the options for socializing were large. Ethelbert Miller, the poet and literary activist, helped bring Vertigo Books into being, as did local bookseller and publisher Derrick Hsu and journalist, A'Lelia Bundles.

Vertigo Books became a key meeting space for the local literary scene in the city. It was also a big friend to African American poets and writers. If an African American poet published a book, Vertigo Books would try to have them do a reading at the store, even if the poet was not a nationally known literary superstar. Vertigo Books did fetch crowds for well-known Black poets such as Amiri Baraka, Sonia Sanchez, and Ntozake Shange. Amiri Baraka was a regular at the store, even though he lived and worked in New Jersey / New York. Few poets and intellectuals missed stopping by the store.

The store opened in November 1991 without much fanfare, when Ethelbert Miller, dressed in a suit with a bowtie, helped declare to the city that Vertigo Books was open for business and cultural exchange. The store is the stepchild of Common Concerns Bookstore, which, like Vertigo, tried to feed the progressive edges of political Washington, DC, and be a place to gather and talk until it closed in 1991. Poet and journalist Jonetta Rose Barras described Vertigo Books as "a retail microcosm of black intellectual life—a place where identity and commerce come together."[5] It was a place of "art critiques" and "political discussions" about books and what is written in them.[6]

Vertigo Bookstore achieved this kind of stature in the city among poets, especially because it was much more visible and its ability to organize big book signings with the likes of Terry McMillan or Colin Powell was interspersed with impromptu Saturday readings or weekly literary events with all kinds of poets. Most important, for the legion of Black poets in the area, Vertigo Books always welcomed poetry even if poetry does not have a super-selling market. For the store's fifth anniversary, deemed a Barber Shop Bash, Ta-Nehisi Coates hyped the event appropriately in the *Washington City Paper*:

> Vertigo is DC's citadel for progressive intellectuals, Etheridge Knight wannabes, and E. Lynn Harris lovers. . . . Plus, the bookstore hosts the phattest reading series in all Go-Go City. A place that can pull that off for just one year gets crazy props. But dig it: It's been five years since Vertigo opened its doors. This Saturday, the domicile of dizziness throws what promises to be the most literary of birthday bashes with its "Fifth Annual Barbershop Bash." The party features some of DC's liveliest metaphor-makers. The roster will feature DC poetry don Kenny Carroll, "O.G." Brian Gilmore, and literary rookie of the year Yona "Young-buck" Harvey. Even if you're only semiliterate, you ain't gonna wanna miss this one.[7]

That reading was just one of hundreds at the store during its incredible run.

Local poet Gaston Neal was a regular at the store, just hanging out and talking politics, culture, and life. Amiri Baraka read and signed books at the store countless times, as did Sonia Sanchez. African American poetry anthologies of note were launched at the store. Ethelbert Miller's *In Search of Color Everywhere*, Natasha Tarpley's *Testimony*, and Daniel Wideman and Rohan B. Preston's *Soulfires: Young Black Men on Love and Violence* all found a healthy and welcoming audience at Vertigo Books during its heyday.

When Vertigo Books finally did close, it had relocated to College Park, Maryland, and the die was cast. It still had great books and readings, but the vibe of downtown in the city was gone. Bridget Warren bid the city, poets, and all the other writers and readers farewell in a long message on social media:

> After seventeen and half years, the time has come. Curtains down and goodbye—in two weeks, Vertigo Books will close. Starting today, EVERYTHING IN THE STORE IS 20% OFF. If you've been eyeing that special something, come in and grab it now, before someone else does. And our new rules for the next couple weeks: no checks, no returns, and no exchanges. Please note: we will be closed Easter Sunday, April 12, our usual hours will resume Monday . . . Why are we closing? There are many reasons, but basically, not enough people buy books here.[8]

When Vertigo Books finally closed in April 2009, it reflected changes in the city and book culture in general. The community space idea had blossomed, but the downtown rents also rose as well as gentrification came to the city that was once over 70 percent African American. From when Vertigo Books opened in 1991 to when it closed in 2009, the African American population decreased from 65 percent to 50 percent.[9] The days of "Chocolate City," in terms of census numbers, were over.

In a certain way, Karibu Books, a popular bookstore for African American poets during the 1990s and into the millennium, was also facing similar challenges from the start. In its early days, Karibu Books sold books on the campus of Howard University from a table covered with mud cloth. Karibu was also a fixture at the 8Rock Cultural Arts Center right in the city's Anacostia Corridor on poetry night. Hoke (Brother Yao) Glover, a poet, could be found at the center making early connections along with his partner, the accountant Simba Sana.

Born and raised in Prince George's County, right outside Washington, DC, Yao was a poet even back then and very well respected as he worked on his craft. He would eventually obtain a master of fine arts (MFA) degree in Creative Writing from the University of Maryland. He was a very good poet even before he left the academy. Sana's talents were in numbers, with a college degree and experience at accounting firms.

Sana, born Bernard Sutton, grew up in Washington and attended Gonzaga High School. With his mother's assistance, Sana was able to escape the poverty of DC to become a successful businessman and accountant. He graduated from Mount St. Mary's College in Maryland. Sana and Glover were both well-read and were mission oriented.

Karibu Books, like Drum and Spear many years before, eventually became a gathering place for Black poets, their poetry, intellectuals, activists, and others. Many African American poets, including myself, found the store a welcoming venue and supporting community institution for African American poetry. Karibu Books eventually grew from that table kiosk on the campus of Howard University to several kiosks to several bookstores that sold books by and about African Americans.

The store became a major presence in the DC area. Even with the expansion of chain stores like Borders and Barnes and Noble, Karibu Books survived because of its focus on Black writing, writers, and life. Its stores were outside the city, so the intentional policies of Washington, DC, to change its demographics did not initially have much impact.

Glover, his then wife, Karla, and Sana, provided DC with a gem of a bookstore chain for fifteen years. They defied the odds. Karibu Books came into being in 1993,[10] right after Vertigo Books. The store had a political, cultural, and economic agenda, including community education and independence. Pan-Africanism and Black Nationalism were the ideological engines for the store's approach but were in no way hateful or dismissive. In fact, these ideas were building blocks for the strength of the chain in the community.

"We consistently enmeshed African culture wherever we could into the business fabric. This approach led us to choose the name 'Karibu,' which means 'welcome' in Kiswahili, as the company's name," Glover wrote in his digital journal *Free Black Space*. "We also used Akan Adinkra symbols in our logo designs and had African priests and African American Christian ministers bless each store."[11]

Karibu Books was also flexible in its desire and willingness to be community oriented. Karibu partnered with the Africa Development Organization (ADO), and spearheaded a Lorton Prison Study Group. Both efforts worked with the local Washington, DC, prison system and used literature and politics to "increase knowledge of African and African American culture." These efforts are like the work and agenda of Drum and Spear Bookstore, the bookshop that opened right after the 1968 riots in DC. Black poets from the city participated in the ADO Program that Karibu Books sought to implement. I was lucky enough to be occasionally invited to participate in Karibu's work at Lorton Prison along with the poet Joel Dias-Porter (DJ Renegade).

Karibu also, like Drum and Spear Books, sold African-centered books. That was its biggest service during an important era of literary history in the city and the country. Glover calls bookselling political and has kept from what the store tried to do. It wanted to promote culture and independence for African people in America in everything it did each day. Naturally, Karibu Books supported African American poetry and poets in the DC area.

Many African American poets read their poetry at Karibu's stores and organized events. Joel Dias-Porter read his poetry many times at Karibu stores, as did Kenneth Carroll. Camille Dungy, poet, essayist, and creative writing professor known for her nature writings, read and held a book signing at the store's Landover location.

It helped that Glover was a poet who took the craft seriously and began to publish his work in various places. Glover, the author of two books of poetry and many other publications, now teaches creative writing at Bowie State University in Prince George's County, Maryland, just outside the city.

Karibu Books also supported Black poetry in other ways. In 2001 the store published *Jungle Nights and Soda Fountain Rags: Poem for Duke Ellington*, my second collection of poetry. It also published Joel Dias-Porter's *4,000 Shades of Blue* collection and helped produce Dias-Porter's poetry jazz CD project, *LibationSong*. *LibationSong* was another triumph for Dias-Porter and his imaginative and ambitious approach to poetry. The *Washington City Paper* (Sarah Godfrey) wrote that on the recording, Dias-Porter "marries jazz from local acts with the hard edge of his spoken-word performances."[12]

There were, of course, other bookstores in and around the city—too many to name, in fact. But a few to mention that did poetry include Sisterspace, Olsson's Books, Politics and Prose, Yawa Books, Pyramid Bookstore, Lammas, and Dar Es Salaam Books. Sisterspace Books, while just one physical location, was probably the strongest of this remaining group and the most memorable. Its focus was mostly on books by and about African American women, and it made a big impact on literature in the DC area, as well as being a safe space for African American women poets. It was a community—bookstore, gathering space, a literary and social village.

Faye Williams and Cassandra Burton opened Sisterspace and Books as a Black feminist bookstore "in a consignment boutique at 1354 U St., NW in November 1994." Williams and Burton "built up the store's library of books for, by and about black women" and then "moved to 1515 U Street, NW, where it would remain until August 2004." While it was a bookstore, it was also an "organizing space for black women" where "conversations about the 'troubles and joys women carry,'" were convened. The space also started a "dissertation support group, classes in computer fluency, GED, and literacy, among other services. Such projects led to the creation of the African American Women Resource Center, Sisterspace not-for-profit organization."[13] Rapid gentrification of the city drove the store out of the U Street area much to the frustration of the store's patrons and supporters.

The Dog

When the poet Cornelius Eady was appointed as Jenny McKean Moore professor at George Washington University (GWU) for the 1996–97 academic year, few could have imagined the impact and importance of the moment. Eady was a well-known and rising poet at the time with several critically acclaimed books and publications across America's literary landscape. DC had an energized poetry scene and was full of Black poets with things to write and speak. The Jenny McKean Moore workshop was also a big deal in the city and nationally.

"The Jenny McKean Moore professorship was established through the Jenny McKean Moore Fund. It was established in honor of the late Jenny Moore, a playwriting student at GWU who left, in trust, a fund that has, for more than 40 years, encouraged the teaching and study of creative writing in the English Department." It allowed the university to bring a writer (poet, fiction writer, or nonfiction writer) to live and teach on campus "every other year." According to the fund, the selected "writer brings a unique experience to the GWU community, teaching a free community workshop for adults along with creative writing classes for GWU students. The fellow is known as the Jenny McKean Moore Writer-in-Washington."[14] Luckily, for poets in Washington, DC, and several African American poets at the time, Eady was the writer in Washington for 1996–97. For Eady, the feeling was mutual. "It was a really great gig," he said. "It really appealed to me." Eady lived in a house on campus and the workshops occurred in the house, in the living room. It was "outreach to the community," he said. It was the university coming to a city of poets.

Eady also noted that it was perfect timing. He and poet Toi Derricotte were already contemplating starting some kind of writing retreat exclusively for Black poets in the United States. Their frustration at the lack of diversity for the various writing retreats in America, the prestigious writing retreats, reached a fever pitch.

African American writers had trouble getting into the majority white writer retreats, though the retreats did not feel like safe, welcoming spaces for their artistic expression either. Eady and Derricotte were both thinking about doing something but just had no idea what they were conjuring. The Jenny Moore workshop, according to Eady, where many local Black poets attended, was part of the answer. Eady believed that Jenny Moore was affirmation that something for just Black poets could work, and in 1996 he and Derricotte launched the African American Writers Retreat known now as Cave Canem.[15]

Eady and Derricotte's thinking was a thought that had come up many times over the years. It wasn't something that other poets hadn't pondered, and African Americans always have gathered in workshop settings or in other kinds of spaces to pursue creative writing and the arts. The idea of placing greater importance on creative arts in African American circles and doing it has always been there. For people that poet Amiri Baraka called "the masters of the arts,"[16] it was an itch to be scratched.

As far back as 1951, African American educational spaces had begun to place higher value on creative writing as a "serious field of academic specialization."[17] However, historically Black writers were not provided support and the resources to pursue creative writing in a serious manner, even in African American cultural and educational circles.[18] And there was so much to deal with in America.

Many creative writing institutions and academic outlets were already in existence at majority white colleges at this time, when Black educators finally began to mull it all over.[19] Black writers and educators remained hesitant mostly. Black studies programs emerged in the 1960s and 1970s in reaction to racism and exclusion in America but not creative writing programs.[20]

Institutions of this nature had to rely on individual efforts of various individuals to create community workshops, writing salons, and in the case of what Eady and Derricotte would eventually establish via Cave Canem—a weeklong writing retreat for African Americans—it has become quite a statement.

Many of the Black poets in the Jenny Moore Workshop in DC that year would attend Cave Canem in 1997. It was quite a gift to the city's Black poetry scene. It was like the natural next step.

By 1996, Eady felt that all they needed was a place to hold the retreat. That came through Father Francis Gargani, a friend of Derricotte, who could provide space at a monastery in the scenic hills of upstate New York. Gargani, an ordained priest in the Redemptorist Order, provided the space at a Redemptorist monastery in Mount Esopus, New York. In their original call for poets back in 1995, Eady and Derricotte wrote that "Cave Canem was created to offer a comfortable setting for African American poets to write and share their poems in daily workshops and readings. The faculty will choose 20–24 participants based on their manuscripts."[21] The first retreat was held June 9, 1996–June 15, 1996. Joel Dias-Porter, living in DC at the time, attended the 1996 workshop, as did poets Valerie Jean and Monica Hand.

The name Cave Canem means "Beware the Dog" and was inspired by a trip Eady and Derricotte took to Italy and viewed the ruins of the city of Pompeii. They were now convinced that Cave Canem, the name they lifted from their trip to Pompeii, would become real. Herman Beavers, a poet and English professor, had been thinking along the same lines on writing retreats and he told Eady as much. Beavers would attend the first retreat.

The mission of Cave Canem since 1996 has never changed: "Remedy the underrepresentation and isolation of African American poets in the literary landscape."[22] The first group of fellows at Cave Canem, workshopped their poetry to "a faculty of renowned poets—at Mount St. Alphonsus Seminary, in Esopus, NY."[23]

In the 1997 fellowship class, an almost unthinkable number of poets from Washington, DC, were invited to attend the retreat. Much of it is a credit to the close-knit nature of the Black poetry scene in DC nurtured over the years.

Elizabeth Alexander, a DC poet, was on the faculty. Dias-Porter, Jean, and Hand returned and were joined by Brandon Johnson, Ernesto Mercer, Toni Asante Lightfoot, Holly Bass, Yona Harvey, R. Erica Doyle, Imani Tolliver, Robin Dunn Bryant, and myself in summer 1997. We spent a week at writing workshops and doing readings with other Black poets from all over the country. Although the full contingent of poets from Washington, DC, were not originally from the city, the poets were living and writing in DC when they came to Cave Canem. It was again part of that tradition that goes back to Paul Laurence Dunbar and Georgia Douglas Johnson.

Cave Canem was a shining moment for the city of Black poets in 1997. The African American poets, while organized and energetic in their city, cohesive, and welcoming, understood the sting of racial alienation. The reason why the DC Black poetry scene was so cohesive and energetic across generations was because of the city of Washington, DC's segregated history. We understood exactly what Cave Canem could offer. Ta-Nehisi Coates, also a very good and active poet on the DC scene in 1997, covered the now important 1997 retreat for the *Washington City Paper* as a reporter.

"This year Cave Canem added University of Chicago professor Elizabeth Alexander and Bucknell instructor Afaa M. Weaver (né Michael Weaver) to its faculty roster. And as an indication of the strength of the District's writing scene, one fourth of the writers in attendance at last month's retreat were from DC," Coates, still a student at Howard University at the time, wrote. And yes, Coates was correct when he noted in that same article then that "whenever a poet from DC" stepped up to read, "the contingent of DC writers" yelled, "2-0-2! Ruff it off!" It was an ode to the famous Washington, DC, telephone area code 202. Coates called these moments a "reading. . . straight out of Gutbucket City . . . a Baptist service under the cloak of polite verse."[24]

It was not a sign of disrespect to other poets and cities either. It was just an acknowledgment to one another of the work the poets from Washington had put in over the decades to nurture their poetry community. The Black poets in DC understood the mission of Cave Canem because in a sense they had lived it in the nation's capital. They were poets in the majority African American city, managed by African Americans, yet resources for Black art in the town seemed to elude them over the decades. They understood the need to build your own institutions and forge a new autonomous path.

As Coates added in his article on the retreat, "One thing the DC contingent of writers doesn't lack is community. This is the city that spoon-fed talent to the Harlem

Renaissance. Alain Locke, Zora Neale Hurston, Langston Hughes, and Jean Toomer all had ties to DC before migrating north." Coates also noted that DC "boasts one of the strongest open-mike scenes in the country" and "the African American Writers Guild is headquartered here, and at least one workshop" specializing in Black poetry. Both Eady and Pulitzer Prize–winning poet Tyehimba Jess have said that before there was "C.C.," a nickname for Cave Canem, "there was DC."[25]

18

"Fierceness"

If there is one aspect of the African American literary scene that allowed it to evolve and thrive since the days of Dunbar, it is its ability to evolve and develop alliances. Sterling Brown went as far as to note that Black progress in the city "has not concerned" just African Americans. "White humanitarians . . . protested his enslavement and abuse, and farsighted statesmen have worked toward integration in the total pattern."[1]

In addition, Brown wrote that this bond on at least some levels assisted in "schooling" Black children and that this could not have happened in the city without "cooperation" between Blacks and whites.[2] As Brown further stressed as far back as the 1930s, the progress made by Black people in the city made them want to simply become full citizens. The talented artistic Blacks of the city were writers, scholars, and professionals of their trade who just happened to be Black.[3] They were very valued residents of the nation's capital.

Within the African American poetry community and artistic community, the same could be said of those who were gay, lesbian, or considered LGBTQ. They were not necessarily discriminated against by the overall African American community, but society itself did seek to marginalize them in the world and in Washington, DC. Yet poets and performance artists who were LGBTQ were essential to the city's poetry scene and the Black poetry scene. They were valued.

But the city's Black LGBTQ community still did its own thing over the years. Though they were part of the poetry community, they were also autonomous. It was an assertion of their own magic, especially so in the 1980s. Essex Hemphill, Garth Tate, Michelle Parkerson, Wayson Jones, and many others had been making their marks since the 1970s, and then the 1980s arrived and their spirit escalated. Their imprint is still felt today. Hemphill fought just as hard against racism as he did homophobia and violence on the page and in performance. Parkerson was no different. Parkerson's 2021 film, *Fierceness Served! The Enik Coffeehouse Experience,* captures one such special effort by the LGBTQ community to be independent.

Fierceness is many things, but it begins with Ray Melrose, who opened his home in the city's H Street NE Corridor as a community space for many Black LGBTQ artists back in the 1980s and 1990s. It was like many of the other literary spaces that emerged during the 1980s—a private effort rooted in art, love, and community. Melrose's efforts back then are known as the ENIKAlley Coffeehouse.[4] According to Ryan J. Lambe in his 2023 dissertation, "Performative Space/Transformative Space: Race, Affect, And Amateur Performance In U.S. Queer Open Mics," spaces such as the ENIKAlley Coffeehouse "make space for marginalized people to heal the trauma of marginalization."[5]

The coffeehouse was located at 816 I Street NE in the heart of another of the city's historical African American communities. The space opened on January 1, 1982, and it was organic in nature, just an idea.[6] Louis Hicks, a museum director and someone who found peace at the coffeehouse, remembers the time of the coffeehouse very well. "This was 1988 . . . Marion Barry was a dominant figure," Hicks recalls in the film. "Ray Edmunds and the crack epidemic was really raging." Hicks says that Melrose, his friend, rescued him, and gave him a place to live at the coffeehouse. Hicks was a graduate student at the time but has since worked in the arts in the metropolitan DC area. He, like most, saw the space as a safe space and especially so for African Americans of the LGBTQ community.

Tania Abdulahad, a social worker, and member of a Black Lesbian group known as Sapphire Sapphos, also met at the coffeehouse. She found it ideal for the moment. "We came in 1983, and we were probably here until '86 or '87."[7] The city was quite violent at the time and dangerous, yet the coffeehouse thrived, as did the people who came and communed in the spirit of art and humanity. Parkerson's film captures the spirit of it all. The film is a "local history of a Black LGBT performance venue, rehearsal space, and meeting place for artists and political organizations in Washington, DC" during this period. The film seeks to revisit a moment that "was the epicenter of a cultural renaissance that paralleled The Harlem Renaissance."[8]

The film documents a snippet of the artistic expression of African American LGBTQ poets from the 1980s and 1990s. Among the artists included directly or indirectly in the film are Essex Hemphill, Wayson Jones, Michelle Parkerson, Garth Tate, and Christopher Prince. These are the Black artists who not only made their own world of art but also were an important part of the overall sonic explosion of spoken word creativity that rose up in the DC area. The coffeehouse had regular events, including poetry readings and performances by artists, with significant audience participation. It is almost strange in a city where the Black poetry scene was quite insular and cohesive that many Black poets did not know about Melrose's spot.

Wayson Jones and Hemphill during this period were regular collaborators. Jones's power as an artist is self-evident in the film. Considering Hemphill died in 1995, it is Jones who can articulate the spirit of the coffeehouse back at that time. In Parkerson's film, Jones said, "magic happened" in the coffeehouse, "in the loft . . . and in the downstairs performance space."[9] Jones describes the coffeehouse as "home" even though it all occurred during the days of "crack cocaine" and "the days of HIV and AIDS."[10]

"But we thrived in that environment," Jones said. "We thrived in an environment we created for ourselves."[11] The space was not just home for art and culture; it was a gathering ground for political organizing. The Black LGBTQ community was quite active at the time, and its politics was reflected in its art and vice versa. It was necessary because of the federal government's failure to embrace the AIDS crisis with a sense of decency.

The coffeehouse was also a place for LGBTQ artists to workshop their performance pieces, according to Parkerson. If an artist had a show coming, they would do it first at the coffeehouse. One of the groups Jones and Hemphill participated in was known as Cinque, and they did, in fact, do test runs of their performances.

The coffeehouse can probably be considered an apex of LGBTQ poetry and spoken word art in the city, though perhaps one apex among several. But because of HIV and AIDS, the Black male gay community in DC and the artists were hit hard by tragedy. Ray Melrose, the curator of the space, died in 1994 of AIDS complications, and Essex Hemphill died the following year. Before he died, Hemphill, an artist many call a "genius," was able to help bring numerous important anthologies into the world and writings.[12] Two notable anthologies are Joseph Beam's *In the Life: A Black Gay Anthology* (1986) and *Brother to Brother: New Writings by Black Gay Men* (1991).

Among the poets and performance artists who found a safe space in a very African American Washington, DC, were many non-Black poets. Asian American poets, Afro-Latino poets, and Latino poets. Ethelbert Miller's Ascension Series was helpful in bringing together poets of many nationalities as one poetry community. The intermingling of poets from all backgrounds was also in action outside Ethelbert Miller's efforts. Poets came together with shared goals to produce great art and to share it with the world. DC Space, the famous arts venue in the city, was responsible for much cultural intermingling. It was a space focused on art, expression, and freedom, most of all, and poets found their voice there and in the city.

Some of the more notable poets are Eric Antonio (Filipino), Silvana Straw (Italian American), Sami Miranda (Puerto Rican), Lori Tsang (Chinese American), Quique Avilés (Salvadoran), Jose Padua (Filipino), and Tony Medina (Puerto Rican). All these poets are important to the city's poetry landscape. Some of these poets also identified as Black. This made their role in the local poetry scene all the more diverse and significant.

Quique Avilés was one of the most popular poets and spoken word artists during the city's rising spoken word movement. Avilés, a Salvadoran American, came to the city after US imperial activities in Central America. He settled in Washington and quickly became a well-sought-out performer on the local scene after attending Duke Ellington School of the Arts. He founded "the LatiNegro Theater Collective, an ensemble of African American and Latino young artists" shortly after. In 1999, "he co-founded Sol & Soul, an arts and activist organization, and served as its Artistic Director until 2005," and has been a fixture on the city's performance poetry scene ever since, providing at least ten one-man performances.[13]

Lori Tsang, a Chinese Jamaican American poet, was a regular presence on the DC poetry scene and a solid presence at African American venues in the 1990s. A lawyer by day at the Federal Energy Commission but also a filmmaker, Tsang created strong poetry rooted in her own experiences as an American and Chinese American with strong ties to Jamaica.

It is in Jamaica where her family ties are strongest. She was raised by her Chinese Jamaican mother and an "American" Chinese father in Connecticut and Indiana.[14] As a result of her willingness to enter multicultural spaces, Tsang has been widely published in journals across the spectrum of literary expression.[15] Tsang was a member of the Modern Urban Griots poetry performance collective, which had ties to the city's larger spoken word scene. She also formed a poetry performance group called the All Blues Jazz Poetry Ensemble, a collaboration between Tsang and Jamaican American poet-musician Sydney March.[16]

Silvana Straw, a poet and performer who was a star of the local Slam scene in the city, was also closely associated with the African American poetry and spoken word scene. Straw performed with Avilés, Reuben Jackson, and Michelle Parkerson, proving her versatility as an artist. Many years later, Straw would curate a retrospective two-day poetry series in the city at Dance Place in 2014. The show, "Ghosts of DC Past," demonstrated Straw's connections to all the city's poetry and performance communities.

Eric Antonio was also a regular voice in African American venues in the city. The poet Lori Tsang wrote that Antonio was so versatile as a writer and so free in performance that he could deliver "a decidedly unpoetic diatribe against U.S. immigration policy one week, and a poignant, artfully crafted tribute to his stepfather the next week."[17] Antonio was born in the Philippines and immigrated to the United States in 1974. When he attended George Washington University in DC for graduate school, he found his way to the city's poetry scene.

Two other poets who were regulars across the city scene but who figured prominently in African American venues as well were Jose Padua and Sami Miranda. Jose Padua, a Filipino American poet, was a rock star on the Washington poetry scene and an exceptional writer. He read and would read just about anywhere in Washington, DC, and in New York City. After many years writing and reading, Padua's first collection of poetry, *A Short History of Monsters*, was published in 2019 by the University of Arkansas Press.[18] Sami Miranda, from the South Bronx, New York, has been part of the DC poetry scene for decades now. He is not only a popular poet in general but is as well a key part of the Black poetry scene in the city and one of the prime movers of the current poetry that gets heard by the public. Miranda is a longtime schoolteacher, writer, artist, poet, and, most recently, director of the American Poetry Museum, the key arts space in the city for poets, especially Black and Brown poets.

B-More

The city of Baltimore ("B-More"), northern neighbor of Washington, DC, was one of the feeder cities to Washington over the years, and DC, in turn, became a cultural landing strip for Baltimore poets. It can be said as well that Baltimore is a poetry ally of DC's African American poets and the scene that was built over the years. Peter J. Harris, a native of Washington, DC, moved to Baltimore after college at Howard University, and only then did he take up poetry after studying journalism.

After college, Harris worked for the *Baltimore Afro-American*, an African American newspaper. He became part of a community of Black men in that city before he moved to California. In 1993 his DC-Baltimore connections helped him publish one of his very great books of poetry: *Hand Me My Griot Clothes: The Autobiography of Junior Baby.*

The book created a buzz for Black poets far away from Harris in his hometown of Washington, DC, and in Baltimore. It was again one of those attempts to do something on the page that had yet to be done before. The book was published by Black Classic Press of Baltimore, an independent African American press created by Paul Coates. Coates had worked for many years at Howard University and started Black Classic Press in 1978 to publish "classic" books by African American and African writers that had gone out of print.

Hand Me My Griot Clothes struck a chord with many Black poets in Washington because of the language. The book talked to you like people talk on street corners. It was conversation as verse. Junior Baby, the narrator and subject of examination in the book, was a modern Black man, with wisdom and endurance in America. Award-winning poet Nikki Finney described Harris as a poet with "a deep Mississippi Ocean for a heart . . . who feeds the reader a rich black soup, swimming with all the caramelized parts of us."[19]

Hand Me My Griot Clothes would win the PEN Oakland Award, in 1993, for Multicultural Literature. Harris would continue to publish poetry and other writings mostly from Los Angeles, but he was never too far away from his city in spirit and tradition. When It's Your Mug had its final reading before the venue closed, Harris was the featured reader, which was appropriate.

Many years later, Harris would publish a literary magazine called *The Drumming Between Us*, a publication about Black love and erotic poetry. It was a way of connecting with communities outside his poetry circle in the city. Harris would publish some of the poets who regularly read at It's Your Mug in *The Drumming Between Us*. Harris would later write that he was trying to document "some of the humidity of that evening" in the room the venue's final night.[20] A Washington, DC, poet who had grown up across the water from the cafe in a neighborhood called Anacostia laid it on thick again that night, as one of the city's most important poetry venues ever turned out the lights for the very last time.

Black Classic Press also published several other important poetry books that are important to the history and advancement of Washington's Black poetry scene. Paul Coates founded the company in 1978 because he saw a need. His initial investment was only $300. Coates was working at Howard University at the time in the Moorland-Spingarn Library. His wife then, Cheryl Coates, helped him start the press. Coates was advised not to do it, but he didn't listen.

In 2002 the press would publish *Beyond the Frontier: African-American Poetry for the 21st Century*. E. Ethelbert Miller edited the book. Miller and Coates had been friends for years via Howard University. Miller had connected with so many poets when he edited *In Search of Color Everywhere* that he could do another anthology that included even more poetry and poets, many of whom were not published in the first anthology. It was also good that an African American press had begun to publish poets. The contributions made by Coates and Black Classic Press proved critical to maintaining veteran voices on the DC scene. But opportunities for Black poets to be published locally were lacking twenty-seven years after Jack Foley made his point. Black Classic would fill the void some by publishing the work of poet Laini Mataka.

Laini Mataka was from Baltimore like Coates. She was born Wanda Robinson and became a dynamic spokenword poet in the 1970s. Black Classic Press published four volumes of her poetry, including *Never as Strangers* (1988), *Restoring the Queen* (1994), *Bein a Strong Black Woman Can Get U Killed* (2000), and *The Prince of Kokomo* (2015). In 1971, as Black poets began collaborating with musicians, Mataka was at the forefront of recording two such albums, *Black Ivory* (1973) and *Me and a Friend* (1977), on Perception Records out of New York City. *Black World* magazine endorsed *Black Ivory* when it was released, writing that "one should listen to the album . . . during those rare quiet, reflective evenings." Mataka (Robinson) is described as a "mature" poet who speaks with "perception and honesty."[21]

In 1977 she also published a chapbook, *Black Rhythms for Fancy Dancers*.[22] Mataka has been a fixture in Washington DC's literary scene and has even worked in public schools teaching young people creative writing. She is a Washington, DC, institution in her own right, even though she is from nearby Baltimore. She is a bit of a gift to the city to the south of B-More.

One of Mataka's running partners on the poetry scene was Kimberly A. Collins. Collins, originally from Philadelphia, has been a steady presence on the DC scene since the 1990s. Yet Collins found her way also to Baltimore to teach at Morgan State University. It expanded her audience and reach on the literary scene. Her 2017 collection of poetry, *Bessie's Resurrection*, was part of that expansion. Collins also began doing writing workshops seeking healing for participants since the 1990s.

Among the other poets with Baltimore links who made important contributions to the DC scene include Lucille Clifton, who taught at historically Black Coppin State and read on Ethelbert Miller's Ascension Series. Clifton seemed like she was part of the city sometimes as she was so well known by local poets. She taught for many years at St. Mary's College in southern Maryland. Poets from Washington, DC, including many African American poets, regularly made trips to the college for readings and conferences because it was so close to the city.

Reginald Harris, poet and librarian at the Enoch Pratt Free Library, also had a presence in the city. Most important, Harris, through the library, helped bring reading opportunities for DC poets in Baltimore. Many of the poets were African American poets who found Baltimore to be a dynamic city full of art and poetry as well. Harris, a Cave Canem fellow, also helped to coordinate the annual Cave Canem reading in Baltimore at the Enoch Pratt Library.

Ta-Nehisi Coates, the MacArthur genius and journalist, was a regular on the DC poetry scene in the 1990s. Coates, born in Baltimore, and son of Paul Coates, of Black Classic Press, connected with many African American venues, institutions, and poets during his time in Washington. He also worked for DC WritersCorps and published a few poems before focusing on reportage and journalism. His accomplishments today are extraordinary. His commitment to being and working as a public intellectual, writing and creating in various sectors of the entertainment and literary world, is impressive. Perhaps it sounds dishonest, but from the first time Coates read his poetry at It's Your Mug as a Howard University student, many on the DC poetry scene were certain he would rise high in the literary world.

James "Otis" Williams, writer, poet, bluesologist, and educator, also brought Baltimore connections to Washington, DC. While he was born in Mississippi, he attended college at Morgan State University in Baltimore. He eventually began working at the University of Maryland in the 1980s and directed the Nyumburu Cultural Center at the college.[23] He mentored many students and young Black writers including DC's Darrell Stover. According to Ethelbert Miller, Williams was doing the same work that the Ascension Series was doing in the city via Howard University. Williams was doing that work at the University of Maryland. His sudden death in 1997 cut short what was likely a longer life of service and literature to not just the students at the University of Maryland but the many poets in Washington he had come to know.

The cities of Washington, DC, and Baltimore always have had a bit of historical rivalry. Baltimore, the working-class, tough town full of ethnic diversity and Southern African American culture and Washington, the up South city full of paper-pushing elites, and a large African American striver population, always in search of mental freedom. The cities could not be more different. But as for poetry, Black poetry, the cities shared common goals and pursuits that fed both cities. The alliance could not be more clear and obvious and was built before Washington, DC, even became an actual city.

19 Corps of Writers

It was inevitable that the community creative writing phenomenon known as the DC WritersCorps would happen. It was also no surprise that Black poets in and around the city would flock to the program to contribute.

DC has always been full of writing workshops for all kinds of writers. It is also a city that has tried to be innovative in reaching out to the city's marginalized youth. The city's colonial status and racial segregation always made that a challenge, though nothing ever stopped the efforts. But the DC WritersCorps is important because it became a home for many African American poets in the 1990s and into the millennium for a while.

Kenneth Carroll, the Washington poet and community presence, recalls interviewing for the job of site coordinator for the DC WritersCorps program at poet Carolyn Forché's house. Even though Carroll was interviewed, there was little doubt about who was the right person for the job. The site coordinator for the DC WritersCorps' job was to create community workshops in the city that would uplift people who were down and out.

WritersCorps was part of President Bill Clinton's AmeriCorps program, "a domestic peace corps," where citizens would be afforded an opportunity to work directly on issues and challenges in society as citizens. When Clinton signed the National and Community Service Trust Act of 1993 into law and created the Corporation for National Service, he said all the key buzzwords like "service" and "young people" and "Peace Corps."[1] The WritersCorps was just a small piece of the law's mission, but in Washington, DC, in the violent 1990s where crack cocaine ruled the streets, DC WritersCorps was a balm to all that pain.

DC WritersCorps, mission was simple: "Transform lives through the written word."[2] Poets of all backgrounds found that joyous. The WritersCorps began in three large urban cities—San Francisco, New York, and Washington, DC. The National Endowment for the Arts (NEA) and the Corporation for National Service partnered on the initiative, and Associated Writing Programs (AWP) managed the three sites. A. B. Spellman, the poet now living and working in DC, was second in command at the NEA when the DC WritersCorps began. He helped design the DC site.[3] Carroll was the ideal site coordinator because poetry was a part of his life, and he was part of the city from birth.

Carroll was already doing writing workshops, as were the poets Joy Jones, Darrell Stover, Joel Dias-Porter (DJ Renegade), and Toni Blackman. Joy Jones, a longtime poet in the city, had already organized one of the key workshops of DC WritersCorps. It was already up and running at St. Elizabeths Hospital. Carroll, Stover, and others would also become part of Jones's workshop.

By 1996 the DC WritersCorps had opened workshop locations at twenty-three sites in the city with twenty-five writers.[4] One example of the work the poets were doing through the DC WritersCorps was a workshop founded at Barry Farms Recreation Center. That workshop began to take shape (1994) when Carmen James Lane, at the Humanities Council of Greater Washington, wanted to start a workshop for young people in Barry Farms. Lane knew Carroll and did not hesitate to reach out.

"Kenny is a forerunner of writers who began to see themselves as agents for social change and service . . . to use humanities in a time of crisis," Lane said.[5] When Lane got in touch with Carroll, he was doing what he was always doing: writing poetry, working, and organizing community programs for young people.

Stover's work with the DC WritersCorps was also an easy pivot. His workshop dossier was extensive by that point. Well before the WritersCorps, he had convened a writing workshop for young Black boys at Oak Hill Detention Facility. He wrote about his travels for *The Washington Post*. "I go to Oak Hill, Cedar Knoll, and other detention facilities to provide activities beyond television and ping-pong," Stover wrote of his experience. "I see my time with these young African American men as more than an opportunity to gain some converts to poetry writing and reading, more than just a discussion of the latest rap music. I want these young men to see their own role in the oral tradition that was born on the African continent where griots (poet-historians) to this very day tell centuries-old stories."[6]

Stover started going to Oak Hill in 1992. He would travel to the facility six times per week sometimes. Once he joined the DC WritersCorps, expansion of his workshop was a no-brainer. *The Washington Post* essay he penned led to a workshop at Lorton Reformatory because residents there saw his article and reached out.

The Lorton Reformatory workshop was the direct result of efforts by Stover, Carroll, and Judy Lyons, who served as the administrator for the high school programs at the facility. For two years, a combination of myself, Dias-Porter, Ta-Nehisi Coates, and Stover drove from Washington, DC, down to Lorton Prison in Lorton, Virginia. The workshop was held in the Medium Facility.

We conducted writing workshops. We gave the residents a chance to express themselves on the page. We inspired them by showing videos, by teaching them poetry forms, and by allowing them to feel like human beings rather than numbers in the system.

Eventually, our efforts but mostly the creative energy of the residents resulted in an anthology called *Medium*.[7] It is probably our proudest moment during the entire two years of the workshop. The workshop had challenges. Some of the residents who attended were not literate. Security at the facility was always an issue. Yet the anthology we produced is evidence of the importance of persistence. It is also evidence that lives were being tossed away into America's criminal justice system.

DC WritersCorps organized other workshops at the Mitch Snyder Homeless Shelter on D Street in the city. Those workshops, Clean and Sober Streets, provided individuals in recovery with an outlet for their writing aspirations. Jeffrey McDaniel, a poet in recovery, worked at that location as did many others. Some other locations for the DC WritersCorps included Ballou Senior High School, Leckie Elementary School, Johnson Middle School, Cardozo Senior High School, Banneker High School, House of Ruth Battered Women's Shelter, Moss Hollow Summer Camp, and New York Avenue Presbyterian Homeless Seniors Program. Hundreds of residents in the city benefited from the efforts of the poets.

Dias-Porter, through the African American Writers Guild (AAWG), was already teaching a workshop in the city under a small grant written by Carroll when he came into the WritersCorps.[8] His self-designed Rapping and Writing workshop for teens was a new twist and was just the kind of program that set WritersCorps apart from past efforts. It became popular quickly. It reflected the power of hip-hop culture to reach a younger audience who greatly needed something to bring beauty to their lives. Washington, DC, was a troubled, violent, and splintering city in the early 1990s, and the children and everyone needed programs that uplifted them. DC WritersCorps was one such program.

Over the more than a decade of its existence, the best poets came through the DC WritersCorps, and some of the best African American poets did as well. Holly Bass, Laini Mataka, Reuben Jackson, Isaac Colon, Kimberly Collins, Gary Lilley, A. Van Jordan, Imani Tolliver, John Murillo, Joel Dias-Porter, Ta-Nehisi Coates, and so many others came to the city to live, write, and teach writing to people.

Rudy McCann, Andy Fogle, Craig Czury, Jeff McDaniel, Joe Ray Sandoval, Ryan Grim, Nancy Schwalb, Jeanie Tietjen, Sheila (Shea) Ashdown, Chris Llewellyn, Emmitt Cunningham, Yona Harvey, Lisa Pegram, Craig Czury, Darrell Stover, Ruth Dickey, Tanya Nyman, and many others also were part of the DC WritersCorps, running workshops and giving young people a chance to talk through art to the world. Workshops already in existence thrived, and new workshops popped up on a whim. Poets entered the schools and connected with students in classroom workshops, and workshops came together at homeless shelters and recreation centers.

Many of these individuals are some of the country's most well-known poets today. Many of them are African American poets who stayed in the Washington area for years and continued to give back. The program put front and center young African American children and the marginalized in the city. Approximately seventy writers and poets would teach and volunteer with DC WritersCorps.

The late poet Reuben Jackson fondly recalled his years teaching in the program.

"How my students approached their work—whether reciting, revising, or writing new pieces with such grace and confidence. They were (and are) the Middle School Students I never was."[9]

Jackson's humorous comment is common among poets who worked in the program for little or no compensation. Nearly all of DC WritersCorps writers were successful poets and were living the lives of poets.

Lisa Pegram, who worked at the DC WritersCorps for ten years, is one of the major players in the program, who pivoted to a career in poetry and writing afterward. Pegram originally began working at DC WritersCorps teaching but soon was the director for the program and would spend a decade working tirelessly with Carroll to make literature happen in DC marginalized communities. Today, Pegram is a writer, editor, and literary consultant with multiple projects always in action. Even though like many Washington, DC, African American poets she has moved out of the city, she remains connected to her home and is frequently there for programs.

Initially, the DC WritersCorps was administered by AWP at George Mason University via the NEA. But as bureaucracies evolve in the nation's capital, Kenneth Carroll's organization was passed around like a hot potato. The cultural wars of previous years always made the bureaucrats pushing arts funding and programs fearful of being defunded or splashed on the headlines of the nation's news outlets. But DC Writers Corps was all about the good, the youth, and saving them from their own country's excesses. There was little reason to fear, in theory.

Lamond-Riggs Public Library, located uptown, right in my own neighborhood, already had a popular workshop for poets when DC WritersCorps started. Carroll urged his writers to come over and lead workshops, and they did. Ta-Nehisi Coates, Yona Harvey, Joel Dias-Porter, Darrell Stover, Toni Asante Lightfoot, and A. Van Jordan were just some of the DC WritersCorps poets who came regularly. Other poets, equally as talented, came to the workshop regularly as participants. This included Brandon Johnson, Jennifer Smith, Robin Dunn (Bryant), Mike Devine, Monica Hand, Lauren Anita (Arrington), and James "Maina" Lee. The workshop at Lamond-Riggs proved to be quite special, as it was also located right in the neighborhood where I was born and raised.

Each Saturday morning between 1995 and 1997, except for holidays, and the summer months, the Lamond-Riggs Library WritersCorps would meet with an energized group of poets. The workshop became so popular and well known by all sorts of poets that it was given the name the Woodshed. The name was a tribute to what jazz musicians often said when they were not on stage performing: they were "sheddin'" or practicing or trying to get better. In addition to the workshop, the WritersCorps and the African American Writers Guild partnered to sponsor poetry readings, panels, and film screenings all focused on poetry and African American poetry at the Lamond-Riggs Library.

Poets in the workshop were also able to find places to read away from the library. On more than one occasion, Vertigo Books sponsored open readings by members of the workshop. Michael (Mike) Devine, a full professor today at State University of New York (SUNY Plattsburgh), came regularly to the WritersCorps at Lamond-Riggs. Devine, while not African American, was firmly part of the African American poetry scene in the city because of the DC WritersCorps workshop at the library. He was a student at nearby Catholic University at the time. Van Jordan, a poet in DC WritersCorps at various locations, is now a full professor in creative writing at Stanford University. Yona Harvey is the same at Smith College in Massachusetts.

Another interesting spinoff from the Lamond-Riggs workshop was a short-lived journal known as *The Bridge: poems, beats, and riffs*. While the journal only lasted two issues, it published some of today's major writers. A. Van Jordan is published in issue 1, and Ta-Nehisi Coates, a contributing editor, contributed a review of Wu-Tang Clan's second album, *Wu-Tang Forever*.

In addition to Coates, Elanna Haywood assisted with production, and Yaphet Brinson, the local hip-hop punk rock poet, was the publication's layout artist. Other poets included in *The Bridge*'s two issues are Doralee Brooks, Kenneth Carroll, and Reuben Jackson. The journal sought to act as a networking vehicle for poets nationwide.

DC WritersCorps continued for eleven years. Funding was always difficult. Carroll admitted that sometimes he didn't get paid. It was a labor of love for him. Poets came to teach in the program from across the country.[10] That is the significance of the DC WritersCorps; it did humane things for those participating in the workshops. These were mostly young people.

One of the crowning moments for DC WritersCorps was its Middle School Slam Poetry League. This annual event, underwritten by Borders Books and the Fannie Mae Foundation, was a source of pride and financial support for Carroll's program. When Borders Books went bankrupt and Fannie Mae had its own financial challenges, DC WritersCorps did struggle forward, but the end was coming. It is to Carroll's and Pegram's credit that it stayed in operation for so long. Poet Silvana Straw, the wordsmith from the days of the Slam poetry revolution, also helped keep the program afloat through her philanthropic work.

The Slam League was the creative idea of Nancy Schwalb and MaryAnn Brownlow, who was directing community affairs at Borders Books downtown. Brownlow was also instrumental in the publication of the WritersCorps anthology, *Paint Me Like I Am*, by Harper Collins. The anthology, first published in 2003, remains in print.

Every middle school in the city became involved in the Slam League. Carroll got poet Jeff McDaniel and Joel Dias-Porter to design the Slam competition because they both were veterans of the phenomenon as performers. "That always raised $5000 or even $10,000 for the programmers every year," Carroll said of the Slam League.

Nancy Schwalb's workshop at Hart Middle School through the DC WritersCorps survived the down period at DC WritersCorps. Schwalb had worked at Hart Middle School during her days at DC WritersCorps. Although she worked at other sites, mostly Hart Middle School was her location. Today, over twenty-five years later, the

Hart after-school writing workshop, known as the DC Creative Writing Workshop (DCCWW), continues to do its work. The young writers in the program perform their poetry each year, and the program produces an anthology of writings.[11]

Nancy Schwalb was a student at George Mason University when WritersCorps was founded. According to Schwalb, she had no idea what the WritersCorps was when she applied to work there in the early 1990s. Schwalb, a writer, activist, and teacher, was hired by Carroll as well.[12] While Schwalb is Jewish and not African American and not a poet, when she and the DC WritersCorps connected as employee-employer, it was an important moment for Black poetry in the city. It remains an important moment as Schwalb's work continues today, even though DC WritersCorps stopped its programs years ago for lack of funding.

"I loved DC," Schwalb says of the early 1990s when it all came together. "I didn't know it at the time but that was the apex."[13] Schwalb is referring to the city itself, the majority Black city locals still called "Chocolate City." Schwalb's workshop in the WritersCorps would be located at Hart Middle School in upper Southeast Washington. Hart is across the river from the federal city and was in one of the most challenging communities in the city. Violence and poverty dominated the streets where the children in Schwalb's creative writing program lived and existed daily.

DCCWW also is a magnet for African American poets to give back to the community. Schwalb called it a "rite of passage" to teach in the workshop. Poets Derrick Weston Brown, Alan King, Patrick Washington, Reginald Dwayne Betts, and several other local DC Black poets have worked at Hart over the years. Even with the many writers that DC WritersCorps helped spawn, it is programs like Schwalb's that are equally if not more important. DCCWW is a direct descendant of what Carroll started back in mid-1990s. Carroll also notes other programs in existence today that are doing exactly what he was trying to do at the DC WritersCorps. "This is what makes it all worth it," Carroll said. "We helped many programs get started with what we were already doing at the WritersCorps."[14]

The DC writer Marita Golden was only a poet for a short time, but as a writer she was also an institution builder who helped poets. She created two organizations that were very important to African American poetry in the city. For this reason, her life and work have taken on an expansive role in African American literature and writing in the city.

The first was the AAWG, formed in 1987. The second organization and one that is important to all African American writers in DC and elsewhere, is the Zora Neale Hurston / Richard Wright Foundation. It almost seems like the Guild was a test run for the Hurston/Wright Foundation. The Guild, which I joined in 1988 and where I served in various roles for ten years, was more focused on supporting local writers in Washington with workshops, readings, and networking. Golden also brought a national reach to the organization. The Hurston/Wright Foundation, founded in 1990, sought to do all of what the Guild was doing and more.

Clyde McElvene, a bibliophile and businessman, had heard Golden on the radio talking about African American literature and got in touch. McElvene and Golden created the foundation in 1990 and began the hard, arduous work of establishing an African American institution of great importance. The foundation's mission from the beginning and today is to "develop, nurture, and sustain the world community of writers of African descent."[15] For several years, the foundation did all sorts of things, but eventually it has settled into what it does best: nurture and celebrate writers.

An annual Legacy Awards program is usually held in the Fall in Marita Golden's hometown, Washington, DC. There are online courses and workshops. There is also a Writers Week held in the summer where established writers conduct workshops for up-and-coming writers for a week. There are readings during that week and oftentimes opportunities to meet individuals from the book industry who tell writers how they might be able to get published.

Many well-known writers have come through the Hurston/Wright community and are now enjoying amazing careers as writers. The award-winning novelist Tayari Jones started out as just a young writer seeking community when she submitted her work to the Hurston/Wright Foundation and was awarded the foundation's award for debut fiction in 2002. Other notable winners of Hurston/Wright Legacy Awards are Chris Abani, Sanderia Faye, and Kwame Dawes. As for poetry, some notable winners include Claudia Rankine, Lucille Clifton, Rita Dove, Terrance Hayes, and Shara McCallum.

The inclusion of Legacy Awards in the poetry category demonstrated the foundation's commitment to all kinds of writing. Writers Week for the foundation also proved a special time for poets and many in the Washington, DC, area. The foundation almost always brought in the best of African American poetry. Tim Seibles, A. Van Jordan, and Nikky Finney are three poets who taught workshops during the foundation's Writers Week over the years. Hoke (Brother Yao) Glover was a regular at many Hurston/Wright events and he served on the foundation's board as well, giving poets a presence with one of the most important national literary organizations.

In 2006, when the foundation offered a writing workshop for teens, I directed the workshop. This was also the year I met Reginald Dwayne Betts, another poet younger than me but also quite an important writer. Betts's story as a poet and writer is right out of the purpose of Hurston/Wright and the Washington, DC, metro area. Betts was born and raised in Suitland, Maryland, an African American suburban city just outside the city. Betts was an outstanding student but at age sixteen committed a transgression that landed him in prison for eight years. Betts eventually fell in love with poetry and writing while incarcerated, and when he was released he hit the ground running. He began working for Karibu Books with the poet Brother Yao. His presence at the Hurston/Wright Foundation Summer Writers Week was evidence of his commitment. He completed a book and a memoir both detailing his journey to literary relevance. He would obtain an MFA degree from the University of Maryland and work for Nancy Schwalb at the DCCWW.

But Betts was hardly finished. He published another collection of poetry, obtained a law degree from Yale, and then was awarded a MacArthur Genius Grant in 2021. He continued to advocate for those incarcerated. He served the Obama administration on juvenile justice issues. He co-wrote a law review article on mass incarceration. And Betts got married and had two children and continues to press forward, making each previous accomplishment seem like a beginning rather than an end.

To Golden's credit, again demonstrating her commitment to all genres of African American writing, the foundation is now directed by the poet Khadijah Ali-Coleman. Ali-Coleman is a native Washingtonian who also lived in its surrounding suburbs like many poets. Ali-Coleman is an artist and administrator, and that is something that does not always happen smoothly. But Ali-Coleman is leading the foundation well into the future. The foundation is not just doing the work it has always done; it is doing more such work. Ali-Coleman also continues to produce her own art. She has performed and presented her own work all over the city's venues. Ali-Coleman, who performed as Khadijah Moon, remembers the scene back to Mango's and has never lost touch with it.[16]

The Roosters

> They arrive one by one on Monday nights, check their egos at the door, and prepare for a workshop that offers honest and intensive criticism. We are all serious about our work, but no one takes themselves too seriously.[17]

Those are the words of Renée Stout, the contemporary artist of paintings and sculptor in Washington, DC, for over forty years. Stout, who maintained a studio in the city across the street from the So Others May Eat (SOME) headquarters, is speaking of the workshop called the Black Roosters. The workshop began in 1997 in Stout's artist studio. It produced a mini anthology called *The Black Rooster Social Inn: This Is The Place* (Spike and Pepper Books). The publication was the work of four poets and Stout: Joel Dias-Porter, Ernesto Mercer, Gary Lilley, and Brandon Johnson. Stout provided the visuals for the book. It is not an entirely unique book, but it does possess qualities of risk-taking by five artists hitting their stride as creators. It is, and was, one of those moments.

Joel Dias-Porter, one of the poets who participated in the special workshop and the publication of the book, describes the experience as quite spontaneous:

> After some reading in town on a Monday night, we were looking for a place to watch Monday Night Football. We considered a sports bar and then Renée invited us to her place. We watched the game and had some good discussions and Renée said we were welcome to come back. So we started watching Monday Night Football at her spot every Monday and when the games weren't good we would talk about whatever, including a bunch of poetry talk.

> One week somebody pulled out a poem and we discussed it. When football season was almost over Renée said we could keep coming back if we wanted to and then we basically turned it into a workshop.[18]

The Black Rooster Social Inn: This Is the Place, the workshop and the publication, was yet another of those special organic moments from the history of African American poetry in the city. It just happened and the literature was produced, providing the snapshot in time of the life of some artists trying to be heard.

Terrance Hayes, who knew all the members of the collective, including the visual artist Renée Stout, was so intrigued by what the artists did over the years that he wrote a poem about it. Hayes himself first began coming to DC in 1997 and got to know Kenneth Carroll and Joel Dias-Porter very well and remained in touch with many poets in the city. Hayes is probably one of the top poets writing in the world today. He has been the recipient of most of the literary world's highest achievements, including the National Poetry Series (2001), the National Book Award (2010), and a MacArthur Fellow Award (2014). His poem individually recognizes the art and poetry that came together under the interesting conditions in the late 1990s. As it turns out, Hayes's literary offering is the highest tribute to the moment:

THE FUTURE OF THE BLACK ROOSTER COLLECTIVE (for Brian Gilmore)
The night before the legendary Black Rooster Collective reunites to present a dazzling group poem and artwork for Michelle Obama's presidential inauguration, the poets gather in DC for a workshop (a.k.a: a panicked inaugural poem making session) just as they used to at the end of the prior century.

::

Brandon D. Johnson, a.k.a. The Brain, Gary Lilley, a.k.a. The Bluesman, Ernesto Mercer, a.k.a. the Priest, and Joel Dias-Porter aka DJ Renegade, a.k.a. the Gambler arrive the night before carrying pages of poetry waiting to be arranged to tell a tale about America.

::

Commissioned to make a portrait of the first lady, Stout's piece is both painting, sculpture and installation made of bamboo and chocolate, revolving iron clock gears, a floor covered in thousands of diamond sunflower seeds, and a US President flag lapel piecing the petal of a Day Lilly.

::

Bluesman Gary Lilley proposes the group poem respond to the piece, but Renegade thinks it's a gamble. It's not quite true that the black rooster poets bring nothing but poetry. Having found his poems in bus stops, rest stops, boxcars, crossroads, airports and ports mouths, the bluesman brings the music of American landscapes and a twelve-string guitar.

::

Joel Dias-Porter the Renegade Black Rooster who has lived in a house of cards (which is to say, a house of math, and a house of intuition, a house of odds and angles) considers every possible arrangement and language for the poem the four are commissioned to compose. When considering their poem's vivid color motif, for example, Dias-Porter calculates the impact of every existing color and hue.

::

Priest Ernesto Mercer, the Black Rooster who has lived in all the houses of the Eternal, the tents and tabernacles, the corner blocks and bulwarks, the riverbanks and dancefloors of the Eternal—where Eternal is a synonym for God and Goddess, John Coltrane, and Alice Coltrane with the same heart—the priest whose name is like Earnest Mercy brings a soulfulness to the poem they make. His spirit is part Prince in "Erotic City," part monk in a monastery, part Monk in "Birdland."

::

Brandon Johnson, the Brain, who still finds poems close to the ground of the District of Columbia where others wandered and returned, brings a complicated local flavor along with two big bespectacled eyes observing his life and the lives of his loves. The group works for much of the night trying to include Johnson's image of black yard dog to the black rooster, poet, Kenny Carroll dressed as Marcus Garvey astride an enormous black panther and another describing Ethelbert Miller as the W. E. B. Du Bois of DC. The poets wonder if Brian Gilmore will appear. "Gilmore," they cheer like a prayer when stuck on a word, "Gilmore," they cheer like a handshake the instances they agree.

::

Late past the witching hour the night before Michelle Obama's inauguration, the black rooster poets fuss, fidget, weep, sleep, stitch, and hammer their magnificent recollections of witness into a single poem: their decades figuring the absence and presence and mysteries of love, the orders and systems of government, religion, music, sports and film; the violences and silences of all systems of order, the levity and gravity of dirt, but the fifth black rooster, Renee Stout sleeps peacefully because her piece is complete.[19]

—*Terrance Hayes*

20

Millennium

On November 20, 2000, after twenty-six years, E. Ethelbert Miller presented the last Ascension poetry reading. The reading was convened at the Folger Shakespeare Library in downtown Washington, DC. The fact that it was held at the Folger Shakespeare Library was a statement about how much the series had become an integral part of the city's overall poetry scene. The series had begun in April 1974 as a space to feature Black and Third World writers, but now it was much more than that. The series now spoke for poetry nationally and for the entire city. Miller had nurtured a safe space that had not just presented poetry but had brought people together.

The end of the Ascension Series and the disappointment many poets and locals felt also spoke to what had been built since the days of Paul Laurence Dunbar: a true autonomous poetry community that existed within and around the city. The Black poetry scene in DC was part of the overall poetry ecosystem in the area, but it also was a community that stood out on its own.

Jennifer King, manuscripts librarian in Special Collections at George Washington University's Gelman Library, wrote years ago that "the DC poetry community is diffuse and difficult to define."[1] King is correct about the overall community in DC. Yet the African American community, as Miller's reading series demonstrated (one aspect among many), is a defined entity and has a strong sense of continuity.

Much of this has to do with the distinct nature of the city as being a historical Jim Crow city but also one where historically African American life had the ability to evolve, grow, and develop easier than in the deep South and even in some northern towns. This allowed the Black poetry scene to develop as a cross-generational scene that sustained over time throughout the twentieth century. It is also the case that alliances were made easier in DC between Blacks and whites who had common goals. These alliances continue to this day.

On the last Ascension reading, Miller brought out two old friends to woo another Washington literary audience: Afaa Michael Weaver of Baltimore and Ahmos Zu-

Bolton, his running buddy from the early days at Howard and the Institute for the Arts and Humanities. It was a great night of poetry but also a bittersweet evening.

Most poets in the city had come to expect the regular Ascension reading, and now there would be no more readings. Though I connected with the series in the second half of its life, I saw many memorable events and poets. Amiri, Amina, and Ras Baraka, the "first family of African American poetry," as Miller called them. June Jordan. Essex Hemphill. Kenneth Carroll. Jennifer Smith. Bernice Reagon, the founder, and leader of the a capella singing legends Sweet Honey in the Rock. The Dark Room Collective. The list of poets covered half a century of Black poetry in America and the world.

No matter how one felt about the poetry, Miller had delivered a wide array of poetry for all kinds of audiences. He had connected poets throughout the city. The fact that the final reading was held at the Folger Shakespeare was also part of the progress made in the city when it came to African American poets and access to venues and resources. Miller had forged a literary alliance, and now today, Teri Cross Davis, an African American poet, is director of the Folger Poetry Series. Black poets regularly read there more often.

The Washington Review, a local literary journal, devoted an entire issue to the end of the Ascension Series.[2] The poet Kim Roberts served as editor.[3] The list of contributors included local poets, friends, and critically acclaimed academics. In the issue, the poet Calvin Forbes's comment was a question: "Who's going to take the weight?"[4]

Forbes wanted to know what would fill the void left by the end of the series. Kenneth Carroll noted that reading in the Ascension was his "first featured reading" as a poet, while Rebecca Villarreal recalled standing before the audience at her Ascension reading "with more experience and confidence, thanks to the . . . generous friendship of Ethelbert."[5]

The end of the Ascension did free Miller up to commence a furious record of publications. He would publish two memoirs—*Fathering Words: The Making of An African American Writer* (St. Martin's Press, 2000) and *The Fifth Inning* (Busboys and Poets / PM Press, 2011). His quantity of poetry is steady after he bowed out as a host and producer of his own poetry reading series.

In addition to a steady record of published poems, short essays, and blogging, Miller published a trilogy of poetry collections inspired by baseball—*If God Invented Baseball: Poems* (2018), *When Your Wife Has Tommy John Surgery and Other Baseball Stories* (2020), and *How I Found Love Behind The Catcher's Mask: Poems* (2022)—that was published by City Point Press. He was nominated for a Grammy award in 2023 in the spoken word category. He would also serve on the board of many of the more prestigious literary and/or political organizations in the country, including the Associated Writing Program, the Institute for Policy Studies, and the Pen/Faulkner Foundation.

In October 1999, just before the Ascension Series ended, poet and cultural organizer and activist Gaston Neal died. Neal had been sick for a while by the time of his death, so it did not surprise anyone. But it was still a big loss for the many poets, political activists, jazz fans, and cultural workers in the city who had known Neal since his early days.

Poet Kenneth Carroll wrote of Neal in the days following his death: "Gaston Neal's importance to the Washington, DC arts community is without question. . . . Gaston helped to create or forge institutions like The New School of Afro-American Thought and Drum and Spear Bookstore. He was also instrumental in starting what became the DC Commission on the Arts and Humanities. . . . Gaston Neal's life was art and action."[6]

As Neal had requested, at his memorial service he was carried into the church in a wooden box. Baba Ngoma, a local African drummer, led a procession of poets, musicians, intellectuals, and activists into Rankin Chapel on the campus of Howard University. Neal wanted young poets to read at his service and they did, as did his longtime friend the poet Amiri Baraka.

In the lead-up to Neal's death after a three-year struggle with cancer, Neal's many friends and the many communities he nurtured were able to pay him appropriate tribute with a day of music, poetry, and love called "Scattered Pieces of the Action," held at Howard University's Cramton Auditorium on July 13, 1997.[7]

Poets Amiri Baraka, Askia Muhammed, Sonia Sanchez, Greg Tate, Joel Dias-Porter, Sekou Sundiata, and Quincy Troupe are among those who showed up to help Neal in his most challenging hour. On the jazz-blues side, Nap Turner, Sunny Sumter, Bobby Parker, Andrew White, Joe Bowie, and Craig Harris were some of the musicians who performed. It was a party celebrating two of Neal's cultural obsessions: poetry and jazz.

Neal, over the years, had remained busy with poetry and jazz so it made perfect sense. In 1996 Neal was part of local saxophonist Fred Foss's release *The Journey*. Foss and Neal were friends, and the poem Neal provided is "To the Northstar," a tribute to Harriet Tubman. The historical relevance of the tune is Black folklore: Tubman guided the Africans through her Underground Railroad by following the North Star in the sky. Neal's lifelong friend the poet and jazz critic A. B. Spellman, in the liner notes to the Foss album,[8] wrote that Neal provided a poem to the recording "strong enough to stand on its own but which came alive in performance like . . . Bird's 'Koko.' "[9]

Neal's most impressive performance partnership during his waning days was probably the occasional jam session with local Washington, DC, tap dancer Johne (pronounced "Jahnay") Forges (pronounced "Forjay"). Forges, born and raised in New Orleans, and Neal, the performance jazz poet, were always an ideal match. They did a call and response where poetry was challenged by the rhythm and tapping of a dancer's tap shoes and vice versa.

Right before Neal died, Tony Gittens, his partner from the days of Drum and Spear Bookstore and the New School of Afro-American Thought, awarded Neal the Mayor's Arts Award for Excellence in Literary Arts. Neal threw a party at his house and put word out for anyone who wanted to come by his house.[10]

Poet Yaphet Brinson's death, also in late 1999, was a shocker. Where Neal had been able to work at poetry for decades, Brinson was just finding his space on the city's art's scene when he got ill. Brinson, like many Black poets, came to the city to be a student at Howard University. He was originally from New York and New Jersey. Brinson made hip-hop music a singular influence on his poetry and on his punk culture. His collection of poetry *Different Dementions* is the best example of Brinson's cutting-edge poetry that foretold part of the future of African American poetry in Washington, DC.

Brinson also was an early innovator of presenting poetry through digital websites when hardly anyone even knew about the internet. Brinson was a writer of haiku over the years, though this part of him was not as well known as his poems with an urban edge alluding to mosh pits and African history. He worked in Kenneth Carroll's DC WritersCorps program teaching community workshops. His biggest motivation as a writer seemed to always be love between African Americans. He wrote about his love of African American people while a student at Howard University in an essay, "Striving for Unity," published in *The Hilltop Newspaper*. Brinson describes Howard University as a "microcosm of society";[11] with "so much that is being pressed on black people (read: racism), there exists animosity that exists . . . within all sectors of campus."[12]

And not long after the death of Neal and Brinson, M'Wilie Askari, the poet and street wordsmith, also died. It was the summer of 2000. Askari was an elder poet on the African American poetry scene going back decades. In the 1990s he spent much of his time with younger poets at the various venues. Askari was a poet I first saw read back in the late 1980s. His death did not result in the massive appearance of Black Arts Movement (BAM) legends in the city to send him off. However, Askari had the same kind of respect in the local African American poetry scene among some of the young poets that Gaston Neal had during his time. Poet Patrick Washington and others paid tribute to Askari on June 3, 2000, and appropriately scattered Askari's ashes on U Street, the spoken word and poetry strip where he reached out to and sought to mentor many of the young African American poets who were new to the poetry world.[13]

In the Tradition

If there is one constant to the African American poetry scene in the city, it is that sense of cross-generational community that so many of the city's Black poets feel in the city. The community is tight-knit, but all the poets are not the same age, and many were not originally born in the city. It has come together cohesively because of the solid foundation and values laid out decades ago long before any of the city's newest voices ever were born. Sterling Brown was a publishing poet and scholar during the initial Harlem Renaissance period. He continued to write, teach, and mentor all day through the BAM in Washington, DC. May Miller as well has a similar historical arc in the city and the literary circles.

Gaston Neal, E. Ethelbert Miller, and Marita Golden were writers in the city in the late 1960s and into the 1970s, and they remained supportive mentor writers into the late 1990s. Golden and Miller remain part of the current literary scene in Washington, particularly the African American literary scene. This is the cross-generational history of the Black poetry world in the city.

Poets such as Venus Thrash (died in 2021), Derrick Weston Brown, Fred Joiner, Alan King, Melanie Henderson, Ebony Golden, Lisa Pegram, Sam Jefferson, Darrell Perry, Patrick Washington, Charles McClain, and Tiffany Thompson are just a few of the African American poets who were beneficiaries of the solid legacy. And each of them, like the many poets before in the city, took their own path into the world of Black poetry in the city.

"I arrived in DC to get my MFA in Poetry from American University," Derrick Brown writes recently. "Another fellow poet in my Program, Ebony Golden and I started checking out open mics through the local City Paper." Brown met Venus Thrash and Alan King at this time.[14] Brown didn't come expecting magic, but he did find it. He calls his growth as a poet in the city a "natural progression." He began to meet writers and found venues and in 2006, Brown released his first chapbook, *The Unscene.*

According to Brown, one of the first spaces where he read was at a dive called the Kaffa House located in the U Street Corridor. Poet Ernesto Mercer, Brown said, organized many of the readings at Kaffa House. Mercer, a veteran on the DC scene by this point, was also part of the cross-generational vibe in the city.

Brown eventually began hosting his own reading series in the city called A Piece of 8, which was an ode to the 8Rock Cultural Center where Kenneth Carroll had programmed poetry and spoken word events.[15] After A Piece of 8' Brown through a connection with Andy Shallal's Busboys and Poets, began hosting 9 on the Ninth, another very popular open microphone series in the city. Shallal was supportive of Brown's efforts, helping with the publication of Brown's 2011 book, *Wisdom Teeth,* via PM Press.

Alan King, Brown's running partner, had a similar but different journey. He was a student at the University of Maryland, College Park when his "Big Sister" (the person helping new students with orientation) learned he wrote poetry.[16] She identified venues for King. King became a regular poet at the venues in the city, even though he lived in the DC suburbs in Fort Washington, Maryland.

"The arts scene embraced me and raised me as a young poet," King said. His first reading was the popular venue Bar Nun in 1999.[17] He would eventually publish two chapbooks, *Transfer* and *The Music We Are.* King describes the DC Black poetry scene as "nurturing." He also said that "the writers don't have egos like those in NYC. The literary scene exists in pockets."[18]

Lisa Pegram, a multidimensional poet and artist now, fully understands what a poet has access to in DC. It is rooted in the history and, again, the values laid down early. "There is this intergenerational family kind of thing that we sometimes take for granted," Pegram said. "In DC everything is connected."[19] Pegram said she felt very taken care of when she was developing as a poet and cultural worker. She spent one summer when fifteen working for the Institute for the Preservation of African American Writing. She was paid to write and present readings around the city along with other poets. Older writers and cultural workers ran the organization, which immediately provided her with that long connection back to the days of Sterling Brown, May Miller, and Paul Laurence Dunbar.

Pegram attended National Cathedral High School along with another African American poet in the city, Tiffany Thompson.[20] Thompson told Pegram about a poetry venue in the 1990s called It's Your Mug, or "The Mug," Toni Lightfoot's creation. Pegram and Thompson began regularly attending and participating in the energy that was happening at the venue. It was the beginning of something, even though they didn't quite know what that was at the time. This is what led to Pegram becoming one of the key poets in the city but also her work at DC WritersCorps with Kenneth Carroll for a decade.

Meanwhile, other Black poets similarly situated in the city artistically were also itching to be more involved in the scene. Sam Jefferson, Darrell Perry, Charles McCain, and Patrick Washington began reading regularly at just about every venue. They soon called themselves and were known around as Generation 2000. Jefferson (now Kemit Mawakana) was a lawyer who was always writing poetry and other things. He wound up at It's Your Mug during its heyday years of 1994–1996.[21] He loved it. Their connection to It's Your Mug proves the continuum that existed in the city was real over the decades.

Once the scene shifted to U Street, with venues like Bar Nun, Kaffa House, and Mango's, Mawakana, Washington, and the other members of Generation 2000 continued their work on the downtown poetry scene. Eventually, Perry and Washington recruited Tiffany Thompson and Lisa Pegram into Generation 2000. Perry, Washington, and Mawakana were looking for the voices of young Black women, and Thompson and Pegram were the ticket.

The group traveled all over for gigs—New York and Vermont were two places asking for their talents. They also hit the college circuit and performed in Brooklyn, New York, at the Brooklyn Moon Cafe. They performed at It's Your Mug in the final days of that venue with the rapper Priest of Freestyle Union as part of the show that night as well. "It seemed like back then you could read poetry and hear poetry every night," Mawakana said.[22]

Mango's was hosted by Raquel Brown. Kaffa House was hosted by Ernesto Mercer or Generation 2000. Matthew Payne and his collective called The Movement were holding court at Bar Nun. Venues started and stopped, and others began.

Aldon Nielsen, the poet and literary critic, remembers a similar time in the 1970s when there was poetry everywhere in the capital city. Gil Scott-Heron was in town, making records and teaching at University of the District of Columbia (UDC). C.L.R. James, the Trinidadian intellectual, was also teaching at UDC, according to Nielsen, and Ahmos Zu-Bolton and Ethelbert Miller were at Howard University starting the Ascension series. For Black poets, it was a moment where what had been nurtured previously in the city got more connected.

Generation 2000, with Mawakana, Pegram, Thompson, Perry, Washington, McClain, and others, made a name for itself quickly with its diverse mixture of poets and spoken word artists. Patrick Washington was more rapper than poet, as was Darrell Perry. Mawakana wrote tight, humorous verses. He became famous for the phrase "Clap Cocaine" on the poetry scene. The term referred to the support poets received at open mic readings from the audience even if their poetry was not strongly embraced.

The respectful applause at poetry readings was one of the reasons people came out and kept coming out. Mawakana eventually published a collection of poetry entitled *Crucifixion of My Soul.* In 1998, The *Washington City Paper* described him as "a Hoya, not a Wizard," and a poet who "now dabbles in socially conscious spoken-word poetry rather than hip hop."[23] Mawakana did play for the storied Georgetown Hoyas Men's Basketball program under John Thompson, and that by itself got attention even though on the poetry scene being part of Generation 2000 was enough.

Generation 2000 gave way to other manifestations of literary art. Perry and Washington broke away and formed the Poem-Cees, a hip-hop duo, and Pegram and Thompson went to the next phase as well outside of Generation 2000, which had earned so much success it only made sense to multiply. This next group of poets not only left their artistic mark on the city; they left behind a trail. Poem-Cees produced several recordings beginning in 2003 with *I.O.U. Street.* Washington was invited onto HBO's *Def Poetry Jam,* and then Poem-Cees (Washington and Perry) got invited onto the program as well. Poetry and hip-hop had become one, and then it got its respect from poets and poetry.

Washington was also instrumental in the "Great Day on U Street" project.[24] This occurred when as many Black poets as possible who were active in the city or had been active at some point took a photograph in front of the historic Lincoln Theater. They followed the photograph up with a reading at the Lincoln Theater that same day. The idea is from the famous "Great Day in Harlem," when New York–based jazz musicians gathered and took a photo in Harlem on August 12, 1958.[25] That photo was featured in *Esquire* magazine that year.

Kyle Dargan, a younger African American poet, scholar, and professor at American University, is one of the poets in the "Great Day on U Street" poetry project photo in DC. Dargan came to the city of Washington, DC, in 2006. His book *The Listening* had been the recipient of the 2004 Cave Canem Poetry Prize. In 2007, his collection *Bouquet of Hungers* was the recipient of the Hurston/Wright Legacy Award for Poetry.[26] He helped to organize poetry events at the White House with President Barack Obama and First Lady Michelle Obama.[27] He was on PBS with Bill Moyers, and he was also smart enough to invite local poets to his university classroom to talk and discuss poetry.

Dargan is an example of a Black poet in the city, teaching at the university level, trying to maintain a presence in the local poetry community as well. It is a difficult challenge, especially for poet-academics who do not teach at Howard University or the UDC. Dargan has done about as good a job as any to nurture connections and become an important component in the day-to-day work of literature in the city.

The Folger Legacy

Teri Ellen Cross Davis, a poet and native of Cleveland, Ohio, also was able to find her way in the city by taking a route that can be called tough. Davis is a very good poet and quickly settled into the city and the area as a poet. Like her husband, the poet Hayes Davis, Cross Davis attended the Cave Canem Poetry Retreat for African American poets. Hayes is from Philadelphia, but he has been in the DC area so long, he, like Teri, is an integral part of the scene. They are always doing readings and supporting poets and their work in literature.

In October 2005 Davis was appointed director of the Folger Shakespeare Library Poetry Series (the Folger Reading Series). It was important that an African American poet was appointed to the post but also even more important that it was Davis. Davis is not just a good poet, but she is quite familiar with the developing cadre of Black poets in the United States. The Folger Reading Series had been operating since 1970, and it did have Black poets over the years. However, for many of the locals, it would have been much more representative to have far more local African American poets invited over the years, especially when the city was culturally dominated by the over 70 percent Black population for two decades.

Davis, much to her credit, just brought in some very good poets to read and many African American poets who were surging at their craft. In 2012 when the Dark Room Collective reconvened itself for a nationwide tour, the poets appeared at the Folger thanks to Davis. Terrance Hayes, who started coming to the city in 1997, also read at the Folger along with the Affrilachian poet Frank X Walker. Other African American poets who read at the Folger during Davis's time directing the series include Rita Dove, Yusef Komunyakaa, and Nikki Finney, poets who have won literary awards of note in the country.[28]

Before Davis arrived in the 2000s, the Folger invited Black poets to read, but only a handful were local poets. Also, during the 1970s and 1980s, when African American poetry activity in the city was significant and quite influential nationally, the Folger did not invite many Black poets. The few exceptions included Ethelbert Miller, who read at the Folger in 1978, and May Miller, Lucille Clifton, Sterling Brown, and Garth Tate, who also read there.[29]

Ethelbert Miller was also responsible for getting more Black poets on the Folger stage. But Teri Ellen Cross Davis met the challenge presented at the Folger and also in her own writing career. She has published two books of poetry: *Haint* (Gival Press, 2016), winner of the 2017 Ohioana Book Award for Poetry, and *A More Perfect Union*

(Ohio State University Press, 2021). Davis has created her own unique artistic curation at the Folger involving more African American poets. She has had a reading devoted to Afrofuturism and a conversation between poetry legends Sonia Sanchez and Lucille Clifton. Davis also had a reading pairing poets Tyehimba Jess and Quincy Troupe with musicians.[30]

Teri's husband, Hayes Davis, while not from DC also established himself on the city's poetry scene as his wife, Teri's, poetry life got busy with poetry and literary curating. In fact, Hayes Davis had been in Washington so long he has become an expected presence. He also obtained his MFA in creative writing from the University of Maryland, College Park. He was part of the It's Your Mug poetry scene in the mid-1990s performing with the Modern Urban Griots in the late 1990s. Davis's book of poems *Let Our Eyes Linger* was published in 2016 by Poetry Mutual Press. His work has appeared in *New England Review, Poet Lore, Auburn Avenue, Gargoyle Magazine, Beltway Poetry Quarterly, Delaware Poetry Review, Kinfolks, Fledgling Rag,* and several anthologies.[31]

One very important and memorable event Teri Cross Davis has presented has been a poetry reading dedicated to Rev. Dr. Martin Luther King Jr. The reading is aptly called Not Just Another Day Off. The first such event was held in January 2007, just as Davis had begun her work.[32] It is always held at the time of the King Holiday celebration and has become one of those expected gatherings of like-minded poets. At the very first of these Dr. King readings, her husband, Hayes Davis, was there as well making the event come together, part of his own contribution with his wife to the history of the Washington, DC, Black poetry scene. Teri calls him the "First Man" of the Folger Poetry Series.

21

The Changing Same

In the summer 2014, I took my family on a trip to visit the Paul Laurence Dunbar National Site in Dayton, Ohio. I had always wanted to go visit the site, and because I always came to visit Washington, DC, in the summers (I was working in Michigan at the time), it was not out of the way.

We spent a full day at the national site that is Dunbar's home but is now a museum maintained by the National Park Service. The full life Dunbar squeezed into thirty-three years is on complete display everywhere. As we strolled through the museum and then his home that he purchased for his dedicated mother, Matilda, and where he wrote and died, I could only think of his legacy and Washington, DC. I thought of the early poets inspired by him such as May Miller and William Waring Cuney. I recalled the many exposed to his legacy like Sterling A. Brown, who represented the city most of all and respected Dunbar's professionalism and art but wanted to go his own way in the world and did.

The venues and institutions related to Black poetry in DC have changed or are gone. Ethelbert Miller's essential Ascension Series has been gone for over twenty years. 8Rock, It's Your Mug, DC Space, and many other legendary arts spaces are gone now and only exist in the memory of those who made them sing. There are new venues and new groups of poets; the various institutions that made the Black poetry scene special over the years continue to evolve. Black poetry is even more alive in Washington, and most of all it is an accumulation of all the poets, the literary activists, the arts institutions, and the people.

The city has changed politically. Mayor Marion Barry, the mayor who stood with the city's people and artists, fell from grace in 1991 and never recovered. In 2014 he died. He received a most honorable and appropriate hero's exit from "Chocolate City" despite the disappointing end to his purposeful life. Chuck Brown, the man who created go-go, the music and culture, the man responsible for "Chocolate City," also passed away in 2014. I came all the way from Michigan to pay my respects to the "Godfather of Go-Go."

In 1999 Anthony Williams, a man who came out of nowhere, took over as mayor of the city and set the city on a course for aggressive gentrification and austerity. In the twenty years since he has taken office, the African American population decreased from 60 percent to 40 percent. This was by design.

Williams specifically supported policies that changed the demographic characteristics of the city back to the numbers from the pre-civil-rights period.[1] Subsequent mayoral leadership, including the current mayor (as I write this), Muriel Bowser, did the same as Williams. This is the city where the African American poets and their historically constructed and nurtured poetry scene took its next steps.

Considering how Black poetry has been consistently pushed aside in the city and has lacked resources that matched its population numbers over the years, the scene itself knows how to fight back. It struggles on and builds alliances. It seeks its own spaces, and most of all it does not compromise its commitment to producing great poetry and words true to the city's history and culture. The high school named for Paul Laurence Dunbar is still educating the city's youth and it is now in its third iteration.

The Poets, Then and Now

Maybe the greatest tribute to two of the city's most important poets, Sterling A. Brown and Waring Cuney, is the fact that in the twentieth century, they are still being studied and celebrated. For Cuney, as one might expect, it was someplace far away from Washington, DC, where he was born, despite his being born there in 1906.

In the Dutch city of Leiden, a poetry project was commenced in 1992 with poems in English installed on walls in the city. Waring Cuney's poem "Charlie Parker," was installed on a wall in 2005 and became a bit of a social media phenomenon.[2] According to Ed Visser, a writer in the city of Leiden at the time of the installation, the mural commemorated the fiftieth anniversary of the American bebop pioneer Charlie Parker.[3] Visser said that the Cuney mural of his poem "Charlie Parker" was installed in May 2005. Considering Cuney's attraction to music as an artist and his life as a songwriter and poet, it was an appropriate choice by the curators. And, finally, much of the poetry Cuney wrote during his life is now available to the public through the first full-length biography written about him.

As for Brown, his reputation only has grown exponentially since his death in 1989. He has been honored countless times, including a special issue of the journal *Callaloo* and a symposium at the Library of Congress. He was also honored at the Americanist Symposium in 2007 when his masterwork *Southern Road* was celebrated on the seventy-fifth anniversary of its publication.[4] Poet Evie Shockley was part of the event, as was Professor Brad Evans of Rutgers University. Evans presented a paper on the collection called "Sterling Brown and Modern Anthropology."[5] Meredith McGill, an English professor at Rutgers University, organized the symposium,[6] and praised Brown's work in *Southern Road* as part of American literature and lore, something that had been lost over time. It is Brown's life work that exposed this fault line over and over.

Brown was perfectly comfortable writing in the vernacular of ordinary people and writing about ordinary people. *Southern Road* is a testament to this ideal. However, because of the development of writing and publishing, Americans had lost touch with the reality of poetry as it is gathered and expressed. It had become controlled by those who wrote it down and could write it down on paper. Brown's work in *Southern Road* was about the folklore and literature, the writing, and the people who made the writing come to life.

On the current scene in the city and the area, there remains a constant flow of poets, both from the past, who are still dedicated to the art, and new poets, equally as committed. Bomani Armah is one of the city's poets who is stretching the limits of spoken word / Slam culture to educate. Armah is a poet, educator, hip-hop artist, and citizen.[7] He educates children and ignites their creative impulses through hip-hop music and poetry, written and spoken. His underground recording "Read a Book," a hip-hop-fueled anthem to promote literacy, is the perfect example of how Armah is carving out a new path in the city.

Maria Fernanda is another example of a poet who has pressed into the scene without fear or expectation. "I started learning about artists in the poetry scene through attending Duke Ellington School of the Arts," Fernanda said.

> The DC poetry scene showcased slam and performance poetry more than anything when I was growing up. It was beautiful. I remember seeing myself as an artist who recited their work and, as a result, was not sure where my work and I would fit in the town where I grew up. While interning at the Library of Congress Poetry and Literature Center, I met the remarkable artist Holly Bass. She is a guiding light and incredible mentor to many. She exposed me to the various genres of poetry, fellowships, and the various DC poetry histories, such as It's Your Mug and more.[8]

The poet and spoken word artist Kenneth Carroll III (Kenny Carroll) is another young Black poet staying busy on the DC poetry scene. Carroll III was DC Youth Poet Laureate in 2017 and is the son of Kenneth Carroll, the poet and DC WritersCorps site coordinator. Young Kenny's impact on the current poetry scene in the city demonstrates a changing literary landscape but also the power of history. His father is still part of the local scene and still presents his poetry, but now his son has come along and joined the tradition. Kenny Carroll is now a regular around the city doing readings and workshops.

Up at Howard University the tradition continues to evolve as well. The school remains an integral part of the city's shifting African American poetry scene. Linette Marie Allen began reading her poetry at Howard University when she was nineteen but soon found her way to the city. Allen, a native Washingtonian, lived in Southeast Washington, DC, and commuted to Howard University in the daytime. Yao Hoke Glover, who was also a young poet at the time and mostly associated with the 8Rock

Cultural Center, introduced her to the local scene. Allen, now an award-winning poet and MFA graduate from the University of Baltimore, describes it like this:

> I ventured off campus to do readings at 19 . . . local poets with something to say, afrocentric poets, Toni Blackman and others . . . HU also had a hand in my introduction to serious poets . . . Poets were really accessible then . . . I met Maya Angelou at 18 or 19 as well at the National Prayer Breakfast, in Washington, DC . . . I'll never forget it. It was like poets all around me, all the time, back then. DC was heaven.[9]

While Allen was absent from the local scene for many years, she, like many of the city's Black poets, eventually returned to poetry and literature. She lives in Baltimore, has obtained an MFA in writing and publishing, and has now reconnected with the Black poetry scene in DC, Baltimore, and other cities. Her publication credits over the last few years are substantial. Yet like many others, her poetic career began here in Washington, DC, at the small venues of the loud, boisterous lovers of Black poetry.

In 2003 Howard University hired Tony Medina, the Bronx, New York City, poet and literary scholar. Medina became the first creative writing professor at the storied college. Medina was a well-known poet in the Washington area going back at least the early 1990s. His poetry was published in the anthology *In the Tradition: An Anthology of Young Black Writer*, edited by Ras Baraka and Kevin Powell, and he came to the city to read for that book. Over the years, I crossed paths with Tony Medina many times at readings in the DC area and in New York. He published children's books, poetry collections, and anthologies. In all, Medina has published more than twenty-five books across literary genres.

At Howard, Medina immediately opened his class to anyone who wanted to attend, and countless local Washington, DC, Black poets took him up on the offer. Melanie Henderson, a several-generation Washingtonian attended; as did Alan King; Fred Joiner; Randall Horton; and Truth Thomas, the poet, singer, and publisher. Medina didn't waste words either. He challenged the poets who sat before him to publish or perish, and they took him at his word. He told them to build poetry institutionally in the city, and they did. In the meantime, he also became part of the Washington poetry scene. "The DC Poetry scene is one of the most vibrant, eclectic, community-oriented scenes in the nation," Medina has said.[10]

It was important that Medina had come to Howard University also because E. Ethelbert Miller would leave the university under less-than-decent circumstances in 2015, when the school laid off eighty-four staff members. For many in the local arts community, the decision was misguided, considering the legacy Miller had built at the school. Miller took it all in stride and moved on. For forty years, Miller had served the school and the school's cultural mission to African American students. The roster of students who graduated from the school and credit him with helping them become better writers and artists is extensive.

Medina's arrival was not a swap, as Miller was there when Medina was there. But Medina was able to have his own impact on the Washington, DC, metro area poetry scene and is still having it. Medina's charge to the poets resulted in many efforts to promote literature from and in the city

The poet Truth Thomas founded a small press to publish literature. The press, Cherry Castle Publishing LLC, located in Columbia, Maryland, immediately engaged in important literary work in and around DC. Thomas published one of his own collections, *Speak Water*, in 2012. Thomas's *Speak Water* was awarded an NAACP Image Award for Poetry for that year.

Thomas also published a collection by Curtis L. Crisler, a well-known and widely published African American poet from Gary, Indiana. Crisler's book, *"This" American-ah*, proved that Cherry Castle Publishing LLC was ambitious. This was also apparent in 2022, when Thomas published an anthology of poetry entitled *Where We Stand: Poems of Black Resilience*.[11]

Melanie Henderson is an editor of the anthology, along with Thomas and Enzo Silon Surin. Henderson is a humble star on the Washington, DC, poetry scene with a unique voice and a steady commitment to poetry. Her 2011 collection of poetry, *Elegies for new york avenue*, won the Main Street Rag Award that year. Henderson is the poetry editor for Cherry Castle Publishing LLC. She was born in Washington at Howard University Hospital. She has always lived in the city. "My roots can be traced back five generations in the city," Henderson said.[12] Henderson, like many others, connected with Tony Medina's poetry class on the Howard University campus. Henderson came up on the Black poetry scene in the U Street Corridor but also read all over the DC area and is constantly a part of the Black poetry community's important literary projects and publications.[13]

American Poetry Museum

The city's poetry scene is old enough now to not only have a history but also be able to document that history. The American Poetry Museum (APM) was a central part of that task the moment it was founded by Jon West-Bey in 2004. APM represents the many important developments that occurred as a new century of poetry began in the city.

Jon West-Bey wanted to marry his two passions into one, and he did despite the efforts of a few people to talk him out of his project. West-Bey discovered poetry in the 1990s when he was at Virginia Commonwealth University in Richmond, Virginia. He also began working with a group of spoken word poets called the Jazz Poetry Society. Eventually, the Jazz Poetry Society connected with the DC poetry scene and the poetry collective Generation 2000.[14]

West-Bey became close friends with the poet Patrick Washington. Collaborations between West-Bey's poetry group and members of Generation 2000 created a permanent connection to the city. West-Bey also set a goal back then to found and direct his own museum before he turned thirty. That goal was met when West-Bey founded APM in Southeast Washington, DC, in 2004. West-Bey devoted his seventy-five-page graduate school thesis to writing a blueprint for the museum.

According to West-Bey, the museum became a "pop up" institution where public programs would be convened at various locations. West-Bey did his due diligence and sought consultation of others, but the early years were tough. Funding a museum that focused on poetry and one that did not have a physical building led many to discourage his efforts. But Ethelbert Miller did not try to talk West-Bey out of his idea and encouraged him to press forward.[15]

Despite the challenges in financial resources and a permanent space, West-Bey, along with poet Fred Joiner, succeeded mostly in maintaining APM. In the early days, Joiner began a regular museum reading series and curation called "Intersections" that focused on poets and allowed the audience and Joiner to engage the poet in a dialog after the reading. This was the partnership West-Bey and Joiner forged. West-Bey had APM, and Joiner's part of the institution was the Center for Poetic Thought. To put the focus on poetry and treat it like high art was a bold statement. It was just as unique as the museum space itself.

APM eventually obtained a permanent space in Southeast Washington, DC. APM was a small, well-lighted arts space in a part of town known for a high rate of crime and poverty. It was a storefront space, larger than normal, but would have likely gone to waste but for the efforts of West-Bey and Joiner.

The audience for the events were arts and literary junkies. Joiner let the poets read, and then he engaged in a conversation with them before the audience. Joiner asked questions, gave the poet space to riff on their poetry, their art. Each featured night took on its own character. APM had financial challenges, but it endured.

Somehow, West-Bey kept the museum open and collected poetry and items related to poetry. Videotapes of poets reading, spoken word anthologies on compact disks, books, photographs, and other archival items related to poetry were collected from all kinds of sources. It was a novel idea that had teeth.

In 2020 both founder Jon West-Bey and Fred Joiner stepped down from running APM.[16] Local poet and artist Sami Miranda took over the day-to-day operations. Miranda, poet, artist, schoolteacher, husband, and father, originally from the Bronx via his Puerto Rican ancestry, found DC to be his home as an artist. Miranda's energy and drive as a multidisciplinary visionary pushed APM forward. Poets Brandon Johnson and Reuben Jackson assisted with programs.

APM relocated to a permanent location at 716 Monroe Street NE, #25 in the city. It has a similar feel to the original space in Southeast Washington. A small stage, well lit, right down in the city, but back among other artist spaces. Visual art adorns the walls of APM's tight space. Local artists benefit from the traffic of poets. And the poetry is constant. Musicians also hang tough in APM among the regular schedule of poetry events. A jazz trio organized by Pepe Gonzalez, the bass player, or Emory Diggs, another well-known bass player adept at working with poets, is common.

APM's ability to navigate the new terrain results from the history in the city of poets and artists, such as its current director, Miranda, being committed to the survival of the art. West-Bey's vision, for now, is safe.

Another less archival space in the Washington, DC, area is the restaurant/community space chain Busboys and Poets. The chain was founded by Andy Shallal, a local Iraqi American businessman. Shallal opened the first Busboys and Poets at 14th and V Street NW in 2005. The various restaurants located in the city and outside the city in Springfield, Virginia, Columbia, Maryland, and Hyattsville, Maryland, are part "progressive political bookstore" and "performance space."[17]

Shallal decided to open Busboys and Poets in the U Street Corridor as the city was in transition demographically. The city was rapidly changing due to post-civil-rights government programs that put the focus on luring new and younger residents, who were, by nature, transient. Older residents, the individuals responsible for the city's unique political culture, were cast aside by successive political administrations.

Shallal is a local. His restaurant Cafe Luna was a favored spot of artists in the city, and he was a longtime part of the metropolitan, international city. He was a regular at poetry readings on the DC poetry scene, especially at Mango's, one of the city's more famous venues in the 1990s. Shallal loved African American poetry back to the days his family first came to America when he was a boy. He recalls studying the Harlem Renaissance in grade school even when he could barely speak English. He knew Langston Hughes poems by memory and when asked, he would recite them.

When he decided to open a restaurant community space in the city's famous U Street Corridor, he at first tried to open it at Bohemian Caverns, the former jazz club of legend in the city. Somehow it never worked out. Shallal believes that was a good thing, considering the legendary status of Bohemian Caverns. Shallal's first Busboys and Poets outlet opened appropriately below what is now known as Langston's Lofts. The property was marketed using the memory of Langston Hughes's famous residency in the city during the Harlem Renaissance in the 1920s. Shallal was struck by the fact that some of the loft residents had never heard of Langston Hughes the poet. It was clear that the city was changing fast. Shallal had read Hughes's memoirs, *The Big Sea* and *I Wonder When I Wander*, so he knew how important Hughes's life and legacy was to the city and the world.[18]

Busboys and Poets opened in August 2005. The muckraking sportswriter Dave Zirin and former NBA basketball player Etan Thomas, who was also a poet, were the featured guests for the first night. Zirin and Thomas had a conversation, and Thomas read poetry. Busboys and Poets was SRO that night. "The place wasn't even officially open yet," Shallal said. "We had no liquor license, no business license, but it was quite a night."[19] Busboys and Poets never looked back. It has become important in the city on a variety of levels. "I wanted to preserve what we had at Mango's," he said. "I was a regular there."[20]

Shallal talked to Ethelbert Miller and Eve Anderson several times about the name

Busboys and Poets, and the name eventually stuck despite some initial reservations about the name from Anderson. Those who know the history of Hughes's famous visit to Washington, DC, in 1924 got it from the start. The original location had a performance room where the poetry and theater and politics were held, and that room was also the mural room. The walls are covered with pictures of progressive legends of the world like Martin Luther King Jr., Mahatma Gandhi, Howard Zinn, and Joan Baez. The progressive politics are in your face. In 2006, while I was teaching at Howard University School of Law, one of my students asked to do a program on gentrification there. We did it. The venue was packed, and the discussion was hot and engaging. Shallal's spaces have done similar things with poetry over and over for the last nineteen years.

As another example, the poetry conference and social justice organization Split This Rock (STR) found Busboys and Poets outlets to be useful to its work. STR traces its roots to the international protests by poets against the war in Iraq in 2003.[21] Many poets in the DC area connected with the national protest movement against the war that began at the time.[22] The by-product of the poetic dissent was an anthology called *DC Poets Against the War*. The organization STR emerged from the energy of that dissent and began organizing conferences promoting social justice. Black poets found opportunities to present their poetry on events organized by STR. This is just one example of the work of Busboys and Poets as well.

Yet African American poets have been critical of Busboys and Poets. Some point to the arrival of the venues in certain neighborhoods as the ominous sign of gentrification; others contend it has sucked all the live poetry activity from smaller venues. To his credit Shallal has listened and has not been unafraid of dialog and discourse. It is, to a certain degree, what Busboys and Poets is supposed to be about anyway.

One of the controversies, over providing compensation to performers, especially poets, was accepted as an issue and was addressed. The efforts of poets Thomas Sayers Ellis and Kyle Dargan were instrumental in making this issue important and worthy of a solution. If anything, their dissent along with that of many others was noted by Shallal, and he accepted the challenge.

While some local activists and some poets remain critical of Shallal's outlets, Busboys and Poets stays committed to artists and the people of the city to have a safe space to speak and express themselves through art that is overtly political. It has been the location of some truly extraordinary events, including WPFW-FM 89.3's birthday salute to the poet Sonia Sanchez in 2022. Whenever progressive writers and voices come to the city, Shallal's space is ready to open its doors and provide a venue.

In a 2015 dissertation, the original restaurant was described as a "model for diversity" (quoting *Research Magazine*), where "any given day, people of all races, genders, sexual orientations, and generation spend time." Derek Hyra, an academic at Virginia Tech University, wrote that "Andy has succeeded in creating an atmosphere where no one feels threatened." In "racially diverse, gentrifying neighborhoods," such a place possibly could "foster meaningful social interactions across differences and can ease tensions in transitioning communities."[23] The city has never had anything like it in the past with the numbers of spaces the venue offers. While various poetry spots have come and gone, Shallal continues to support literature and politics despite some criticism.

When the anthology *Full Moon on K Street* was published in 2010, it was easy to track the history of poetry in Washington, DC. *Full Moon on K Street* was edited by Kim Roberts, a local poet, cultural historian, and publisher/editor. It was published by Plan B Press. For years Roberts served as editor/publisher of *Beltway Poetry Quarterly* (founded in 2001). The publication would provide poets across the metropolitan DC area with great opportunities to get their work out into the world. But as good as *Beltway Quarterly* had been, *Full Moon on K Street* told a story. It helped that it was basically a spinoff from *Beltway Poetry Quarterly*.

According to a review in *The Washington Post*, *Full Moon* was "the first anthology of modern poetry to be wholly for, about and by current and former Washington residents—teems with poets who've distilled the region's lifeblood into verse over the past 50 years."[24] It that sense it was a snapshot. The city, after all these decades of poetic evolution and demographic shifting, remains a transient town. It is only natural with the government here.

The anthology begins at the start of the twentieth century and groups the poets according to the year they were born. The first poet in the book, born in 1899, is none other than May Miller, the Dunbar High School and Howard University graduate who went on to do it all in the world of literature, including teaching public education in Baltimore. Next is Sterling Brown, born 1901 in Washington, DC, and today the most important DC poet.

The anthology proceeds from there, and while it includes all kinds of poets of various ethnic and demographic backgrounds, it is one of the few anthologies that reflects the true historical span of the city. At the beginning of the book, Black poets are quite prevalent because of Howard University, the Renaissance, and the momentum created by the early migratory period to the city by African Americans after the Civil War. As the city becomes more and more of a city, the true home of America's federal government, the mixture changes. Ann Darr (1920), Grace Cavalieri (1933), Gaston Neal (1934), Ahmos Zu-Bolton (1935), and A. B. Spellman (1935) are all published in the anthology. "All the poems were written by past or current residents of the city," Roberts writes, "who can best provide that intimate view, and all are contemporary."[25]

Eventually, *Full Moon* reflects the change of population in the city to a majority African American city. After Ethelbert Miller's (1950) poem appears in the book, there is a proliferation of African American poets. Lesser-known poets, such as Alan Spears (1964), Esther Iverem (1960), and Venus Thrash (1969), are included and so many others who lived in the city and wrote on the scene.

"Ghosts of DC's Past" was the brainchild of performance poet Silvana Straw. It was two days of poetry at Dance Place in Northeast Washington, DC, on October 25–26, 2014.[26] The poets for the two nights were Straw, Jeffrey McDaniel, Jose Padua, Quique

Avilés, Michelle Parkerson, Kenneth Carroll, Joel Dias-Porter (DJ Renegade), Ernesto Mercer, Brian Gilmore (myself), and Patrick Washington. The event was not just a great night of poetry in the city, but it defied most of the history of poetry in the city where it existed in segregated spaces. But the spoken word / Slam movement had challenged that back in the 1990s. McDaniel and Straw had curated poetry events at the Black Cat back in the '90s that always featured a diverse mix of poets and a diverse audience. Straw had recaptured that spirit. "I felt like we were time traveling," Straw said after the event. "Something happens when these people come together. For me, in many ways, it was the same Saturday night and Sunday night as it was in '94 and '95."[27] For just those two nights, a tiny piece of history had been captured. It was something to savor, something worth remembering. It was a beginning, as the next generation of poets in the city navigate the poetry scene that they will design for themselves.

Straw is not alone in trying to create an important moment for poetry in the city. For the African American poets who were part of the event and that moment not long ago when spoken word poetry surged in popularity, Straw's efforts are historically important. These kinds of sentiments are the same for other African American poets who are part of the city's history and who also are trying to preserve the history. Toni Asante Lightfoot continues to return to the city where she was born to commemorate the poetry venue It's Your Mug. In July 2023 Lightfoot organized a reading at a new venue, Bloombars, to celebrate thirty years of It's Your Mug. The venue's stage had gone dark in August 1996, but the spirit of what had happened there continued. Lightfoot's reading also recognized the other venues from the recent history of the city's poetry scene. 8Rock, Bar Nun, Mango's, and Kaffa House were also recognized for their moment in time.

African American Poetry

Finally, in May and June 2022, Peter J. Harris, the first poet I met after my reading in the Ascension Poetry Reading Series (Ascension #92) in October 1988, arrived in his hometown for a three-month residency. The residency, sponsored by the Nicholson Project, enabled Harris to curate two readings and an exhibition at APM. Harris's artistic effort was called "See You . . . Come by Tens."[28] The exhibition was part poetry, photography, history, culture, love, and happiness of African American men and boys. Harris has devoted most of his creative efforts over the past twenty years to exploring the happiness of Black men.

Harris's residency and curation of poetry in the city where he had been born culminated with the choir poem featuring Kenneth Carroll, his son, Kenneth Carroll III (Kenny Carroll), Melvin Brown, Harris, and me. Harris selected the poetry; it included his own poetry and the poetry from Sterling Brown's famous poem "Old Lem." The event and where it was presented represented precisely what African American poetry is about and has been about in the city.[29]

According to the Nicholson Project, "Harris's . . . drew inspiration from his deep involvement with and belief in the power of embracing the presence and happiness of Black men and boys."[30] For Harris to include the poetry of Sterling A. Brown, the city's most important literary figure, and to hold the reading just down the street from Brown's house was the ultimate tribute. It said so much about how far Black poets and their poetry had come in the city and how the poets and their poetry had survived and thrived as a community. The event was held at perhaps the city's must authentic venue for African American poetry in the city today, the American Poetry Museum.

Harris's residency and programs also made clear that the legacy of Black poets and poetry in Washington, DC, was safe and secure. All that the African American poets in the city needed to do now was continue what they had been doing since the days of poets like Georgia Douglas Johnson, May Miller, Jean Toomer, Waring Cuney, and Sterling Brown. The standard has been set for decades; there is nothing to do but to embrace it.

Timeline

1872
Paul Laurence Dunbar is born, June 27 in Dayton, Ohio, on Howard Street. The same year, Washington, DC, achieves territorial government status in the United States; it will last for two years.

1877
The Reconstruction Era, in the United States, comes to an end. It is mostly a period of time to bring Black Americans into society following the end of chattel slavery in 1865. Southern governments regain control of their states and reenter the Union. The legal rights Black Americans have gained following the end of the Civil War slowly begin to be dismantled. The last of the federal troops end their occupation of southern states.

1882
All remaining civil rights laws passed during Reconstruction (1863–77) are declared unconstitutional by the US Supreme Court.

1896
Plessy v. Ferguson decision is handed down by the US Supreme Court. The decision declares that "separate but equal" facilities in the United States are constitutional. This decision marks the official beginning of legalized segregation in the United States.

Dunbar comes to Washington, DC, for an extended visit. He resides in the city, writes, works, and marries the New Orleans writer Alice Ruth Moore, who by then is teaching in Manhattan.

1899
May Miller is born in Washington, DC, January 26, 1899.

1901
Sterling Brown is born in Washington, DC, May 1, 1901.

Dunbar publishes his essay "The Negro in Washington" in *Harper's Weekly*.

1901–03
Dunbar's marriage to Alice Dunbar comes apart, and Alice Dunbar leaves the city. In poor health, Paul also leaves the city and does not reside there for an extended period afterward. He will spend time in Colorado but will eventually return to his hometown of Dayton, Ohio.

1906
Dunbar dies at his home in Dayton, Ohio, of tuberculosis.

William Waring Cuney, the poet and songwriter, is born in Washington, DC.

1910
Writer and socialite, Georgia Douglas Johnson moves to Washington, DC, from Atlanta, Georgia.

1914
May Miller is published for the first time in *The Washington Post*.

1917
The Howard University literary society Stylus is formed.

1920
Washington, DC,'s storied M Street High School is renamed after Paul Laurence Dunbar.

1923
Jean Toomer, born in Washington, DC, in 1906, publishes his seminal work, *Cane*. It is arguably the most important publication of the Harlem Renaissance period except for Alain Locke's *The New Negro* in 1925.

Lewis Grandison Alexander's article "Japanese Hokkus" appears in the December issue of *The Crisis* magazine. The article also includes eight poems by Alexander, where he is exploring the hokku form.

1925
The New Negro is published. Edited by Howard University professor Alain Locke, the publication is a momentous cultural shift in history and literature.

Langston Hughes lives in Washington, DC, between 1924 and 1926. He gets a job at the Wardman Park Hotel. He achieves a bit of notoriety while there and meets Waring Cuney and other Black poets.

1932
Sterling A. Brown's first book of poetry is published. *Southern Road* will go on to not only influence American poetry but also change Black poetry in the United States.

1935
Sterling Brown begins working with the Works Progress Administration during the Great Depression. He serves until 1938.

1936
Poetry Week begins to be recognized in Washington, DC.

1941
Numerous Black writers at Howard University form a writing workshop known as the Writers Group. Georgia Douglas Johnson, May Miller, and Owen Dodson are part of the group at various points.

Josh White releases an album of protest songs called *Southern Exposure*. The poet Waring Cuney writes the lyrics to many of the songs. The album enjoys great critical acclaim.

1942
The African American anthology textbook *The Negro Caravan* is published. The editors are Sterling A. Brown, Arthur Davis, and Ulysses Lee.

1944
Sterling A. Brown publishes his famous essay "Count Us In" in the anthology *What the Negro Wants*, edited by historian Rayford Logan.

1945
World War II ends. Waring Cuney returns from military service in the Pacific. Dolores Kendrick graduates from Paul Laurence Dunbar High School. Gwendolyn Brooks is awarded the Pulitzer Prize for her poetry collection *Annie Allen*.

1948
Owen Dodson starts teaching at Howard University.

1953
The *Thompson's Restaurant's* case is decided by the local courts. The case effectively desegregates eateries and lunch counters in the city once reserved for whites only. The case is a precursor to the *Brown v. Board of Education* decision in May 1954.

1957
Percy A. Johnston arrives to study at Howard University. He will be instrumental in the establishment of the Howard Poets on the campus of the university.

1959
Dasein Poets and Howard Poets emerge as creative forces in the city. Beat poetry is also in its heyday in the city.

1961
Amiri Baraka's collection *Preface to a Twenty Volume Suicide Note* is published. It includes the poem "One Night Stand," an account of a poetry reading at Howard University involving Baraka, Allen Ginsberg, Gregory Corso, and Ray Bessemer. A. B. Spellman and Gaston Neal are also part of the trip.

1962
Rosey E. Pool's anthology *Beyond the Blues* is published. Numerous Washington, DC, Black poets are included, such as Waring Cuney, Georgia Douglas Johnson, and Sterling Brown.

1966
Poet and activist Gaston Neal founds the New School of Afro-American Thought. The school, located in the city's U Street Corridor, becomes a magnet for Black poetry in the city and political activism.

1967
Langston Hughes visits the area for the final time at the Madeira School, in suburban Washington, DC (Virginia). He dies in May 1967.

1968
Drum and Spear Bookstore is founded and opened for business just days after riots in the city following the killing of the Reverend Dr. Martin Luther King Jr.

E. Ethelbert Miller enrolls as a student at Howard University in Washington, DC.

1971
Understanding the New Black Poetry by Stephen Henderson is published. Henderson, a Professor at Howard University, and protégé of Sterling Brown, is one of the most important literary critics of the twentieth century.

1974
Howard University's Institute for the Arts and Humanities is created and begins conducting programming.

E. Ethelbert Miller launches his Ascension Poetry Reading Series. The series will eventually hold 133 poetry readings.

1976–78
Detroit poet Robert Hayden serves as the poetry consultant to the Library of Congress.

1981
Sterling Brown's *Collected Poems* is published.

1986
Ethelbert Miller publishes *where are all the love poems for dictators?* It is a book like many books of poetry at the time that reflects the difficult politics of the day involving Cold War politics and imperialism.

1989
Sterling Brown dies in Takoma Park, Maryland.

1992
8Rock Cultural Arts Center is opened in Anacostia, Washington, DC, in July 1992. Poets Kenneth Carroll, Jacquie Jones, Judy Cohall, and lawyer and community organizer Peter Clare are the organizers and curators of the arts at the center.

Reuben Jackson wins the Columbia Poetry Prize for his collection *fingering the keys.*

1994
It's Your Mug Reading Series begins in the Georgetown section of Washington, DC. Its curator is Toni Asante Lightfoot (Patricia Harvey), a native of the city.

Barry Farms writers workshop starts. Joel Dias-Porter (DJ Renegade), Toni Blackman, and Kenneth Carroll are instrumental in getting the workshop started.

1995
DC WritersCorps Program begins in three US cities. The program, part of Bill Clinton's AmeriCorps Program, allows poets and writers to teach writings in underserved communities. Washington, DC, New York, and San Francisco are the three cities selected. DC poet Kenneth Carroll is the site coordinator for Washington.

1997
Nine poets from Washington, DC—including Brandon Johnson, Holly Bass, and Toni Asante Lightfoot—are accepted into and attend the Cave Canem African-American Summer Workshop Fellowship.

1999
Dolores Kendrick is named the city's second poet laureate in May 1999.

Poets Gaston Neal and Yaphet Brinson both die in Washington, DC.

2000
Ethelbert Miller's Ascension Poetry Reading Series holds its last reading after twenty-six years. It takes place at the Folger Shakespeare Library.

2001
Kim Roberts creates her digital literary magazine, *Beltway Poetry Quarterly*. It will consistently feature African American poets as contributors and editors.

2003
Tony Medina, Bronx, New York, poet, comes to teach at Howard University, the first creative writing professor on the Howard University faculty.

2004
Jon West-Bey establishes the American Poetry Museum in the city's Brookland neighborhood just down the street from Sterling A. Brown's house.

2005
The first Busboys and Poets restaurant/community space opens at Fourteenth and V Streets.

2010
Retrospective anthology *Full Moon on K Street* is published by Plan B Press. The anthology is edited by poet Kim Roberts. It includes many of the city's leading poets of the twentieth century and beyond.

2012
Dark Room Collective reads at the Folger Shakespeare Library celebrating over twenty years of dedication and creativity by African American poets.

2014
"Ghosts of DC's Past" poetry performances are held in October.

Marion Barry, "Mayor For Life," dies in Washington, DC.

2017
Dolores Kendrick, DC's second poet laureate, dies in Washington, DC.

2021
Sterling A. Brown Papers are donated to Williams College in Williamstown, Massachusetts.

2023
Jean Toomer's book *Cane* turns 100 years old.

2024
Reuben Jackson dies in Washington, DC.

Photo Gallery

Paul Laurence Dunbar, 1896. Courtesy of the Ohio Historical Association.

May Miller (date unknown). Courtesy of May Miller and Kelly Miller Collected Papers, Stuart A. Rose Manuscript, Archives, and Rare Book Library, Emory University.

19 CLASS BOOK 22

STERLING ALLEN BROWN
"Brownie"

ΦBK; Debating Team; Adelphic Union; Rice Book Prize; Sophomore Honors (2); Second Prize Junior Moonlight Oratorical Contest (3); Classical Society (1, 2, 3, 4).

Sterling Allen Brown was born in Washington, D. C., on the first of May, 1901. From the most accurate information we have, he spent his youth reading Horatio Alger, Jr., but after he had succeeded, at the age of twelve, in throwing a dollar across the Potomac River, his parents were so impressed that they decided to send him to Williams.

In the S. A. T. C. his face was turned, for the first time, towards the higher things of life, and he bought a victrola, with a large flock of "Jazz" records. His career, at this point, bears out the old saw which says that the most trivial things influence the lives of the greatest men. One evening, when Sterling was sitting entranced by the strains of "You can't get lovin' where there ain't any love", one of his neighbors, much disgusted at hearing this unverified platitude for the seventh time in an hour, threw a book at him, and his fate was sealed; his career was predetermined from that hour, for the book was Moody and Lovett's *History of English Literature*. Brownie opened the book, and was soon lost in the mysteries of Romanticism; thus was literature first thrown at him, as both Mr. Maxcy and Mr. Licklider have been doing ever since. We understand he is going to teach Literature; may he give as many "A's" as he has received!

Future Occupation: Teaching Literature.

Address: 2464 Sixth Street, N. W., Washington, D. C.

Sterling A. Brown, yearbook photo, 1948. Courtesy of Sterling A. Brown papers, Williams Archives, Williams College, Williams, Massachusetts.

Young middle school student at Bruce Monroe Middle School, Washington, DC. Used with permission of Scurlock Studio Records, Archives Center, National Museum of American History, Smithsonian Institution.

Poet E. Ethelbert Miller reading for WPFW-FM 89.3 benefit circa 1988. Used with Permission of Darrell Stover.

Darrell Stover at DC Space, 1984. Used with Permission of Darrell Stover.

Cover of Free DC Workshop anthology. Cover Art by Mark Montgomery. Courtesy of Mark Montgomery.

From left to right: Kenneth Carroll, Amiri Baraka, Gaston Neal, Joel Dias-Porter, and Brian Gilmore at Vertigo Books, undated photo. Used with permission of Michael Wallace.

From left to right beginning up front: Lori Tsang, Ta-Nehisi Coates, James "Maina" Lee, Robin Dunn Bryant, Jane Alberdeston, and Brian Gilmore at DC WritersCorps writing workshop, The Woodshed, at Lamond-Riggs Library, 1996. Used with permission of Brandon D. Johnson.

Toni Asante Lightfoot (Patricia Harvey) with Twain Dooley, spoken word poetry event, undated photo. Used with permission of Brandon D. Johnson.

Poet Deheija Maat, State of the Union, 1997. Used with permission of Brandon D. Johnson.

Notes

Chapter 1

1. Paul Laurence Dunbar, "We Wear the Mask," *The Complete Poems of Paul Laurence Dunbar* (Dodd, Mead and Company, 1895; public domain).

2. Gossie Harold Hudson and Rebekah Baldwin, "An Unpublished Letter Written to Paul Laurence Dunbar," 1894, *Journal of Negro History* 55, no. 3 (July 1970): 215–17.

3. "An Afro American Poet Laureate: Paul Laurence Dunbar, Poet, in Reading His Works," *Washington Post*, October 20, 1896, 12.

4. The Library of Congress, Robert Heberton Terrell Papers, http://rs5.loc.gov/service/mss/eadxmlmss/eadpdfmss/2010/ms010253.pdf, accessed May 12, 2022.

5. Robert H. Terrell, "Debut of a Negro Poet," *Washington Post*, October 5, 1896, 4.

6. "An Afro American Poet Laureate," 12.

7. "An Afro American Poet Laureate," 12.

8. Paul Laurence Dunbar, "Ode to Ethiopia" (1895) (public domain).

9. Paul Laurence Dunbar, "When Malindy Sings," Wright State University digital holdings, 1896 version, https://corescholar.libraries.wright.edu/dunbar/7/, accessed May 12, 2022.

10. Dunbar, "When Malindy Sings."

11. Eleanor Alexander, "Introduction," in *The Heart of Happy Hollow* (Harlem Moon Broadway Books, 2005).

12. Ralph Story, "Paul Laurence Dunbar: Master Player in a Fixed Game," *College Language Association Journal*, September 1983, 33.

13. Quoted in Story.

14. "Dunbar's Dialect Verse," *Washington Post*, December 16, 1896, 7.

15. "Dunbar's Dialect Verse," 7.

16. Wilda D. Logan, "Fifteenth Street Presbyterian Church, Washington DC, Finding Aid," Moorland-Spingarn Library, Howard University, https://dh.howard.edu/cgi/viewcontent.cgi?referer=&httpsredir=1&article=1073&context=finaid_manu, June 1980, accessed May 12, 2022.

17. "Dunbar's Dialect Verse," 7.

18. Henry Louis Gates Jr., *Reconstruction*, PBS documentary, pt. 1.

19. Gates.

20. Gates.

21. Benjamin Brawley, *Paul Laurence Dunbar: Poet of His People* (University of North Carolina, Chapel Hill Press, 1936).

22. Gene Andrew Jarrett, *Paul Laurence Dunbar: The Life and Times of a Caged Bird* (Princeton University Press, 2022).

23. Brawley, 15.

24. Brawley, 19.

25. Constance McLaughlin Green, *The Secret City: A History of Race Relations in the Nation's Capital* (Princeton University Press, 1967), 119.

26. Green, 120.

27. Tingba Apidta, *The Hidden History of Washington DC, The Reclamation Project*, 1996, 31–32.

28. Apidta, 47.

29. Green, 121.

30. Green, 121.

31. Mark A. Sanders, *A Son's Return: Collected Essays by Sterling Brown* (Northeastern University Press, 1996), 35.

32. J. Saunders Redding, *To Make a Poet Black* (Cornell University Press, 1988), 56.

33. Addison Gayle Jr., *Oak and Ivory: A Biography of Paul Laurence Dunbar* (Doubleday, 1971).

34. Brawley.

35. Young was the first librarian of Congress required to be confirmed by the US Senate.

36. "Library Places All Filled," *Washington Post*, October 6, 1897, 10.

37. Paul Laurence Dunbar, "The Negro in Washington DC," *Harper's Weekly*, January 13, 1901, 2000, 32.

38. Dunbar, "The Negro in Washington DC," 32.

39. Dunbar, "The Negro in Washington DC," 32.

40. Dunbar, "The Negro in Washington DC," 32.

Chapter 2

1. May Miller Sullivan, "The Washingtonian," used by permission, The Estate of May Miller—Miller Newman, Literary Executor.

2. "Wedding Bells," *Colored American*, October 10, 1903, 5.

3. Arthur Davis, J. Saunders Redding, and Joyce Ann Joyce, *The New Cavalcade, African American Writing from 1760 to the Present*, vol. 1 (Howard University Press, 1991), 416.

4. "Wedding Bells," 5.

5. Davis, Redding, and Joyce.

6. "New Colored Poet," *Washington Post*, December 21, 1902, 17.

7. James Weldon Johnson, ed., *The Book of American Negro Poetry* (Harcourt Brace/Jovanovich, 1922).

8. *Indianapolis Freeman*, November 13, 1913, 3.

9. Grace Lucas-Thompson, "What Are Our Women Doing?" *Indianapolis Freeman*, April 3, 1915, 3.

10. H. W. Johnson, "Better Babies Insure a Better Race," *Indianapolis Freeman*, July 31, 1915, 1.

11. R. W. Thompson, "The Passing Show in Washington," *Indianapolis Freeman*, September 25, 1915.

12. Thompson.

13. "News of the Nation's Capital," *Savannah Tribune*, July 21, 1917.

14. "News of the Nation's Capital."

15. From Georgia Douglas Johnson, "Hegira," in *Selected Works of Georgia Douglas Johnson* (G. K. Hall and Company, 1997). The book notes that this version of the poem was taken from a book originally published in 1922.

16. Jessie Faucet, "*The Heart of a Woman* by Georgia Douglas Johnson and William Stanley Braithwaite," *Journal of Negro History* 4, no. 4 (October 1919): 467–68.

17. *The Crisis*, July 1918, 128–30.

18. Davis, Redding, and Joyce, 350.

19. Georgia Douglas Johnson, *The Heart of a Woman* (Boston Cornhill Company, 1918).

20. May Miller and Kelly Miller Papers, Rose Library, Emory University, Atlanta Georgia, collected papers of May Miller, Collection 1080, Box 1, Item 1.

21. May Miller and Kelly Miller Papers, Collected papers of May Miller, Box 1, Item 1.

22. Davis, Redding, and Joyce, 272.

23. Davis, Redding, and Joyce, 272.

24. Letters and documents received from Myra Sklarew, Brian Gilmore Papers, Gelman Library—Special Collections, George Washington University, Washington, DC.

25. Sklarew letters.

26. Sklarew letters.

27. Sklarew letters.

28. Grace Cavalieri interviews "May Miller," 1989, provided to author via digital file.

29. Miller interview.

30. May Miller and Kelly Miller Papers, Collected papers of May Miller, Box 1080, File 1, Item 1.

31. May Miller, "Wireless in Squirreldom," *Washington Post*, October 4, 1914, M.

32. Miller, "Wireless in Squireldom."

33. Keith Leonard, *Fettered Genius: The African American Bardic Poet from Slavery to Civil Rights* (University of Virginia Press, 2006), 50–52.

34. Leonard.

35. Leonard.

36. Leonard.

37. Leonard.

38. Leonard, quoting Gloria T. Hill, *Three Women of the Harlem Renaissance* (Indiana University Press, 1987), 90.

39. Leonard, quoting Hill, 90.

40. George Derek Musgrove and Chris Myers Asch, "Democracy Deferred," *Statehood Report*, March 2021, 12–14, https://assets.website-files.com/5df7f915fcb12b538aa0494f/60541fb1af8047a0fde84ad7_Democracy%20Deferred.March.2021.pdf.

41. Musgrove and Asch, "Democracy Deferred."

42. Musgrove and Asch, "Democracy Deferred."

43. Kathleen L. Wolgemuth, "Woodrow Wilson and Federal Segregation," *Journal of Negro History* 44, no. 2 (April 1959): 158–73.

44. Wolgemuth, 158–73.

45. W. E. B. Du Bois, "My Impressions of Woodrow Wilson," *Journal of Negro History* 58, no. 4 (October 1973): 453–59.

46. Du Bois, "My Impressions of Woodrow Wilson."

47. Mu-So-Lit, Repository, Moorland-Spingarn Library, Howard University, Washington, DC.

48. Mu-So-Lit.

49. "In the Nation's Capital," *Indianapolis Freeman*, May 27, 1911.

50. "Colored High School," *Washington Bee*, December 25, 1915.

51. "The Dunbar High School," Mrs. Helen Davis's Letter to the Commissioners, *Washington Bee*, January 29, 1916.

52. "The Dunbar High School."

53. "Board of Education," *Evening Star*, July 12, 1916, 2.

Chapter 3

1. John Chandler Griffin, *Biography of American Writer, Jean Toomer* (Mellen Press, 2002), 15–31.

2. Griffin, 28, 42.
3. Mark Whalan, ed., *The Letters of Jean Toomer, 1919–1924* (University of Tennessee Press, 2006), 3.
4. W. E. B. Du Bois, *Black Reconstruction* (The Free Press, 1935), 468–74.
5. Du Bois, 469.
6. Du Bois, 469.
7. Du Bois, 469.
8. Du Bois, 469.
9. Nellie McKay, "Introduction," in *Jean Toomer, A Critical Evaluation* (Howard University Press, 1988), 3–5.
10. Jean Toomer, *Cane*, Project Gutenberg, released in 2019, https://www.gutenberg.org/cache/epub/60093/pg60093-images.html.
11. Whalan, 5–6.
12. Whalan, 5–6.
13. Whalan, 6–7.
14. Whalan.
15. Griffin, 79.
16. Steven Mintz, *The Historical Ethnography of Black Washington, DC*, vol. 52 of *A Historical Ethnography of Black Washington, D.C., Records of the Columbia Historical Society, Washington, DC*, 1989 (Historical Society of Washington, DC), 235–53.
17. Mintz, 245.
18. Mintz, 245.
19. Mintz, 245.
20. Mintz, 245.
21. John Hasse, *Duke Ellington's Washington* (Omnibus Press, 1995).
22. Griffin, 71–75.
23. Whalan, 27–28.
24. Whalan, 27.
25. Whalan, 27.
26. Griffin, 79.
27. "Booklovers Hour," *Evening Star*, November 20, 1922, 29.
28. "Books and Authors," August 12, 1923, *New York Times*, BR26.
29. "New Books," November 10, 1923, *New York Age*, 8.
30. "New Books," 8.
31. Floyd G. Calvin, "Book Review," December 22, 1923, *Pittsburgh Courier*, 16.
32. Calvin, 16.
33. Display ad, *New York Times*, September 23, 1923.
34. Display ad, *The New York Times*.
35. Display ad, *The New York Times*.
36. Waldo Frank, "Foreword," in *Cane*, by Jean Toomer, orig. 1st printing (Liverlight, 1923), vii.
37. Frank, ix.
38. Frank, ix.
39. Gerald H. Strauss, "Cane," in *Masterpieces of African American Literature* (Harper Collins, 1992), 91.
40. Strauss, 91–95.
41. Toomer, *Cane*.
42. Abraham Chapman, ed. *Black Voices* (Penguin Group, 1968), 63.
43. Chapman, 63.
44. Kenneth Carroll, email exchange, May 2022.

45. James Weldon Johnson, ed., *The Book of American Negro Poetry* (Harcourt Brace/Jovanovich, 1922, 1931).

46. Johnson, *The Book of American Negro Poetry*, 40.

47. John S. Lash, "The Anthologist and the Negro," *Phylon* [1940–1956] 8, no. 1 (1947): 68–76.

48. Lash, 71.

49. "Book Review of *The Book of American Negro Poetry* by James Weldon Johnson," *Journal of Negro History* 8, no. 3 (July 1923): 347–48.

50. Jim Kacian, "A Brief History of the Haiku in the United States," Haiku Foundation of America, https://www.thehaikufoundation.org/omeka/files/original/8cd4850b0d0799d6c3c72cd025fc8111.pdf, accessed May 20, 2022.

51. Lewis Grandison Alexander, "Japanese Hokkus," *The Crisis*, December 1923, 67–68 (public domain).

52. Alexander, Poets.org, "Lewis Grandison Alexander," https://poets.org/poet/lewis-grandison-alexander.

53. Alexander, "Japanese Hokkus," *The Crisis*, December 1923, 67–68 (public domain).

54. John Thompson Jr. (with Jesse Washington), *I Came as A Shadow: The Autobiography of John Thompson Jr.* (Henry Holt, 2021) 65.

55. Thompson, 65.

56. Thompson, 43.

57. Thompson, 43.

58. Thompson, 42.

Chapter 4

Epigraph: Grace Cavalieri interviews "May Miller," 1989, Cavalieri's personal collection, provided to author via digital file.

1. Dr. Albert C. Barnes, "Negro Art and America," *Survey Graphic*, March 1925 (Black Classic Press reprint 1980), 668.

2. Alain Locke, *The New Negro* (Dover Publications, 1925, 2021), 16.

3. David Levering Lewis, *When Harlem Was in Vogue* (Oxford University Press: 1979), 29–30.

4. Mark Whalan, ed., *The Letters of Jean Toomer, 1919–1924* (University of Tennessee Press, 2006), 19–20.

5. Alain Leroy Locke, "Enter the New Negro," *Journal of Negro History* 39, no. 4 (October 1954): 332–34.

6. Locke, "Enter the New Negro," 332–34.

7. Moorland-Spingarn Collections, Howard University, Stylus Literary Society (document), dhu.hua.ybk_1934_Organizations.pdf, accessed, June 10, 2022.

8. Jeffrey C. Stewart, *The New Negro: The Life of Alain Locke* (Oxford University Press. 2018), 82–90.

9. Alain Locke, *Survey Graphic Magazine*, March 1925 (repr. Black Classic Press, 1980).

10. Whalan, 19–20.

11. Lawrence Rubin, "Washington and the Negro Renaissance," April–May 1971, *The Crisis*, 79–82.

12. Rubin.

13. Brian Gilmore, "Seventh Street Blues," *Washington Post*, January 27, 2002, https://www.washingtonpost.com/archive/lifestyle/2002/01/27/the-seventh-street-blues/87837194-d6df-4311-8405-7a91852a7d06/, accessed June 1, 2022.

14. Langston Hughes, *The Big Sea*, Thunder's Mouth Press, 1940, 1986, 203.

15. Gilmore, "Seventh Street Blues."
16. Hughes, *The Big Sea*, 204
17. Gilmore, "Seventh Street Blues."
18. Hughes, *The Big Sea*.
19. Gilmore, "Seventh Street Blues."
20. Josephine Tighe Williams, "Discovery of New Writer of Poetry at Washington Hotel," *Washington Star*, December 13, 1925, 94.
21. Hughes, *The Big Sea*, 216.
22. Hughes, *The Big Sea*, 216.
23. Georgia Douglas Johnson Papers, Moorland-Spingarn Library, Howard University, Washington, DC, Box 162-2 (Series B).
24. Valerie Boyd, "Zora Neale Hurston: The Howard University Years," *Journal of Blacks in Higher Education*, no. 39 (Spring 2003): 104–8.
25. Dickinson College, digital archives, https://archives.dickinson.edu/people/esther-popel-shaw-1896-1958, accessed May 28, 2022.
26. Anne P. Rice, ed., *Witnessing Lynching: American Writers Respond* (Rutgers University Press, 2003), 282.
27. "Clarissa Delaney," *New Amsterdam News*, March 18, 2021, https://amsterdamnews.com/news/2021/03/18/clarissa-scott-delany-poet-verge-greatness/, accessed December 20, 2022.
28. Dunbar High School Yearbook collection, Charles Sumner School Archives, Washington, DC (1928 edition).
29. Clarissa Scott Delany, "Solace," *Opportunity Magazine*, National Urban League, 1926, https://scalar.lehigh.edu/african-american-poetry-a-digital-anthology/clarissa-scott-delany-solace-1927.
30. "Superbly Poised for Life; and Quietly She Left it—," *Pittsburgh Courier*, November 5, 1972, 1, https://www.proquest.com/historical-newspapers/superbly-poised-life-quietly-she-left/docview/201873638/se-2.
31. "Superbly Poised for Life."
32. J. C. Byars, ed., *Black and White* (Crane Press, 1928).
33. E. E. F., "Anthology of Capital Verse Reveals Poets from All Walks of Life," *Washington Post*, January 1, 1928, S9.
34. E. E. F., S9.
35. E. E. F., S9.
36. Donald Jeffrey Hayes, "Interracial Poetry," *Chicago Defender*, February 18, 1928.
37. "Chat: Mary White Ovington: Board of Directors of the N.A.A.C.P. Caroling Dusk," 1927, *Philadelphia Tribune*, December 29, 15.
38. "NC Magazine Gives May issue to Race Writers," *Norfolk Journal and Guide*, April 28, 1928, 1.
39. Stewart, 307.
40. Andrew Donnelly, "Langston Hughes on the DL," *College Literature* 44, no. 1 (Winter 2017): 30–57.
41. Elizabeth McHenry, *Forgotten Reader: Recovering the Lost History of African American Literary Societies* (Duke University Press, 2002), 274–75.
42. McHenry, 275.

Chapter 5

1. Census records obtained from DC Public Library (MLK Jr. Main Branch).
2. Carter G. Woodson, "The Cuney Family," *Negro History Bulletin* 11, no. 6 (March 1948): 123–48.

3. Woodson, 123–25.
4. Woodson, 123.
5. Woodson, 123.
6. Woodson, 123.
7. Woodson, 123.
8. *The Reflector* (Armstrong High School Yearbook) (Class of 1923 edition).
9. *The Reflector.*
10. *The Reflector.*
11. *The Reflector.*
12. Cynthia Davis and Verner D. Mitchell, *Images in the River: The Life and Work of Waring Cuney* (Texas Tech University Press, 2023), 124.
13. Davis and Mitchell, *Images in the River*, 124.
14. Davis and Mitchell, *Images in the River*, 124.
15. Waring Cuney, "No Images," *Storefront Church* (1973), Paul Breman papers, Special Collection, Chapin Library, Williams College, Williamstown, MA, Waring Cuney Boxes (public domain).
16. Paul Breman, "Introduction to *Storefront Church*," *Storefront Church*, by Waring Cuney (Heritage Series, 1973).
17. Lorenzo Thomas, "Whose Images: Waring Cuney and the Harlem Renaissance's Idea of a Poet's Work," University of Houston, author copy of essay shared with author independent of publication.
18. Anna Nussbaum, ed., *Afrika Singt* (Vienna and Leipzig, 1929).
19. "Isaac L. Rice, Financier, Dies," *New York Times*, November 3, 1915, https://timesmachine.nytimes.com/timesmachine/1915/11/03/105045863.pdf, accessed May 23, 2023.
20. Cynthia Davis and Verner D. Mitchell, "Eugene Gordon, Dorothy West, and *The Saturday Evening Quill*," *CLA Journal* 52, no. 4 (June 2009): 393–408.
21. Davis and Mitchell, "Eugene Gordon."
22. Email exchange with Mary Meekins, February 11, 2006.
23. Email exchange with Mary Meekins, February 11, 2006.
24. Carter G. Woodson, Zoom discussion with Cynthia Davis and Verner Mitchell, June 8, 2023.
25. Zoom discussion with Cynthia Davis and Verner Mitchell.
26. "Out of Town Society News," *New Amsterdam News*, August 25, 1927, 5.
27. *Four Lincoln University Poets* (Lincoln University Herald, 1930).
28. St. Clair Drake and Horace R. Cayton, *Black Metropolis: A Study of Negro Life in a Northern City* (University of Chicago Press, 1945, 1933).
29. Drake and Cayton, xviii.
30. Drake and Cayton, 394–95.
31. Rev. Sterling N. Brown, *My Own Life Story* (Hamilton Printing, 1924), https://docsouth.unc.edu/neh/brownsn/brownsn.html, 6.
32. Brown, *My Own Life Story.*
33. Joanne V. Gabbin, *Sterling A. Brown* (University of Virginia Press, 1985), 14–16.
34. "a feeling of pride, fellowship, and common loyalty shared by the members of a particular group" (Encyclopedia.com, Oxford University Press, https://www.encyclopedia.com/humanities/dictionaries-thesauruses-pictures-and-press-releases/esprit-de-corps).
35. Mark A. Sanders, ed., *A Son's Return: Selected Essays of Sterling A. Brown* (Northwestern University Press, 1955, 1996), x.
36. Sterling A. Brown, "Count Us In," in *What the Negro Wants*, ed. Rayford Logan (University of North Carolina Press, 1944).
37. Sterling A. Brown, "Didn't He Ramble?," in Sanders, ed., *A Son's Return*, 16.

38. "For A Certain Youngster," *Oracle*, March 25, 1933, Omega Psi Phi Fraternity, https://library.williams.edu/2021/09/22/friendship-heights-duke-ellington-sterling-a-brown/, accessed May 1, 2023, 33.

39. Darren J. McManus, "Sterling A. Brown's Legacy of Hope" (quoting John F. Callahan, "Reconsideration: Sterling Brown," review of *The Collected Poems of Sterling A. Brown*, ed. Michael S. Harper, *New Republic*, December 20, 1982, 25–28), thesis submission, Master of Arts degree, Florida Atlantic University, 1993, digital source, University of Maryland Library.

40. Sterling A. Brown, "The New Negro in Literature," in Sanders, ed., *A Son's Return*, 185.

41. Brown, "The New Negro," 185.

42. Sterling A. Brown, "Athletics and the Arts," in Sanders, ed., *A Son's Return*, 127.

43. Constance McLaughlin Green, *Secret City* (Princeton University Press, 1967), 219.

44. James Weldon Johnson, ed., *The Book of American Negro Poetry* (Harcourt Brace/Jovanovich, 1931), 247.

45. Johnson, *The Book of American Negro Poetry*, 247.

46. Johnson, *The Book of American Negro Poetry*, 247.

47. Johnson, Introduction to *Southern Road: Poems by Sterling A. Brown* (Harcourt, Brace and Company, 1932, repr. Beacon Press, 1974), xxxv–xxxvii.

48. B. A. Botkin, *Folk-Say IV: The Land Is Ours* (University of Oklahoma Press, 1932).

49. Biography of George Goetz, New York Public Library Archives, V. F. Calverton, https://archives.nypl.org/mss/459, accessed May 28, 2022.

50. Sterling Brown Papers, Williams College collection, Williamstown, MA, email, July 10, 2022, original copy with author.

51. Grace Cavalieri interviews Sterling Brown, copy provided by Cavalieri, with author, date undetermined. In addition, Amber Easter Gautier Zu-Bolton's dissertation provided insight: Amber E. Zu-Bolton, "All Trails Lead to Sterling: How Sterling Brown Fathered the Field of Black Literary and Cultural Studies, 1936–1969" (2019), University of New Orleans Theses and Dissertations, 2711, https://scholarworks.uno.edu/td/2711.

52. Louis Untermeyer, "New Light from an Old Mine," *Opportunity* magazine, August 1932, 250.

53. Louis Untermeyer, Poet, Poetry Foundation website, https://www.poetryfoundation.org/poets/louis-untermeyer, accessed June 1, 2022.

54. Johnson, *The Book of American Negro Poetry*.

55. Wallace Thurman, "Books To Read: Southern Road, Sterling Brown," *National News*, June 2, 1932, 1–2.

56. "*Southern Road* by Sterling Brown (brief notices)," *Poetry Magazine* 44, no. 2 (May 1934): 115.

57. "A New and Notable Negro Book of Poetry," *New York Times*, May 15, 1932, BR13.

58. "A New and Notable Negro Book of Poetry," BR13.

59. "Southern Road, Sterling Brown's First Book, Praised," *Pittsburgh Courier*, September 3, 1932, 2.

60. Sterling Brown Papers, Boxes 413, 315.

61. Henry Louis Gates Jr., "Book Review of *The Collected Poems of Sterling A. Brown* by Michael S. Harper," *Black American Literature Forum* 15, no. 1 (Spring 1981): 39–42.

62. Gates Jr., 39–42.

Chapter 6

1. Paul Gardullo, Michelle Delaney, Jacqueline D. Serwer, and Lonnie Bunch III, eds., *Picturing the Promise: The Scurlock Studio and Black Washington* (Smithsonian Books, 2009).

2. Gardullo et al., *Picturing the Promise*.

3. Brian Gilmore, "Poetry Week," in Gardullo et al., *Picturing the Promise*, 98–99.

4. National Register of Historic Places application for Bruce-Monroe School, https://planning.dc.gov/sites/default/files/dc/sites/op/publication/attachments/Bruce%20School%20application%20form.pdf, accessed June 2, 2023.

5. Gilmore, "Poetry Week."

6. "Book Notes," *New York Times*, November 15, 1934, 19.

7. Sterling A. Brown papers, Special Collections, Williams College, Williamstown, MA, copies provided by Sylvia Brown, Special Collections.

8. Waring Cuning, "After Prayer Meeting," December 16, 1935, Boston, MA, Sterling A. Brown papers, copies of poems provided courtesy of Williams College.

9. Sterling A. Brown, *Evening Star*, April 1979, via Robert Malesky's blog, November 2014, https://bygonebrookland.com/2014/11/02/oleary-column-prompts-telling-response-from-sterling-brown/, accessed August 2022.

10. Brown, *Evening Star*.

11. Sandra Fitzpatrick and Maria R. Goodwin, *The Guide to Black Washington* (Hippocrene Books, 1990).

12. Fitzgerald and Goodwin, *The Guide to Black Washington*.

13. Lawrence P. Jackson, *The Indignant Generation: A Narrative History of African American Writers and Critics, 1934–1960* (Princeton University Press, 2013).

14. Jackson, 38–39.

15. Sterling A. Brown, "Negro Character as Seen by White Authors," *Journal of Negro Education*, January 1933, 179, 198.

16. Joanne Gabbin, *Sterling A. Brown: Building the Black Aesthetic Tradition* (University Press of Virginia, 1985, 1994), 6.

17. Jerre Mangione, *The Dream and the Deal: The Federal Writers' Project, 1935–1943* (Little, Brown and Company, 1972).

18. Mangione, *The Dream and the Deal*, 29.

19. Federal Writers' Project and Works Progress Administration, *Washington, City and Capital* (US Government Printing Office, 1937).

20. Mangione, *The Dream and the Deal*, 210.

21. Mangione, *The Dream and the Deal*, 210.

22. Federal Writers' Project and Works Progress Administration, 90.

23. Federal Writers' Project and Works Progress Administration, 87.

24. Langston Hughes papers, Digital archives, Correspondence to and from Waring Cuney, Yale University (Digital Collections), https://archives.yale.edu/repositories/11/archival_objects/335116, accessed April 3, 2023.

25. Arna Bontemps Papers, Syracuse University Library, Special Collections, Letter from Arna Bontemps to Waring Cuney, copy provided by Syracuse University to author via mail.

26. Arna Bontemps Papers, Bontemps letter to Cuney.

27. William Smallwood, "New York and Quaker City Vie for Week's Social Leadership," *Afro-American*, May 21, 1938, 8.

28. Elijah Wald, *Josh White: Society Blues* (University of Massachusetts Press, 2000), 80–90.

29. Liner notes, quoted in Wald, 80–90.

30. Wald, 81–82.

31. Wald, 81–82.

32. "Paul Robeson Among Artists to Appear at W.C. Handy Festival," *Chicago Defender*, October 25, 1941, 9.

33. "Youth Committee Holds Meeting," *Chicago Defender*, October 18, 1941, 8.

34. "Richard Wright to Tell of Hitler's Threat to America," *Atlanta Daily World*, November

7, 1941, 1.

35. Documents received from US Army, by request from National Archives.

36. Sterling A. Brown, Arthur P. Davis, and Ulysses Lee, eds., *The Negro Caravan* (Dryden Press, 1941, 1969).

37. Brown, Lee, and Davis.

38. Rayford W. Logan, ed., *What the Negro Wants* (University of North Carolina Press, 1944).

39. Sterling A. Brown, "Count Us In," in Logan, ed., *What the Negro Wants,* 308.

40. Brown, "Count Us In," in Logan, ed., *What the Negro Wants,* 308.

41. Race riots occurred in Detroit in 1943.

42. Brown, "Count Us In," in Logan, ed., *What the Negro Wants,* 308.

43. Sterling A. Brown, "A Son's Return," in *The New Negro in Literature,* ed. Mark A. Sanders (Northeastern University Press, 1996), 199.

44. "Delores Kendrick," Poets.org, https://poets.org/poet/dolores-kendrick; Elizabeth Abel, Barbara Christian, and Helene Moglen, eds., *Female Subjects in Black and White: Race, Psychoanalysis, Feminism* (University of California Press, 1997); Lucille Clifton and Dolores Kendrick, "Channeling the Ancestral Muse," in *Soul Talk: The New Spirituality of African American Women,* ed. Akasha Hull (Inner Traditions, 2001).

45. Abel, Christian, and Moglen, *Female Subjects in Black and White.*

46. Ike Kendrick, obituary, *Washington Post,* December 20, 1993.

47. Dunbar Yearbook, Charles Sumner School Archives, Washington, DC (1945 edition).

48. "Keep A-Pluggin' Away," first two of four stanzas (public domain), Dunbar school archives.

49. Lauri Ramey, ed., in consultation with Paul Breman, *The Heritage Series of Black Poetry, 1962–1975: A Research Compendium* (Routledge, 2008), 111–14.

50. "Evening with the Poets," *Hilltop Newspaper,* February 9, 1949, 2, Moorland-Spingarn Library, Howard University, Washington, DC.

51. "Evening with the Poets," 3.

52. Gertrude Martin, "Hughes Edits Poetry Quarterly," *Chicago Defender,* February 25, 1950, 7.

53. Alberto Casey, *Dos siglos de poesía norteamericana* (Coordinación de Difusión Cultural, Dirección de Literatura / UNAM, 1950).

54. Bill Chasehavis, "All Ears," *New Amsterdam News,* July 17, 1943, 8.

55. Lawrence D. Reddick, World War II Project, Schomburg Center, New York, MG 490, Box F10.

56. Lawrence D. Reddick, Box F10.

57. Lawrence D. Reddick, Box F10.

Chapter 7

1. Mark A. Sanders, ed., *A Son's Return: Selected Essays of Sterling A. Brown* (Northeastern University Press, 1996), 184–197.

2. Sterling A. Brown, "The New Negro in Literature," in Sanders, ed., *A Son's Return,* 199.

3. Arthur P. Davis, "Integration and Race Literature," *Phylon* (1940–1956) 17, no. 2 (1956): 141–46, 144.

4. Davis, 144.

5. May Miller and Kelly Miller Papers, Rose Library, Emory University, Atlanta, GA, B 36.

6. Myra Sklarew, *Over the Rooftops of Time: Jewish Stories, Essays, Poems* (State University of New York Press, 2003), 90–92.

7. The United States rendered this decision in the case of *Shelley v. Kraemer,* 334 U.S. 1 (1948).

8. *Hurd v. Hodge* is a racially restrictive covenant case that originated in the District of Columbia. It was decided on the same day as *Shelley v. Kraemer* (see note 7).

9. "Text of Decision Outlawing Negro Segregation," *New York Times*, May 18, 1954, 15.

10. D. V. Cohn, "The Year the Whites Left the City; Fear, Peer Pressure, Bias Helped Fuel Fast Flight out of Town Series: THE CENTURY; Washington Comes of Age; Occ: [FINAL Edition]," *Washington Post*, July 19, 1999, https://www.proquest.com/newspapers/year-whites-left-city-fear-peer-pressure-bias/docview/408484984/se-2.

11. Cohn.

12. Editor of *The Washington Evening Star, The Negro History Bulletin*, "Segregation in the District of Columbia," reprinted from *The Evening Star*, October 19, 1952.

13. Editor of *The Washington Evening Star*.

14. Myra Sklarew," Howard Poets in Perspective," *Beltway Poetry Quarterly*, Fall 2014, https://www.beltwaypoetry.com/howard-poets/, accessed May 2022.

15. Percy Johnston, *Six Cylinder Olympus* (Jupiter Hammond Press, 1961).

16. Johnston, *Six Cylinder Olympus*.

17. Percy Johnston, *Concerto for Girl and Convertible* (Continental Press, 1960).

18. Winston Napier, "The Howard Poets," *Beltway Poetry Quarterly*, http://washingtonart.com/beltway/howardpoets.html, accessed May 23, 2022.

19. Interview with Dolores Kendrick, January 2006.

20. E. Y. Wood, "Black Abstraction: The Umbra Workshop and an African American Avant-Garde," 2004 (order No. 3122073), ProQuest Dissertations & Theses Global (305182869), https://www.proquest.com/dissertations-theses/black-abstraction-umbra-workshop-african-american/docview/305182869/se-2. Wood references Aldon Nielsen's scholarship in the dissertation cited.

21. *Dasein* 1, no. 1, Sawyer Library, Williams College, Williamston, MA.

22. Napier.

23. "Poets of Dasein," *Washington Star*, June 29, 1963, A-13.

24. "Poets of Dasein."

25. *Dasein*, Sawyer Library, Williams College, Williamston, MA.

26. Johnston's works include *Concerto for Girl and Convertible, Sean Pendragon Requiem* (Dasein-Jupiter Hammon, 1964), and *Six Cylinder Olympus*. He also produced *Afro American Philosophies: Selected Readings from Jupiter Hamilton to Eugene C. Holmes* (Monclair State College Press, 1970); *Phenomenology of Space & Time: An Examination of Eugene Clay Holmes's Studies in the Philosophy of Time and Space* (Dasein Literary Society, 1976); and *William Shakespeare: Pioneer of Modern Free Verse* (New Merrymount Press, 1977).

27. Instant messenger exchange with DeBravo, January 22, 2023.

28. *Burning Spear: An Anthology of Afro Saxon Poetry* (Jupiter Hammond Press, 1963). The poets in the anthology are Lance Jeffers, Percy Johnston, Walter DeLegall, Oswald Govan, Leroy Stone, Alfred Fraser, Nathan Richards, and Joseph White, poets who were published in the journal *Dasein*. The publisher, Jupiter Hammond Press, is part of the Dasein Literary Society. The cover was designed by the visual artist and painter Yvonne Pickering, who also contributed to the journal *Dasein*.

29. Rosey Pool, ed., *Beyond the Blues: New Poems by American Negroes* (Hand and Flower Press, 1962). The anthology includes poets Gwendolyn Brooks, Langston Hughes, Margaret Walker, Sterling A. Brown, Dudley Randall, Amiri Baraka (as LeRoi Jones), Audre Lorde (her name is spelled "Lord"), and Robert Hayden.

30. J. Welfred Holmes, "Beyond the Blues review," *CLA Journal* 6, no. 3 (1963): 222–24, http://www.jstor.org/stable/44324426.

31. Holmes, 224.

32. Holmes, 224.
33. Holmes, 223.
34. Rosey Pool, ed., *Is ben de nieuwe Neger: Gedichten, rijmen, liedjes en dokumenten uit 300 jaar verzet van de Amerikaanse Neger* (I am the New Negro: Poems, rhymes and songs from 300 years of resistance) (Bert Bakker Daamen, 1965).
35. Carl Bode, “Speaking to Blacks About Themselves,” *Washington Star*, February 18, 1973, 139.
36. Charles H. Nichols, *Arna Bontempts Langston Hughes: Letters 1925–1967* (Athena Books, 1990), 454.
37. Bontemps did write Cuney on occasion to try to get approval to publish work. Cuney did not respond quickly or at all. I obtained two letters from Syracuse University (Arna Bontemps Papers, Syracuse University Library, Special Collections) via fax many years ago. Copies remain in possession of the author.
38. Marguerite Cartwright Papers, Tulane University Library—Amistad Research Center, Tulane University, New Orleans, copies of poems written by Cuney provided electronically by the library.
39. Information pertaining to the song written by Cuney and recorded by Ives verified via ASCAP online records. See https://www.discogs.com/release/24231869-Burl-Ives-One-Hour-Ahead-Of-The-Posse-This-Time-To-morrow?srsltid=AfmBOoqDcPutQrTnaM3hhoBv3lR5pMeRS8FfwfyyW6Muj6vKR_sGwu2G.
40. Email exchanges with Breman, 2005.
41. Breman email exchange, 2005.
42. Paul Breman Heritage Collection, Williams College, Williamstown, MA, Box 3, Folders 1–36.
43. William Waring Cuney, *Puzzles* (De Roos Utrecht, 1960).
44. Cuney, *Puzzles.*
45. Cuney, *Puzzles.*
46. Cuney, *Puzzles.*
47. Cuney, *Puzzles.*
48. Cuney, *Puzzles.*

Chapter 8

1. The Poetry Foundation, “The Beat Poets,” permanent collection, https://www.poetryfoundation.org/collections/147552/an-introduction-to-the-beat-poets.
2. Interviews with A. B. Spellman, phone, April and May 2023.
3. Spellman interviews.
4. John S. Wilson, “Jazzmen’s Quartet,” *New York Times*, November 20, 1966, https://archive.nytimes.com/www.nytimes.com/books/97/08/03/home/jazz-bebop.html.
5. Spellman interviews.
6. Spellman interviews.
7. “Student-Faculty Forum Discusses Beat Generation, *Hilltop Newspaper*, November 29, 1958, 1.
8. Primus St. John, “Notes on the Beatnik Generation,” *Hilltop Newspaper*, November 29, 1958, 6.
9. Leroy Stone, “Notes on the Beatnik Generation,” *Hilltop Newspaper*, November 29, 1958, 6.
10. Amiri Baraka: St. Claire Bourne, producer, *In Motion* (Icarus Films, 1983).
11. Spellman interviews.

12. LeRoi Jones(Amiri Baraka), *Preface to a Twenty Volume Suicide Note* (Corinth Books / Totem Press, 1962).

13. *Hilltop Newspaper* archives, online photo by James Wilson, March 1959 section.

14. According to Mark Opsasnick, in *Coffee, Confusion and Jim Morrison: The Forgotten History of Hip Coffee Houses and Beatnik Poets in the Nation's Capital*, "Coffee 'n' Confusion" became the focal point for the city's "beatnik" contingency and is noted today for having been the site of the very first public performance of rock and roll legend Jim Morrison, who, as a teenager, gave an original poetry recital on the dank coffee house's cramped, makeshift stage: http://joeb-tallyho.blogspot.com/2010/04/coffee-and-confusion-bill-walker-lester.html.

15. Amiri Baraka, "A Post Racial Anthology," review of *Angles of Ascent: A Norton Anthology of Contemporary African American Poetry, Poetry Magazine*, found at https://www.poetryfoundation.org/poetrymagazine/articles/69990/a-post-racial-anthology, accessed December 2, 2022.

16. Sonya M. Toler, "Poet, Activist Nick Flournoy Dead at 58," *New Pittsburgh Courier*, city edition, July 8, 1998.

17. William Raspberry, "New School Stresses Negro Heritage," *Washington Post*, October 26, 1966, B-1.

18. Raspberry, B-1

19. James Mosby, "Interview with Gaston Neal, July 1, 1968," The Civil Rights Documentation Project, online transcript, Archives Unbound, Gale Publishing, DC Public Library digital holdings, 1-11.

20. Mosby.

21. Michael Kernan, "The Poetry and Rage of a Black Nationalist: Viewpoints," *Washington Post*, May 26, 1971, C-1.

22. Mosby.

23. Mosby. In addition, Neal confirmed many times his commitment to a mental hospital.

24. Marya McQuirter, administrator and creator, *1968 Remembered*, website exhibit, https://www.dc1968project.com/blog/2018/12/22/23-november-1968-amp, accessed May 1, 2023.

25. McQuirter.

26. Carl Irving, "Beatnik Officer Faces Pals in Court," *Washington Star*, April 28, 1960, 1.

27. Raspberry, B-1.

28. Amiri Baraka, *The Autobiography of LeRoi Jones*(Lawrence Hill Books, 1984, 1986), 295.

29. "Any Day Now: Black Art and Liberation," *Ebony*, August 1969, 54.

30. Larry Neal, *Visions of a Liberated Future* (Thunder's Mouth Press, 1989), 60–64.

31. Amiri Baraka and Larry Neal, *Black Fire: An Anthology of African American Writing* (William Morrow, 1968), 278–82.

32. Baraka and Neal, *Black Fire*, 413–14, 666.

33. Leroy F. Aarons, "Negro Arts and History School Will Open Today in Cardozo," *Washington Post*, October 15, 1966, B-5.

34. Aarons, B-5.

35. Mosby, 7–11.

36. Community Research Inc. and Don Freeman, *Under the Radar: The New School of Afro American Thought*, documentary (2011).

37. *Under the Radar.*

38. James Clark Moone, "The Problem of Designing an African American Studies Program in the U.S. Public Schools: The Challenge for New Direction. A Case Study of the Washington DC Public Schools, 1969–1974," order No. 7630119, Howard University, 1976, 112–13.

39. Mosby, 8–11.

40. William Clopton Jr., "A Tribute to Langston Hughes with a Dividend," *Washington Post*, June 19, 1967, B-1.

41. *The Baltimore Afro-American*, October 14, 1967, 18.

42. "Afro School Founder Gets Jail on Gun Charge," *Jet* 35, no. 12 (December 26, 1968): 50.

43. Floyd B. Barbour, ed., *The Black Power Revolt* (Collier Books, 1969).

44. Gaston Neal, "1967: TODAY," *Washington Post*, January 26, 1969, https://www.proquest.com/historical-newspapers/1967/docview/147714349/se-2.

45. Barbour, *The Black Power Revolt*, 300.

46. Elias Rodrigues, "The Black Arts Movement's Revolution in the South, *Nation*, January 10, 2022.

47. Rodrigues.

Chapter 9

1. Interview with Marita Golden, August 10, 2022.

2. Marita Golden, *Migrations of the Heart* (Ballantine Books, 1983), 16.

3. Ben Gilbert and *Washington Post* staff, *Ten Blocks from the White House* (Frederick A. Praeger, 1968), 13–30.

4. Interview with Karl Carter, August 2023.

5. Judy Richardson, Anthony Gittens, and Marita Golden were all interviewed via telephone for this section on Drum and Spear in 2006, 2006, and 2022, respectively.

6. Interview via phone, Judy Richardson, August 2019.

7. Adrienne Manns, "Ghetto Book Shop Finds Untapped Literary Mart." *Washington Post*, August 27, 1968, https://www.proquest.com/historical-newspapers/ghetto-book-shop-finds-untapped-literary-mart/docview/143393623/se-2.

8. Manns.

9. Golden interview.

10. Golden, *Migrations*, 23.

11. Lurma Rackley, "A Lab of Blackness," *Evening Star*, December 26, 1971, 33.

12. Simba Sana, "African Centered Bookstores as Weapons of Culture: Applying the Thought of Amilcar Cabral to the Development of Cultural Institutions in the U.S" (MA thesis, Howard University, 1998).

13. Sana, 54–55.

14. Joshua Clark Davis, "The F.B.I.'s War on Black Bookstores," *Atlantic*, February 19, 2018, https://www.theatlantic.com/politics/archive/2018/02/fbi-black-bookstores/553598/, accessed May 3, 2021.

15. Davis.

16. Interview with Jonetta Barras, August 16, 2023.

17. Monroe W. Karmin, "Calm in the Capital," *Wall Street Journal*, June 23, 1967, 1.

18. Amber E. Zu-Bolton, "All Trails Lead to Sterling Brown" (thesis, University of New Orleans), https://core.ac.uk/download/pdf/275815458.pdf, accessed May 22, 2022.

19. Karmin, "Washington may have Racial Peace, Thanks to Apathy, Prosperity Though Summer Stirs Fears, City's Many Negroes Seem Unlikely to Heed Extremists Awaiting Stokely Carmichael Calm in the Capital: Outlook Good for Racial Peace in Washington," *Wall Street Journal*, Jun 23, 1967, https://www.proquest.com/historical-newspapers/calm-capital/docview/133201410/se-2, 1.

20. *The Cricket: Black Music in Evolution*, 1968–69 (Blank Forms Edition, 2021).

21. *The Cricket*.

22. *The Cricket*.

23. Bernard W. Bell, "New Black Poetry: A Double Edged Sword," *CLA Journal* 1971, no. 15, "Black Studies III: A Special Number" (September 1971): 37–43, 37.

24. Bell, 37, 38, 39.

25. Chris Myers Asch and George Derek Musgrove, *Chocolate City: A History of Race and Democracy in the Nation's Capital* (University of North Carolina Press, 2017), 382–83.

26. Kenneth Carroll, "The Meanings of Funk," *Washington Post*, February 1, 1998, https://www.washingtonpost.com/wp-srv/local/longterm/library/dc/chocolate/funk.htm, accessed May 27, 2022.

27. Carroll, "The Meanings of Funk."

28. Stephen Henderson, *Understanding the New Black Poetry* (William Morrow, 1971).

29. Mercer Cook and Stephen E. Henderson, Th*e Militant Black Writer in Africa and the United States* (University of Wisconsin Press, 1969).

30. Joseph Jenkins, "Book Review of *Understanding the New Black Poetry*," *Baltimore Afro-American*, March 17, 1973, A-1.

31. Hollie I. West, "Contemporary Black Poetry," *Washington Post*, May 18, 1973, E-2.

32. Barry Beckham, "Review: *Understanding the New Black Poetry*," *New York Times Book Review*, April 1, 1973, 32.

33. Poem provided by Karl Carter.

34. Email exchange with Karl Carter, July 10, 2022.

35. Poem reprinted here by permission of the author, Karl Carter. © 2023 Karl Carter. "Markings: In Memory of Mrs. Vashti Cook," *Présence Africaine*, Nouvelle série, No. 73 (1er TRIMESTRE, 1970), 128.

36. Brian Gilmore and Larry Neal, "In Service of Art," *Beltway Quarterly* 15, no. 4 (2014), https://www.beltwaypoetry.com/larry-neal-in-service-of-art/, May 2018.

37. Harry L. Jones, "Review of Hoodoo Hollerin' Bebop Ghosts by Larry Neal," *CLA Journal* 20, no. 2 (December 1976): 310–12.

38. Marcus Baram, *Gil-Scott Heron: Pieces of a Man* (St. Martin's Press, 2014), 102–15.

39. Phillip Herzbrun, "Devices in the Arsenal," *Evening Star*, August 15, 1971, C-7.

40. Jacqueline Trescott, "A Three Day Tribute," *Evening Star*, April 17, 1972, B-3.

41. Email exchanges with Aldon Nielsen, 2022–23.

42. David Nicholson, email exchange.

43. Robert Daniel McClure, "'Who Will Survive in America?': Gil Scott-Heron, the Black Radical Tradition, and the Critique of Neoliberalism," *National Political Science Review* 17, no. 2 (2015): 3–26, https://www.proquest.com/scholarly-journals/who-will-survive-america-gil-scott-heron-black/docview/1747344864/se-2.

44. McClure.

45. Jack Hamilton, "Pieces of a Man," *Transition*, no. 106 (2011): 113–26, https://doi.org/10.2979/transition.106, A-117.

46. Hamilton, A-117.

47. Baram, 102–15.

48. Baram, 117, 125.

49. Baram, 113, 216, 217.

50. Email exchanges with David Nicholson.

51. *Hilltop Newspaper*, April 18, 1969, 9.

52. Askia Muhammed, "Poet Gaston Neal Wins 'Oscar,'" *Washington Informer*, October 21–27, 1999, 1–2.

53. Gus Constantine, "The Shouting Is Replaced," *Evening Star*, January 12, 1971, 18.

54. Constantine, 18.

55. Earl Byrd, "Pride's Two Man Art Team," *Evening Star*, December 13, 1971, 19.

56. June Jordan, Stephen Henderson, E. Ethelbert Miller, and James Borders, "A Basic and Necessary Forum, Reviewed Work(s): *Hoodoo #7*," Energy Earth Communications, Inc. by *Obsidian* 6, no. 1/2 (Spring, Summer 1980): 255–58.

57. Adesanya Alakoye, *Tell Me How Willing Slaves Be* (Energy Black South Press, 1976).

58. Alakoye, inside cover.

59. Treva B. Lindsey, "Saturday Night at the S Street Salon," *Colored No More* (University of Illinois Press, 2017), 111.

60. Lindsey, 111.

Chapter 10

1. Donna Lundry, "Incantation and Parody," *Washington Post*, October 12, 1976, B6.

2. Interview with Dolores Kendrick, January 2006.

3. E. Ethelbert Miller, "My Life," *Washington History* 32, no. 1/2, "Meeting the Moment: SPECIAL ISSUE" (Fall 2020): 38–41.

4. Miller, "My Life," 38–41.

5. E. Ethelbert Miller papers, Gelman Library—Special Collections, George Washington University, Washington, DC, Box 89, Stephen Henderson files.

6. Ethelbert Miller, Survey response, "DC Black Poets," 2021–23.

7. E. Ethelbert Miller, ed. *Transition* 1 (1972).

8. Interview with E. Ethelbert Miller, December 2023.

9. Ethelbert Miller, "That was the week that was," *Hilltop Newspaper*, February 18, 1972, 3.

10. Priscilla R. Ramsey, "E. Ethelbert Miller," *Afro American Poets Since 1955*, ed. Trudier Harris and Thadious M. Davis (Gale Research Company, 1985).

11. Jack Foley, "Poetry in Washington: Mass Transit BlackBox," *Washington Post*, July 27, 1975, 157.

12. Christopher J. King, Brian O. Buckley, Riya Maheshwari, and Derek M. Griffith, "Race, Place, and Structural Racism: A Review of Health and History in Washington, DC," *Health Affairs* 41, no. 2 (February 2022): 273, https://doi.org/10.1377/hlthaff.2021.01805.

13. Miller interview.

14. Charles Jarmon, "Andrew Billingsley: Essays and Tributes," in *Confronting Blackness: Howard University, Institute for the Arts and Humanities and Stephen Henderson* (Black Classic Press, 2021), 97–104.

15. Jarmon, 97–104.

16. Third World Press Foundation website, https://thirdworldpressfoundation.org/product/rise-vision-comin-cd/, accessed May 2, 2023.

17. *Black World*, December 1973, 93–96.

18. *Black World*, August 1974, 50.

19. Miller interview.

20. E. Ethelbert Miller, *Fathering Words: The Making of an African American Writer* (St. Martin's Press, 2000), 96.

21. Ahmos Zu-Bolton, ed., *Hoodoo* no. 4 (Energy Black South Press, 1975).

22. Eugene Redmond, letter to E. Ethelbert Miller (February 29, 1976), E. Ethelbert Miller papers, Box 175, Eugene Redmond folder (F-3).

23. Moorland-Spingarn Library, Howard University website, https://dh.howard.edu/iah_alc74/#:~:text=In%20May%201974%2C%20led%20by,the%20second%20African%20Liberation%20Day.

24. "Ascension #3 Program, *Black World*, March 1975, 84, scanned copy, Google digital.

25. "A Calendar of Literary Events," *Washington Post*, August 31, 1975, C-5.

26. E. Ethelbert Miller papers, Box 43, Ishmael Reed folder.

27. E. Ethelbert Miller papers, Box 30, Calvin Forbes files.

28. E. Ethelbert Miller papers, Box 174 (1), Thulani Davis files.

29. Jacqueline Trescott, "Of Poetry and Power," *Washington Post*, March 7, 1980, B-1.

30. "Radio," *Washington Post*, January 6, 1981, B-6.

31. Richard Harrington, "Poetry to Their Ears," *Washington Post*, December 13, 1982, C-8.

32. Paula Tarnapol, "Weekend's Best," April 18, 1930, *Washington Post*, W-3.

33. Richard Harrington, "A Little Help," *Washington Post*, August 30, 1983, B-7.

34. E. Ethelbert Miller papers, Box 89, Darrell Stover files.

35. Elizabeth Kastor, "Ethelbert Miller: Poet, at Large," *Washington Post*, March 11, 1987, C-1.

36. Kastor, C-1-4.

37. Megan Rosenfeld, "Black Pepper and Spice," *Washington Post*, August 28, 1971, C-7.

38. Interview with Michelle Parkerson, March 31, 2023.

39. Parkerson interview.

40. Keith Gilyard, *John Oliver Killens: A Life of Black Literary Activism* (University of Georgia Press, 2011).

41. Miller interview.

42. Miller interview.

43. Essex C. Hemphill, *Obsidian II*, no. 3 (Winter 1977, 1975–82): 69.

44. Essex Hemphill, "Song for Rapunzel," *Callaloo*, no. 6 (May 1979): 21.

45. "Literary Calendar," *Washington Post*, December 30, 1979, BW8.

46. Culture File, "Lectures and Readings," *Washington Post*, April 28, 1978, W-13.

47. W. Royal Stokes, "Arrangements in Jazz," *Washington Post* (1974–), March 2, 1986, https://www.proquest.com/historical-newspapers/arrangements-jazz/docview/138900854/se-2.

48. W. Royal Stokes, "Sonnets and Street Talk," *Washington Post* (1974–), April 30, 1986, https://www.proquest.com/historical-newspapers/sonnets-street-talk/docview/138765030/se-2.

49. K. Swisher, "The Storm over a Stanza; Poet, Official Spar over Mayor's Arts Awards Incident: [FINAL Edition]," *Washington Post*, September 28, 1987, https://www.proquest.com/newspapers/storm-over-stanza-poet-official-spar-mayors-arts/docview/306936853/se-2.

50. K. Swisher, "East Side, West Side; New York Gets Primed for a Festival of Firsts: [FINAL Edition]," *Washington Post*, November 9, 1987, https://www.proquest.com/newspapers/east-side-west-new-york-gets-primed-festival/docview/306953329/se-2.

51. Jacqueline Trescott, "'Langston': Poet versus Premier; Disputed Film to Open Here: [FINAL Edition]," *Washington Post*, December 9, 1989, https://www.proquest.com/newspapers/langston-poet-versus-premiere-disputed-film-open/docview/307209328/se-2.

52. Octave Stevenson and Peter H. Share, eds., *City Celebration 1976: Poetry Anthology* (MLK Public Library, 1977).

53. Octave Stevenson, ed., *The Poet Upstairs* (Washington Writers Publishing House, 1979).

54. J. C. Rosenberger, "Collection of Poetry Is Published," *Richmond Times-Dispatch*, January 20, 1980, 101.

55. Rosenberger, 101.

56. Julia Cameron, "Michael Harper: In the Middle of a Great Sad," *Washington Post*, April 3, 1973, B-9.

57. Correspondence of E. Ethelbert Miller, Richard Peabody Papers, Gelman Library—Special Collections, George Washington University, Washington, DC, Box 13.

58. Kenneth Carroll, Darrell Stover, Reuben Jackson, 2009 inaugural poet and DC local Elizabeth Alexander, Joel Dias-Porter (DJ Renegade), Maxine Clair, Afaa Michael Weaver,

Brandon D. Johnson, and Sydney March, poet-jazz musician, are some of the notable African American poets published in *Gargoyle*.

59. Afaa Michael Weaver and Brian Tate are two poets who were recorded by Peabody.

60. Essex Hemphill Papers (Nethula Collection), Moorland-Spingarn Library, Howard University, Washington, DC, Box 6-F 1-20.

61. Essex Hemphill Papers (Nethula Collection), Box 6-F 1-20.

62. Ann Corbett and Bob Samek, "Personalities," *Washington Post*, February 26, 1979, B-3.

63. Essex Hemphill Papers (Nethula Collection), Box 6–all folders.

64. Jonetta Barras, survey responses, "DC Black Poets," July 2023.

65. *Free DC (The Writers Workshop)* (Free DC Press, 1978).

66. "Book Party Scheduled," *Evening Star*, November 18, 1976, 28.

67. "District Calendar," *Evening Star*, May 10, 1979, DC-2.

68. "Poetic Performance," *The Evening Star*, June 29, 1979, DC-2.

69. Jonetta Barras survey responses.

Chapter 11

1. James Spady, "UMUM Fete for Sterling Brown in Washington, DC," *Black Scholar* 8, no. 5 (March 1977): 40–44.

2. "Pure Sterling," *Washington Post*, May 1, 1979, 1, ProQuest, accessed May 29, 2024.

3. Hollie West, "Day of the Wordmaster," *Washington Post*, May 2, 1979, B-6.

4. West, B-6.

5. "Sterling A. Brown," Stephen E. Henderson, *Ebony*, October 1976, 128–36.

6. William Waring Cuney, *Storefront Church* (Black Heritage Series, Paul Breman, 1973).

7. Email exchanges with Paul Breman, 2006.

8. Marguerite Cartwright Papers, Tulane University Library—Amistad Center, Tulane University, New Orleans, Box 4, Folder 6.

9. Rosey Pool Papers, University of Sussex Library.

10. Correspondence, Waring Cuney (not yet catalogued), Sterling A. Brown Papers, Williams College, Williamstown, MA.

11. Correspondence, Waring Cuney (not yet catalogued), Sterling A. Brown Papers.

12. Adeline Norris, Obituary, *Wisconsin State News*, December 11, 2008.

13. Richard Tillinghast, "Book Review of The First National Poetry Series: *The Collected Poems* by Sterling A. Brown; *Any Body's Song* by Joseph Langland; *Denizens* by Ronald Perry; *Folly River* by Wendy Salinger; *Silks* by Roberta Spears," *Sewanee Review* 89, no. 2 (Spring 1981): 265–70.

14. Sterling A. Brown, "Introduction," *Collected Poems* (Harper and Row, 1979), xv.

15. Samuel W. Allen, "Book review of *Collected Poems of Sterling A. Brown*," *Massachusetts Review* 24, no. 3 (Autumn 1983): 649–57.

16. Joseph McLellan, "Poetic Justice at Last: The Joyful Poems of Sterling Brown: Sterling Brown's Joyful Poems of 50 Years Ago, *The Collected Poems of Sterling A. Brown*," *Washington Post*, September 4, 1980, 2, ProQuest, Web 29, accessed May 2024.

17. McLellan, 2.

18. Cornelius Eady, "Introduction," in *The Collected Poems of Sterling A. Brown, Triquarterly* (Northwestern University Press, 2020).

19. "Folger Poetry Series," *Evening Star*, January 18, 1970, 37.

20. *Evening Star*, January 16, 1971, 21.

21. *Evening Star*, August 11, 1975, 1.

22. *Evening Star*, August 11, 1975.

23. E. Ethelbert Miller, biography, Wikipedia, https://en.wikipedia.org/wiki/E._Ethelbert_Miller, accessed June 1, 2022.

24. Pinkie Gordon Lane, "Foreword," in *Dust of Uncertain Journey* by May Miller (Lotus Press, 1975).

25. Lauri Ramey, ed., in consultation with Paul Breman, *The Heritage Series of Black Poetry, 1962–1975: A Research Compendium* (Ashgate Publishing Company, 2008), 173–75.

26. Chris Myers Asch and George Derek Musgrove, *Chocolate City: A History of Race and Democracy in the Nation's Capital* (University of North Carolina Press, 2017), 355–83.

27. Myers Asch and Musgrove, 249.

28. Historically, Washington, DC, residents could not vote for president and had no control over local affairs. They also had no voting representation in Congress. All these goals would be achieved by 1974, when the city obtained home rule, the right to vote, and a nonvoting representative in Congress. Among those who fought hard for these rights including Marion Barry, David Clarke, Polly Shackleton, Walter Fauntroy, and Walter E. Washington. This is only a small portion of the individuals who helped the city's residents obtain some of their full citizenship rights.

Chapter 12

1. Interview with Darrell Stover, May 2023.

2. "Radio," *Washington Post*, November 22, 1979, C-15.

3. According to *The New York Times*, Dial-A-Poem began operating in New York City in January 1969: "Dial a Poem," *New York Times*, January 17, 1969, B-12.

4. Stover interview.

5. Larry Neal, "The Movement," *Washington Post, Times Herald*, January 26, 1969, 148, https://www.proquest.com/historical-newspapers/movement/docview/147720513/se-2.

6. "Foreword," in *Visions of a Liberated Future: Black Arts Movement Writings*, by Larry Neal, "The Wailer," Amiri Baraka (Thunder's Mouth Press, 1989).

7. Stover interview.

8. Stover interview.

9. Michael Goldfarb, "Poetry in Motion," July 18, 1982, *Washington Post*, https://www.washingtonpost.com/archive/lifestyle/style/1982/07/18/poetry-in-motion/d102d0dc-1e93-4fa7-a88c-5ed4547190f4/, accessed May 1, 2023.

10. W. Royal Stokes, "Free Verse?," *Washington Post*, November 6, 1984, D-9.

11. E. Ethelbert Miller papers, Gelman Library–Special Collections, George Washington University Library, Washington, DC, Box 46, Darrell Stover files.

12. E. Ethelbert Miller papers, Box 46, Stover files.

13. "Writers Guild Corners the Market on Poetry," *Washington Post*, August 1987, J 01.

14. E. Ethelbert Miller papers, Stover files.

15. In addition to Stover, Joy Jones, Steve Monroe, Kenneth Carroll, Caprece Jackson, Salvadoran American poet Quique Avilés, Leslie Lewis, and Doc Lewis all performed. Kenneth Carroll appeared with his group By Any Means Necessary.

16. E. Ethelbert Miller papers, Stover files.

17. E. Ethelbert Miller papers, Stover files.

18. The Spoken Word, *Bad Beats, Sacred Rhythms* (The Spoken Word, 1993).

19. Reuben Jackson survey responses, "DC Black Poets," 2023.

20. Reuben Jackson, *fingering the keys* (Gut Punch Press, 1991).

21. "Sterling Allen Brown Named D.C. Poet Laureate," *Jet*, June 4, 1984, 30.

22. Interview with Haile Gerima, July 20, 2023.

23. Gerima interview.

24. Ethelbert Miller and Octave Stevenson interview Gwendolyn Brooks (*The Writing Life Series*, Howard County Public TV, 1986).

25. Ethelbert Miller interview with Gwendolyn Brooks.

26. "Literary Calendar," *Washington Post*, September 1, 1985, https://www.proquest.com/historical-newspapers/literary-calendar/docview/138551847/se-2.

27. Jacqueline Trescott, "The 40 Year Quest of a Poet," *Washington Post*, September 25, 1985, D-1.

28. Darrell Stover, *Record of the Green Hat Chronicles* (Melolips Press, 1989).

29. Stover.

30. Stover.

31. Stover.

32. E. Ethelbert Miller papers, Gelman Library—Special Collections, George Washington University Library, Washington, DC, Box 31, Brian Gilmore Papers.

Chapter 13

1. Maxine Clair, "Reincarnation" (MA thesis, American University, 1984).

2. "Literary Calendar," *Washington Post*, August 30, 1987, BW-13.

3. "Community Events," *Washington Post*, October 15, 1987, DC-8.

4. "Listings," *Washington Post*, November 29, 1987, BW-14.

5. E. Ethelbert Miller papers, Gelman Library–Special Collections, George Washington University, Washington, DC, Box 26, Maxine Clair folder.

6. E. Ethelbert Miller, *where are all the love poems for dictators* (Open Hand Publishing, 1986), back cover.

7. Book jacket, back cover, Kwelismith, *Slavesong: The Art of Singing* (Anacostia Repertory Company, 1989).

8. Kwelismith, *Slavesong*.

9. "On Record," *Washington Post*, April 15, 1988, W-23.

10. Anne Gowen, "Artists, Patrons, Honored by the Mayor," *Washington Times*, November 1, 1991, E-2.

11. William Booth, "AIDS Report Draws Tepid Response," *Science*, n.s., 241, no. 4867 (August 12, 1988): 778.

12. Marcellus Blount, "The Preacherly Text: African American Poetry and Vernacular Performance," *PMLA* 107, no. 3, "Special Topic: Performance" (May 1992): 582–93.

13. James Alexander Robinson, "Giving Voice: The Power of Words in African American Culture," *Smithsonian Magazine*, September 16, 2016, https://folklife.si.edu/magazine/freedom-sounds-giving-voice-the-power-of-words-in-african-american-culture.

14. Ahmos Zu-Bolton and Kirsten Mullen, "Review of THE CLEARING AND BEYOND and WINDY PLACES, by May Miller and Henry Blakely," *Obsidian* 3 (1975–82, 1977): 75–78, http://www.jstor.org/stable/44490175.

15. Zu-Bolton and Mullen, "Review."

16. Qtd. in Henry Louis Gates Jr. and Evelyn Brooks (Higginbotham), eds., *Harlem Renaissance Lives from the African American National Biography* (Oxford University Press, 2009), 353.

17. Patricia Gaines-Carter, "New Generation Discovers May Miller," *Washington Post*, December 26, 1986, B-12.

18. Gaines-Carter, B-12.

19. Beth Brown, Review, *College Language Association Journal*, September 1984, 101–9.

20. Zu-Bolton and Mullen, "Review."

21. Alphine W. Jefferson, "Black America in the 1980s: RHETORIC VS. REALITY," *Black Scholar* 17, no. 3 (1986): 2–9, http://www.jstor.org/stable/41067268.

22. Jefferson.

23. Charles Sumner School Archives exhibit, "McKinley Tech Library and the making of a writer," Kenneth Carroll.

24. Ernesto Cardenal, Poetry Foundation, https://www.poetryfoundation.org/poets/ernesto-cardenal, accessed May 12, 2023.

25. Biographical information on Jennifer E. Smith provided by her sister, Karen Dickeson, email, June 2023.

26. Dickerson communication.

27. Black American Literature Forum, August 1985 issue, 109–14.

28. Jennifer E. Smith, "For All the 'They Think They Conscious' Writers Who Applauded Wilson Goode at a Conference Celebrating Black Writing," in *Fast Talk Full Volume*, ed. Alan Spears (Gut Punch Press, 1993). (Permission provided by Karen Dickerson.)

29. "May 13, 1985 Move Bombing," Zinn Education Project, https://www.zinnedproject.org/news/tdih/move-bombing/, accessed June 1, 2023.

30. Kenneth Carroll, "Supermax," 1997. (Poem provided by author.)

Chapter 14

1. Ta-Nehisi Coates, "Slamming Open-Mic Poetry," *Washington City Paper*, August 2, 1996, https://washingtoncitypaper.com/article/286987/slamming-open-mike-poetry/, accessed May 12, 2022.

2. Qtd. in Javon Johnson, *Killing Poetry: Blackness and the Making of Slam and Spoken Word Communities* (Rutgers University Press, 2017), 1–2.

3. Carly (Frankie) Laird, "A Poetry of Embodiment," *Writing on the Edge* 30, no. 1 (Fall 2019): 27–43.

4. Laird, 27–43.

5. E. Ethelbert Miller, *In Search of Color Everywhere: A Collection of African American Poetry* (Stewart, Tabori, and Chang, 1994).

6. Lorenzo Thomas, "Review of *In Search of Color Everywhere*," *African American Review* 31, no. 2 (Summer 1997): 357–59.

7. Rudolph P. Byrd, "Defining the Field of Thought and Vision," *Callaloo* 12, no. 2 (1994): 643–45, 743.

8. Byrd, 643–45.

9. E. Ethelbert Miller papers, Gelman Library—Special Collections, George Washington University, Washington, DC, Box 113, Alan Spears files.

10. Alan Spears, ed., foreword, in *Fast Talk, Full Volume: An Anthology of Contemporary African American Poetry* (Gut Punch Press, 1993).

11. Fred Chappelle, "Taking Sides: Six Poetry Anthologies," Reviewed Work(s): *Against Forgetting: Twentieth-Century Poetry of Witness* by Carolyn Forché; *A Gathering of Poets* by Maggie Anderson, Alex Gildzen and Raymond Craig; *The Rag and Bone Shop of the Heart: Poems for Men* by Robert Bly, James Hillman and Michael Meade; *Men of Our Time: Anthology of Male Poetry in Contemporary America* by Fred Moramarco and Al Zolynas; *Fast Talk, Full Volume* by Alan Spears; *African-American Poetry of the Nineteenth Century: An Anthology by Joan R. Sherman, Georgia Review* 48, no. 2 (Summer 1994): 361–84.

12. Kevin Powell and Ras Baraka, eds., *In the Tradition: An Anthology of Young Black Writers* (Harlem River Press, 1992).

13. Howard Ramsby, "What Happened with African American Poetry from 1977 to 1987?" *Cultural Front*, May 12, 2012, https://www.culturalfront.org/2012/06/what-happened-with-african-american.html, accessed June 1, 2023.

14. Qtd. in Mel Watkins, "Hard Times for Black Writers: Black Authors' Queries," *New York Times*, Feb 22, 1981, 2, https://www.proquest.com/historical-newspapers/hard-times-black-writers/docview/121888458/se-2.

15. Watkins.

16. "A Presidential Assault on the Arts: [Letter]," *New York Times*, June 4, 1981, https://www.proquest.com/newspapers/presidential-assault-on-arts/docview/424124715/se-2.

17. "50% Cut in U.S. Arts Aid Drafted by Budget Head: Cuts Must be Approved 'Arts Have Abiding Value' Public Broadcasting Proposals," *New York Times*, February 7, 9, https://www.proquest.com/historical-newspapers/50-cut-u-s-arts-aid-drafted-budget-head/docview/121501455/se-2.

18. Grace Cavalieri, "A Child of Two Cultures," *Italian Americana* 37, No. 2 (Summer 2019): 147–49.

19. Some of the poets who were recorded by Cavalieri and/or appeared on *The Poet and Poem* include Ethelbert Miller, Kenneth Carroll, Darrell Stover, Brandon Johnson, Abdul Ali, Kwame Alexander, Holly Bass, Lucille Clifton (Maryland), Kyle Dargan, Twain Dooley, Thomas Sayers Ellis, Reginald Harris (Baltimore), Le Hinton (Baltimore), Reuben Jackson, Carolyn Joyner, Dolores Kendrick, Alan King, Laini Mataka, Sami Miranda, Venus Thrash, Fred Joiner, Maritza Rivera, Michelle Parkerson, and Askia Muhammed.

20. D. Kevin McNeir, "WHUR Radio Pioneer and DMV Legend Joe Gorham Dies at 69," *Washington Informer*, https://www.washingtoninformer.com/whur-radio-pioneer-and-dmv-legend-joe-gorham-dies-at-69/, accessed June 2, 2023.

21. A native Washingtonian, Kimberly Washington earned her undergraduate degree in English from the UDC and her master of social work from the University of Maryland, Baltimore. Kimberly was the creator/co-host of *Soul Conversations*, on Washington, DC's community radio station WPFW 89.3 and worked as a producer at WHUR 96.3 for close to a decade.

22. McNeir, "WHUR Radio Pioneer."

23. Randall Horton, social media comment, January 24, 2022, Facebook.

24. Joe Gorham's introduction to *Spoken Word at Joe's Place*, WHUR Radio, n.d.

25. Other personalities and institutions that used poetry to communicate and advance poetry through the medium of radio include Mark Thompson, the Sirius X One radio personality, WDCU-FM before it closed, WPFW on many other programs, and WAMU-FM 88.5. Danny Queen, a poet, and Kenneth Carroll produced a poetry/political program on WPFW-FM for years featuring young high school students. Carroll's show was produced and presented by teenagers from Carroll's creative writing classes at Duke Ellington School of the Arts.

26. Nadine Winter, "For the Record," *Washington Post*, January 11, 1990, A-28.

27. Carlos Sanchez, "DC Police Say Jump in Homicides May Be Seasonal," *Washington Post*, November 20, 1990, B-05.

28. Interview with Eugene Wooden, July 6, 2023.

29. Desson Howe," Festival Focus on Issues," *Washington Post*, April 28, 1995, https://www.washingtonpost.com/archive/lifestyle/1995/04/28/festivals-focus-on-issues/e1a3b06b-a283-47e0-9983-b004a7470941/, accessed May 29, 2023.

30. Holly Bass, "Voices That Carry," *Washington City Paper*, April 28, 1995, https://washingtoncitypaper.com/article/294834/voices-carry/, accessed June 1, 2022.

31. Terrence Nicholson aka SUB-Z, web page, https://www.jammincolors.com/composers/terence-sub-z-nicholson, accessed June 23, 2023.

32. Richard Stratton and Kim Wozencraft, eds., *SLAM: The screenplay and filmmakers' journals* (Grove Press Books, 1998), 14, 23–70.

33. Kehinde David Chaytor, *Rhythm, Rhyme & Life: Spoken Word and the Oral Tradition* (Bunce Island Media, 2002).

34. Natalie Hopkinson, "A Few Words For Every Occasion," *Washington Post*, July 13, 2000, G-33.

35. Others in the film include Patrick Washington, Joy Jones, Twain Dooley, Jane Alberdeston, Brandon Johnson, Holly Bass, E. Ethelbert Miller, Nana Malaya, Nomsa Mdalose, Gayle Danley, Ferricia Fatea (student/poet), Kenneth Carroll, and Gaston Neal.

36. Chaytor.

Chapter 15

1. Natalie Hopkinson, *Go-Go Live: The Musical Life and Death of a Chocolate City* (Duke University Press, 2012), xii.

2. Hopkinson, xii.

3. Keith D. Leonard, "Postmodern Soul: The Innovative Nostalgia of Thomas Sayers Ellis," *Contemporary Literature* 56, no. 2 (2015): 340–71, http://www.jstor.org/stable/24735011.

4. Leonard, 344.

5. Charles Roswell interviews Thomas Sayers Ellis, in "A Mixed Congregation," *Callaloo* (Autumn 2004): 884–96.

6. E. Ethelbert Miller papers, Gelman Library—Special Collections, George Washington University, Washington, DC, "The Dark Room Collective" Box/Files. Other members of the collective include Sharan Strange, Kevin Young, Natasha Trethewey, Tracy Smith, John Keene, Major Jackson, Patrick Sylvain, Carl Phillips, Janice Lowe, and Bethany White.

7. Interview with Peter Clare, May 2023.

8. Clare interview.

9. Trey Ellis, "The New Black Aesthetic," *Callaloo* no. 38 (Winter 1989): 233–43.

10. Ellis, 234.

11. Clare interview.

12. Clare interview.

13. David Mills, "Putting Down Roots in Anacostia," *Washington Post*, July 24, 1992, D-1.

14. Mills.

15. Mark Jenkins, "Gangsta Mack Cinema: Perpetuating Negative Images or Expanding Opportunities," *Washington City Paper*, December 3, 1993, https://washingtoncitypaper.com/article/291148/gangsta-mack-cinema-perpetuating-negative-images-or-expanding-opportunities/, accessed March 21, 2023.

16. Tracy E. Hopkins, "A Cultural Haven—Poets and Hip Hop Lovers Gather to Work on the Flow of Their Rhymes," *Washington Times*, July 20, 1994, C-10.

17. Interview with Kenneth Carroll, August 2023.

18. Carroll interview.

19. Carroll interview.

20. Kerry L. Goldmann, "Keepers of the Culture at 3201 Adeline Street: Locating Black Power Theater in Berkeley, California," *California History*, no. 1 (February 2021): 98–120, https://doi.org/10.1525/ch.2021.98.1.98.

21. Goldmann.

22. Patricia Harvey, survey responses, "DC Black Poets," May 2022.

23. Harvey survey responses.

24. Harvey survey responses.

25. Harvey survey responses.

26. Holly Bass, "Rhymin' and Readin'" *Washington City Paper*, February 3, 1995, https://washingtoncitypaper.com/article/293564/rhyme-and-readin/, accessed March 12, 2023.

27. Ta-Nehisi Coates, "Slamming Open-Mic Poetry," *Washington City Paper*, August 2, 1996, https://washingtoncitypaper.com/article/286987/slamming-open-mike-poetry/, accessed June 12, 2022.

28. Brandon Johnson, survey responses, "DC Black Poets."

29. Fred L. Joiner, survey responses, "DC Black Poets," September 2022.

30. Alan King, "Ernesto Mercer's Journey," Alan King's Blog, https://alanwking.com/2011/08/22/ernesto-mercers-journey-towards-and-beyond-gunpowder-a-match/, accessed May 1, 2023.

31. Joy Alford (J. Joy "Sistah Joy" Matthews), survey responses, "DC Black Poets," September 21, 2022.

32. Patricia, D. McCoy, " 'Poetry Extrvaganza Day' Celebrated in D.C.," *The Washington Afro American*, January 18, 2011, https://afro.com/poetry-extravaganza-daycelebratedin-d-c/.

33. "The Week," *Washington Post*, October 26, 2003, M4.

Chapter 16

1. E. Ethelbert Miller papers, Gelman Library—Special Collections, George Washington University, Washington, DC, Box 89, Stephen Henderson files.

2. Delores B. Stephens, "Stephen Henderson 1925–1997," *Journal of Negro History* 85, no. 4 (Autumn 2000): 318–19.

3. Stephens, 318.

4. Stephen E. Henderson, "The Blues as Poetry," *Callaloo* no. 16 (October 1982): 22–30.

5. Henderson, "The Blues as Poetry," 22.

6. Henderson, "The Blues as Poetry," 22.

7. Henderson, "The Blues as Poetry," 25.

8. Henderson, "The Blues as Poetry," 22.

9. Stephen Henderson, *Understanding the New Black Poetry* (William Morrow and Company, 1973).

10. Kenneth Carroll, *So What! For the White Dude Who Said This Ain't Poetry* (Bunny and Crocodile Press, 1997).

11. Herbert Woodward Martin, "Review: *Fast Talk, Full Volume: An Anthology of Contemporary African American Poetry*, by Alan Spears," *African American Review* 31, no. 2 (Summer 1997): 360–62.

12. John Gehring, "Outside Art," *Education Week* 24, no. 37 (May 18, 2005): 25–29.

13. Gehring.

14. Bob Garfield, "Poetry in Commotion," *Washington Post*, August 1, 1993, N-24.

15. Henry Allen, "It's Rhyme Time Live," *Washington Post*, December 21, 1992, C-1.

16. Andy Fogle, social media response to questions regarding Washington, DC, spoken word scene in the 1990s.

17. Jeffrey McDaniel, "Washington DC Poetry Slam, 1993–95," *Poetry Magazine*, June 13, 2007, https://www.poetryfoundation.org/harriet-books/2007/06/washington-dc-poetry-slam-1993-95, accessed May 12, 2023.

18. Richard L. Schurr, *Parodies of Ownership: Hip-Hop Aesthetics and Intellectual Property Law* (University of Michigan Press, 2009), 17.

19. Schurr, 17.

20. Schurr, 44.

21. Kwame Alexander and Kalamu ya Salaam, *360 Degrees of Black Poets* (Alexander Publishing, 1998).

22. Interviews with Joel Dias-Porter, June and July 2023.

23. DJ Kool, "Pressed Against the Glass," DOH Entertainment 1990, YouTube video, https://youtu.be/U3NNzXhXDXw?si=NsBkRNUvYnt83Zdl.

24. Dias-Porter interviews.

25. Digital chat with Joel Dias-Porter aka DJ Renegade, June 2023.

26. Jelani Cobb, "Times Up," *Washington City Paper*, September 20, 1996, https://washingtoncitypaper.com/article/286368/times-up/, accessed June 10, 2023.

27. Joel Dias-Porter, "21 Black Jacks." Used by permission of Joel Dias-Porter.

28. Deborah A. Ring, *Contemporary Black Biography: Toni Blackman* (Gale Cengage Learning, 2011), 13–15.

29. Eric Brace, "Toni, Toni, Toni," *Washington Post*, October 3, 1997, 13.

30. Brace, 13.

31. Brace, 13.

32. Brace, 13.

33. Toni Blackman, "So What?," YouTube video, https://www.toniblackman.com/music-videos, accessed May 3, 2023.

34. *Obsidian II* 10, no. 1/2 (Spring–Summer, Fall–Winter 1995): 264–70.

35. Yao Glover, "Yaphet Brinson," Free Black Space, http://freeblackspace.blogspot.com/2016/05/yaphet-brinson-back-cover-outro-from.html, accessed May 22, 2023.

36. Gayle Danley letter to Ethelbert Miller, April 10, 1995, E. Ethelbert Miller's papers, Gelman Library—Special Collections, George Washington University, Washington, DC, Gayle Danley files.

37. Gayle Danley, "Artist Statement," Young Audiences website, https://www.yanjep.org/artist/poetry-pros-gayle-danley-for-soul-sessions/, accessed May 27, 2023.

38. Gayle Danley, *Passionate: poems you can feel* (Brilliance Productions, 1997).

Chapter 17

1. "Washington's Poet Laureate," *Washington Post*, February 27, 1893, 6.

2. Qtd. in Robin Bingham, "Sweet Child of Rhyme," *Washington City Paper*, October 27, 2000, https://washingtoncitypaper.com/article/265840/sweet-child-of-rhyme/, accessed May 12, 2022.

3. Interview with Andy Shallal, July 2023.

4. " 'The Humble Prose of Living': Rethinking Oral/Written Relations in the Echoes of Spoken Word, Anne Haas Dyson, English Education," *Literocracy: A New Way of Thinking About Literacy and Democracy* 37, no. 2 (January 2005): 149–64, 149.

5. Jonetta Rose Barras, "Independent Thought," *Washington City Paper*, September 8, 1995, https://washingtoncitypaper.com/article/297027/independent-thought/, last accessed May 2, 2022.

6. Barras.

7. Ta-Nehisi Coates, "Fifth Annual Barber Shop Bash," *Washington City Paper*, December 6, 1996, https://washingtoncitypaper.com/article/285194/fifth-annual-barbershop-bash/, May 2, 2022.

8. Facebook post.

9. US Census Bureau 2020, "Quick Facts—Washington DC," https://www.census.gov/quickfacts/fact/table/washingtoncitydistrictofcolumbia/PST04522, accessed, May 12, 2023.

10. Sara Gebhardt, "For Karibu Books, A Community Bash," *Washington Post*, March 6, 2003, T25.

11. Hoke (Brother Yao) Glover, *Free Black Space*, July 7, 2015, http://freeblackspace.blogspot.com/2015/07/exhausting-means-of-struggle-part-1-of.html, accessed May 1, 2023.

12. Sarah Godfrey, "DJ Renegade," *Washington City Paper*, February 7, 2003, https://washingtoncitypaper.com/article/255355/dj-renegade/, accessed May 22, 2023

13. "Books and Bonding: At D.C. Bookstore, Black Women Find Haven of Literature and Sisterhood," *Washington Post*, March 18, 1997.

14. Jenny McKean Moore website, GWU, https://english.columbian.gwu.edu/jenny-mckean-moore-professorship, accessed June 2, 2022.

15. Interview with Cornelius Eady, July 24, 2023

16. Comment at readings.

17. Phillip Butcher, "Creative Writing in the Negro College," *Journal of Negro Education* 20, no. 2 (Spring 1951): 160–63.

18. Butcher, 161.

19. John Keene, "BLACK STUDIES, ALL STUDIES: What Can Black Studies Teach Creative Writing?," in *Teaching Black: The Craft of Teaching on Black Life and Literature*, ed. Ana-Maurine Lara, and Drea Brown (University of Pittsburgh Press, 2021), 39–42.

20. Keene, 37.

21. Advertisement, *Ploughshares* 21, no. 4 (Winter 1995/1996).

22. Cave Canem website, https://cavecanempoets.org/mission-history/, accessed March 12, 2023.

23. Cave Canem website, accessed March 12, 2023.

24. Ta-Nehisi Coates, "Heirs of the Dog," *Washington City Paper*, July 11, 1997, https://washingtoncitypaper.com/article/282262/heirs-of-the-dog/.

25. Conversation with Jess.

Chapter 18

1. Sterling A. Brown, "The Negro in Washington," in *A Son's Return: Selected Essays of Sterling A. Brown*, ed. Mark Sanders (Northeastern University Press, 1996), 25–45, 45–46.

2. Brown, "The Negro in Washington."

3. Brown, "The Negro in Washington."

4. Michelle Parkerson, "Fierceness Served," https://www.thecoffeehousedc.com/ourstory, accessed May 22, 2023.

5. Kyle J. Lambe, "Performative Space / Transformative Space: Race, Affect, and Amateur Performance in U.S. Queer Open Mics" (PhD diss., University of Santa Cruz, March 2023).

6. R. C. Dolinsky, "Lesbian and Gay DC: Identity, Emotion, and Experience in Washington, DC's Social and Activist Communities (1961–1986)," ProQuest Dissertations & Theses Global (755690853), 2010, https://www.proquest.com/dissertations-theses/lesbian-gay-dc-identity-emotion-experience/docview/755690853/se-2.

7. Parkerson, "Fierceness Served."

8. Parkerson, "Fierceness Served."

9. Parkerson, "Fierceness Served."

10. Parkerson, "Fierceness Served."

11. Parkerson, "Fierceness Served."

12. Parkerson, "Fierceness Served."

13. Lannan Center for Poetics and Social Practice, Georgetown University, "Quique Avilés," https://lannan.georgetown.edu/past-guests/quique-aviles/, accessed May 1, 2023.

14. Lori Tsang bio, Bourgeon, https://bourgeononline.com/2021/11/four-poems-by-lori-tsang/, accessed September 12, 2023.

15. Lori Tsang, *The Women's Review of Books* 19, no. 10/11 (July 2002): 1–3.

16. Sydney March, *Stealing Mangos* (Mica Press, 1997).

17. Lori Tsang, "Griot Police," *Washington City Paper*, August 9, 1996, https://washingtoncitypaper.com/article/286899/griot-police/, accessed, May 22, 2023.

18. Jose Padua, *A Short History of Monsters: Poems by Jose Padua* (University of Arkansas Press, 2019).

19. Peter J. Harris, *Hand Me My Griot Clothes: The Autobiography of Junior Baby* (Black Classic Press, 1993).

20. Peter J. Harris, *Drumming Between Us* 3, no. 1 (Spring 1997).

21. "On Record," *Black World*, March 1972, 79.

22. Sarah Godfrey, "I Usta Be Wanda Robinson," *Washington City Paper*, https://washingtoncitypaper.com/article/239663/i-usta-be-wanda-robinson/, accessed May 8, 2023.

23. "Otis Remembered," Nyumburu Cultural Center website, https://nyumburu.umd.edu/otis-remembered, accessed September 22, 2023.

Chapter 19

1. Legislative History of the National and Community Service Trust Act of 1993 P.L. 103-82 (1993).

2. *Tell the World* (Harper Collins 2008).

3. Johnathan Katz, "A Description of a Possible National Agenda for Literary Activities in the United States Based on an Analysis of Systems Governing Literary Participation," ProQuest Dissertations & Theses Global (304381350), https://www.proquest.com/dissertations-theses/description-possible-national-agenda-literary/docview/304381350/se-2.

4. Adrienne T. Washington, "Teens Get Literary Lifeline," *Washington Times*, October 21, 1996, C-6.

5. Washington, C-6.

6. Darrell Stover, "Boys Town," *Washington Post*, May 16, 1993, https://www.washingtonpost.com/archive/opinions/1993/05/16/boyz-town/d00c5f14-9b2a-4fd7-be15-75d7e5eb2b1a/, accessed June 12, 2023.

7. Brian Gilmore, Ta-Nehisi Coates, Joel Dias-Porter, and Darrell Stover, *Medium: Writings from Lorton Prison—DC Writers Corps* (DC WritersCorps, 1997).

8. Interviews with Joel Dias Porter, June and July 2023.

9. Email exchanges with Reuben Jackson, September 2023.

10. Andy Fogle teaches high school in New York now. Jeffery McDaniel is a professor of creative writing at Sarah Lawrence College. John Murillo, author of two critically acclaimed books of poetry, teaches at Wesleyan College. Laini Mataka still lives in Washington, DC, writing and reading her poetry. Most of the poets who passed through the DC WritersCorps remain active poets and teachers nationwide. Students who participated in workshops are now writers and work in academia.

11. Full disclosure: the author is on the board of the DC Creative Writing Workshop.

12. Interview with Nancy Schwalb, July 2023.

13. Schwalb interview.

14. Interview with Kenneth Carroll, August 2023.

15. Hurston/Wright Foundation, https://www.hurstonwright.org, accessed July 2023.

16. Khadijah Ali-Coleman, https://khadijahali-coleman.com/Poet-Laureate, accessed July 2023.

17. "New in Paperback," *Washington Post*, May 24, 1998, https://www.washingtonpost.com

/archive/entertainment/books/1998/05/24/new-in-paperback/8f84445f-1e4e-4f59-9862-a83663dbc689/, accessed June 1, 2023.

18. Email exchange with Joel Dias-Porter, June 28, 2023.

19. Terrance Hayes, "The Future of the Black Rooster Collective," 2023 (unpublished). Used by permission of the author.

Chapter 20

1. Jennifer King, "Let Me Count the Ways: Documenting the Poetry Community in Washington DC, A Case Study," *Archival Issues* 33, no. (2011): 57–67.

2. Kim Roberts, Editor, "The Ascension Reading Series," *Washington Review* 26, no. 6 (April/May 2001).

3. Roberts, "The Ascension Reading Series."

4. Roberts, "The Ascension Reading Series," 8–9.

5. Roberts, "The Ascension Reading Series," 8–9.

6. Kenneth Carroll, "Gaston Neal," *Beltway Poetry Quarterly*, https://washingtonart.com/beltway/neal.html#:~:text=Gaston%20Neal%27s%20importance%20to%20theWashington,and%20Drum%20and%20Spear%20Bookstore, accessed January 2, 2021.

7. Flyer for "Scattered Pieces of the Action," in E. Ethelbert Miller papers, Gelman Library—Special Collections, George Washington University, Washington, DC, Box 101, Gaston Neal files.

8. A. B. Spellman, Liner Notes, *The Journey* (Musical recording, July 13, 1995).

9. Spellman, liner notes.

10. "Gaston Neal Receives Award," *Washington Informer*, October 1999.

11. Yaphet Brinson, "Striving for Unity," *Hilltop Newspaper*, April 26, 1991, A-5.

12. Brinson, "Striving for Unity," A-5.

13. Patrick Washington, "It's Your Mug—30th anniversary reading—BloomBars," July 2023.

14. Derrick Weston Brown, survey responses, "DC Black Poets.".

15. Brown survey responses.

16. Alan King, survey responses, "DC Black Poets."

17. King survey responses.

18. King survey responses,

19. Interview with Lisa Pegram, Zoom, March 2023.

20. Pegram interview.

21. Interview with Kemet Mawakana, phone, August 2023.

22. Mawakana interview.

23. Neil Drumming, "Samuel the 7 Foot Poet," *Washington City Paper*, August 14, 1998, https://washingtoncitypaper.com/article/276670/samuel-the-7foot-poet-jefferson/.

24. Patrick Washington, "Patrick Washington," in *Creative Suitland*, October 2019, https://creativesuitland.org/blog/patrick-black-picasso-washington-poet-of-many-faces, accessed June 2023.

25. John Leland, "58 Jazz Giants in One Immortal Image," *New York Times*, September 25, 2018, https://www.nytimes.com/2018/09/25/lens/great-day-in-harlem-art-kane-jazz.html.

26. American University website, Kyle Dargan webpage, https://www.american.edu/cas/faculty/kd6017a.cfm.

27. Kyle Dargan webpage.

28. Folger Reading Series list, "1970–2023, Folgerpedia," https://folgerpedia.folger.edu/Previous_poetry_readings_at_the_Folger.

29. Folger.

30. Interview with Teri Cross Ellen Davis, December 2023.

31. Hayes Davis, "Presence," *Common Lit Magazine*, 2016, https://www.commonlit.org/en/texts/presence.

32. Not Just Another Day Off, https://folgerpedia.folger.edu/Not_Just_Another_Day_Off.

Chapter 21

1. Steven Overly, Delece Smith-Barrow, Katy O'Donnell, and Ming Li, "Washington Was an Icon of Black Power," *Politico*, April 15, 2022, https://www.politico.com/news/magazine/2022/04/15/washington-dc-gentrification-black-political-power-00024515.

2. Email exchange with Ed Visser, December 23, 2005.

3. Visser email exchange.

4. Email exchanges with Evie Shockley, July 11, 2023–August 1, 2023.

5. Shockley email exchanges.

6. Shockley email exchanges.

7. The official website of Bomani Armah, https://notarapper.com.

8. Maria Fernanda, survey responses, "DC Black Poets." Fernanda has read, among many places, at Busboys and Poets, Spit Dat, and at the Split This Rock Poetry Festival in 2022.

9. Linette Marie Allen, email exchange, July 2023.

10. Tony Medina survey responses, "DC Black Poets." See also Shanae L Harris, "Employee of the Week: Tony Medina," *Hilltop Newspaper*, February 11, 2005, A-4.

11. The anthology reflects the troubled times of American life as reflected in poems about racism, police violence, violence, and social failure. Many of the poets included are from Washington, DC, or connected to the city in some way: Fred Joiner, Sami Miranda, Melanie Henderson, Venus Thrash, Lisa Pegram, Kimberly Collins, and Cedric Tillman.

12. Melanie Henderson, survey responses, "DC Black Poets."

13. Henderson also founded the journal *Tidal Basin Review* and edited publications from Central Square Press. Henderson, along with Fred Joiner, Lisa Pegram, and Enzo Silon Surin, is part of the chap-journal *The New Verse Poets Mixtape: Volume One: The 4X4* (Central Square Press, 2016).

14. Interview with Jon West-Bey, July 25, 2023.

15. Interview with Jon West-Bey, August 2023.

16. Today, West-Bey is "a curator, museum consultant, and owner of West-Bey Consulting in Washington, DC. He has curated over 60 exhibitions and produced and managed numerous award-winning public, educational, and multimedia programs over multiple disciplines, including history, art, literature, and cultural studies." https://www.linkedin.com/in/jon-west-bey-98819436/.

Fred Joiner, a poet originally from Philadelphia, continues to write poetry from North Carolina.

17. Tom Sietsma, "Weekly Dish," *Washington Post*, October 5, 2005, Fb5.

18. Interview with Andy Shallal, June 2023.

19. Shallal interview.

20. Shallal interview.

21. Joe Knowles, "Poets Against the War," *In These Times*, https://inthesetimes.com/article/poets-against-the-war, accessed June 2, 2023.

22. Sam Hamill, poet and co-founder of the prestigious literary publisher Copper Canyon Press, was invited to a White House literary symposium. Incensed by President George W. Bush's war plans, Hamill wrote in an open letter to his colleagues: "I believe the only legitimate

response to such a morally bankrupt and unconscionable idea is to reconstitute a Poets Against the War movement like the one organized to speak out against the war in Vietnam." He asked "every poet to speak up for the conscience of our country and lend his or her name to our petition against this war." The response was extraordinary. By March 1, when poetsagainstthewar.org, the website Hamill and friends set up to receive poems, stopped accepting submissions, more than 12,000 poems had been posted. *The Monthly Review*, Poets Against the War, https://monthlyreview.org/author/poetsagainstwar/.

23. Qtd. in S. Bourdeaux, "A Place at the Table: The Role of Historic Sites in Gentrifying Neighborhoods. Our Stories: Shaw Through the 1970s," PhD diss., 2015, ProQuest Dissertations & Theses Global (1695282760), https://www.proquest.com/dissertations-theses/place-at-table-role-historic-sites-gentrifying/docview/1695282760/se-2.

24. Dan Zak, "What's the Verse That Could Happen in DC?," February 7, 2010, *Washington Post*, https://www.proquest.com/newspapers/whats-verse-that-could-happen-d-c/docview/410311927/se-2.

25. Kim Roberts, ed., *Full Moon on K Street* (Plan B Press, 2010).

26. "October 30, 2014 (Page SS2-22 DC)," *Washington Post*, October 30, 2014 (final edition), https://www.proquest.com/newspapers/october-30-2014-page-ss2-22-dc/docview/1938306497/se-2.

27. "October 30, 2014 (Page SS2-22 DC)."

28. Peter J. Harris, "Remembering Peter J. Harris," https://www.thenicholsonproject.org/2023-peter.

29. The Nicholson Project, a key player in the curation of Harris's work, described "See You . . . Comes by Tens," as a project "conceived and curated by our current artist-in-residence, Peter J. Harris, in collaboration with the American Poetry Museum." Harris, "Remembering Peter J. Harris."

30. The Nicholson Project, in Harris, "Remembering Peter J. Harris."

Selected Bibliography

Archives

Toni Blackman Papers, Gelman Library—Special Collections, George Washington University, Washington, DC.

Arna Bontemps Papers, Special Collections, Syracuse University Library, Syracuse, NY.

Sterling A. Brown Papers, Special Collections, Williams College, Williamston, MA.

Paul Breman Heritage Collection, Williams College, Williamstown, MA.

Marguerite Cartwright Papers, Tulane University Library—Amistad Research Center, Tulane University, New Orleans.

Owen Dodson Papers, Moorland-Spingarn Library, Howard University, Washington, DC.

Brian Gilmore Papers, Gelman Library—Special Collections, George Washington University, Washington, DC.

Essex Hemphill Papers (Nethula Collection) Moorland-Spingarn Library, Howard University, Washington, DC.

Langston Hughes Papers, Yale University (Digital Collections), https://archives.yale.edu/repositories.

Georgia Douglas Johnson Papers, Moorland-Spingarn Library, Howard University, Washington, DC.

Toni Lightfoot Papers, Gelman Library—Special Collections, George Washington University, Washington, DC.

May Miller and Kelly Miller Papers, Rose Library, Emory University, Atlanta, GA.

E. Ethelbert Miller Papers, Gelman Library—Special Collections, George Washington University, Washington, DC.

Lawrence D. Reddick World War II Project, 1943–1953, New York Public Library—Schomburg Center.

Richard Peabody Papers (*Gargoyle Magazine*), Gelman Library—Special Collections, George Washington University, Washington, DC.

Books

Poetry and Anthologies

Abel, Elizabeth, Christian Barbara, and Helene Moglen. *Female Subjects in Black and White: Race, Psychoanalysis, Feminism.* University of California Press, 1997.

Adoff, Arnold, ed. *I Am the Darker Brother.* Aladdin Paperbacks, 1968.

Asch, Chris Myers, and George Derek Musgrove. *Chocolate City: A History of Race and Democracy in the Nation's Capital.* University of North Carolina Press, 2017.

Baraka, Amiri, and Larry Neal, eds. *Black Fire: An Anthology of African American Writing*. William Morrow, 1965.

The Black Rooster Collective. *The Black Rooster Social Inn: This Is the Place*. Spike and Pepper Books, 1997.

Brinson, Yaphet. *Different Dementions*. Double Negatives Press, 1991.

Brown, Derrick Weston. *Wisdom Teeth*. Busboys and Poets Press, 2011.

Brown, Sterling A. *The Collected Poems of Sterling A. Brown*. National Poetry Series, 1981.

Brown, Sterling A. *Southern Road: Poems*. Harcourt, Brace and Company, 1932.

Brown, Sterling A., Arthur P. Davis, and Ulysses Lee, eds. *The Negro Caravan*. Dryden Press, 1941, 1969.

Byars, J. C., *Black and White*. Crane Press, 1927.

Carroll, Kenneth, *Never Piss Off a Poet*. Shattered Wig, 1990.

Carroll, Kenneth, *So What! For the White Dude Who Said This Ain't Poetry*. Bunny and Crocodile Press, 1997.

Carter, Karl W. *Southern Road and Selected Poems*. Self-published, 2014.

Carter, Karl W. *Traveler & Other Poems*. Word Tech Editions, 2022.

The Cricket: Black Music in Evolution, 1968–69. Blank Forms Edition, 2021.

Cuney, William Waring. *Puzzles*. Paul Breman, 1960.

Cuney, William Waring. *Storefront Church*. Paul Breman, Black Heritage Series, 1973.

Davis, Arthur, J. Saunders Redding, and Joyce Ann Joyce, eds. *The New Cavalcade: African American Writing from 1760 to the Present*. Vol. 1. Howard University Press, 1991.

Dias-Porter, Joel (DJ Renegade). *Ideas of Improvisation*. Thread Makes Blanket Press, 2022.

Dodson, Owen. *Powerful Long Ladder*. Farrar, Straus and Giroux, 1946.

Dunbar-Nelson, Alice. *Violets and Other Tales*. 1895.

Ellis, Thomas Sayers. *Crank Shaped Notes*. Arrowsmith, 2021.

Ellis, Thomas Sayers. *The Maverick Room*. Graywolf Press, 2005.

Ellis, Thomas Sayers. *Skin, Inc.: Identity Repair Poems*. Graywolf Press, 2010.

Four Lincoln University Poets. Lincoln University Herald, 1930.

Gilbert, Derrick I. M. *Catch the Fire: A Cross-Generational Anthology of Contemporary African American Poetry*. Riverhead Books, 2008.

Gilmore, Brian. *elvis presley is alive and well and living in harlem*. Third World Press, 1993.

Gilmore, Brian. *Jungle Nights and Soda Fountain Rags: Poem for Duke Ellington*. Karibu Books, 2001.

Gilyard, Keith, and Anissa Wardi. *African American Literature*. Penguin Books, 2004.

Hand, Monica A. *Me and Nina*. Alice James Books, 2012.

Harris, Peter J., *Hand Me My Griot Clothes: The Autobiography of Junior Baby*. Black Classic Press, 1993.

Harris, Peter J. *SongAgain*. Beyond Baroque Books, 2022.

Henderson, Melanie. *Elegies for new york avenue*. Main Street Rag, 2011.

Horton, Randall. *the lingua franca of ninth street*. Main Street Rag, 2009.

Howard Poets. *Burning Spear: An Anthology of Afro Saxon Poetry*. Jupiter Hammond Press, 1963.

Hughes, Langston, and Arna Bontemps, eds. *The Poetry of the Negro*. Doubleday and Company, 1970.

Johnson, Georgia Douglas. *Selected Works of Georgia Douglas Johnson*. G. K. Hall and Company, 1997.

Johnson, Georgia Douglas Camp. *The Heart of A Woman, and Other Poems*. Boston Cornhill Company, 1918.

Johnson, James Weldon, ed. *The Book of American Negro Poetry*. Harcourt Brace/Jovanovich, 1922, 1931.

Johnston, Percy E. *Concerto for Girl and Convertible*. Continental Press, 1960.
Jones, LeRoi. *Preface to a Twenty Volume Suicide Note*. Corinth Books / Totem Press, 1961.
Jordan June, ed. *Soulscript: Afro-American Poetry*. Zenith Books, 1968.
Kendrick, Dolores. *now is the thing to praise*. Lotus Press, 1984.
Kwelismith. *Slavesong: The Art of Singing*. Anacostia Repertory Company, 1989.
Lightfoot, Toni Asante. *Steel Drum Memoirs*. Self-published chapbook.
Locke, Alain, ed. *Survey Graphic Magazine*. Survey Associates, 1925; reprinted by Black Classic Press, 1980.
Locke, Alain, ed. *The New Negro*. Dover Publications, 1925, 2021.
Madhubuti, Haki R. *Liberation Narratives*. Third World Press, 2009.
Madhubuti, Haki R. *Taught by Women: Poems as Resistance Language New and Selected*. Third World Press, 2020.
Major, Clarence, ed. *The New Black Poetry*. International Publishers, 1969.
Miller, E. Ethelbert. *First Light: New and Selected Poems*. DuForcelf, 1994.
Miller, E. Ethelbert. *In Search of Color Everywhere: A Collection of African American Poetry*. Stewart Tabori and Chang, 1994.
Miller, E. Ethelbert. *where are all the love poems for dictators?* Open Hand Publishing, 1986.
Miller, May. *Halfway to the Sun*. Lotus Press, 1988.
Miller, May. *The Ransomed Wait*. Lotus Press, 1983.
Neal, Gaston. *The Poetry of Gaston Neal: A Sampler*. The HR Consortium, 1996.
Neal, Larry. *HooDoo Hollerin' BeBop Ghosts*. Howard University Press, 1968.
Parkerson, Michelle. *Waiting Rooms*. Common Ground Press, 1983.
Pool, Rosey E. *Beyond the Blues: New Poems by American Negroes*. Hand and Flower Press, 1962.
Redmond, Eugene. *Drumvoices: The Mission of Afro-American Poetry*. Anchor Books/Doubleday, 1976.
Roberts, Kim. *By Broad Potomac's Shore: Great Poems from the Early Days of Our Nation's Capital*. University of Virginia Press, 2020.
Spears, Alan. *Fast Talk, Full Volume: An Anthology of Contemporary African American Poetry*. Gut Punch Press, 1993.
Spellman, A. B. *Things I Must Have Known*. Coffee House Press, 2008.
Stover, Darrell. "SciPoet." *Somewhere Deep Down When*. Melolips, 2011.
Thomas, Truth. *Speak Water*. Cherry Castle Press, 2012.
Toomer, Jean, *Cane*. Project Gutenberg, released in 2019. https://www.gutenberg.org/cache/epub/60093/pg60093-images.html.
Yanes, Moses. *Community of Friends*. Yanes, 1975.
Yao, Bro. (Hoke S. Glover III). *One Shoe Marching Towards Heaven*. Africa World Press, 2020.

Biography and Memoir

Baraka, Amiri. *The Autobiography of LeRoi Jones*. Lawrence Hill Books, 1984, 1986, 1997.
Baram, Marcus. *Gil-Scott Heron: Pieces of a Man*. St. Martin's, 2014.
Betts, R. Dwayne. *A Question of Freedom: A Memoir of Learning, Survival and Coming of Age in Prison*. Avery–Penguin Group, 2009.
Brawley, Benjamin. *Paul Laurence Dunbar: Poet of His People*. University of North Carolina Press, 1936.
Ellington, Duke. *Music Is My Mistress*. DaCapo Paperback, 1973.
Gilyard, Keith. *John Oliver Killens: A Life of Black Literary Activism*. University of Georgia Press, 2011.
Golden, Marita. *Migrations of the Heart*. Ballatine Books, 1983.

Griffin, John Chandler. *Biography of an American Writer, Jean Toomer*. Mellen Press, 2002.
Hales, Douglas. *A Southern Family in Black and White: The Cuneys of Texas*. Texas A&M University Press, 2003.
Hasse, John. *Duke Ellington's Washington*. Omnibus Press, 1995.
Hughes, Langston. *The Big Sea*. Thunder's Mouth Press, 1940, 1986.
Jarmon, Charles, *Andrew Billingsley: Scholar and Institution Builder. Essays and Tributes*. Black Classic Press, 2021.
Mangione, Jerre. *The Dream and the Deal: The Federal Writers' Project, 1935–1943*. Little, Brown and Company, 1972.
Rampersad, Arnold. *The Life of Langston Hughes*. Vol. 1: *1902–1941—I, Too Sing America*. Oxford University Press, 2002.
Stewart, Jeffrey C. *The New Negro: The Life of Alain Locke*. Oxford University Press, 2018.
Thompson, John (with Jesse Washington). *I Came as a Shadow*. Henry Holt and Company, 2020.
Wald, Elijah. *Josh White: Society Blues*. University of Massachusetts Press, 2000.

Criticism and Nonfiction

Barbour, Floyd B., ed. *The Black Power Revolt*. Collier Books, 1969.
Bassett, John E. *Harlem in Review*. Susquehanna University Press, 1992.
Bernard, Emily, ed. *Remember Me to Harlem: The Letters of Langston Hughes and Carl Van Vechten 1925–1964*. Knopf, 2001.
Botkin, B. A., ed. *Folk-Say IV: The Land Is Ours*. University of Oklahoma Press, 1932.
Du Bois, W.E.B. *Black Reconstruction*. Free Press, 1935.
Federal Writers' Project and Works Progress Administration. *Washington, City and Capital*, US Government Printing Office, 1937.
Fitzpatrick, Sandra, and Maria R. Goodwin, eds. *The Guide to Black Washington*. Hippocrene Books, 1990.
Gabbin, Joanne V. *Sterling A. Brown: Building the Black Aesthetic Tradition*. University Press of Virginia, 1985, 1994.
Gardullo, Paul, Michelle Delaney, Jacqueline D. Serwer, and Lonnie G. Bunch, eds. *The Scurlock Studio and Black Washington: Picturing the Promise*. Smithsonian Books, 2009.
Gilbert, Ben, and the Washington Post Staff. *Ten Blocks from the White House*. Frederick A. Praeger, 1968.
Harper, Michael S., ed. *The Collected Poems of Sterling Brown*. TriQuarterly Press / Northwestern University Press, 2020.
Harris, Trudier, and Thadious M. Davis, eds. *Afro-American Poets Since 1955*. Gale Research Company, 1985.
Henderson, Stephen. *Understanding the New Black Poetry*. William Morrow and Company, 1973.
Hopkinson, Natalie. *Go-Go Live: The Musical Life and Death of a Chocolate City*. Duke University Press, 2012.
Jarrett, Gene Andrew. *Paul Laurence Dunbar: The Life and Times of a Caged Bird*. Princeton University Press, 2022.
Johnston, Percy E. *Afro-American Philosophies*. Montclair State College Press, 1970.
Lewis, David Levering. *When Harlem Was in Vogue*. Oxford University Press, 1979, 1981.
Locke, Alain. *A Decade of Negro Self Expression*. Facsimile Publisher (printed), 1928.
Logan, Rayford W., ed, *What the Negro Wants*. University of North Carolina Press, 1944.
McKay, Nellie, ed. *Jean Toomer, A Critical Evaluation*. Howard University Press, 1988.

McHenry, Elizabeth. *Forgotten Readers: Recovering the Lost History of African American Literary Societies.* Duke University Press, 2002.
McKinley, Catherine E., and Joyce I. Delaney, eds. *Afrekete.* Anchor Books Doubleday, 1995.
Miller, Baxter, ed. *Black American Poets Between Worlds, 1940–1960.* University of Tennessee Press, 1986.
Mintz, Steven. *Historical Society, Washington, D.C., 1989.* Vol. 52 [The 52nd separately bound volume] of *A Historical Ethnography of Black Washington, D.C., Records of the Columbia.* Historical Society of Washington, D.C., 1989.
Napier, Winston, ed. *African American Literary Theory,* NYU Press, 2000.
Neal, Larry. *Visions of a Liberated Future: Black Arts Movement Writings.* Thunder's Mouth Press, 1989.
Nielsen, Aldon Lynn. *Black Chant: Languages of African American Post Modernism.* Cambridge University Press, 1997.
Parks, Gregory S. *Black Greek Letter Organizations.* University of Kentucky Press, 2008.
Ramey, Lauri, ed., in consultation with Paul Breman. *The Heritage Series of Black Poetry, 1962–1975: A Research Compendium.* Routledge, 2008.
Rice, Anne P., ed. *Witnessing Lynching, American Writers Respond.* Rutgers University Press, 2003.
Sanders, Mark A., ed. *A Son's Return: Selected Essays of Sterling A. Brown.* Northeastern University Press, 1955, 1996.
Sandler, Matt. *The Black Romantic Revolution: Abolitionist Poets at the End of Slavery.* Verso Books, 2020.
Whalan, Mark, ed., *The Letters of Jean Toomer, 1919–1924.* University of Tennessee Press, 2006.
Williams, Edward Christopher. *When Washington Was in Vogue.* Amistad, 2004.

Correspondence

Linette Marie Allen, July 2023, via email.
Paul Breman, via email, 2005.
Karl Carter, August 2023.
Peter Clare, via email.
DeBravo, January 22, 2023, via instant messenger.
Joel Dias-Porter, June 28, 2023, via email.
Yona Harvey, via email.
Mary Meekins, February 11, 2006, via email.
David Nicholson, via email.
Aldon Nielsen, July 2022, via email.
Michelle Parkerson, via email.
Reuben Jackson, via email.
A. B. Spellman, 2023, via email.
Ed Visser, December 23, 2005, via email.

DC Black Poets Survey Responses, 2021–2023

Alan Spears
Michelle Bond
Derrick Weston Brown
Terrance Hayes

Maria Fernanda Chamorro
Valerie Jean Turner
Alan King
Reuben Jackson
Eric Easter
VeTalle J. Fusilier
Deirdre Cross
Makalani Bandele
Valencia Robin
Sun Singleton
Alison Meehan
Pages Matam
DeAngelo Starnes
T. C. Hails
Audrey Hipkins
Melanie Henderson
Vonnie Wright
Robin Michel Caudell
Linette Marie Allen
Charles Edwin Roberson
Amanda Johnston
Lisa Marie Simmons
Heather Buchanan
Tony Medina
Calvin Reid
Holly Karapetkova
William Lawrence Tucker Jr.
Dr. John Walton Cotman
E. Ethelbert Miller
Khadijah Ali-Coleman
Jennifer King
Donald Illich
Erica B. Donaldson-Ellison
Kim Roberts
Alyss Dixon
Joel Johnson
Fred L. Joiner
Kahlil Hernandez
Brandon D. Johnson
Melissa Tuckey
Jordan E. Franklin
Andy Fogle
Jeff Epton
Georgia Stewart McDade
Christopher D. Stackhouse
Aldon Lynn Nielsen
Kenneth May
Jabari Asim

Jeffrey Renard Allen
Kurt Billoups
Gregory Woodward Luce
Chess Reis
Azora Muntasir
Patricia Harvey (Toni Asante Lightfoot)
Naomi Ayala
Nancy Schwalb
Sarah Browning
David Nicholson
Joel Dias-Porter (DJ Renegade)
L. Miller Newman
Curtis L. Crisler
Kwame Alexander
Jon West-Bey
Yona Harvey
Truth Thomas
Crystal Williams
Jeffrey McDaniel
Joseph Ross
Lisa Page
Richard Peabody
Tyehimba Jess
Sandra Beasley
J. Joy "Sistah Joy" Matthews (Joy Alford)
Barras, Jonetta

Dissertations and Theses

Arimitsu, Michio. "Black Notes on Asia: Composite Figurations of Asia in the African American Transcultural Imagination, 1923–2013." PhD diss., Department of African and African American Studies, Harvard University, Cambridge, MA, November 2011.

Bailey, Johnny L. " 'As Proud of Our Gayness, as We Are of Our Blackness': The Political and Social Development of the African American LGBTQ Community in Baltimore and Washington, D.C., 1975–1991." PhD diss., Morgan State University, Baltimore, MD, 2017.

Borchardt, Gregory W. "Making D.C. Democracy's Capital: Local Activism, the 'Federal State,' and the Struggle for Civil Rights in Washington, D.C.." PhD diss., University of Notre Dame, Notre Dame, IN, 2005.

Dolinsky, Rebecca C. "Lesbian and Gay D.C.: Identity, Emotion, and Experience in Washington D.C.'s Social and Activist Communities, 1961–1986." PhD diss., University of California–Santa Cruz, June 2010.

Gooding Jr., Frederick W. "American Dream Deferred: Black Federal Workers in Washington, D.C., 1941–1981." PhD diss., Georgetown University, Washington, DC, June 2013.

Jackson, Kyle A. "Gentrification and the Decline of African American Arts and Culture in Washington D.C.." In partial fulfillment of the requirements for the degree of Master of Science in Arts Administration, Drexel University, Philadelphia, PA, June 2016.

Jensen, Hilmar Ludvig, "The Rise of the African American Left: John Davis and the National Negro Congress." PhD diss., Cornell University, Ithaca, NY, May 1997.

Zu-Bolton, Amber Easter Gautier. "All Trails Lead to Sterling: How Sterling A. Brown Fathered the Field of Black Literary and Cultural Studies, 1936–1969." A thesis submitted to the Graduate Faculty of the University of New Orleans in partial fulfillment of the requirements for the degree of Master of Arts in History, University of New Orleans, New Orleans, LA, December 2019.

Films and Videos

Bourne, St. Clair. *In Motion: Amiri Baraka*. Icarus Films, 1983.

Chaytor, David. *Rhythm, Rhyme & Life: Spoken Word and the Oral Tradition*. Chaytor, 2000.

Levin, Marc. *Slam*. Trimark Pictures, 1998.

Miller, E. Ethelbert & Octave Stephenson. *A Conversation with Gwendolyn Brooks*. Library of Congress, 1986.

Parkerson, Michelle. *Fierceness Served! The Enik Coffeehouse Experience*. 2021.

Riggs, Marlon. *Tongues United*. 1989

Wooden, Eugene. *Voices Against Violence*. Digital Underground, 1995.

Interviews (all interviews conducted by Brian Gilmore)

Barras, Jonetta Rose, August 2023.

Carroll, Kenneth, May 2022, May 2023, and August 2023.

Carter, Karl, August 2022, August 2023.

Clare, Peter, May 2023.

Dargan, Kyle, March 2023.

Davis, Tery Ellen Cross, December 2023.

Dias-Porter, Joel, June and July 2023.

Eady, Cornelius, July 2023.

Forde, Ken, August 2022.

Gerima, Haile, July 2023.

Gittens, Tony, 2006.

Golden, Marita, August 2022.

Harris, Peter J., May 2023.

Kendrick, Dolores, January 2006.

Mawakana, Kemet, August 2023.

Miller, E. Ethelbert, August 2023, December 2023.

Parkerson, Michelle, March 2023.

Pegram, Lisa, March 2023.

Richardson, Judy, August 2019, 2006.

Roberts, Kim, 2022.

Shallal, Andy, June and July 2023.

Schwalb, Nancy, July 2023.

Spellman, A. B., April and May 2023.

Stover, Darrell, May 2023.

West-Bey, Jon, July 2023.

Wooden, Eugene, July 2023.

Journals and Reviews

African American Review
Alehouse
Black American Literature Forum
The Black Scholar
Callaloo
College Literature
GW Studies
Journal of Black Studies
Journal of Negro Education
Massachusetts Review
Obsidian / Obsidian II
Présence Africaine
Sewanee Review
Souls

Magazines

Ebony
Jet
Negro Digest / Black World
Opportunity
Saturday Evening Post
Survey Graphic

Newspapers

Afro American (*The Washington Afro American, Baltimore Afro American*)
Atlanta Daily World
Boston Globe
Colored American
Dunbar Newsreel
Evening Star
Hilltop Newspaper
Indianapolis Freeman
New Amsterdam News
Pittsburgh Courier
Washington Bee
Washington Post
Washington Review
Washington Star
Washington Times

Talks and Interviews (by others)

Ethelbert Miller and Octave Stevenson interview Gwendolyn Brooks. *The Writing Life Series.* Howard Public TV, 1986.

Grace Cavalieri interviews "May Miller," 1989.
Grace Cavalieri interviews Sterling Brown (undated audio file, copy with author, provided by Cavalieri).
Mosby, James. "Interview with Gaston Neal, July 1, 1968." The Civil Rights Documentation Project, online transcript, Archives Unbound, Gale Publishing, DC Public Library digital holdings, 1-11.
Sayers Ellis, Thomas. Charles Roswell interviews Thomas Sayers in "A Mixed Congregation." *Callaloo*, Autumn 2004, 884–96.
Woodson, Carter G. Zoom discussion with Cynthia Davis and Verner Mitchell, June 8, 2023.

INDEX

Page numbers for images appear in italics.

About the Author

Brian G. Gilmore is a native of Washington, DC, born and raised. He is the son of Wilmer I. Gilmore and Dorothy Pearl Gilmore. He is a graduate of Archbishop Carroll High School in Washington, DC., and Frostburg State University in Frostburg, Maryland, 1987. Both bard and barrister, he is a 1992 graduate of the University of District of Columbia David A. Clarke School of Law. He is the author of four books of poetry: *elvis presley is alive and well and living in harlem* (Third World Press, 1993); *Jungle Nights and Soda Fountain Rags: Poem for Duke Ellington* (Karibu Books 2001); *We Didn't Know Any Gangsters* (Cherry Castle Publishing, 2024), a 2014 NAACP Image Award nominee and a 2015 Hurston/Wright Legacy Award nominee; and *come see about me, Marvin* (Wayne State University, Press 2019), a Michigan Notable Book Award recipient for 2020. He is a regular contributor to *The Progressive* magazine, has practiced public interest law in the District of Columbia, Maryland, and Michigan for thirty years, and has served as a full-time clinical law professor at Howard University School of Law and Michigan State University College of Law for sixteen years. Currently, he is senior lecturer at the University of Maryland, College Park in the MLAW Program teaching law and society. He lives in Maryland with his family.